INTRODUCTIONS TO ENGLISH LITERATURE

GENERAL EDITOR: BONAMY DOBRÉE

VOLUME II

THE ENGLISH RENAISSANCE
1510–1688

THE ENGLISH RENAISSANCE

1510—1688

By
V. DE SOLA PINTO
Emeritus Professor of English, University of Nottingham

With a Chapter on Literature and Music by
BRUCE PATTISON
Professor of Education in the University of London

THE CRESSET PRESS
LONDON

COPYRIGHT © BY V. DE SOLA PINTO 1938, 1951, 1966

Published in Great Britain by
The Cresset Press 11 Fitzroy Square London W.1

First published 1938
Second edition, revised, 1951
Third edition, revised and reset, 1966

Printed in Great Britain by
Butler and Tanner Ltd, Frome and London

TO
REGINALD MAINWARING HEWITT
lo buon maestro e il duca mio

ACKNOWLEDGMENTS

I WISH to acknowledge with thanks the valuable help which I have received from Mr F. C. Francis, of the Department of Printed Books, the British Museum, in the preparation of the bibliographical part of this book, from Mr F. W. Bateson, who has allowed me to see the proof-sheets of part of the *Cambridge Bibliography of English Literature*, and from Professors R. M. Hewitt and R. R. Betts and Mr J. B. Leishman, who have read parts of my work in manuscript and have given me most valuable advice and suggestions.

V. DE S. P. (1938)

My thanks are due to the readers of the first edition of this book who have kindly helped me by pointing out mistakes and suggesting amendments. I wish particularly to acknowledge my debt to the late Canon F. E. Hutchinson, who gave me a long and very useful list of corrigenda, and to F. W. Bateson's great *Cambridge Bibliography of English Literature*, which has been available in its complete form for the preparation of this edition.

V. DE S. P. (1950)

In preparing the third edition of this book I have again received valuable help from a number of sources, which I acknowledge with thanks. These include certain indispensable works of reference: *The Cambridge Bibliography of English Literature, Vol. V, Supplement*, edited by George Watson, *The Annual Bibliography of English Language and Literature*, edited for the Modern Humanities Research Association, and *The Year's Work in English Studies*, edited for the English Association. I wish especially to record with deep gratitude my debt to a long list of corrigenda and addenda generously placed at my disposal by Dr Holger Nørgaard of the University of Copenhagen. I have been glad to embody a great many of Dr Nørgaard's corrections and amendments in my revision of the earlier chapters of my Bibliography.

V. DE S. P. (1962)

CONTENTS

CHAPTER		PAGE
	Editor's Preface	xiii
I	Renaissance and Reformation	1
II	The Elizabethans	31
III	The Seventeenth Century	71
IV	Literature and Music	104

STUDENTS' GUIDE TO READING

	Students' Guide to Reading	133
	List of Abbreviations	135

RENAISSANCE AND REFORMATION

I	The Humanists	141
II	The New Poetry up to the Accession of Elizabeth (1558)	148
III	The Protestant Reformers	156

THE ELIZABETHANS

IV	Early Elizabethan Poetry	165
V	The Translators	177
VI	Chronicles, Antiquarian Works and Voyages	193
VII	Later Elizabethan Poetry	202
VIII	Tudor Drama Up To Shakespeare	219
IX	Elizabethan Secular Prose	236
X	William Shakespeare	248
XI	Elizabethan Divines	270

CONTENTS—*continued*

THE SEVENTEENTH CENTURY

CHAPTER		PAGE
XII	Philosophical Writers	281
XIII	Metaphysical Poetry	293
XIV	The Later Drama up to the Civil War	304
XV	Secular Prose of the Seventeenth Century	319
XVI	Religious Prose of the Seventeenth Century	332
XVII	Poetry from Carew to Oldham	342
XVIII	John Milton	354
XIX	Restoration Drama	373
XX	John Dryden	386
	Index	395

EDITOR'S PREFACE

IF there is a danger of literature becoming separated from life, and at times the danger becomes actuality, there is a still greater one of the same thing happening in the study of literature. For one thing, it is apt to become that most arid of studies, literary history, in which history is largely, and literature, in any real meaning of the word, entirely ignored. The literature of the past is only of value in so far as it has significance to-day, just as history is only of use if it can throw a light upon the contemporary scene. But in the same way as history becomes illuminating by study, by finding out not only what people did, but why they did it, what circumstances, thoughts and emotions brought them to act, so we enlarge the boundaries within which the literature of the past has value if we gain an insight into the circumstances, thoughts and feelings which produced not only the writers, but also the readers of any particular period.

People of different ages speak different languages; not that the words are necessarily different, but the implications are. We of the twentieth century mean very little when we speak of the 'social virtues', whereas to an eighteenth-century writer the phrase implied a whole philosophy of civilization. For us to understand what Donne meant when he wrote:

> *On man heaven's influence works not so,*
> *But that it first imprints the ayre,*
> *Soe soule into the soule may flow. . . .*

we have to be at least aware of a whole body of philosophic thought, we might say of philosophic apprehension, to which most of us are likely to be strangers, but which was common at the beginning of the seventeenth century. Thus one of the objects of literary study should be to enable us to translate the language of another day into that of our own, which we can only do if we realize that these divergencies of expression are not merely a question of literary allusion, but of what entered the minds of educated people every day, coloured the spectacles through which they looked at life, and moulded the form in which they uttered their feelings. Thus it is not altogether idle to ponder why Ben Jonson should have written:

EDITOR'S PREFACE

> *What gentle ghost, besprent with April dew,*
> *Hails me, so solemnly, to yonder yew.*
> (Elegy on Lady Jane Pawlett)

while Pope should have preferred:

> *What beck'ning ghost along the moonlight shade*
> *Invites my step, and points to yonder glade?*
> (In Memory of an Unfortunate Lady)

for there is a reason which lies deeper than personal idiosyncrasy.

It has become a platitude to say that an age is reflected in its literature, and like all platitudes the saying has ceased to have any force. Moreover, an age is often much better represented by what is no longer read, than by the works which we still take from our shelves. If, for instance, we try to reconstruct the Restoration period from the plays of the time, we shall get a view which is, to say the least of it, misleading: the age is far better represented by the turgid flood of pamphlets which issued from the inkpots of Penn and Muggleton, Thomas Hicks, John Faldo, and a dozen other forgotten and vituperative sectarians. We tend to read Dryden's plays, or certain of the satires, in preference to his other work; but he is far nearer his age in *Religio Laici* and *The Hind and Panther* than in his now more popular writings. And if each age brings forth its own recognizable progeny, how is it that Milton and Etherege appeared together? or Thomas Hardy and Max Beerbohm? Each age has so many facets, that it is difficult to pitch on any as being its outstanding mirror though each age will have certain peculiarities not shared by the others. But these peculiarities are often merely the surface of fashion, accidental rather than essential, and until we know something of the age, we cannot tell which peculiarity, when explained, can have any significance for us.

Yet, if it is dangerous to regard literature as the looking-glass of its time, every age has certain problems which seem to it to be of major urgency. In the Shakespearian age it was to incorporate the 'new learning' into life; later in the seventeenth century, the politico-religious issue was the important one; the eighteenth century, again, was lured by a vision of civilized man. That is to say that each age has its philosophy, its scale of values. But philosophy, which to some extent conditions literature, is itself conditioned, partly by the way people live, and partly by the influx

EDITOR'S PREFACE

of thought from foreign countries, though it is as well to remember that such thought will only penetrate or take root in a country already prepared for it. Therefore, the way people live, their social and political grouping, their economic formation, to some extent determine the way they write. Much has lately been made of the influence of economics: too much, for Marx cannot account for Milton, and it is as easy to argue that the economic development of the eighteenth century was due to the idea of the universe as defined by Newton as that 'Dutch finance', commercialism, and the expansion of trade, gives a clue to the philosophy of history which runs through Gibbon's *Decline and Fall*. Yet economics have an effect on literature; we can see it to some extent in *Piers Plowman*, and without the rise of the middle classes at the end of the seventeenth century we could not have had Defoe, Steele, or Addison; the polite essayist could not have come into being, quite apart from whether or not he preached the bourgeois virtues.

The influence of foreign thought is a subject that has loomed too large, perhaps, in most histories of literature, mainly because literature has on the whole been treated as separate from life. The influence of something on somebody has been a favourite subject for theses, and the answers have been as dubious as the theme has been ill-defined. Because Chaucer, having read Dante's

> Quali i fioretti di notturno gelo
>   chinati e chiusi, poi che il sol gl'imbianca,
>   si drizzen tutti aperti in loro stelo;
>
> tal mi fec' io. . . .
>
>   (*Inferno* II, 127. . . .)

or, more probably, the corresponding lines in the *Filostrato* of Boccaccio, proceeded to sing

> *But right as floures, thorugh the colde of night*
> *Y-closed, stoupen on hir stalkes lowe,*
> *Redressen hem a-yein the sonne bright,*
> *And spreden on hir kinde cours by rowe;*
> *Right so gan.* . . .
> . . . .*Troilus.* . . .
>
>   (Troilus and Criseyde, II St. 139)

EDITOR'S PREFACE

that is not to say that Chaucer was influenced by Dante or by Boccaccio, indeed no prettier contrast to the *Divine Comedia* could be found than *The Canterbury Tales*, though it is clear that there is some connection between them and the *Decameron*. No one really familiar with the comedy of France and England in the seventeenth century, with an understanding of what they were up to, can believe that the English were influenced by the French to more than a superficial degree. Nevertheless, the thought of one country, or of one individual, can very profoundly affect a period, and the scepticism of Montaigne is apparent throughout the seventeenth century from Shakespeare to Halifax. In the same way, German thought obscured the clarity of Coleridge, and puffed the thought and style of Carlyle to an almost intolerable smokiness.

The writer, therefore, is, besides being a unique individual, the product of the forces of his time. However much we may regret it, we have to abandon Shelley's contention that 'poets are the unacknowledged legislators of the world', though we need not altogether throw over the position; for though, no doubt, thought does sometimes influence action, it is more usually the successor of deeds, and it will not be denied that Locke is a child of the Revolution just as Hobbes was of the Great Rebellion. It is truer to say with Arnold that poetry is a criticism of life, though not quite true, for literature is, rather, a growth from life itself, a part of life, not its harvest only. We can go further and say that it is so ravelled with life that it can be described also as the soil and the seed. But that metaphor should lead to such confusion is enough to indicate how closely tangled with life literature is, how complex the relation between them, and how impossible it is to separate one from the other.

．　　．　　．　　．　　．　　．　　．　　．　　．　　．

The object of the Introductions in this series is to give the student some idea of the soil out of which the works of literature grow, so as to be able to grasp with fuller understanding the books mentioned in the Bibliographies. This, then, is not yet another History of English Literature, but rather, to exaggerate a little, a History of England in which not kings, battles, diplomatic or constitutional struggles, nor even, economic development, are given pride of place, but literature. As is suitable to our age in

EDITOR'S PREFACE

which economics have come to be given a high place as determinants not only of our lives, but of our manner of thinking and feeling, and even of our religion, economics will be given more stress than they have hitherto been allowed in books on literature, but not, as some would no doubt wish, to the exclusion of everything else. For instance, though the question of the control of money no doubt played a larger part in the Great Rebellion than we were most of us brought up to believe, it would be absurd to neglect the religious elements in the struggles. Indeed, as Professor R. H. Tawney has shown, it was religion itself that largely determined the economic trend of the eighteenth century. The effect of religion on literature is more easily traceable; it begins with Beowulf and runs through the whole most markedly in the periods where the Church to a large extent stamped the nature of society, or when controversy raged high, as it did from the Reformation—or at least from the time of the *Marprelate Tracts*—to the foundation of the Bank of England. Philosophy also plays an important part, not only as being the matter of much admirable writing, but also in the general attitude towards life exhibited by writers who unconsciously, rather than in full awareness, absorbed the ideas of their time. But philosophy again is affected by economics, for no one can doubt that the individualism of the nineteenth century was largely the result of the Industrial Revolution, and that Carlyle's Cromwell must own as forebears Adam Smith and James Watt. Science also can affect literature, and without Huxley there would probably have been a different Hardy.

Another addition to the view of literature is made in these volumes by giving due place to the sister arts where they rose to any height, or seem to have importance with respect to writing. Thus music had an effect on poetry in the seventeenth century, while painting and architecture affected the poetry, and perhaps the prose, of the eighteenth. Wherever, in short, the literary 'movement' of a time seems congruous with that of the other arts, they are included in the survey. Most important of all, however, is the social background, the changes of milieu indicated, say, by the decay of the guilds or the rise of nationalism; for these are the things which most affect the way people live, and therefore what they will most wish to write and to read.

The Bibliographies which form the major part of each volume

EDITOR'S PREFACE

are designed to give the reader a detailed view of the literature of each period; and being classified and commented on will enable him to study or to enjoy either any special branch, or the whole literature of the period. Only the specialist can read everything; but the aim of this series is to enable anyone who so wishes to get a clear idea of any one period by reading with a certain degree of fervour for a year, a clear notion not only of what was written, but, so to speak, of why and how, from what impulses, with what objects, and in what conditions morally speaking. It is hoped by this method to integrate literature with life, and so give the writings of the past that meaning without which to read is to be baffled, and to miss that greatest of all pleasures, a sense of unity of feeling with the writer of any work. Lacking this, literature is too far separated from living, and can have but little value.

The manner in which English literature has been split up in this series no doubt demands an explanation. There are many ways in which it can be split up. This has been done variously, sometimes rather arbitrarily by centuries or other irrelevant measuring rods, more often by grouping it around great figures: The Age of Wordsworth and so on; or by literary movements: The Romantic Revival, for instance. These divisions have their uses, but for our purpose here they tend to subordinate life to literature. It is admitted that there is an element of arbitrariness in the present divisions also, but the object is to relate literature to life, disregarding movements which may only be different aspects of the same thing. The divisions here correspond in the main with social sense; roughly indeed, with what reservations you will, and contradictions of a rule which cannot be rigid, since human nature refuses to fit into compartments.

In the first period, after the Conquest, you can say with some plausibility (though it is in this period that our structure is weakest) that literature was much more diffused among different classes; it was written for no particular brand of person. Everyone would read *Piers Plowman*, or applaud the miracle plays. There is, it is true, much that is courtly about Chaucer, but there is much that is not. When we get to Spenser, say, we feel that literature is being written for an aristocracy: the drama still maintained its general appeal (though even as early as the moralities and interludes there is a shift away from the people), but it became more and more aristocratic, till under Charles II it was entirely courtly.

EDITOR'S PREFACE

This period, then, we can describe as the aristocratic period: Donne, Jeremy Taylor, Sir Thomas Browne, Milton, are writers for an aristocracy, and this social sense we may say was established by the Tudors, and exploited by the Stuarts, till it came to an end at the Revolution of 1688. Then, with great suddenness, there appeared a literature written by the middle class, of the middle class, and for the middle class: the pamphleteers, the essayists, and soon Defoe and the novelists. Even the drama changed with startling rapidity, with the anti-aristocratic satire of Farquhar, and the sentimental comedy of Steele.

The ideas of the middle class, with its strong sense, as it then had, of an organized society, gave place in the last century to the idea of individualism, due partly to the French, and partly to the Industrial Revolution. It had been begun by the romantic poets with their break-away from the idea of 'society' so dear to the eighteenth century. It might grieve Shelley to think that he was the forerunner of the excellent Dr Smiles, but so it is. At all events, individualism dominated literature until the War of 1914-18. But even before that it was breaking down (having somewhat oddly consorted with a blatant imperialism), as can be seen from the plays of Mr Bernard Shaw, and still more, perhaps, from the novels of Mr E. M. Forster. The post-War period had its own characteristics; a new twist was given to the human view by investigations into psychology, ethnology, physics, and by the Russian Revolution.

There are, of course, several objections to this sort of division: odd elements appear everywhere: you cannot, for instance, rank Bunyan among aristocratic writers. But some division has to be made along chronological lines. It may be objected that the first period needs at least two volumes; it is so long and so varied. That is true, but the number of works which remain which can be of interest to the general reader are comparatively few, and it was thought better to devote more space to our more recent heritages, as being both fuller of works we are likely to read, and as having a closer influence upon our present-day approach to living.

BONAMY DOBRÉE

THE ENGLISH RENAISSANCE

CHAPTER I

RENAISSANCE AND REFORMATION

HUMANISM

CHRISTIAN Europe in the Middle Ages lived, as it were, within a magic circle. Geographically the circle was closed on the north by the frozen seas, on the west by the Atlantic and on the south and east by the Mohammedan power. The medieval conception of the universe, too, was the closed system of Ptolemy with the earth at the centre and the heavenly bodies fixed to solid spheres revolving round it. Intellectually the boundaries were determined by the fact that all books were written by hand, whereby literary culture was thus confined to a very limited class. The same metaphor can be applied to the world of the spirit which was fenced in on all sides by the strong barriers of Catholic orthodoxy. This closed and limited world had originally been a refuge for the peoples of Europe after the collapse of the Roman Empire and the chaos that followed. Within its bounds a great civilization had arisen in the West. It was the civilization that has left us the Gothic cathedrals, the ancient universities, the painting of the Italian and Flemish 'primitives', the teaching of St Francis, the philosophy of St Thomas Aquinas and the Schoolmen, and the poetry of Dante and Chaucer. But in the fifteenth century that civilization, though still producing much that was admirable in art, in learning and in religion was decaying from within. Individualism and nationalism, two new and rapidly growing forces, were beginning to sap the foundations of the communal and international organization of medieval society. The Holy Roman Empire, which had attempted to unite Christendom, had failed hopelessly as a political force. The Church, though enormously wealthy and powerful, was corrupt and lethargic, and had suffered terribly in prestige by the schism which set up rival Popes at Rome and Avignon. Italy, France and England were in a state of political chaos. In the world of the intellect too it had become apparent that the limits imposed by medieval tradition were becoming too narrow and were beginning to resemble the walls of a prison rather than of a refuge and a defence. In Italy, there had been flourishing since the fourteenth century the great intellectual movement called humanism. Humanism was the attempt to transcend the limits of the medieval mind by studying the ancient civilizations of Greece and Rome and rebuilding European culture according to the patterns provided by them. Such studies were called 'humanism' or 'humanity' (Latin, *humanitas*, Italian, *umanismo*, *umanità*), because they dealt with the purely human and secular wisdom of the ancients as opposed to the 'divine' studies of medieval theologians. The civilizations of antiquity had never, indeed, been forgotten, but in fifteenth-century Italy they seemed to rise again out of the mists of the past in all the dazzling splendour of a new dawn. The study of Greek had already begun to be revived in Italy in the fourteenth century. It received a great stimulus from the fall of Constantinople, which was taken by the Turks in 1453. Many Greek refugees came to Italy, and Greek scholars lectured to large audiences at the Italian universities on the philosophers and poets of ancient Hellas. At Florence, Marsilio Ficino, with the encouragement of the ruling family of the Medici, founded his Florentine Academy in imitation of Plato's Academy at Athens. Italian scholars transcribed, edited and translated the great works of ancient Greek authors. It was felt that Plato, Aristotle, Sophocles and Demosthenes were more truly modern than any of the medieval authors. They were admired, not because they were ancient, but because they represented the kind of civilization that men now wanted to build in the future. Then the art of printing was invented in Germany about 1450, and it became possible to multiply books with a rapidity and an accuracy hitherto undreamed of, and to sell them at a price which would place them within the reach of every scholar. The summit of the ambition of Chaucer's Oxford scholar was to possess twenty books. Now for the same price a scholar could buy several hundred. The Italian Renaissance was not only a revival of scholarship. It was an artistic and scientific revival. It produced a new and splendid poetry, and still more splendid achievements in painting and sculpture. By reviving the geographical and astronomical methods of the ancients, it broke through the limits of the closed universe and the closed Europe of the Middle Ages. Astronomers rediscovered the spherical shape of the earth and found out that it was a planet of the sun and not the centre of a universe. Their discoveries suggested to explorers and merchants the possibility of reaching the fabulous wealth of Asia by sailing into the unknown West. In the last decade of the fifteenth century Europeans burst through the Eastern and Western limits of the medieval world. In 1492 Columbus reached the West Indies, and in 1497 Vasco da Gama rounded the Cape of Good Hope and reached India by sea. These discoveries were the result not of intellectual curiosity but of the urge to economic power. The expeditions were organized by men whose eyes were fixed on the wealth of the East, the land of spices and jewels, of silks and precious metals. The medieval social and economic structure had been founded in theory, at any rate, on the analogy of the human body. Lord and priest, knight, burgher and peasant, were all necessary, though unequal parts of the organism and were bound together by mutual obligations. This functional conception of society was being undermined in the latter part of the fifteenth century by a vast economic revolution. In the Italian and South German cities modern capitalism and large scale finance had already come into existence. Priests and Schoolmen might denounce usury and popes might issue bulls rebuking the spirit of mammon, but such protests were of little avail against the operations of great business houses like the Medici and the

Fuggers. All over Western Europe the medieval social order was beginning to crumble before the desire for personal gain, the aggrandizement of the individual at the expense of his neighbour.

Five years after Columbus reached the West Indies, Erasmus, then a young, unknown Dutch student, later to become the great scholar whose work was to inaugurate a new humanism in Northern Europe, visited England for the first time and stayed with Prior Richard Charnock at Oxford. Writing to a friend two years later he describes the country in the following words:

'I find the climate both pleasant and wholesome; and I have met with so much kindness and so much learning, not backward and trivial, but deep, accurate, ancient, Latin and Greek, that but for the curiosity of seeing it, I do not now so much care for Italy. When I hear my Colet I seem to be listening to Plato himself. In Grocin who does not marvel at such a perfect round of learning? What can be more acute, profound and delicate than the judgment of Linacre? What has nature ever created more gentle, more sweet, more happy than the genius of Thomas More?'

The England that Erasmus found so attractive at the end of the fifteenth century (has the climate changed or was his praise of the weather a piece of flattery?) had certainly made a remarkable recovery from the political and social chaos of the Wars of the Roses. It had been ruled since 1485 by Henry VII, the first of the Tudor monarchs. This shrewd and able king had deprived the great feudal barons of much of their power, and surrounded himself by new men sprung chiefly from the middle class. These men already began to form a new aristocracy of wealth which replaced the feudal and military aristocracy of the Middle Ages, and was later to rise against the Crown itself. For the present, however, they formed the strongest bulwark of the New Monarchy on which they were entirely dependent. Henry developed the practice (already begun by Edward IV) of calling to his Council only the men of his choice and of excluding from it the great nobles. Through the Council he set up a centralized despotism, working not through a professional army and civil service, but through the voluntary support of the whole nation, and especially of the propertied classes who feared nothing so much as a reversion to the chaos of the previous age. The communal rule of the medieval guilds and corporations and the feudal rule of the medieval barons was replaced by the administration of the Justices of the Peace, local squires, who were responsible to the Court of the Star Chamber, which in its turn was responsible to the King's Council. At the other end of the scale were the Petty Constables (like Shakespeare's Dull and Dogberry) who executed the orders of the Justices and, like them, were unpaid amateurs.

This patriarchal despotism was an attempt to set up a new sort of social solidarity in place of the decayed medieval structure. The Tudor monarchs succeeded in infusing remarkable vigour into the system, but everywhere it came into collision with the new conception of the ownership of property as an absolute right carrying no obligations, and in the seventeenth century the power of the property owners was to destroy the remains of the Tudor experiment. Henry VII encouraged trade, and made commercial treaties with foreign powers. The wool and cloth trades benefited especially by his policy, and the English became not only great producers of wool (as they had been for centuries), but also manufacturers and exporters of cloth. One of the results was the conversion of much of the arable land into sheep runs, and hence the depopulation of a large part of the countryside, and ever recurring distress among the peasants, leading to numerous risings and described in moving terms by such writers as More, Latimer and Crowley. This was the beginning of the creation of a wage-earning class, the modern type of 'proletariat', which hardly existed in the Middle Ages.

Another result of the prosperity of trade was a great influx of wealth into the country. The lovely stone villages of the Cotswolds and the noble Tudor farms of the Thames Valley are memorials of that prosperity. Much of the new wealth was spent on the building and adorning of churches, abbeys, chantries and colleges at Oxford and Cambridge. Some of the greatest achievements of English architecture were built or finished in the reign of Henry VII, the Divinity schools and Magdalen Tower at Oxford, Henry VII's Chapel at Westminster, the royal chapel at Windsor and a host of noble churches in the Thames Valley and East Anglia. But the greater part of the beauty produced in that age has disappeared. A Venetian envoy who visited England in 1500 was surprised not only at the wealth of the merchants, but at the abundance of rich ornaments in the churches and monasteries. Many of the great churches and monasteries of the late fifteenth and early sixteenth centuries are still in existence, but nearly all that glory of English craftsmanship which adorned them was swept away at the Reformation, and of the great monasteries and friaries only a few gaunt ruins remain.

Before the reign of Henry VII some Englishmen like John Tiptoft, Earl of Worcester and Bishop Grey, had been in touch with Italian humanism, but it was at the end of the fifteenth century that humanism for the first time became a significant force in English life. The old king was no friend to the new movement. His mind was essentially medieval, and the New Learning was not likely to make much headway at his court. Its patrons during his reign were the two great churchmen, Archbishop Morton and his successor Archbishop Warham. The hopes of the humanists were fixed on the Prince Henry who became Prince of Wales on the death of his brother Arthur in 1502. When his father died in 1509 Henry was seventeen. He was handsome, popular, a sportsman, a lover of music, and a good scholar. He had shown marked favour to the humanists. When Erasmus was in Italy he had written a Latin letter to him in his own hand. It seemed that a golden age was going to begin in England. Lord Mountjoy, Erasmus's English pupil and patron, sent a letter to his old master where he describes the prospects of England at Henry's accession in glowing language.

The importance of the Court, 'the establishment and surroundings of the sovereign with his councillors and retinue', to quote the definition of the Oxford dictionary, throughout the whole of this period can hardly be exaggerated. The court was not merely the focus of high society, it was also the centre of both political and of cultural life, 'foster mother', as Coleridge writes 'of the State and the Muses'. All important officers of the state were chosen by the sovereign and the only way in which it was possible to succeed in a public career was to obtain the sovereign's favour. The Tudor policy of personal government made the court even more important than it had been in the Middle Ages. It is, perhaps, not without significance that the earliest recorded use of the adjective 'courtly' dates from the latter part of the fifteenth century. It was the only large assembly of wealthy, educated and powerful people in the kingdom. Its ornamental functions were hardly less important than its political. The courtiers had to amuse their master as well as to serve him, and it was their duty also to display his glory to the world. Henry VII was miserly, and his court had no splendour. But he amassed a large fortune, and Henry VIII proceeded to spend it in creating one of the most brilliant and extravagant courts in Europe. He loved learning, and he also loved pleasure and ostentation. His favourite was Thomas Wolsey, a young Oxford priest whom he promoted rapidly. Wolsey became a Cardinal and Lord Chancellor in 1515. He was proud and ambitious, as great a lover of luxury and pleasure as Henry himself and, like the king, a learned man and a generous friend to the New Learning.

The opening years, then, of the reign of Henry VIII were years of triumph and high hopes for the humanists. In 1512 John Colet, now Dean of St Paul's, preached a noble sermon before Convocation 'Of Conformation and Reformation', in which he made a strongly-worded attack on the corruptions of the Church, and especially on the greed, avarice and evil lives of priests and monks. He was even bold enough to preach against war on another occasion when Henry was preparing a great military expedition against France.

1516 was the great year of the humanist reformers. It was the year of the publication of More's famous Latin work, *Utopia*, at Louvain, and of Erasmus's great critical edition of the New Testament. The international character of the group is marked by those two publications. They stood for the unity of Europe and a republic of letters that transcended national boundaries. *Utopia* is the manifesto of early English humanism. It is a picture of an imaginary island discovered in the Western world of marvels then recently found by Columbus, Vespucci and Cabot. This island is inhabited by a people who have reached 'excellent perfection in all good fashions, humanity, civil gentleness, wherein they go now beyond all the people of the world'. Utopia is a pagan nation governed on purely rational principles. All the way through the book the contrast is pointed between this nation of wise, just and gentle heathens, with their well-ordered polity and their spacious, clean houses and cities, and the ignorant, rapacious, superstitious Christian English of More's own time with their social and economic disorder, their filthy narrow streets and insanitary dwellings. It is a book full of subtle irony and noble idealism, and here more than anywhere else can we find the essential qualities of the English humanists, their zeal for social, political and ecclesiastical reform, their longing for the sweet reasonableness of ancient philosophy, their profound religious feeling and moral fervour.

These were indeed golden years for humanism when Wolsey was founding new colleges at Oxford and the saintly and enlightened Bishop Fisher was encouraging the New Learning at Cambridge. More was high in the king's favour. He became a privy councillor, held various important offices under the Crown, and served Henry on diplomatic missions to the Continent. The king treated him with the easy familiarity of a personal friend and delighted in discussing learned matters with him. His own household, which included his second wife, his son, his daughters and their husbands and other relatives, and which was often visited by Erasmus, became a centre of light and learning, a school where Latin, Greek, logic, philosophy, theology, mathematics and astronomy were taught. This household, too, was closely connected with the beginnings of the English secular and romantic drama. More had been interested in the drama from his youth, and when he was a page in Cardinal Morton's household we learn that he would 'sodeynly sometymes step in among the players, and never studyinge for the matter, make a part of his owne there presently among them, which made the lookers on more sport than all the players besides'. One of the plays acted in Morton's palace when More was there was almost certainly *Fulgens and Lucres* by Henry Medwall, chaplain to the Cardinal. The play is the earliest known drama in England that can be called purely secular. It is significant that it is based on a translation of a Latin humanist dialogue written in Italy, and is thus the first link between the English drama and the Italian Renaissance. Crude as it is, its double plot and combination of serious and comic elements foreshadow in a remarkable way the practice of Shakespeare and the great Elizabethans. The development of the secular and courtly drama in Henry VIII's reign seems to have been largely due to the influence of More and his circle. Most of the best extant plays of the period were printed by John Rastell, More's brother-in-law. Rastell himself was author of a play called *The Four Elements*, full of allusions to contemporary learning and reflecting the enthusiasm of More's circle for education in its prologue, which contains a plea for the writing of learned books in English, so that

All subtell science in Englýsshe might be lernyd.

Such plays as *The Four Elements*, though entirely secular, retained the allegorical form of the late medieval 'morality' plays. The group of clever and amusing farces, based partly on French originals and ascribed to John Heywood, who married Rastell's daughter, mark a still further emancipation from medieval tradition. In several of these plays the characters are no longer abstractions but contemporary types, the greedy, rascally Pardoner, the cozening Friar, the honest layman Johan Johan or Neighbour Prat. It is not impossible that More himself may have written these farces; it is at least highly probable that he had a hand in their composition.

Poetry as well as learning and the drama awoke as from a long sleep at the court of Henry VIII. The old court poetry of the degenerate Chaucerian school had reached its last stage of decay in the dreary allegories of Stephen Hawes. The lively genius of Skelton gave it a momentary resurrection, and also experimented in other ways suggested by medieval Latin poetry, but the time was now ripe for a poetry of a less medieval and a more definitely humanistic kind. The long-winded, late-medieval allegories were abandoned, and a group of courtier-poets inaugurated a new fashion of writing short poems of a more subjective kind dealing particularly with love. A large part of their poetry is probably lost. Tudor courtier-poets did not generally have their works printed, but circulated them in manuscript. What survives we owe chiefly to the enterprise of a printer called Richard Tottel, who printed his famous anthology of early-Tudor courtly poetry, *Songs and Sonettes written by the ryght honorable Lorde Henry Haward late Earl of Surrey, and other*, usually known as *Tottel's Miscellany*, in 1557, the last year of Queen Mary's reign, long after the death of most of the contributors.

The two members of this group to whom an important body of poetry can definitely be ascribed are Sir Thomas Wyatt and the Earl of Surrey. Of others such as Sir Francis Bryan and Lord Vaux hardly anything is known, except the fact that they wrote poems in the new manner. The pioneer was certainly Sir Thomas Wyatt (the name is also spelt Wyat and Wiat). The son of a faithful servant of Henry VII, he had held official positions at Henry VIII's court since he was little more than a boy. In 1527 he accompanied an English embassy to Italy and visited Ferrara, Bologna, Florence and Venice. Soon after his return he was appointed High Marshal of Calais, then an English possession. There can be little doubt that Wyatt's visit to Italy in 1527 was comparable in its effect on English poetry with those of Chaucer a century and a half before. For the second time English poetry was kindled into new life by contact with Italian civilization. We have no details of Wyatt's Italian tour beyond the fact that he was taken prisoner by the Spaniards and escaped, but it is highly significant that the famous book of Baldassare Castiglione called *The Courtier* (*Il Cortegiano*) had recently been written and was circulating in manuscript at this time. *The Courtier* is one of the works that spread the ideals of the Italian Renaissance all over Europe. It gives a picture of life at the cultivated court of the Duke of Urbino, and professes to describe conversations between the Duke and Duchess and members of their family with certain distinguished humanists, such as Giuliano di Medici, Bernardo Bibiena and Pietro Bembo, on the subject of the character of the Perfect Courtier. *The Courtier* is a treatise on the Art of Fine Living which placed the Italian humanist ideal at its highest before the whole of Europe. This ideal is purely aesthetic and intellectual, not moral and religious like the humanism of More and his friends. Literary criticism in Italy was also very active when Wyatt was there. It has been conjectured that, just as Chaucer may have met Petrarch, Wyatt may have come into contact with the great critics of the Italian Renaissance Navagero and Trissino. These writers were both humanists who were interested in the development of vernacular literature. Trissino's *Poetica*, in particular, gives a careful account of the Italian verse forms, including the sonnet.

Puttenham, the Elizabethan critic, describes Wyatt and his friend Surrey as the 'chieftaines' of the new literary movement, who 'having travelled into Italie, and there tasted the sweete and stately measures and stile of the Italian Poesie as novices newly crept out of the schools of Dante, Ariosto and Petrarch, they greatly pollished our rude and homely maner of vulgar Poesie from what it had been before and for that cause may be justly said the first reformers of our English numbers'. Puttenham is wrong in his statement that Surrey visited Italy as well as Wyatt, but he is right in his emphasis on the revolution in technique that these poets carried out. Dante and Ariosto had little effect on Wyatt, but Petrarch had a very great influence on him. It may seem strange that an English poet seeking for new inspiration in Italy in the early sixteenth century should have been affected particularly by a poet such as Petrarch who died in 1374, and was a contemporary of Chaucer. We must remember, however, that Italy was far ahead of the rest of Europe in the development of the new civilization. Petrarch, though he only learnt a little Greek in his old age, was one of the saints of humanism. He had been to his age what Erasmus was to the age of Henry VIII. Unlike Erasmus, however, he was a great poet in the vernacular language as well as a brilliant scholar and master of Latin prose and verse. His famous Italian sonnets and lyrics have an exquisite finish and elegance of form and style that made them the admiration and despair of European poets for centuries. In his hands poetic art in a vernacular language seemed to have reached the standard of craftmanship that had previously been attained only by the great Greek and Roman poets. It was not, however, only the workmanship of Petrarch's poems that attracted the attention of sixteenth-century poets. It was also the conception of courtly love to which they gave expression. This conception was undoubtedly derived from Dante, the early Tuscan poets, and their predecessors, the troubadours of Provence, but in Petrarch's hands it underwent a change that made it appear to be something new and exciting to the men of the Renaissance. It was more personal, more complex, and more introspective. The vogue of *Petrarchismo* was at its height in

Italy at the very time of Wyatt's visit. In 1525 Vellutello had published the first elaborate life of the poet and Bembo, the great humanist, had recently edited his poems. Soon, like Byron three centuries later, Petrarch was to fascinate Europe by the 'pageant of his bleeding heart'. When Mercutio mockingly compared Romeo's mistress to Petrarch's Laura, every educated member of Shakespeare's audience understood the allusion.

Wyatt is not a great poet, but he is a great and a memorable pioneer. He abandoned the conventions of the long poem and the allegory which had hampered the late-medieval poets and had produced the monstrosities of Lydgate and Hawes. He gave a new dignity and a new power to the short poem: 'That to have wel written in verse, yea and in small parcelles, deserveth great praise, the works of divers, Latins, Italians and other doe prove.' These are the words which Tottel uses in the preface to his famous anthology. Poetry 'in small parcels', the short, subjective poem dealing especially with courtly love, was to be the normal form of secular lyrical poetry for a century and a half. Wyatt introduced into English poetry the sonnet, which is the most compact and satisfying of all conventional forms for the short poem. The sonnet had been Petrarch's favourite verse form, and its use became the mark of Petrarchan love-poetry all over Europe in the sixteenth century. Chaucer had known Petrarch's sonnets, but, when he translates one in his *Troilus and Criseyde* (ll. 1400-20), he uses his own seven-lined narrative stanza and makes no attempt to naturalize the sonnet in English. As far as we know, Wyatt's are the first English sonnets. His handling of the form is usually wooden and awkward and his sentiment seems mostly to be quite conventional. He imitates the conceits and verbal wit of Petrarch and the Petrarchans, but he entirely fails to achieve their warm sensuous colour or delicate music. Nevertheless a line or two here and there in the sonnets show that he is a genuine poet. When Petrarch, in his 137th sonnet, compares his soul to a ship tempest-tost in a storm of trouble that hides the eyes of his love as a storm hides the stars from a mariner he writes a pretty but undistinguished line:

Celansi i duo miei dolci usati segni.

Wyatt in an otherwise clumsy translation transforms this conceit into a line worthy of Shakespeare:

The stars be hid that led me to this pain.

His true gift, however, is revealed in his songs and lyrics. His achievement was not only the naturalizing of the sonnet and other verse forms such as terza rima (used in a single fragment of Chaucer) and ottava rima; it is also the re-establishment of English prosody, which had collapsed as a result of the linguistic changes of the fifteenth century, and the foundation of a new school of English lyrical poetry. As a result of the changes that transformed the language in the fifteenth century Chaucer's delicate metrical art became incomprehensible. The sounded final e of middle English words and the accent on the final syllable in words of romance origin (such as 'favour' and 'honour'), had almost disappeared by the beginning of the sixteenth century. The result was that the early printed texts of Chaucer such as Pynson's of 1520 (which Wyatt probably read) often turned Chaucer's exquisitely harmonious lines into doggerel which was supposed to be due to the barbarous age in which he lived. This mistake was to last for centuries, and even Dryden, who wrote such a noble appreciation of Chaucer's genius, could only ascribe to his metre 'the rude sweetness of a Scottish tune'. The loose doggerel line thus came to be considered the mark of Chaucerian poetry, and a glance at almost any poem in rime royal (the fashionable Chaucerian stanza) written in the late fifteenth or early sixteenth century will reveal the chaos into which English prosody had fallen.

> *Sapience bade me marvel nothing*
> *For she would show me the signification*
> *Why he so sat by short reckoning,*
> *According to a moralization.*

Dignified poetry could never be written to a tune like that, and when Puttenham calls Wyatt and Surrey the 'first reformers of our English numbers' he means that they delivered English verse from this kind of hobbling movement. Wyatt was certainly helped by the Italians, and he often imitates carefully the movement of Italian verse; he was helped too by Pynson's edition of Chaucer which, in spite of its bad text, provided him with models of verse infinitely superior to the works of the degenerate Chaucerians of the fifteenth and sixteenth centuries. His third source of inspiration was the popular song and the fine English musical tradition that had come down from the Middle Ages.

Wyatt's best work is to be found in his lyrics. A few of them like 'Farewell, my lute', 'Forget not yet', and 'They flee from me' are masterpieces. In these poems Wyatt is the successor of a long line of anonymous medieval minstrels who naturalized in English the short riming stanzas of Latin and French medieval lyric poetry. His best work has their sweetness and spontaneity, their perfect command of metrical form, and the freshness of their simple language; and to these qualities Wyatt adds a courtly grace and delicacy, the dignity of a man of learning and culture. It was this union of the popular tradition of lyric poetry with the courtly that was to achieve such great things in the Elizabethan age, and it seems to have been Wyatt who discovered the secret. His young friend and disciple Henry Howard, Earl of Surrey, was the heir of the great Duke of Norfolk, one of the most powerful nobles in England. Surrey was a man of a different stamp from the 'depe-witted Sir Thomas Wyatt'. He was a hot-tempered turbulent young noble and was described as 'the most foolish proud boy that is in England'. But he was a remarkable poet, a finer craftsman than Wyatt, though he never attains the magic of Wyatt's finest lyrics. In its union of the chivalrous spirit with humanism his poetry anticipates that of Sidney. He is more definitely a humanist poet than Wyatt. Petrarch influences him, and like Wyatt he translates from the Italian, but Latin poetry meant more to him than it did for the elder poet. He translates from Martial, from Horace and from Virgil and his translations have something of the lucidity, the conciseness and the elegance of the originals. If Wyatt had the glory of bringing the sonnet into English poetry, it is to Surrey that we owe our great epic and dramatic measure of blank verse. His translation of two books of Virgil's *Æneid* is doubly significant, as the first English verse translation of Virgil (a Scottish version by Gavin Douglas was printed a few years before Surrey's and probably written much earlier), and also as the first example of the unrimed English decasyllabic line which was to be the chief instrument of Shakespeare and Milton. Blank verse is symbolic of English humanist poetry, which was to combine medieval tradition with lessons learnt from the classics. The abandonment of rime was doubtless due to the influence of Greek and Latin verse. The structure of the line itself, however, is derived not from Homer or Virgil, but from the medieval poets, Chaucer and his French and Italian masters.

THE ARREST OF HUMANISM: THE REFORMATION

The fair promise of the early English Literary Renaissance, the humanism of Sir Thomas More and his friends and the revived poetry of Wyatt and his followers was to be destroyed by the social, economic and religious revolution which began in the latter part of Henry VIII's reign and continued until the accession of Elizabeth. Whatever the ultimate causes of this upheaval may have been, it was certainly precipitated by the desire of Henry VIII for a male heir and his passion for Anne Boleyn. All the children of his first wife Catherine of Aragon died in infancy, except one daughter, and by 1518 it became evident that Catherine would bear no more children. The problem of the succession was a vital one for England. It must be remembered that Englishmen had not at that date had any experience of the rule of a successful queen.

It was universally believed that only a male heir could secure an undisputed succession, and the memories of the terrible dynastic wars of the fifteenth century were still fresh in men's minds. Henry had for long been infatuated with Anne Boleyn, a dark-eyed, vivacious maid of honour of the Queen and a relative of the great family of the Howards. In 1524 he formed the plan of divorcing Catherine and marrying Anne. According to Canon Law this could only be done by obtaining an annulment of the first marriage from the Pope. Before her marriage to Henry Catherine had been married for a few months to Prince Arthur, his elder brother, who had died in 1502. The Roman Church did not permit marriage to the widow of a deceased brother, but Pope Julius II had granted Henry a dispensation from this rule. Now Henry contended that the dispensation had been illegal and should be set aside. There can be little doubt that he and others believed that the marriage with Catherine had been cursed, as all the male heirs who had been born had died in infancy. Catherine was an aunt of the Emperor Charles V, who was also King of Spain, and the most powerful ruler in Europe. The Emperor was indignant at Henry's attempt to divorce his aunt. Pope Clement VII was in the power of Charles, whose army had recently captured and sacked Rome. There were attempts at negotiation with the Pope and the Emperor. At last the Pope consented to the setting up of a legatine commission in London, under the presidency of Wolsey and the Italian cardinal Campeggio. Before the commission could pass sentence it was adjourned by the order of the Pope who, under pressure from the Emperor, now ordered Henry to attend a trial at Rome. Henry refused indignantly, and his wrath fell on Wolsey, who had always been detested by Anne Boleyn. He was stripped of all his offices of State and most of his wealth, and had to retire from court to his Archbishopric at York. Catherine was banished from the king's palace, and Anne, who had been living with the state of a queen, was finally married to Henry in 1533, in defiance of the Pope.

The quarrel between the English King and the Pope over

the divorce coincided with a great religious revolution on the Continent and a social and economic revolution in England. We have already seen that Erasmus and his English friends More and Colet were ardently desirous of purifying the Church from the corruption into which it had fallen and awakening it from its spiritual lethargy. Erasmus's famous edition of the orignal Greek text of the New Testament, which appeared in 1516, contained notes bitterly attacking the condition of the Roman Church and even questioning some of its doctrines. The book had effects beyond anything that Erasmus dreamed of or desired. It seems to have been the spark which kindled into a flame a vast body of discontent against the Church that had been smouldering for some time in Germany. In the following year Martin Luther, an Augustinian monk who was moved to indignation by the sale of indulgences and other abuses of the ecclesiastical system, nailed his famous theses to the door of the church at Wittenberg and thus began a religious revolt which spread like wildfire through Germany. The monks said that Erasmus laid the egg and Luther hatched it; Erasmus retorted that the egg he laid was meant for a hen and Luther hatched a game-cock. The Reformation now began to assume a different aspect from the purifying and modernizing of the Church contemplated by the Erasmian reformers. In Germany, and later in other countries, it became an attack not only on the abuses of the Church but on the Church itself. This revolutionary movement had at first very little effect in England except on a few scholars like William Tyndale. Between 1517 and 1529 England seemed of all European countries to be the most firmly attached to the Pope. Before the divorce controversy became acute Henry posed as the paladin of the Church; he wrote a Latin book against Luther and received from the grateful Pope the title of Defender of the Faith. But two forces were working to undermine this alliance between England and the Papacy. One was Henry's desire to possess Anne Boleyn. The other was the strong anti-clerical movement in England. This movement was not at

RENAISSANCE AND REFORMATION

first Protestant, though afterwards it gathered force by the spread of the Protestant doctrine. It was due partly to honest indignation at the immense power and wealth possessed by the Church and the way in which their power and wealth were abused, and partly to the baser motive of envy of the Church's possessions and the desire of private persons to enrich themselves at its expense. The families which had become rich by breeding sheep and manufacturing and exporting cloth consisted of hard-headed business men, aggressive individualists who looked with indignation on what appeared to them to be a waste of broad lands and vast treasure on the maintenance of idle monks and nuns and friars. The king, too, by his reckless extravagance had squandered the whole of the vast sums accumulated by his father and needed money badly. The great religious orders whose houses and possessions had been admired by the Venetian envoy in Henry VII's time were a tempting bait. Closely connected with them were other religious and semi-religious corporations such as the chantries and the guilds, which also had large possessions. In fact, the old medieval communal life, wealthy, to a certain extent corrupt, and helpless, was confronted by the power of aggressive private capitalism in the first flush of its lusty youth. That power allied itself with the king who had been alienated from the Church on account of the divorce. The parliament summoned in 1529, sometimes called the Reformation Parliament, began the great revolution. In the year when it was summoned a certain barrister called Simon Fish published a vigorous, cleverly-written but scurrilous pamphlet called *A Supplication for the Beggars*, which the king is said to have read and enjoyed. It is a violent attack on the alleged idleness, greed and corruption of the 'Bishops, Abbots, Priors, Deacons, Archdeacons, Suffragans, Priests, Monks, Canons, Friars, Pardoners, and Summoners'. Fish lays particular stress on the great possessions of the Churchmen, 'the goodliest lordships, manors, lands and territories are theirs, beside this they have the tenth part of all corn, meadow, pasture, grass, wool, colts, calves, lambs, pigs, geese and chickens'. He goes on to reckon up (with gross exaggeration) the immense amounts of money annually paid to the Church for offerings, masses, and all the various and elaborate spiritual services performed by priests and monks for the faithful.

Fish's pamphlet is the beginning of the new literature of Protestant capitalism. It is highly significant that he reproaches the monks with laziness, and desires to make them work for their living. The ideal of the contemplative monk in his cell, which appealed so strongly to the medieval mind, had now come to appear ridiculous. The new ideal was that of the energetic man of affairs with his mind set on the acquisition of wealth. Fish and his friends had their way in the Parliament of 1529. This parliament was completely subservient to the king, and violently anti-clerical. It drew up a petition setting forth a long list of abuses of ecclesiastical power. It passed bills severely curtailing the ancient privileges of the clergy and it gave its warm support to Thomas Cromwell, a remarkable man who succeeded Wolsey as Henry's chief minister. Cromwell was a clever, unscrupulous politician who had served as a common soldier in Italy, and is said to have boasted of his indebtedness to Machiavelli's *The Prince*, a book which expresses the ruthless intellectualism of the Italian Renaissance, as Castiglione's *The Courtier* had expressed its aesthetic humanism, and holds up as the ideal for rulers the conception of *virtù* or energy entirely divorced from morality. It was Cromwell who organized the great spoliation of the Church. By a piece of legal chicane the whole nation, on account of Wolsey's acceptance of the office of papal legate, was judged by the law officers of the Crown to have incurred the penalties of the statute of Praemunire which forbade any appeal to Rome from an English ecclesiastical or civil court. The nation was pardoned, with the exception of the clergy, who had to purchase their pardon by acknowledging Henry as Head of the Church and Clergy of England, and by paying an immense fine amounting to about a million of modern money. What John Richard

Green, an English historian by no means favourable to the Roman Catholics, calls a 'reign of terror' began. Parliament confirmed Henry's new ecclesiastical title by passing the Act of Supremacy which conferred on him the title of the 'only supreme head on earth of the English Church'. This became one of the King's official titles, and the denial of it was pronounced to be High Treason, punishable by the terrible penalties attached to this crime in the sixteenth century. Cromwell set to work to make this ecclesiastical supremacy no mere title but a reality. His aim was to turn the vast and complex organization of the Medieval Church into a department of the State under the direct control of the centralized Tudor monarchy. Cromwell's policy had now placed the vast possessions of the monastic orders at Henry's mercy. Wolsey had already dissolved a few of the smaller convents. A commission was set up to inquire into the condition of the religious houses, but the inquiry was a farce. Between 1536 and 1542 all the religious houses and their immense possessions in land, in buildings, in gold and silver plate were seized. The country was covered with a network of Cromwell's spies. The total value of the gold and silver plate which was confiscated is estimated at £85,000 or about a million pounds sterling in modern money. The total value of the church property seized was nearly a million and a half, or in modern values between fourteen and fifteen millions. This property was not retained by the Crown, but sold immediately and the result was a great social and economic revolution. In that storm most of the glory of late-medieval art amid which men like More and Colet had been brought up was destroyed. 'The avalanche,' writes Professor R. W. Chambers, 'destroyed not only men's lives but treasures of art which the English nation had been accumulating for eight centuries.' Buildings, manuscripts, stained glass, paintings, woodwork, brasses, work of goldsmith and silversmith, were swept away. Only fragments have survived.

On the ruins of the old monastic system there arose a new plutocracy, the families which had been growing rich under

Henry VII and had long been casting greedy eyes on the wealth of the Church. The old abbey or friary would often become a rich man's house, or else it would be allowed to fall into ruin and a rich man's house would be built close by, while its lands would now form the rich man's estate. Shakespeare has put the whole tragedy of these great ruined monastic buildings into the single line where he uses them as an image for the leafless boughs of autumn:

Bare ruin'd choirs where late the sweet birds sang.

The country house was to be the new centre of English social life and culture, and English literature was to be dominated by its influence for centuries. Many of the great names among what is now the old English aristocracy—Cecils, Herberts, Russells, Sidneys, Sackvilles, Cavendishes—are derived from shrewd squires who bought up church lands under Henry VIII at absurdly low prices, and made fortunes out of them with the help of which some of their sons and grandsons collected libraries, bought pictures from Italy and Flanders, and patronized poets and men of letters.

In 1534 Henry was proclaimed by Parliament Supreme Head of the English Church. Sir Thomas More who had been Lord Chancellor from 1529 till 1532, but had resigned because he could not support the king's divorce policy, refused to take the oath prescribed in the Succession Act, which renounced papal primacy and acknowledged the lawfulness of Anne Boleyn's marriage. His friend, Bishop Fisher, was equally firm in his adherence to the Roman Church. Both were imprisoned in the Tower. Both were beheaded under the provisions of the statute which made it high treason to deny any of the king's titles including his new title of Supreme Head of the Church of England. More met his death with his usual courage, serenity and humour, declaring that he 'died the king's good servant but God's first'. With him died the hope of the early Renaissance in England. His death and that of Fisher sent a thrill of horror though Europe.

It may seem surprising that the champions of the New

Learning died as martyrs for the Old Religion. The fact may be explained by the difference between the conception of reform held by such men as Erasmus and More and the actual 'reformation' carried out by Henry VIII and Cromwell. The humanist reformers would have purified the Church from abuses, but they would have retained its power and influence and its international character. They were not Protestants: they did not want to divide the Church or set up new sects. They were enlightened Catholics, detesting the obscurantism and corruption of the late-medieval Church as much as any Protestant, but equally detesting the nationalism which wanted to cut off the English Church from continental civilization and the aggressive capitalism which wanted to plunder the Church of its wealth. Whatever we may think of their opinions, there is no doubt that their defeat was a great blow to the progress of the new civilization in England. In fact it meant the eclipse of humanism, as it was understood by Erasmus, for a quarter of a century.

The poets fared hardly better than the humanists in the latter years of Henry VIII. Wyatt was imprisoned in 1536 and again in 1541. He was no devout Catholic like More and Fisher, but a friend and supporter of Thomas Cromwell, the Protestant minister. But the savage tyranny of Henry's later years spared neither Protestant nor Catholic. Wyatt died in 1542 worn out at the age of thirty-eight. The young Earl of Surrey was one of Henry's last victims. In 1546 he was arrested on the charge that he had quartered the arms of Edward the Confessor on his escutcheon. The real reason was Henry's jealousy and fear of the Howards, and particularly of the Duke of Norfolk, Surrey's ambitious father. His trial, like most treason trials under the Tudors, was a farce, and he was executed a few days before the king himself died. Thus the reign which had opened with such brilliant promise for humanism closed with the judicial murder of a young man who promised to be the first great English humanist poet, and who, if he had lived, might well have anticipated the achievements of Sidney and Spenser by half a century.

English Protestantism, regarded as a religious force, did not grow out of Henry VIII's spoliation of the monasteries or his assumption of the headship of the Church. Henry's reformation was an 'old Catholic' reformation which abolished the monastic and mendicant orders and repudiated papal supremacy but left nearly all the rest of the Catholic organization and dogma untouched. At the same time, however, genuine Protestantism was appearing in England. The popular medieval Protestant movement of the Lollards, which had flourished in England in the reigns of Edward III and Richard II had died down at the end of the fifteenth century, but it had never been forgotten, and the books of its great leader Wyclif, in spite of all attempts to suppress them, still circulated. The new English Protestantism, however, was largely due to a group of Cambridge scholars who used to meet at an inn called the White Horse at Cambridge about 1521. This group began by reading Erasmus's paraphrase of the New Testament, but soon began to be interested in the new docrines of Luther and was nicknamed 'Germany'. It included William Tyndale, Miles Coverdale, Thomas Cranmer, and Hugh Latimer, the men who created the literature of popular English Protestantism, the translation of the Bible, the English Prayer Book, and a new type of vigorous vernacular sermon.

Tyndale, a fine scholar and a fiery spirit full of revolutionary ardour, came to London from Gloucestershire in 1523 in the hope of obtaining the patronage of Cuthbert Tunstall, Bishop of London, for his projected translation of the New Testament from the original Greek, but the London clergy were thoroughly alarmed by the spread of Lutheran doctrine and Tyndale received no encouragement from ecclesiastical quarters. In 1524 he went to Hamburg and there he finished his translation of the New Testament. He took it to Cologne to be printed, but the Catholic magistrates of that city intervened and before the printing was finished Tyndale and his assistant fled to Worms with the incomplete edition. There the English New Testament was finally printed in full and published. Tyndale's version is not only a translation of scripture. It is also a piece of Protestant propaganda. The notes are strongly anti-Roman. Words with Catholic associations like church, priest, grace, charity and penance are deliberately avoided and the translator substitutes for them words which are accurate renderings of the Greek, such as congregation, elder, favour, love, repentance. Tyndale planned a complete English Bible, and when he had finished translating the New Testament from the Greek, he started a translation of the Old Testament from the Hebrew. He published an English Pentateuch in 1530 and to the second edition added the Book of Jonah. He probably left in manuscript a version of the Old Testament as far as the end of Chronicles. His work was brought to an end in 1535 when he was enticed outside the walls of the free city of Antwerp and executed by the Spaniards.

The importance of Tyndale's Bible translations can hardly be overestimated. The Lollards had produced versions of the Bible from the Vulgate, the Latin translation of the Bible by St Jerome, but Tyndale's translations were the first English versions made from the Hebrew and Greek texts. They are not only notable works of scholarship, they are literary achievements of a very high order. They are in fact the core of the great English Bible which was to be the chief literary influence on the English mind for at least three centuries. The subsequent English versions, culminating in the Authorised Version of 1611 must be regarded simply as revisions and extensions of Tyndale's work, which, in the words of Professor Pollard, fixed 'once for all, the style and tone of the English Bible'. This style and tone are essentially popular. Tyndale is said to have declared that it was his ambition that a boy 'that dryveth the plough' should know more of the scriptures than a priest. His English is therefore remarkably simple, direct and lucid, while the translator's reverence and religious fervour give it a rare dignity. It is not the ornate prose of the Renaissance, but the clear forcible English of common speech in the sixteenth century wrought into unforgettable phrases by a man who had a poet's sense of the power and beauty of words and of speech rhythms. The music of Tyndale's sentences is echoed in countless English masterpieces of verse and prose from Spenser and Shakespeare to Ruskin and Newman.

Tyndale's work was continued by the Yorkshire priest Miles Coverdale, inferior to him as a scholar but almost his equal as a master of English prose style. The 'Great Bible' which was officially adopted in 1539, and placed in the churches by order of Henry VIII consisted of Tyndale's version completed by Coverdale. Coverdale's versions of the psalms were included in the Prayer Books of Edward VI because of their beautiful rhythms and felicitous phrasing, and have been retained in the English Prayer Book ever since.

Thomas Cranmer began his ecclesiastical career as Chaplain to Anne Boleyn and was made Archbishop of Canterbury in 1533. He was not as ardent a reformer as Tyndale, but somewhat of an opportunist who adapted himself with extraordinary skill to all the curious changes in Henry's ecclesiastical policy. In 1542 a Committee of Convocation was set up by Cranmer to consider a reformation of the service books and in 1543 it was decreed that a chapter of the English Bible (the 'Great Bible') should be read in churches every Sunday and Holy day. An English litany was issued officially in 1544. It was not a mere translation of the old Latin litany, but a thoroughly revised version in which most of the invocations to saints were omitted. This was the furthest step in liturgical reform that Cranmer dared to take while Henry was still alive. When the king died in 1547 his son, the boy Edward VI, was in the hands of advisers who were determined to bring about a Protestant reformation. Immediately prayers in the royal chapel were read in English, and a temporary English order of communion was substituted for the mass. With the help of a committee Cranmer proceeded to draw up the first English Prayer Book, which was published early in 1549 and officially adopted by the Act of Uniformity in that year. It was not revolutionary in character, but consisted mainly of translations from the old Latin service books, especially from the Sarum breviary which was very popular in medieval England. When a rebellion broke out in the West, and the Catholic rebels likened the new English service to 'a Christmas game', the Royal message to them (probably written by Cranmer) answered in the following words: 'It seemeth to you a new service: and indeed it is none other than the old: the selfsame words in English which were in Latin, saving only a few things take out.' In the latter part of the reign of Edward VI strong pressure was brought on the government to make it proceed further in the direction of Protestant reforms. Cranmer was much in the company of the foreign Protestant leaders who were in England at that time, while Hooper, Bishop of Gloucester, criticized the first Prayer Book severely. The result of this agitation was the issue of the second Prayer Book of Edward VI, a revised service book of a more decidedly Protestant character, in November 1552. It was this second Prayer Book which was re-issued by Elizabeth, and it has formed the basis of all subsequent revisions.

The English Prayer Book was mainly the work of Cranmer. It has been hardly less influential than the English Bible itself. Like the Bible of Tyndale and Coverdale it combines simplicity with wonderful stateliness, dignity and felicity of phrasing. It must never be forgotten that, from the accession of Elizabeth until the time when the English ceased to be a church-going people, the great prose of the English Bible and the English Prayer Book was heard by almost the whole nation every Sunday and Holy day. Cranmer was also the author of the greater part of the First Book of Homilies, an official collection of printed sermons which were often read in church, and these, too, are noble examples of stately Tudor prose.

The fourth divine whose writings exerted a powerful influence on the English Reformation was Hugh Latimer. The son of a Leicestershire yeoman who had a farm 'of three or four pound by yere at the uttermost', he was probably a pupil at Cambridge of Erasmus, who became Professor of Greek in 1510. Henry VIII made him bishop of Worcester, and showed him much favour at first. In the latter part of Henry's reign, however, he had to resign his bishopric and narrowly escaped with his life. When Edward VI came to the throne he did not return to his bishopric, but remained with Cranmer at Lambeth and devoted himself to preaching. When Catholicism was restored by Mary he was marked down for destruction, and the story of his intrepid bearing at the stake when he was burnt at Oxford in 1555, is well known. Latimer's sermons are masterpieces of vivid, racy, homely prose. He was a man of the people, and he preached to the people in their own language. His sermons are full of humour and anecdote. He makes great use of alliteration and pithy proverbs, and has much in common with Langland and other popular medieval poets. He is noteworthy not only for his attacks on medieval superstitions, but also for his fierce denunciation of the social abuses brought about by the rising tide of capitalism and the spoliation of Church property by favourites of Henry VIII and courtiers of Edward VI, the difficulty of the poor in obtaining justice, and their sufferings through the enclosure of the old common lands. In Latimer we hear for the first time the voice of Protestant democracy, which was to produce the John Bunyans and George Foxes of the next century.

The revolutionary period that began with the attack of Henry VIII and Cromwell on the property of the Church may be said to have continued through the short reigns of his successors, Edward VI and Mary I. Edward was a sickly child, and during his reign the country was governed by rapacious nobles who continued the work of spoliation. The medieval guilds were suppressed and their property plundered and many of the ancient grammar schools suffered the same fate. In fact it has been said that the so-called Edward VI grammar schools that survive in certain English towns are the schools that were lucky enough to escape the depredations of the courtiers of the well-meaning but helpless young king. The Protestant reformers had their own way in this reign, and there was an influx of continental Protestant refugees into the country. Through them England was now in touch with the later and more extreme Protestant movement which originated in south-eastern France and Switzerland. Zwingli the Swiss, and Calvin the Frenchman, were the leaders of this new Protestantism. In 1540 Calvin had published his *Institutio Religionis Christianae*, where he applies to Protestant dogma and Church government a mind as ruthlessly logical as those of the great Catholic Schoolmen of the Middle Ages. Lutheranism had been largely negative in character. Calvinism was a great ordered system of theology, ethics and ecclesiastical organization. The Franco-Swiss Reformation did not influence England much at first, but its doctrine and discipline soon began to make an appeal to a small minority of ardent spirits who were dissatisfied with the *via media* of Cranmer. These men were the spiritual ancestors of the great Puritan movement of the seventeenth century.

Edward died in 1553, and after the brief and tragic interlude of Lady Jane Grey, he was succeeded by his elder sister Mary the daughter of Catherine of Aragon, who restored Roman Catholicism and married Philip II of Spain. Mary's persecution of the Protestants, though hardly more ferocious than Henry VIII's persecution of the papalists and the religious orders, was more spectacular, and the burning of about three hundred persons including Latimer, Cranmer and other distinguished men as well as many humbler but equally brave victims probably popularized Protestantism more than all the preaching of the reign of Edward VI. It gave the new religion a martyrology more vivid and less remote than that of Romanism and this advantage was cleverly and unscrupulously exploited in the lurid narratives of John Foxe's *Acts and Monuments* (The Book of Martyrs) first published in 1563, which was one of the most popular English books for two centuries. It is to be noticed that Mary did not dare to restore the lands and property of the religious orders to their original owners. The new Families were already too strongly entrenched for any sovereign, however ardently Catholic, to dislodge them. Their leader was a clever squire called Sir William Cecil. Like most of his fellows he conformed to Romanism under Mary, but when she died, he and his friends rallied to the support of her sister Elizabeth, Anne Boleyn's daughter, who, though she had been declared illegitimate by Parliament, succeeded without opposition to the throne in 1558. The last year of Queen Mary's reign saw the publication of certain books which may be said to contain nearly all that was saved from the early Tudor literary renaissance. They were Sir Thomas More's English Works collected by his nephew John Rastell in a noble folio and the two black letter octavos in which Richard Tottel published the *Songs and Sonnets* of Wyatt and Surrey and Surrey's blank verse translations from Virgil. The great abbeys were falling into ruin or had been converted into country houses, the glorious craftsmanship of the late fifteenth and early sixteenth centuries had been pitilessly destroyed, but the printing press preserved some remnant at least of the early English humanist movement, and thus laid the foundations of the great literature of the Elizabethan age.

CHAPTER II
THE ELIZABETHANS

ELIZABETH AND HER ENGLAND

WHEN the fanatical, unhappy, half-Spanish Queen Mary died on November 17th, 1558, the Renaissance in England had its second chance. Elizabeth, daughter of Anne Boleyn and half-sister of the dead queen, was a young woman of twenty-five with a fine, dignified presence, a lofty spirit and a ready wit. Like her father she understood the English people. She gloried in the fact that she was 'mere English', and combined something of the vanity of Henry VIII with much of the political wisdom and caution of Henry VII. The extreme English Protestants, who had been in exile on the continent during Mary's reign, hurried home on Elizabeth's accession, which they hailed with jubilation. They looked forward to a revival and a completion of the religious revolution begun by Thomas Cromwell and Cranmer. Fortunately, however, for England, Elizabeth was a child of the Renaissance rather than of the Reformation. Whatever the faults of Henry VIII may have been, he certainly gave his children a good education. Elizabeth had been trained by distinguished representatives of English humanism, whose first centre in England was at Oxford, and then in the latter part of the reign of Henry VIII among a group of brilliant Cambridge scholars. These men form the chief link between the school of More and Colet and Elizabethan learning and letters. Their leader was Sir John Cheke, Professor of Greek at Cambridge, the pupil of Erasmus and the tutor of Edward VI. Cheke's favourite pupil was Roger Ascham, a distinguished writer of English prose, who began his literary career under Henry VIII and ended it under Elizabeth. Ascham's favourite pupil was a certain William Grindal. Elizabeth's teachers were Grindal and Ascham, and under their tuition she became, like Sir Thomas

More's daughters, a learned lady with a thorough knowledge of Greek and Latin literature, and a power of expressing herself forcibly and fluently in Latin, Italian, French and English. 'I thank God,' she said to one of her parliaments, 'I am endued with such qualities that if I were turned out of the realm in my petticoat, I were able to live in any place in Christendom.' The boast was characteristic and not ill-founded. But she had a touch of humanity, even of tenderness, that prevented her from becoming a pedant. This was the quality that endeared her to the English people. They never forgot her little gracious actions on the day of her coronation, when she accepted a branch of rosemary from a poor woman, and smiled when someone shouted 'remember old King Henry VIII'.

When Elizabeth came to the throne England was a poor country and the English were one of the backward nations of Europe. The question of religion divided the nation into two bitterly opposed factions, the Protestants smarting under the Marian persecutions, and the Catholics dreading the revenge that a Protestant government was likely to take for the burning of Cranmer, Latimer, Hooper and Ridley. 'At this time,' writes Stowe, the chronicler, 'the English Nation was wonderfully divided in opinions as well in matters ecclesiastical as in divers points of religion by reason of three changes within the compass of twelve years.' The confusion of mind caused by these violent changes in Church government and dogma might well have led to chaos and to a series of wars of religion such as those which devastated France in the sixteenth and Germany in the seventeenth century. It was from this fate that Elizabeth and her advisers saved England. Cecil and the squires were her supporters because they knew that the tenure of the lands they had acquired from the Church would be endangered by a religious conflict. But Elizabeth was their mistress, not their servant. She would not allow them to plunder her government as the government of Edward VI had been plundered; and she would not allow them to impose on England an alien and revolutionary

Protestantism. She herself was neither a Papist nor a strong Protestant. At bottom she was probably somewhat of a sceptic but the public worship that she favoured was of the Anglo-Catholic type. She quizzed the extreme Protestants as her 'brethren in Christ', and tried to retain the crucifix and the celibacy of the clergy. She would not satisfy the Protestant lust for revenge by executing the Catholic bishops, though she imprisoned them. It was long, too, before she abandoned all hope of reconciliation with the Papacy, and if Rome had been willing to meet her half-way, to recognize the English liturgy and the English Bible, and to give the Anglican Church a considerable measure of independence, it is probable that a reconciliation would have been effected. For Elizabeth was both a 'little Englander' and a 'good European' and had no desire to cut her country off from the community of Christendom. Reconciliation with the Papacy, however, became impossible after the rising of the Catholic Earls of Northumberland and Westmorland in 1569, backed by money from Rome, and the subsequent issue of the Bull of Pope Pius V in 1570, which excommunicated Elizabeth and gave her throne to her cousin, Mary, Queen of Scots. Yet even after these events Elizabeth was willing to employ Protestants and Catholics alike, provided they were loyal and efficient. 'I will open no window into men's consciences,' she said. But unhappily the religious conflict became a political one, and the Jesuits, often brave men and noble martyrs, came to be treated as the agents of a foreign power that was plotting to assassinate the queen. Ardent patriots and Protestants like Walsingham and Sidney chafed at Elizabeth's policy of moderation and compromise, but one of its results was to prevent English civilization and culture from becoming provincial and sectarian. The Elizabethans were able to participate both in the Protestant spirit of free inquiry and the Catholic sense of a European community with a common intellectual and imaginative heritage, and they owed this privilege in a great measure to the character and tastes of the Queen.

The Elizabethan age falls naturally into two parts. The first is a period of preparation, the second a period of achievement. For more than twenty years Elizabeth played for time, keeping several distinguished suitors in a fairly hopeful condition, putting in order England's finances, which Mary had left in a shocking state, strengthening her position both at home and abroad, and above all, keeping on pretty good terms with Spain and refusing to be drawn into the major European war with Philip which the extreme Protestants were trying to precipitate. Her task at home was harder than it may appear when we read of the enthusiasm with which the Londoners greeted her accession. London was the most Protestant part of England and Elizabeth easily gained its heart. But she had also to gain the hearts of a host of factious nobles and Catholic or semi-Catholic squires. Part of her success was due to the splendour and dignity of her court. The court again dominated English life under Elizabeth as it dominated it in the reign of Henry VIII and now it became something different from any previous court in English history.

The worship of Elizabeth, the royal virgin, 'Faith's pure Shield, the Christian Diana', to whose cause the hearts of all true Englishmen were supposed to be patriotically and chivalrously devoted, was both a romantic idyll and a kind of religion, supplying the English Protestants with a badly needed mythology, more national in character than the mariolatry of the counter-reformation, and having the advantage of being incarnated in a living woman. Elizabethan poetry cannot be understood unless we appreciate this fact. When Armado in *Love's Labour's Lost* says, 'I do adore thy sweet grace's slipper,' he is speaking the language of the whole of Elizabethan England. Elizabeth and her court became the focus of the English imagination as well as the centre of political life. Shakespeare may place his scenes of courtly life in Athens, Illyria, Sicily, Denmark or Bohemia, but the grace and the charm of Theseus and Hippolyta, Viola and Olivia, Beatrice, Hamlet and Florizel belong to the court of Elizabeth.

The direct influence on Elizabethan poetry of the gorgeous shows and pageants in which Elizabeth delighted was great, and their indirect influence must have been even greater. They filled the gap left in the popular imagination by the disappearance of the gorgeous ritual and processions of the medieval church, and prevented that drying up of the old pagan joy in colour and drama which Puritanism was to achieve in the next century. When Elizabeth's great favourite, Robert Dudley, Earl of Leicester, entertained her at his Castle of Kenilworth in July 1575, the pageantry lasted for three weeks. She was greeted at the castle gate with a speech in verse spoken by a porter dressed as Hercules. As she crossed the bridge over the pool in front of the Castle, the Lady of the Lake with attendant nymphs floated to her on an island illuminated by torches. In the base court gods and goddesses presented her with birds, fruit, fish and wine. When she entered the castle all the clocks were stopped to show that time stood still while the Queen was at Kenilworth. As she came into the chamber, guns and fireworks were discharged whose noise and flame was heard and seen for twenty miles round. The next day was Sunday, and after church lords and ladies danced before the queen with 'lively agility and commendable grace'. On Monday there was hunting, and the Queen's steed was stopped by a 'salvage man' girt with oak leaves representing the god Sylvanus, who began an immense oration in verse which he continued to recite as he ran by the Queen's horse, declaring that, if his rude speech did not offend her, he would continue to run and speak it for twenty miles! Sylvanus was none other than the poet George Gascoigne, who wrote most of the verses for the pageant and subsequently published an account of 'The Princely Pleasures of Kenilworth'. In 1591, when the Earl of Hertford was the Queen's host at Elvetham, a special lake was constructed with three islands and Elizabeth was diverted by Nereus, five Tritons, Neptune and other marine deities. In the morning when the Queen awoke, she was greeted at her chamber window by three musicians in old English country attire, who sang her the lovely song which Nicholas Breton had written for the occasion:

> *In the merry month of May*
> *In a morn by break of day,*
> *Forth I walked by the wood side,*
> *Whereas May was in his pride.*
> *There I spied, all alone*
> *Phillida and Coridon*
> *Much ado there was, God wot!*
> *He would love and she would not....*

The goddess who was the centre of these elaborate rituals was as human as the Homeric divinities. She spat and swore like her father Henry VIII. She fondled Leicester and her other favourites in the face of the whole court. She hunted and danced superbly, and was proud of her classical scholarship. She had the gift of noble English speech too. When the Commons petitioned her to marry early in her reign, she replied with lofty poetic eloquence: 'If I continue in this kind of life I have begun, I doubt not but God will so direct mine own and your Counsels that ye shall not need to doubt of a Successor which may be more beneficial to the Commonwealth than he that may be born of me, considering that the issue of the best Princes many times degenerateth. And to me it shall be a full satisfaction, both for the memorial of my Name, and for my Glory, also, if, when I shall let my last breath, it be engraven on my Marble Tomb: Here lieth Elizabeth, which Reigned a Virgin, and died a Virgin.' Many years later, when she received the thanks of the House of Commons for her proclamation abolishing the hated monopolies or royal grants giving the sole rights of manufacture and sale of various articles she spoke in the same magical vein:

> Mr Speaker, we perceive your coming is to present thanks to us. Know I accept them with no less joy than your loves can have desire to offer such a present, and do

THE ELIZABETHANS

more esteem it than any treasure or riches; for those we know how to prize, but loyalty, love and thanks, I account them invaluable. And though God hath raised me high, yet this I account the glory of my crown, that I have reigned with your loves.

A queen who could speak like this was worthy to rule the England of Shakespeare, Spenser, Hooker and Bacon. She was more than a queen of England. She was the epitome of her age: sensual, artistic, with a childish love of finery and a childish appetite for pleasure, yet with a cool, calculating intellect that baffled the ablest statesmen in Europe; sordidly mean in some ways, recklessly extravagant in others, at once affectionate, vain, compassionate and cruel. This was Spenser's Gloriana, Raleigh's Cynthia and Shakespeare's fair Vestal throned by the West. Even when she was a gaunt old woman with a red wig and a few black teeth the poets and courtiers worshipped her. That worship was not mere flattery. They rightly saw in her the incarnate spirit of the nation and the age.

. . . .

In the sixty-six years that elapsed between Columbus's voyage across the Atlantic and the accession of Elizabeth to the English throne, a large part of the American continent had been discovered, and Spain, already the first power in Europe with her possessions in Italy and the Netherlands, had erected a great colonial empire in Central and South America.

The first Spanish settlers in the West Indies had been followed by the soldier-explorers, Cortez and Pizarro, who had conquered and annexed the great kingdoms of Mexico and Peru. Now it was found that the New World was rich in gold, silver and precious stones. Great fleets brought these treasures annually to Europe, making the Spanish King the wealthiest monarch in Christendom. Portuguese mariners, too, following in the footsteps of Vasco da Gama, the first modern circumnavigator of Africa, had opened up a great trade with

India and the Far East; and in 1520 the Portuguese captain Magellan rounded South America by the Straits that bear his name, and sailed across the Pacific to the Philippines. As early as 1493 Pope Alexander VI had issued his famous bull dividing the world by a line running from pole to pole a hundred leagues west of the Azores. This line, passing down the Atlantic and cutting off Brazil from the rest of South America, can be seen marked on one of the globes in Holbein's picture of 'The Ambassadors' in the National Gallery. All the newly-discovered land east of it was assigned to Portugal and west of it to Spain. England played only a small part in the first great act of the drama of the discovery of the New World.

Nevertheless, the voyages of the Italian, Spanish and Portuguese navigators completely altered the situation of the islands of north-western Europe. On the ancient and medieval maps Britain is at the farthest extremity of the inhabited world. For the Romans its inhabitants were 'ultimi Britanni' and throughout the Middle Ages they were regarded as living on the outer edge of Christendom. By the middle of the sixteenth century the discoveries in the New World had brought about a great change. The Atlantic was becoming the great highway of the civilized world instead of the Mediterranean, and instead of being, as it were, on the rim of the map of Christendom, England was almost in the centre of it. The British Isles lay between Spain's rich possessions in America and the great commercial and industrial centres in the Netherlands and Germany, and its harbours were, perhaps, better suited for the purposes of Atlantic trade than those of any country in Europe.

Englishmen were not slow to perceive the advantages of their situation, and their determination to acquire a share in the wealth and wonders of the new discoveries is one of the capital factors in the life of the Elizabethan period. The voyage of John Cabot, the anglicized Venetian who reached America with a Bristol ship soon after Columbus, was not forgotten, but the religious discussions, and the economic revolution caused by the seizure of Church property, prevented any important English enterprise of discovery from being undertaken during the first half of the sixteenth century. In a remarkable book published in 1527 Robert Thorne, a friend of the Cabots, who had visited Spain, advised Englishmen to seek a route to the rich lands of Asia by sailing northwards through the arctic seas. 'There is no land unhabitable and no sea unnavigable', he wrote, and his proud words might have been taken as a motto for the English navigators of the coming age. At the end of the reign of Edward VI the Company of Merchant Adventurers was formed at Bristol 'for the discovery of Regions, Dominions, Islands and places unknown'. The governor of this famous company was Sebastian Cabot, the son of John Cabot, who, like his father, had crossed the Atlantic in a Bristol ship, and sailed along the American coast southward to Florida.

The first attempt of the Merchant Adventurers was to find a north-east passage to Asia. Richard Chancellor with one of their ships reached the White Sea, and travelled from there overland to Moscow, where he established trading and diplomatic relations for the first time between England and Russia. Other Englishmen followed, crossing Russia to the Caspian, Persia and Central Asia, and in 1558, the year of Elizabeth's accession to the throne, Anthony Jenkinson reached Bokhara. Then it was supposed that the riches of Cathay, the great kingdom described by Odoric of Pordenone and Marco Polo, the medieval travellers, could be reached by a north-westerly route, and that, just as Magellan had sailed round the southern extremity of America, so some English pioneer might circumnavigate its northern shores. The chief result of this theory was the heroic enterprise of Martin Frobisher and John Davies, who failed to find a north-west passage, but succeeded in discovering much of the northern part of Canada. But in Elizabeth's reign a new school of navigators sprang up. The northern school was in a large measure the result of unwillingness to interfere with the Spanish monopoly in Central and South America, for

Catholic England was on good terms with Spain. The new school, however, was a southern school, and it had learned much from the exploits of French Protestant sea rovers, who had shown that, powerful as Spain might be in Europe, her settlements in the New World were ill defended against a resolute attack. French cruisers had captured many rich Spanish vessels returning from America and from seizing ships they soon proceeded to attack ports. In 1536 a French ship actually captured the great Spanish town of Havana in Cuba and held it to ransom. The French Protestant corsairs were soon joined by Protestant Dutchmen and Englishmen, eager to harry the subjects of the King of Spain, the hated enemy of their religion, and equally eager to seize and share the fabulous wealth of the 'Indies', which he had hitherto monopolized. In the early years of Elizabeth's reign this kind of piracy became a sort of national industry. For centuries English seafaring activities had been of certain well defined types: the Iceland and North Sea fisheries, supported by the great demand for fish on Catholic fast-days, and the ancient wine-trade with Bordeaux. Now since it was almost the mark of a good Protestant to eat flesh on Fridays and Saints' Days the fisheries were ruined, and none of Cecil's legislation could revive the old demand for fish; while piratical attacks on Spanish ships in the Channel and the Atlantic provided a much more congenial occupation than honest trade for the young English seamen of the third quarter of the sixteenth century. They found bold and spirited leaders among the young men of good birth, such as the Cobhams, the Killigrews and the Carews. 'Incredible it is,' writes Camden, 'with how great alacrity they put to sea, and how readily they exercised piracy against the Spaniards.' Philip and his governors in the Netherlands were constantly complaining. Captured Englishmen had been cruelly treated in the prisons of the Inquisition, and there was deep sympathy with the cause of the Dutch Protestants who were rebelling against Spain. The piracies swelled into a sort of vast private war conducted by English buccaneers on all the seas of the world,

THE ELIZABETHANS

a huge enterprise in which most of the nobility and even the Queen herself had a financial interest. One of the results was that enormous wealth poured into England in the form of gold, silver, precious stones, spices, silks, wines and all manner of luxuries.

John Hawkins was the first great sailor of the new southern school of English adventurers. The prototype of a host of successors, merchant, slave dealer, pirate and patriot, he was succeeded by his cousin Francis Drake, the son of a Devonshire parson. In 1570 Drake saw the Pacific for the first time, and vowed that one day he would sail on it in an English ship. His next and most famous voyage was the fulfilment of this vow. In the autumn of 1577 he left England with five vessels and one hundred and fifty men. His state was that of a prince. He dined off silver plate, attended by musicians, and at his table sat a number of young men of good family, sons of those Elizabethan gentlemen, who, as Shakespeare remarked, used to

> *Put forth their sons to seek preferment out:*
> *Some to the wars, to try their fortune there;*
> *Some to discover islands far away.*

It was to these young gentlemen that Drake addressed his famous words: 'I must have the gentlemen to hale and draw with the mariner, and the mariner with the gentleman. What, let us show ourselves all to be of a company.' The Queen was informed of the enterprise and had shares in Drake's venture. The English ships sailed through the Strait of Magellan and fell on the rich undefended Spanish towns of the Pacific sea-board, acquiring an immense plunder. They sailed northwards up the coast of what is now California, where Drake entered into friendly relations with the Indians, who regarded him as their champion against the Spaniards. Finding no north-west passage, he struck across the Pacific to the Philippines and the East Indian Islands, where he traded with the natives, and returned by the Cape of Good Hope. In September 1580 he entered Plymouth Sound, the first

English captain to have circumnavigated the world, with treasure worth over a million. For once Elizabeth cast caution to the winds, received Drake at court, visited his ship at Deptford, and knighted him on board.

The return of Drake in 1580 was the turning point of the Elizabethan age. England was at last ready for the great struggle with Spain. Open war soon followed. Spain made her great effort to conquer the heretic islanders in 1588 and was foiled by the men who served their apprenticeship in the guerilla warfare of the Spanish Main. In 1595 the tables were turned, and Sir Walter Ralegh and the Earl of Essex captured and plundered the great Spanish city of Cadiz. The gaiety and exuberance of spirits displayed by the commanders of this expedition was characteristic of the age. Essex flung his hat into the sea when the order was given to enter the harbour, and Ralegh replied to the Spanish cannonades with fanfares of trumpets. An incidental result was the capture of a great Spanish library which formed the nucleus of the Bodleian library at Oxford.

While Hawkins, Drake and Raleigh were carrying the English flag into the New World of the West, humbler Englishmen were boldly pursuing the old dream of reaching the great and wealthy empires of Asia. When Shakespeare wrote in *Macbeth*:

Her husband's to Aleppo gone, master o' the Tyger. . . .

he is referring to events which were as topical as the achievements of a transatlantic flyer to-day. In 1583 the *Tyger* had sailed from England to the Levant. She landed five of her crew as near to Aleppo as the sea allowed, and these five Englishmen, John Eldred, John Newbery, Ralph Fitch, William Leeds and John Stony boldly set out to reach India by the overland route. Eldred halted between Bagdad and Basrah, and the four others were arrested by the Portuguese at Ormuz on the Persian Gulf and reached India as prisoners. Ralph Fitch escaped, walked over South India, Ceylon and Burma, and returned safely to England with accounts of the splendour of oriental kingdoms and the rich merchandise of the East:

> Sanguis draconis, coral, elephants' teeth, cloves garbled and ungarbled, calicoes, cinnamon, benzoin, benzoar stones, musk, saltpetre, nutmegs, mace, pepper and dust of pepper, silk, olibanum, tincal, seed-lac, shellac, tamarind, myrrh, frankincense, cowries, cassia, fistula, aloes lignine and socatrine, lignum aloes, cubels, ginghams, sallampores, morees, tapseils, niccanees, cardamums, chillies, baftas, taffaties of Persia, agate ware, camphor, Chinese dishes, chequeens, toqueens, ambergris, civets, pearl, rubies, diamonds, myrabalam, China roots, ginger, orris root, cassia lignum, vermilion, indigo, quicksilver, conserves of all kinds.*

On September 24th, 1599, eighty merchants met in Founders' Hall in the City of London. Eldred and Fitch were both present at this gathering which was the inauguration of the great East India Company. Meanwhile a Levant Company had been formed and had established friendly relations with Turkey. Sir William Harborne had gone to Constantinople as the first English Ambassador at the Sultan's court.

Thus, by the end of the sixteenth century, although Englishmen had not yet obtained permanent possession of an acre of soil outside Europe or founded a single successful colony, the nation was conscious of the fact that it was playing a heroic and memorable part in the great adventure of exploring the wonders of the new worlds discovered in the East and the West. 'Which of the kings of this land,' asks Hakluyt proudly, 'before her Majesty had their banners ever seen on the Caspian Sea? Which of them hath ever dealt with the Emperor of Persia, as her Majesty hath done, and attained for her merchants large and loving privileges? Who ever saw an English Ligier in the stately porch of the Grand Signor at Constantinople? Who ever found English consuls

* List of merchandise offered for sale by the East India Company in 1650.

and agents at Tripolis in Syria, at Aleppo, at Babylon, at Balsara, and which is more, who ever heard of Englishmen at Goa before now? What English ships did heretofore ever anchor in the mighty River of Plate?' The achievements of the mariners and the travellers set the whole of the latter life of Elizabeth's reign against a vast background of wonder and enchantment. The little ships, no bigger than modern yachts, sailed out into the ocean with young men from the manor houses and cottages of Elizabethan England and reached countries where the dust might be gold and the pebbles precious stones, where there were anthropophagi, and men with heads that grew beneath their shoulders, and mountaineers dewlapped like bulls. The islands where they landed seemed to be haunted by spirits, to be full of noises, sounds and sweet airs, that gave delight and hurt not, and at any minute the clouds might open and show riches ready to drop on them. Over all the newly discovered regions there still hung the magic and the strange fragrance of romance and legend. In 1594 Queen Elizabeth sent to the Sultana Safiyeh, wife of Amurath III a letter which 'did smell most fragrantly of camfor and ambargriese', and she received a reply that sounds like a love lyric:

> I send your Majesty so honourable and sweet a salutation of peace that all the flocke of Nightingales with their melody cannot attain to ye like, much lesse this simple letter of mine.*

To sail across the Atlantic was like sailing into Hy Brasil or fairyland and to enter the South Seas was like making a descent into Hades; yet living Englishmen were actually making these voyages. Shakespeare's Fairy Queen, Titania, lives in 'India', which may mean either the new 'Indies' of the West or the mysterious ancient 'India' of the East. For Shakespeare fairyland and 'India' seem to be nearly the same thing. The Elizabethan poets had the advantage of living in a

* *Queen Elizabeth and the Levant Company*, by H. G. Rexdale, Oxford 1904, p. 4.

world full of wonders which their contemporaries had seen with their own eyes They had heard trustworthy accounts of such extraordinary and incredible things that it appeared to them that almost anything might be possible. Spenser boldly bases his argument in favour of the existence of fairyland on the new discoveries. He thinks that some might condemn his poem as fantastic, and he answers by pointing triumphantly to the new discoveries:

> *But let that man with better sense advize*
> *That of the world least part to us is red;*
> *And daily how through hardy enterprize*
> *Many great Regions are discovered,*
> *Which to late age were never mentioned*
> *Who ever heard of th' Indian Peru?*
> *Or who in venturous vessel measured*
> *The Amazon, huge river now found true*
> *Or fruitfullest Virginia who did ever view?*

Such a passage as this must not be dismissed as a mere flight of fancy. It is full of significance as a revelation of the effect of the voyages on the English imagination. It helps us to understand the hyperbolical character of Elizabethan literature. For men whose daily life was surrounded by the miraculous, hyperbole was the natural form of expression.

ELIZABETHAN LITERATURE

The development of English literature in the sixteenth century resembles the development of oversea enterprise and discovery. Both sprang out of the collapse of medieval civilization and the simultaneous rapid evolution of a new type of society in a favourable economic and intellectual environment. It is not merely fanciful to compare the first bold voyages of More and Wyatt into new worlds of humanistic prose and verse with Cabot's first bold voyage to the New World across the Atlantic. Except for some isolated attempts, creative effort in literature hung fire during the revolutionary period of religious dissension, and there was a similar slackening in the enterprise of the voyagers. Then with the accession of Elizabeth to the throne a new expansion began at first in a halting and rather unsatisfactory way and finally developed with almost miraculous rapidity and success. Like the voyagers the writers had their north-east and north-west passages such as the Senecan drama and the use of ancient classical metres, and like the voyagers they learned much from these attempts though they failed to reach their objectives. While the Cobhams, the Carews and the Killigrews were engaged in the piracies that formed the starting point of Elizabethan naval power, other young Englishmen were trying to pick up the threads dropped by Wyatt and Surrey and produce a new courtly poetry in the manner of the work recently published in Richard Tottel's anthology, which was in the hands of every cultivated gentleman. Their poems appeared in a series of anthologies with highly poetical titles but rather disappointing contents: *The Paradise of daynty devises* and *A gorgious Gallery of gallant Inventions*. Occasionally there is a faint foreshadowing of the lyrical sweetness of the later Elizabethans, but generally their works may well be described in Sir Philip Sidney's phrase as 'a confused mass of words with a tingling sound of rime, barely accompanied with reason'. At the beginning of Elizabeth's reign the English language was in a curious state. It was growing rapidly like English trade and nautical enterprise and nearly doubled itself in the sixteenth century. New words were pouring in from abroad or being coined at home to express new ideas. Scholars like old Sir John Cheke were alarmed and thought that 'our tung shold be written cleane and pure, unmixt and unmangeled with borrowing of other tunges'. But their complaints had as much effect on the rising tide as Canute's. Writers at first were unable to handle this rapidly growing half-formed language and produced 'a confused mass of words'. George Gascoigne, the poet who acted the part of the 'Salvage Man' at Kenilworth was one of the most versatile and enterprising of these early Elizabethan writers. He was a remarkable pioneer, author of the first English play in prose (a translation of a comedy of Ariosto), the first English version of a Greek tragedy (from an Italian adaptation) and the first English critical essay on poetry. But in all his writings, with the exception of a few lyrics, there is a curious emptiness. His long works are diffuse and exceedingly dull and his short ones trifles, 'toyes' as he himself called them. Another group of writers tried to revive the long heroic poem on a grand scale. Their enterprise was begun in Mary's reign, but they only succeeded in publishing their work after Elizabeth had come to the throne. Their leader was a man of some poetical talent called William Baldwin, but they chose a most unfortunate model in the dreary *Falls of Princes* of Lydgate, a fifteenth-century version in doggerel verse of a Latin prose work of Boccaccio relating the 'tragedies' of famous persons in classical or Biblical history, treated in the manner that Chaucer parodies in his *Monk's Tale*. The plan of Baldwin and his friends was to produce a work similar to Lydgate's dealing with the falls of eminent Englishmen. The whole scheme of the original *Mirror for Magistrates*, as the joint production was called, is in the spirit of the late Middle Ages, a dreary succession of 'tragedies' moralizing on the falls of the great from prosperity. Its chief claim to be remembered is the fact that it attracted the attention of a young man of noble family called Thomas Sackville who appears to have joined Baldwin's committee after the publication of the first edition of *The Mirror for Magistrates*, and to have planned a revision of the whole cumbersome scheme which would have transformed it into a legendary descent into hell, modelled on the sixth book of Virgil's *Aeneid* and Dante's *Inferno*. Sackville never succeeded in carrying out this scheme, but he wrote his famous Induction for the revised poem and a single legend. The Induction is a poem of a grave and tragic beauty, the product of a sombre and powerful imagination written in stately and monumental verse. It is the most impressive piece of narrative poetry between Chaucer and Spenser.

The most interesting and significant literary work of the early part of Elizabeth's reign was not, however, that of the poets. We must look for it rather in the work of the chroniclers and the translators, who amassed rich stores of material for the dramatists and poets of the future. The two books which Shakespeare used more than any others were a chronicle and a translation, Holinshed's *Chronicles of England and Scotland* and North's *Plutarch*. The chroniclers were popular historians whose work really forms part of a great patriotic-antiquarian movement, encouraged and patronized by Archbishop Parker, an eminent Cambridge scholar who was appointed by Elizabeth to the vacant see of Canterbury in 1559. Parker edited a number of the medieval Latin chronicles of England from the original manuscripts and also printed Anglo-Saxon works for the first time. It was by his orders that the first Anglo-Saxon type was cut in England. One motive for this enthusiasm for the study of the past was the desire to show that the Church of England always had a distinctive character and a tradition of independence. Another was the wish to connect the Welsh ancestry of the kings of the house of Tudor with the old legends of the British kings going back to King Arthur and the mythical Brutus of Troy. So we find a line of chroniclers such as Hall, Holinshed and Stow, producing popular historical narratives compounded of myth, tradition and authentic record, strongly nationalistic in sentiment, uncritical, but great storehouses of fascinating legend and anecdote concerning the great figures of English history.

The translators were as conscious of the national importance of their work as the chroniclers. They translated both from modern languages (especially Italian) and from the classics. They opened for their countrymen a window into the enchanted world of classical antiquity which appeared with all the freshness of a new discovery, the world of the gods and the goddesses of Greece and the great soldiers and statesmen and the Roman Empire. Moreover they brought their readers too into contact with the life and thought of contemporary

Europe and especially of Renaissance Italy. In 1570 the puritanical Roger Ascham was shocked to find the London bookshops full of 'fonde bookes of late translated out of the Italian into English'. He is probably referring to William Painter's *Palace of Pleasure* (1566) and Sir Geoffrey Fenton's *Certain Tragical Discourses* (1567). These books are collections of translations, chiefly of Italian 'novelle' or short but highly coloured and sensational stories breathing the spirit of the fierce sensual life of renaissance Italy. They fired the imagination of many young Englishmen, one of whom was William Shakespeare.

The translations from the classics, though not generally scholarly versions, may be said to have completed the work of the early Tudor humanists. Their merits are not accuracy and precision, but fire, vigour and raciness. Their Caesars, Anthonies and Brutuses talk like Leicester, Ralegh and Sidney, and even use Elizabethan colloquialisms and slang. The greatest of them and the most typical is Sir Thomas North's translation of Plutarch's *Lives of the Noble Grecians and Romanes*. Plutarch's *Lives* had an immense significance for the men of the Renaissance. 'To the readers of Plutarch's lives,' it has been truly said, 'the Renaissance became a living reality,' and to the Elizabethan reader of North's Plutarch the Renaissance became not merely a reality but part of his national heritage. North did not translate from the original Greek but from Amyot's fine French version. Yet his book is one of the few translations that can be truly said to have all the merits of an original work. It has a fire and a poetry that are found neither in Amyot nor in Plutarch himself.

The translators not only provided quarries of rich material for the poets and dramatists. They also provided for them a new reading public with a spacious background of knowledge and ideas. Their influence on the language was also of the highest importance. They enriched it with new words and they learned from their great originals the art of using language with power and dignity. They began the process of transforming the clumsy, shapeless English of Gascoigne and

The Mirror for Magistrates into the wonderfully flexible and vivid language of Shakespeare.

When Drake was setting out on his great voyage in 1577 Edmund Spenser had recently come down from Pembroke Hall, Cambridge. He had begun his education at Merchant Taylors' School, where he was well taught by Richard Mulcaster, one of the most intelligent schoolmasters of the day, a scholar thoroughly imbued with the humanist tradition of Erasmus, More and Ascham, and an apostle of what might be called the new humanism of Elizabeth's reign, which aimed, not only at studying, understanding and copying the classics, but at producing a vernacular literature that would emulate the achievements of Greece and Rome. The Cambridge where Spenser studied was a great centre of patriotic, Protestant, humanist and antiquarian learning. Matthew Parker's influence was dominant there; Chaucer and the old English authors were read and admired, and Gabriel Harvey's lectures on rhetoric in the manner of the Italian Renaissance scholars drew crowded audiences. While Drake was circumnavigating America and bursting like a whirlwind on the Spanish colonies of the Pacific sea-board, Edmund Spenser was making voyages no less adventurous into new worlds of the imagination. Like the mariners, he learnt much from foreign predecessors. The Italians provided him with a rich background of humanistic art and learning, while the recent French school of poets called *La Pléiade* of which the leaders were Ronsard and Du Bellay, showed how a European nation without the special advantages of Italy could aspire to emulate the ancients in vernacular works and build up an 'illustrious vulgar tongue' no less rich and beautiful than Greek and Latin.

The first published work of the 'New Poet', as Spenser was called by his friends, was *The Shepheardes Calendar*, which appeared in 1579. The book is one of the most significant in English literary history. It was the starting-point of a poetic tradition that lasted until the beginning of the twentieth century. In it Spenser shows for the first time his extraordinary power of combining various literary elements and fusing them together so as to form a new unity. He takes the ancient pastoral of Theocritus and Virgil (a threadbare antiquity now, but new and exciting in sixteenth-century England) and combines it with the old English tradition of Chaucer and Langland. It is significant that it is Chaucer whom he praises and equates to Virgil by calling him Tityrus. He has gone back behind Lydgate and Hawes, behind the bad pseudo-Chaucerian tradition of the late Middle Ages, to the pure sparkling source of Chaucer's own poetry, which he mingles in a fascinating way with the new wine of the Renaissance. *The Shepheardes Calendar* is the work of a young man excited at the beauty and variety of the material with which he is working. The clumsy, embarrassed English of the early Elizabethan period has suddenly become a new thing full of infinite possibilities. Spenser's friend E.K. who edited *The Shepheardes Calendar* is afraid that English is becoming a mere 'gallimaufray or hodge-podge', but the young Spenser himself is imbued with a spirit of joyous experiment. He makes all kinds of new linguistic ventures, in dialect, in Chaucerian and other medieval words, in borrowings from abroad, in neologisms, even in slang. Before Spenser the Elizabethans had been afraid of the expansion of the English language. Spenser was the first poet who rejoiced in it.

'No one tung is more fine than another naturallie, but by industrie of the speaker which endeavoreth himself to garnish it with eloquence and to enrich it with learning.' Thus argued Mulcaster following Du Bellay, and Spenser puts this doctrine into practice. In the lyric in praise of Elizabeth in the April eclogue we find for the first time the radiance and music of the great Elizabethan poetry. But in *The Shepheardes Calendar* Spenser is only trying his wings. His huge unfinished epic called *The Faerie Queene* was intended to achieve for England what Homer achieved for Greece and Virgil for Rome, but actually nothing could be more unlike a classical epic. Taking his cue from the Italian poet Ariosto, he grafted on to the ancient conception of the heroic poem the lusty shoots of medieval chivalry and romance. 'Hobgoblin run away with the garland from Apollo' was the rather shocked comment of the humanist Gabriel Harvey; but Spenser's instinct was right. English poetry had to be linked to its medieval past as well as to the classics. Richness is the typical Elizabethan literary virtue, not clarity or symmetry. *The Faerie Queene* is not really a chaos, but its plan is so complex and intricate that it is very difficult for a modern reader to enjoy it as a whole. All the diverse and many coloured elements of Elizabethan learning and fantasy are brought together in this enormous, bewildering, magnificent poem. Its gigantic scope is indicated by the fact that the heroine Gloriana is at once the queen of the fairies, Glory and Queen Elizabeth while her lover, Prince Arthur, is the mythical British king of medieval romance, the Earl of Leicester and the Aristotelian virtue of Magnificence. The action takes place in Fairyland, which is also an idealized Britain and the world of the Platonic Ideas. Over its plains and through its enchanted glades ride knights of romance in shining armour who encounter distressed damsels, wicked enchanters, dragons, classical nymphs and satyrs, and Christian hermits. Allegorical pageants like those Elizabeth saw at Kenilworth and Elvetham, but ennobled by the light of a high imagination, pass continually before our eyes. Now it is the Seven Deadly Sins, now the Marriage of the Thames and the Medway, now the Mask of Cupid, and now the pageant of the Seasons and the Months. Spenser was a Puritan humanist, but the most distinctive quality of his poetry is a sort of happy, instinctive, nature-worship, a delight in the beauty and fertility of living things. His most characteristic and significant creation is the Garden of Adonis in the third book of *The Faerie Queene*, that 'joyous Paradise' where

> *Without fell rancor, or fond gealousie;*
> *Franckly each paramor his leman knowes,*
> *Each bird his mate, ne any does envie*
> *Their goodly meriment, and gay felicitie.*

He combines and transmutes the two apparently irreconcilable medieval ideals of chastity and 'courtly love' in his romantic conception of marriage, as typified by such a union as that of Artegall and Britomart. Thus he created the type of love-sentiment that exercised a powerful influence on English writers down to the end of the nineteenth century.

As a story, *The Faerie Queene* is a hopeless failure, but as a succession of glowing word pictures and as a symphony of word music it is still unrivalled. Here English verse has completely regained at last the lovely fluid movement it had lost since Chaucer, whom Spenser nobly praises, as the 'well of English undefiled', and it has found a new splendour, a surprising richness and variety, and a vast range of harmonies, far beyond anything previously known.

The other great builder of the new poetry besides Spenser was his friend and patron Sir Philip Sidney. Spenser came from the middle class, the lesser burgesses whose standard of living and culture had increased enormously during the sixteenth century. Sidney, like Sackville, came from the new aristocracy which had acquired wealth and power through the dissolution of the monasteries and the favour of the Tudor monarchs. He is a natural aristocrat, a man not only of remarkably wide culture, but of exquisite taste and courtesy. His sonnets and lyrics have a remarkable purity and delicacy of style and a note of deep sincerity, that 'inward touch' which he himself contrasts with the manner of those who 'dictionary's method bring' into their rimes. Sidney was the first great English master of the sonnet and the writer of the first really notably English critical essay. His vast unfinished prose romance, *The Arcadia*, may be compared with *The Faerie Queene* both in respect of its bewildering intricacy and the splendour of isolated passages. Like *The Faerie Queene* it is an attempt to combine the heroic narrative with the pastoral idyll. These are the two ideals of the Elizabethan mind: the knight or soldier in search of adventure and conquest, and the shepherd and shepherdess in the greenwood, fleeting the time carelessly as in the golden age.

But the work of Spenser and Sidney only represents the beginning of the great harvest of Elizabethan poetry, that grew up, flowered and decayed in less than forty years. Its most memorable achievement is to be found in the popular drama. By the beginning of Elizabeth's reign English drama had made little advance since the work of Rastell and Heywood in the time of Henry VIII. As yet there was no public theatre, and no really distinguished author had written for the stage. However, one of the results of humanist teaching in the schools and universities had been a great development of the study of the Latin drama and the growth of the practice of acting Latin plays by Terence, Plautus and Seneca, and also of contemporary works both in Latin and the vernacular. These performances were the work of amateur actors, schoolboys or students of the universities and the Inns of Court, and were often given in honour of the visits of royal persons or ambassadors. Their significance lies in the fact that they brought the educated classes into touch with a much more highly developed kind of drama than the older English plays. Only a very few scholars were familiar with the drama of ancient Greece, but from the comedies of Plautus and Terence and the rhetorical tragedies ascribed to Seneca it was possible for Englishmen to learn the lessons of careful dramatic construction, of consistent characterization and of organic unity. The five-act structure, universal in Latin plays, was a much needed corrective for the shapelessness of the native English drama. About the middle of the sixteenth century attempts were made by academic writers to write original plays in English on the Latin model. Nicholas Udall, headmaster of Eton, produced his *Ralph Roister Doister*, and a certain Mr S. of Christ's College Cambridge, *Gammer Gurton's Needle*. These are plays in which the characters and the sentiments are completely English, but the structure that of Latin comedy. The law students of the Inns of Court in London, who included some of the most able and intelligent young men of the time were particularly fond of giving dramatic displays. Early in Elizabeth's reign they produced the first English tragedy on the model of the Latin tragedies ascribed to Seneca which had recently been translated by Jasper Heywood, son of John Heywood, and several other scholars. The tragedy acted by the gentlemen of the Inner Temple before Elizabeth on January 18th, 1561-2, was *Ferrex and Porrex, or the Tragedie of Gorboduc* by Thomas Sackville, author of the *Induction to the Mirror for Magistrates*, and Thomas Norton. Wooden as this play is, it is notable not only as the first English tragedy in the classical sense of the word, but also as the first work in which blank verse, Surrey's great metrical invention, is used for dramatic purposes. *Gorboduc* was the first of a series of frigid academic tragedies written and acted by students of the Inns of Court often before the Queen, who delighted in the academic drama and herself translated part of a chorus from one of the Senecan plays. The demand of the Queen and the Court for dramatic entertainments exercised a powerful influence on the growth of the drama. Besides the plays performed by academic amateurs, interludes of the old kind and other plays were frequently performed by the 'Children of the Chapel' or choir-boys of the Chapel Royal. Richard Edwards, master of the 'Children' from 1561 to 1566, produced interludes in which he attempted to use matter from classical legend, and John Lyly, a much more considerable writer, composed for the 'Children' a series of delicately wrought courtly plays in prose from about 1584 onwards.

Meanwhile remarkable developments in the popular drama were taking place. Companies of players and minstrels had formed part of the retinues of sovereigns and of noblemen since the Middle Ages, and it had for long been customary for them to give performances in public places as well as in royal palaces and noblemen's houses. But the growth of wealth in London and the desire for pleasure in Elizabeth's reign produced a demand for much more elaborate popular theatrical entertainments than anything which had hitherto been known. The law only recognized actors in so far as they ministered to the recreation of the sovereign and members of the nobility, but in the second decade of Elizabeth's reign the companies of professional actors in London, though legally known as the 'Servants' of the Queen, the Earl of Leicester and other great persons, were actually becoming independent commercial ventures, making their profits by entertaining the general public at performances given in the great yards of the London inns. The Puritan clergy and the Puritan City of London waged continual war against the players, and, if it had not been for the protection given to them by the Queen and the nobility, might have suppressed them altogether. In 1574 the Queen issued a royal patent to the Earl of Leicester's players permitting them to play in London or any other city, borough or town. The Common Council of the City replied by forbidding the performance of plays within its 'liberties'. Then James Burbage, the head of Leicester's troupe, made a bold and memorable counterstroke by erecting in 1576 'The Theatre', the first public building of its kind in England, at Shoreditch just outside the City boundaries where the Puritan authorities had no jurisdiction. The 'Theatre' was a wooden building, in appearance very much like the courtyard of a Tudor inn, with a stage that jutted forward into a cobbled and unroofed yard surrounded by galleries. Other theatres were soon erected by rival managers, first the 'Curtain' at Shoreditch, and then a host of others across the river on the 'Bankside' at Southwark, the Rose, the Swan, the Fortune, and the famous Globe, erected by Burbage's sons and owned by them in partnership with William Shakespeare and other actors. The playhouses came into being just at the time of that heightening of the national consciousness that began about 1580 with the return of Drake. There was now a new kind of theatrical audience representing all classes, and its demands produced great changes both in acting and in the drama. To use the words of Granville Barker, 'a new art of emotional acting' came into being. Such men as Richard Burbage (son of James Burbage) and Edward Alleyn seem to have transformed acting into something that combined the qualities of oratory and music. The new theatre and the new acting called for a new type of drama that should combine the dignity and the organic structure of the academic plays with the delicacy of the court drama and the hearty flesh and blood of the popular entertainment. With a slight alteration, Drake's famous words might have been applied to the new drama as well as to the Navy: 'I must have the gentleman to hale and draw with the mariner, and the mariner with the gentleman.' The men who provided the actors with plays of the new kind demanded by the audiences of the fifteen-eighties were a group of young writers who have been called the 'University Wits', young graduates from Oxford and Cambridge who had no desire to take holy orders (hitherto the normal career for a poor scholar), and no court influence to obtain other employment. Loose-living, reckless young bohemians they were, spending much of their time in the London taverns and in shady company. But they lived the life of their age to the full, and their writing is full of the ardour, the insolence and the poetry of youth. One of them, Robert Greene, tells how he first came to write for the stage. He had been deceived by a courtesan and had lost his money in bad company. While he was lamenting his misfortune, he met a gorgeously dressed person who told him he was a player and wanted the services of a scholar. The player said that he used to write morality plays himself, but the public did not care for that kind of thing any longer. They wanted the work of a scholar, and Greene would be well paid if he took pains. The anecdote may be taken to symbolize the alliance between the University Wits and the new type of successful actor, such as the Burbages and Alleyn. The greatest of the scholar dramatists was Christopher Marlowe, son of a Canterbury tradesman, who came to London with a Cambridge degree in 1587 at the age of twenty-three and took the town by storm with his *Tamburlaine the Great*, a play in two parts, both of which were probably acted in the winter of 1587-8. In *Tamburlaine* the whole glory of Elizabethan poetry and Elizabethan adventure makes a sudden and dazzling irruption into the popular theatre. The young dramatist proclaims his intention of freeing the theatre from 'jigging veins of riming mother wits, and such conceits as clownage holds in fee', and he is as good as his word. He has learnt from Spenser the secrets of glowing poetic colour and enchanting word music, but his spirit is very unlike that of Spenser or of Sidney. They were men of the Renaissance, but Puritans too, gentle and courteous Christians. The author of *Tamburlaine* is a new kind of English poet, a mind striving after power, wealth and beauty, exulting in material splendour, full of rapture at the glories of this world, contemptuous of traditional religion, yet aspiring to an ideal existence beyond the fleeting glories of our blood and state. In *Tamburlaine* the Scythian outlaw and conqueror, he paints a picture of his own ideal, the Man of the Renaissance:

> *Of stature tall, and straightly fashioned,*
> *Like his desire, lift upwards and divine....*
> *Pale of complexion: wrought in him with passion,*
> *Thirsting with soverainty with love of armes.*
> *His lofty browes in foldes, do figure death,*
> *And in their smoothness, amitie and life.*

This man is half god, half wanton schoolboy. He can use Bajazeth, the Turkish Sultan, as his footstool, massacre the Virgins of Damascus and harness the kings of Soria and Trebizond to his chariot. But he can also woo and win Zenocrate, daughter of the Sultan of Egypt, with impassioned lyrical speeches and he can speak of intellectual aspiration with the enthusiasm of a Renaissance scholar:

> *Nature that fram'd us of foure Elements,*
> *Warring within our breasts for regiment,*
> *Doth teach us all to have aspyring minds:*
> *Our soules, whose faculties can comprehend*
> *The wondrous Architecture of the world:*
> *And measure every wandring plannets course,*
> *Still climing after knowledge infinite,*
> *And alwaies mooving as the restless Spheares.*

Tamburlaine is the story of a medieval Tartar conqueror, but all through it there are echoes of the rich talk of Elizabethan London, with its taverns full of adventurers who have been to the four corners of the earth and returned with tales of marvels seen by land and sea. The verse is a perfect riot of strange geographical names: Tunis, Barbary, Argier, Gibraltar, Zanzibar, Manico, Cubar, Samarcanda, Babylon, Alexandria, Nubia, Persepolis, Mexico, Morocco, Bithynia. We hear of

> *Christian Merchants that with Russian stems,*
> *Plow up huge furrowes in the Caspian sea,*

of naked negroes drawing a chariot over 'Turky Carpets', and of '*Oblia*, and *Nigra Silva*, where the Devils dance'. In Marlowe's work, English poetry has become bright and translucent, 'all aire and fire', to use the words applied to him by a contemporary. The last remains of late-medieval dullness and opacity have gone. In his second great play, *Doctor Faustus*, Marlowe uses one of the great myths of the Renaissance and creates a kind of intellectual and philosophical Tamburlaine, striving not for wealth and dominion, but for sensuous and intellectual experience. In this play he reveals for the first time in English drama the full possibilities of psychological tragedy, the anguish of a mind at war with itself. There is little tenderness, no humour and no understanding of common humanity in Marlowe's plays, but there is an interesting suggestion of ironic comedy in *The Jew of Malta*, which probably influenced Ben Jonson, and *Edward II* is the first noteworthy attempt to construct a tragedy out of English historical material. The magnificence of the fragment of his unfinished narrative poem, *Hero and Leander*, suggests that he might have found his true bent in non-dramatic verse. He was murdered at the age of twenty-nine in a Deptford tavern, probably as a result of a political intrigue. He had brought into the English drama greatness of spirit and high poetry. Beside him worked other men who made valuable though less spectacular contributions towards the development of a drama that was to be at once poetic and popular. Thomas Kyd's *Spanish Tragedie* is an able piece of stage-craft which showed how the lessons of the academic dramatists could be applied to the popular stage, and Robert Greene made the first successful attempts at romantic and idyllic comedy.

William Shakespeare came from the same stratum of society as Spenser and Marlowe. Like them, he was a tradesman's son, and like Marlowe's, his boyhood was spent in one of the little country towns of Elizabethan England. He had no university education, but he belonged to a class which seems to have been particularly favourably placed for the reception of cultural influences in the sixteenth century. It preserved something of the traditional medieval lore, which was now despised by the aristocracy, and also drank in eagerly the new humanist culture of the Renaissance. It is as natural for Shakespeare to refer to Queen Guenevere and King Cophetua as to Jove and Venus. He probably came to London about 1588 and found employment as an actor. Later he entered into partnership with the younger Burbage and others and became one of the leading members of the Globe Theatre syndicate. Their company, originally the Earl of Leicester's, became the Lord Chamberlain's Men, and finally under James I, the King's Company of Players. Shakespeare was a highly successful actor-manager. He bought a coat of arms which gave him the status of a gentleman, and retired about 1612 to his native town of Stratford-on-Avon, where he died in 1616.

He began his career as a dramatist with a series of plays which showed that he had learnt everything that the University Wits could teach him. He outshines Lyly's courtly comedies in *Love's Labour's Lost*, in *A Midsummer Night's Dream* he takes Oberon from Greene, and carries the romantic play into worlds of enchantment far beyond anything that Greene could have imagined, in *Romeo and Juliet* he achieves the love tragedy that Kyd crudely attempted, and in *Richard III* he shows himself to be the true inheritor of Marlowe's mighty line. But in these plays besides the accomplishment of the aims of the University Wits there is a quality that is different from anything in their works. It is a power of writing words which not merely bring a character to life, but which seem to penetrate to the very heart of humanity itself. It appears already in *Love's Labour's Lost*, when Costard describes Sir Nathaniel:

> There an't shall please you; a foolish mild man; an honest man, look you, and soon dashed. He is a marvellous good neighbour, faith, and a very good bowler: but for Alisander,—alas, you see how 'tis,—a little overparted.

This quality is to be found here and there in all the early plays; in *A Midsummer Night's Dream* and *Romeo and Juliet* it becomes very prominent. The Nurse's speeches are full of it and in Mercutio's words it is tinged with tragic feeling:

> *A plague o' both your houses!*
> *They have made worms' meat of me:* ...

After the University Wits the two great formative influences on Shakespeare's mind were English history and North's *Plutarch*. On the foundation of Holinshed and old plays based on Holinshed and other chronicles he built the great series of English historical plays, *King John*, *Richard III*, *Richard II*, the two parts of *Henry IV* and *Henry V*. These plays are no mere antiquarian reconstructions. They deal with contemporary problems. In the attempts of the English medieval kings to impose unity on their world of warring barons Shakespeare seems to find an image for the attempt of the monarchy of his own day to create national solidarity. The famous patriotic outburst of John of Gaunt in *Richard II* is followed by lines that reveal the writer's passionate indignation at the commercialism which was coming to dominate England:

> *this dear, dear land,*
> *Dear for her reputation through the world,*
> *Is now leased out, I die pronouncing it,*

> *Like to a tenement or pelting farm:*
> *England bound in with the triumphant sea,*
> *Whose rocky shore beats back the envious siege*
> *Of wat'ry Neptune, is now bound in with shame*
> *With inky blots, and rotten parchment bonds.*

The Bishop of Carlisle in the same play prophesies concerning the miseries of anarchy and disunion:

> *O! if you rear this house against this house,*
> *It will the woefullest division prove . . .*

In *Henry V* he conceived a popular, efficient king, who could solve the social problem as Elizabeth had tried to solve it. Henry V is a splendidly drawn hero, but there is something cold and unconvincing about him, and Falstaff, the gigantic embodiment of the free, joyous life of the Elizabethan taverns has to be sacrificed in order that he may triumph. The Shakespeare who had created Falstaff could never remain content with a Henry V. In *Julius Caesar* the great tragic phase of his art begins; it was North's *Plutarch* which revealed to him a heroic conception of human life: the life of the 'antique Roman' who was 'not passion's slave', 'the large discourse, looking before and after', 'the capability and godlike reason'. In the first decade of the seventeenth century he produced the four supreme tragedies of the modern world, *Hamlet*, *Othello*, *Macbeth* and *Lear*. These Shakesperian tragedies are not religious like the great tragedies of ancient Athens. They are tragedies of the individual, the man isolated from society, either like Hamlet through disgust at its rottenness, or like Othello, Macbeth and Lear, through his own unrestrained passions. These plays reveal the spiritual effect of the collapse of medieval social solidarity and of the patriarchal absolutism which tried to replace it. The naked soul of man is left face to face with the mystery of evil. The full horror of that situation is revealed in Macbeth's soliloquy:

> *To-morrow, and to-morrow, and to-morrow,*
> *Creeps in this petty pace from day to day,*

*To the last syllable of recorded time;
And all our yesterdays have lighted fools
The way to dusty death. Out, out, brief candle!
Life's but a walking shadow, a poor player
That struts and frets his hour upon the stage,
And then is heard no more; it is a tale
Told by an idiot, full of sound and fury,
Signifying nothing.*

The climax is reached in the soul-shattering storm of *Lear*, where the isolated human being is seen exposed to all the terrors and miseries of the world and the still more terrible 'tempest in the mind', and here a remedy is hinted when Lear exclaims:

*Take physic pomp:
Expose thyself to feel what wretches feel.*

But no remedy seemed possible to Shakespeare. In *Timon of Athens* we find only a blind anarchic rage against humanity foreshadowing Swift at his bitterest and in *Coriolanus* the spectacle of an aristocratic hero utterly frustrated by a political situation which he cannot comprehend and led to betray his country for the sake of his 'honour'. In the so-called 'romances' Shakespeare escapes from the impasse, not to the 'heights' as the Victorian critic said, but to a strange, unearthly world of poetic fantasy, the fairyland of *Cymbeline* and *The Winter's Tale*. He ended the great series of plays with *The Tempest*, one of the most astonishing of his creations, a myth rather than a fairy story which seems in one of its aspects to symbolize the artistic creation of the poet himself and in another the solution of the social problem by the beneficent 'magic' of science. If Tamburlaine is the Man of the Renaissance in all the vigour of a glorious and exultant youth, Prospero, the magician who has learned to control both the elements and his own passions, is the supreme manifestation in poetry of the full-grown wisdom of humanism, a wisdom irradiated by imagination and endowed with a kind of prophetic quality, which also characterizes the greatest sonnets in the famous collection published under Shakespeare's name in 1609.

Besides Shakespeare, a multitude of dramatists were working for the popular theatre in the last decade of the sixteenth century, and a vast number of plays was produced, many of which have been lost. None of these dramatists have Shakespeare's profound insight into character, his wide humanity or his sense of significant dramatic form. But many of them, such as Chapman, Marston, Middleton, Dekker, Heywood, Massinger, Webster, Beaumont, Fletcher and Ford were fine poets and able dramatists. They wrote Italianate tragedies and comedies founded on the novelle, chronicle plays, Roman plays, dramas of contemporary life and Senecan revenge plays. Their works form a vast jungle full of magnificent blooms of poetry, but also full of tangled undergrowth and impassable swamps. The weakness of these plays lies in the fact that they were generally ephemeral productions written for no other purpose than that of diverting a popular audience. There was no motive for the writers to give their work the monumental quality that distinguishes the drama of ancient Athens. The strength of the Elizabethan playwrights is to be found in their enormous vitality and their imaginative power. Though they were only writing to divert a popular audience, it was an audience that was intoxicated with the wonder and the romance of newly-discovered worlds and with a sense of the greatness of the human spirit. The splendid lines of Chapman's Duke of Byron might be taken as a description of the ideal character of Elizabethan drama, if it is possible to generalize concerning such a vast and heterogeneous mass of writing:

> *Give me a spirit that on this life's rough sea*
> *Loves t' have his sails filled with a lusty wind,*
> *Even till his sail-yards tremble, his masts crack,*
> *And his rapt ship run on her side so low*
> *That she drinks water, and her keel plows air.*

> *There is no danger to a man that knows
> What life and death is: there's not any law
> Exceeds his knowledge; neither is it lawful
> That he should bow to any other law.*

Together with this sense of the greatness of the human spirit there is a sense of the nearness of death and of death's majesty. These plays are not the work of scholars sitting in comfortable studies in a well-policed city, but of men who might be stabbed at any time in the streets or poisoned, or executed after hideous mutilations. 'What would it pleasure me,' asks Webster's Duchess of Malfy, 'to have my throat cut

> *With diamonds? or to be smothered
> With cassia? or to be shot to death with pearls?
> I know death hath ten thousand several doors
> For men to take their exits; and 'tis found
> They go on such strange geometrical hinges
> You may open them both ways; any way, for heaven sake,
> So I were out of your whispering. Tell my brothers
> That I perceive death now I am well awake
> Best gift is they can give or I can take.*

The world was full of marvels, but in the end death was found to be a greater marvel than any of them. The ultimate crown of success for the Elizabethan hero or heroine was not, as it is for the hero or heroine of a modern play or film, the acquisition of comfort or self-esteem, but deliverance from the three thousand furies that live in a great man's breast. They cry with Chapman's hero:

> *Strike, strike, O strike; fly, fly, commanding soul,
> And on thy wings for this thy body's breath,
> Bear the eternal victory of death.*

Elizabethan drama is often tedious, often coarse, often violent and absurd, but it has the superb and unflagging vigour of youth, and it is the mirror of a truly poetic moment in the life of a great nation, when intensity of passionate experience was preferred to comfort and security.

One great figure stands apart from the other dramatists, or rather towers above them like a massive rock in a wild and magnificent sea. Ben Jonson, Shakespeare's friend and younger contemporary, was by far the most learned of the dramatists, a man of immense reading, of a masterful spirit and a strong intellect. With none of Shakespeare's tenderness and humanity, he is a great satiric dramatist, combining ironic realism with a strange vein of fantastic imagination. There is magnificent poetry in his ironic drama of *Volpone* and elsewhere in his plays, masques and occasional verses, but it is perhaps in his prose that his most notable achievement is to be found. In the hands of the dramatists, and especially of Ben Jonson, English prose, which hitherto has been generally stiff and clumsy, though often stately and beautiful, becomes a more flexible and serviceable medium. In such a passage as the following from *The Silent Woman* we can see the beginnings of a new art of English writing:

> Let your gifts be slight and dainty, rather than precious. Let cunning be above cost. Give cherries at time of year, or apricots, and say they were sent you out of the country, though you bought them in Cheapside. Admire her tires: like her in all fashions; compare her in every habit to some deity; invent excellent dreams to flatter her, and riddles; or, if she be a great one, perform always the second parts to her: like what she likes, praise whom she praises, and fail not ... to make the physician your pensioner, and her chief woman.

This prose has not the grace and distinction of the prose of Dryden or Congreve, but it has a clarity and an ease that anticipates their work.

The Elizabethan song is in its own way as rare and astonishing an achievement as the Elizabethan drama. It is the descendant of the English popular song of the Middle Ages and it inherits from it a dewy freshness and happy freedom of spirit, but it is also derived from the courtly lyrics of Wyatt and Surrey and from Italian and classical models with their choice phrasing and careful structure. The two strains of popular and courtly song met and mingled in it, just as, at the same time, through the work of the University Wits, the fusion of courtly and popular drama produced an art of the theatre that was truly national. Music seems to have played a part in the development of the lyric similar to that played by acting in the development of the drama. The great revival of English music in the late sixteenth century is described in a separate chapter in this volume. Here it will be sufficient to say that in the Elizabethan period music played a greater part in the life of English men and women than ever before or since. Every person with any pretence to cultivation could bear a part in the singing of the unaccompanied songs for several voices called madrigals, and there were few ladies and gentlemen who could not play on one of the stringed instruments of the day, such as the lute. The words of the songs were inseparable from the music, which, in the fine phrase of William Byrd, one of the greatest Elizabethan composers, was 'framed to the life of the Word'. Numerous books of Madrigals, Airs, Ballets and Canzonets containing both words and music were published from 1590 until the reign of Charles I and the time of the Civil War, when Milton could still ask, 'Who shall silence all the airs and madrigalls, that whisper softnes in chambers?' Sometimes the songs consist of lines from some well-known poems like *The Faerie Queen*, or even passages of blank verse or prose, but usually they are short lyrics written specially for the occasion, in many instances apparently by the composers of the music. The poetry varies in quality, but the general level is astonishingly high, and certain song-books, such as those of John Dowland and Thomas Campion, contain some of the loveliest lyrics in the English language. The diction is nearly always exquisitely melodious, and the sentiment is that of the Arcadian dream world of the Renaissance where nymphs and shepherds lead joyous lives in the greenwood, and enjoy innocent pagan delights as though Christianity and the Middle Ages had never existed. But this Arcadia is somehow English too. It has the maypole and the customs of the old English countryside like Shakespeare's countries of pastoral romance in *As You Like It* and *The Winter's Tale*, and its shepherds and shepherdesses wear their holiday apparel on Sundays:

Phyllis. *I will gather flowers, my Corydon,*
          To set in thy cap.
Corydon. *I will gather pears, my lovely one,*
          To put in thy lap.
Phyllis. *I will buy my true love garters gay*
          For Sundays, for Sundays,
          To wear about his legs so tall.
Corydon. *I will buy my true love yellow say*
          For Sundays, for Sundays,
          To wear about her middle small.

The songs of the Elizabethan dramatists rival the madrigals and airs of the song-books in their freshness and delicacy. Lyly showed how they could contribute to dramatic effect, and in Shakespearian drama they are not merely ornaments, but an essential part of the life of the plays in which they occur.

Sir Walter Ralegh, in his *History of the World*, wrote that 'The mind of man hath two Ports, the one always frequented by the entrance of manifold vanities; the other desolate and overgrown with grass, by which enter our charitable thoughts and divine contemplations.' Elizabethan life had two 'ports' also. Through one of them passed the glittering pageantry of an exultant imagination, the nymphs and shepherds of Arcadia, the conquerors, the knights and maidens of romance and the revellers of court and tavern; through the other passed a different procession, Jesuits going to the stake, 'silenced' Puritan preachers, Catholic 'recusants', disappointed courtiers, and homeless peasants in their 'looped and windowed raggedness' driven off the land by the enclosures. Thus all through Elizabethan literature we find a streak of profound sadness, of disillusion and sometimes of revolt, contrasting strangely with all the rich fantasy, the

heroic energy and the faith in human greatness. Sir Walter
Ralegh, courtier, poet, soldier, explorer, colonizer, confiden-
tial secretary to the Queen and Captain of her Guard, gives
a fierce and poignant expression in some of his verses to this
'disenchantment of the Elizabethans':*

> *Goe soule the bodies guest*
>   *Upon a thankelesse arrant,*
> *Feare not to touch the best,*
>   *The truth shall be thy warrant:*
> *Goe since I needs must die,*
>   *And give the world the lie.*
>
> *Say to the Court it glowes,*
>   *And shines like rotten wood,*
> *Say to the Church it showes*
>   *What's good, and doth no good.*
> *If Church and Court reply,*
>   *Then give them both the lie.*

Towards the end of the century there was a strong revolt
against the gentle, fluid movement, the sugared melody and
the intellectual emptiness of the Petrarchan, Spenserian and
Arcadian poetry. The living embodiment of that revolt was
John Donne, the writer who might be called the last of the
great Elizabethans and one of the chief prophets of the
coming age. It is a significant fact that he belonged to an old
Catholic family and, though he soon abandoned Romanism,
he had, to use his own words, his 'first breeding and conversation with men of suppressed and afflicted Religion, accus-
tomed to the despite of death, and hungry of an imagined
Martyrdome'. In the last decade of the sixteenth century
young Jack Donne's *Songes and Sonnets*, his daring *Elegies* and
his cynical and disturbing prose *Paradoxes and Problems* were
being handed round in manuscript in London and were
shocking and delighting their readers. His poetry is not the

---

* I owe the phrase, and not the phrase only, to Sir E. K. Chambers's
notable essay with this title in *Sir Thomas Wyatt and some Collected Essays*.

poetry of Arcadia. It is remarkable for its concentrated passion, its intellectual agility, and its forcible dramatic power. Donne had learnt much from the dramatists, and he brings into lyrical poetry their abrupt and vivid colloquialism. With a single scornful line he shatters all the melodious commonplaces of Petrarchan compliment:

For Godsake hold your tongue, and let me love.

He writes of no imaginary shepherds and shepherdesses, but of his own spiritual, intellectual and amorous adventures. He is a realist, not in the sense of one who copies external facts, but of a writer whose chief care is for truth and fidelity to personal experience rather than to beauty. He is often scornful, cynical, disillusioned and sardonic, but he is never tired or feeble. He, too, is an Elizabethan, and he plunges into the new adventure of introspection with the same ardour that carried Drake into the Pacific and Spenser into the enchanted glades of Fairyland.

CHAPTER III

THE SEVENTEENTH CENTURY

THE STUARTS AND THE PURITAN REVOLUTION

'NO Terrours, no enticement, no care of her safety hath removed her from her stedfastnesse ... (she) hath entred herselfe and brought us into *Zoar*. *It is a little one*, but therein *our souls shall live*; and we are in safety, all the Cities of the *Plaine* being in *combustion* round about us.' These words were spoken by Bishop Lancelot Andrewes in a sermon before Elizabeth, and they show us how Englishmen at the end of the seventeenth century assessed the Elizabethan achievement. England was a 'Zoar', a small island of peace and safety amid the fierce strife that was rending Europe—'the Cities of the *Plaine* ... in *combustion* round about us'. On the Continent despotisms were rising everywhere and the old constitutional governments were being crushed out of existence. Only in England Crown, Lords and Commons seemed to stand firmly together at the opening of the new century. Englishmen, however, were not destined to live much longer in their 'Zoar' of national solidarity, and the next half-century showed that it was built on very insecure foundations. The last of the Tudors was a consummate diplomat who knew how to manage her subjects so that in her time there was no open clash between the Tudor system of paternal absolutism and the claims of the lusty property-owning class whose fortunes had been made out of the economic changes of the sixteenth century. The situation was very different when James Stuart, King of Scots, sat in Elizabeth's place. Accepted by the English squires because they dreaded the prospect of a disputed succession, and because his accession to the English throne solved the age-long problem of uniting the English and Scottish crowns, he was an alien, grotesque in appearance, ill-mannered, tactless and undignified. The English court, admired at home and abroad in Elizabeth's time, became the laughing-stock of Europe, and the popular balladmongers drew unflattering comparisons between the 'Queen's old courtier' and 'the new courtier of the King'. This weak, pedantic ruler with his handsome, worthless favourite Buckingham, and after him his son Charles, a man of far nobler character than his father, but inheriting his obstinacy and his failure to understand the English character, were confronted with a rapidly rising tide of discontent, which they were quite incapable of stemming, and which soon broke down the structures of the English monarchy and the English Church so carefully reared by the Tudors. The English revolution of the seventeenth century was both political and religious. The Tudor system of personal government by the monarch through the Council and the Prerogative Courts was confronted by a new theory put forward in the House of Commons that property had inalienable rights, that the traditional Common Law of England was above the Royal Prerogative, and that the House of Commons should control religion and finance, and even give advice on foreign policy. James and his ministers were wasteful and extravagant and needed money. They obtained it by granting trade monopolies to courtiers and to chartered companies, by levying duties and by the revival of obsolete taxes and fines on landed estates. The result was that they united against them the landowners and the traders, a large part of the aristocracy and most of the middle class. Political and economic grievances were accentuated and transcended by a great religious movement. All through Elizabeth's reign there had been a minority of extreme Protestants who were discontented with the Anglican compromise in Church government and who longed to sweep away the remains of the medieval hierarchy and ritual, and erect a Calvinist Jerusalem in England. In the seventeenth century their numbers increased, especially among the traders and artisans. Puritanism was not merely a theory of Church government: it was a way of living. 'It made the world seem to me,' writes that great Puritan

Richard Baxter, 'as a carkass that has neither life nor loveliness. . . . It caused me first to seek God's Kingdom and his Righteousness, and most to mind the One thing needful, and to determine first of my Ultimate End.' The Puritan had to 'determine of his Ultimate End' alone, unaided by priest or liturgy, guided only by the study of the scripture, and he had to pursue his mission, not in retirement from the world like a medieval monk, but by passing through Vanity Fair like Bunyan's pilgrims and testifying to the faith which was within him. Such a religion it has been truly said 'worked like yeast which sets the whole mass fermenting' in the English society of the seventeenth century. It 'went through its slack and loosely knit texture like a troop of Cromwell's Ironsides through the disorderly cavalry of Rupert'.* It appealed especially to the manufacturers, 'the merchants and middle sort of men', because it encouraged the economic virtues, sobriety, thrift, energy and industry.

'Publicans and sinners on the one side, Scribes and Pharisees on the other' was Chillingworth's contemptuous verdict on the two parties in the Civil War, and it is true that there were plenty of philistines and hypocrites among the Puritans and plenty of wastrels and debauchees among the royalists, but, if Puritanism produced a Milton, a Hampden and a Cromwell, the High Anglicans had their saintly George Herbert, their large-minded Falkland and their liberal Chillingworth and Taylor. Their ideal, based on the majestic thought of Hooker, who had built his famous defence of Anglicanism in the latter part of Elizabeth's reign on an appeal to reason, lacked the energy and power of the Puritan philosophy but had far more sweetness and light, and at its best was a kind of aristocratic Christian humanism summed up in the figure of Herbert's country parson whose purity was said to be 'breaking out and dilating itself even to his body, clothes and habitation'.

For a period of eleven years after his break with the Parliament in 1629, Charles with his minister Strafford and his

* R. H. Tawney, *Religion and the Rise of Capitalism*, 1926, p. 231.

Archbishop Laud revived the old absolutist system, carrying it further than any of the Tudors, and in some respects using the power of the Crown to protect the poor against the privileged classes. But Laud in the words of Keith Feiling 'ruined Hooker's appeal to reason by the methods of a provost marshal' and Strafford made himself hated by his policy of 'thorough' which seemed to be paving the way to a military despotism. The attempt to impose high Anglicanism on the Presbyterian Scots was futile and disastrous, and the king's necessities forced him to appeal to Parliament and abandon Strafford and Laud to their enemies the Puritan squires. But even then no reconciliation was possible between Charles's conception of a paternal and authoritarian government in Church and State and the views of the 'Root and Branch' party in the House of Commons who claimed the appointment of ministers by Parliament, the control of the armed forces of the Crown, and the settlement of religion by a national synod.

When the final breach took place in 1641, the nation was fairly equally divided, but the Parliament held London and was backed by the trading classes and the moneyed interests. Moreover, it is highly significant that a majority of the great landowning families who had made their fortunes under the Tudors, Percys, Russells, Sidneys, Herberts, Cecils, Montagues and Cavendishes, were either neutral or hostile to the Crown. 'The king's cause and party,' it was said in Bristol in 1645, 'were favoured by two extremes in that city; the one the wealthy and powerful men, the other of the basest and lowest sort; but disgusted by the middle rank, the true and best citizens.' For a while the war was waged indecisively, but the result was assured when the New Model Army, the army of Fairfax and Cromwell, was organized by the Parliament. This army consisted mainly of extreme Puritans representing a peculiarly English brand of Puritanism, which came to be called Independency. They were too fiercely individualistic to accept the cast-iron ecclesiastical system of Geneva and they tended to adopt what in the middle of the seventeenth century was the new doctrine of toleration, a doctrine which would have been as hateful to Calvin as it was to Laud, but which, curiously enough, was being discussed at the same time by some of the high churchmen such as Jeremy Taylor. In politics these Puritan soldiers were the first English radicals, demanding the abolition of the House of Lords, and manhood suffrage, whilst some of the extremists among them, called the Levellers, were the first English social democrats.

When the King was finally defeated in the field, the Presbyterian politicians in the House of Commons showed themselves to be utterly incapable of producing a workable constitution. The power fell into the hands of the Army and the Independents, who seized the King, tried to negotiate with him, and finally committed the immense tactical blunder of bringing him to trial and executing him, thus turning him into a Royal Martyr, and giving monarchy and Anglicanism a popularity which they had not enjoyed since the time of Elizabeth. But the English people were not ready for the democracy desired by the Puritan extremists, Milton's 'Nation of Prophets, of Sages, and of Worthies', and they had to be content with the firm rule of Cromwell, who tried vainly to make England a Puritan Free State and ended with a revival of monarchy in all but name. Under the Protectorate for the first time in England a fairly wide toleration for all religious sects except 'popery and prelacy' was allowed. The Jews were readmitted, and a great variety of religious communities (Bossuet's 'mille sectes bizarres') flourished. Among them may be noted especially the peculiarly English body of pacifists and believers in the Inner Light called the Society of Friends and early nicknamed the Quakers, the followers of that remarkable apostle George Fox who started his campaign of preaching 'The Word of Life' in opposition to the 'priests' during the Civil War.

When Cromwell died, power was wrested from the weak hands of his son by the Puritan generals, and there was a short period of anarchy, which made both Independency and standing armies hateful to Englishmen. Then General Monk marched on London and practically the whole nation united to recall Charles II.

The tall, swarthy King who stepped ashore at Dover on May 29th, 1660, was not only the heir of Charles I; he was also a modern man, the first modern king, a sceptic and *libertin* in the French sense of the word as well as a libertine in the English, who was far more interested in chemistry and mechanics than in religion.

> *Never was such a Faith's Defender,*
> *He, like a politick Prince, and pious,*
> *Gives liberty to conscience tender,*
> *And doth to no religion tye us.*
> *Jew, Turks, Christians, Papists, he'll please us,*
> *With Moses, Mahomet and Jesus.*

Rochester's lines are not only a satiric sketch of the King's character; they sum up the spirit of the new court. It has often been stigmatized as the centre of a violent reaction of extravagance and debauchery after the Reign of the Saints, and it certainly seemed a sink of iniquity to the Puritans; but it was the last English court which was a true focus of culture, as well as of fashion, and the King's pastimes included not only dallying with the languishing beauties of Lely, but listening to the music of Lully and Grabut and the young Purcell, discussing poetry with Dryden, architecture with Wren and science with members of the newly-founded Royal Society. Perhaps even more important than the court as centres of culture and civilization were the great country houses scattered all over the country,* the homes of those landowners who were now becoming the real rulers of England. In such palaces as Longleat, Welbeck, Bowood, Knole and Chatsworth and in hundreds of less princely but spacious and often beautiful manor houses, there was in the words of H. G. Wells, 'an atmosphere of unhurried liberal inquiry,

* Many of them are described admirably by John Evelyn in his *Diary*.

of serene and determined insubordination and personal dignity, of established aesthetic and intellectual standards'. Here were great libraries, noble picture galleries and gardens, and often scientific collections and laboratories; here was the true source of some of the most valuable achievements of modern civilization, the scientific discoveries which have made the drudgery on which this old aristocratic culture was based to a large extent unnecessary, the freedom of thought and discussion which defeated superstition and intolerance, and above all a new conception of human freedom and social relationships, the 'good life' of humanist philosophy translated into terms of practical reality.

Outside the court, England remained serious, god-fearing and in a large measure Puritan. The characters in Bunyan's allegories are far more typical of the majority of English people in the reign of Charles II than the rakes and harlots of Etherege and Wycherley. But Puritanism was undergoing a curious and significant change. Its ethics were losing the heroic quality of the great days of Milton and Cromwell and were rapidly becoming the ethics of utilitarianism. 'Be wholly taken up in diligent business of your lawful callings,' wrote Baxter, 'when you are not exercised in the more immediate service of God.' Expelled from high society and debarred from the Universities, the Puritans (now coming to be called Dissenters) distinguished themselves especially in commerce, banking and manufacture. After a long struggle they won toleration, and were to become the backbone of Whig and liberal England. Meanwhile a change was also taking place in the Church of England. Some of the most learned and attractive Anglican leaders called 'latitudinarians', began to recommend tolerance, and to try to rationalize Christianity and to link it to Platonic philosophy. These men were mostly Cambridge dons, and they were really reviving an old Anglican tradition that went back to Hooker and beyond him to Erasmus. It is perhaps no accident that the ablest of their books, The *Select Discourses* of John Smith, appeared in 1660, the year of the Restoration, while in 1662 there was published a pamphlet which professed to give an *Account of the New Sect of Latitude-Men*.

In the forty years that followed the Restoration England became a modern country, a capitalist empire, depending largely on foreign and colonial trade, with cabinet government, a two-party system, a national debt, religious toleration, and a 'press' in the modern sense of the word. During the reign of Charles II the national unity which had brought about the Restoration soon collapsed, and the 'Popish Plot' agitation was followed by the crystallization of the two great parties, as they were to remain in essentials for over a century, under the two first great English party leaders, the Tory Danby and the Whig Shaftesbury. Shaftesbury's secretary and physician was a young Oxford scholar called John Locke, who had worked out a theory of government based on the conceptions of 'liberty' and 'property'. The old analogy for the body politic had been the human body, a living organism. The new analogy insisted upon by Locke was a business contract, the so-called 'Social Contract', or agreement by individual owners of property to unite for mutual profit and protection. Society, in fact, was conceived no longer as organism, but as a joint stock company.

In 1681 the demand of the Whigs for the exclusion from the succession to the throne of James, Duke of York, the King's Roman Catholic brother, produced a crisis which threatened the government with a second civil war. But Charles II was a far more astute politician than his father, and he allowed the opposition plenty of rope till it disgusted moderate men by its violence and brutal treatment of the 'papists'. Then he acted with energy and decision. Lord Russell and other prominent Whigs were executed and Shaftesbury was forced to flee to Holland, where he died. Thus the last period of absolute rule by the Stuart kings began. Whether Charles with all his tact and good humour could have continued the experiment is doubtful. When he died in 1685, he was succeeded by his brother James, who, although he was a Roman Catholic, began his reign under the most favourable auspices, and it seemed possible that he might succeed in establishing in England an authoritarian state similar to the France of Louis XIV with whom both he and his brother had intimate relations. But the obstinacy and tactlessness of James recall the characters of his father and grandfather. After suppressing with needless violence the foolish rebellion of Monmouth, he embarked on the hopeless task of forcing Romanism on a nation that detested it and whose anti-Catholic feeling had recently been strengthened by the oppression of the French Protestants after the Revocation of the Edict of Nantes in 1685 and the influx of a large number of them into England. Thus he succeeded in creating again the combination which destroyed Charles I, the alliance of the Money Power of the City with the great landowners of the House of Lords, the squires of the House of Commons and the Puritan shopkeepers and artisans, while on this occasion the revolt was actually blessed by the Anglican Church, which for the first time in its history (not without considerable qualms) found itself in opposition to the monarchy. William of Orange, the Dutch Prince, a grandson of Charles I on his mother's side, who had married Mary, James's Protestant daughter, and had spent his life in organizing a great European coalition against Louis XIV, was invited by representatives of all parties to come over to protect the 'liberties' and 'property' of Englishmen. James fled, and a Convention Parliament declared the throne vacant, offering it to William and Mary and drawing up the Bill of Rights founded largely on the theories of Locke, together with the Toleration Act giving liberty of worship to the Protestant dissenters. Thus the work begun in 1641 was completed. The paternal absolutism of the Crown was finally destroyed in England, and was replaced by the conceptions of the Free State and the limited monarchy, which meant in practice the rule of the Money Power and the propertied classes, though the theory of the natural rights of the individual on which the new settlement was founded meant an immediate extension of personal liberty especially with regard to religion and the press, and paved the way for the development of democracy in the future. Militant and republican Puritanism was dead in England. Its future lay on the other side of the Atlantic, in the little group of colonies that had been growing upon the Eastern American seaboard since the reign of James I, and ultimately was to become the great English-speaking republic of the United States.

LITERATURE IN THE EARLY SEVENTEENTH CENTURY

English literature in the opening decades of the seventeenth century was dominated by three great and masterful minds, those of Ben Jonson, John Donne and Francis Bacon. All were men of immense learning. Jonson, classical scholar and dramatist, was the first great English literary dictator, the predecessor of John Dryden and Samuel Johnson. He gathered round him a brilliant group of young men who met at London taverns ('the *Sun*, the *Dog*, the triple *Tunne*'), and were proud to belong to 'the tribe of Ben'. Among them were not only poets like Carew, Lovelace, Waller, Herrick and Randolph, but lawyers and politicians like the learned Selden, the young Edward Hyde, Lord Falkland, and Maynard, the Puritan barrister who lived to welcome William of Orange in 1688. Under the influence of Jonson there grew up a new English poetic tradition of vigour and perspicuity based largely on Latin models, mingled at first with much 'metaphysical' fantasy, but developing later into the noble art of Dryden. The first-fruits of Jonson's influence outside the drama were those exquisite 'cavalier' lyrics unrivalled in English for limpidity and purity of outline, though often enough marred by the carelessness of the gentlemen-amateurs who wrote them. The finest products of this school of lyric, however, are to be found not so much in the works of the 'mob of gentlemen who wrote with ease' such as Carew, Suckling and Lovelace, as in the exquisitely wrought songs of Robert Herrick, the London jeweller's son, who became a Devonshire parson, and sang with pagan ecstasy

> ... of *Brooks*, of *Blossomes*, *Birds*, and *Bowers*:
> Of *April*, *May*, of *June* and *July*-Flowers.
> ... of *May-poles*, *Hock-carts*, *Wassails*, *Wakes*,
> Of *Bride-grooms*, *Brides*, and of their *Bridall-cakes*,
> Of *Youth*, of *Love*
> ... of cleanly-*Wantonnesse*.

By an irony of chronology Herrick's dainty *Hesperides* appeared a few weeks before the execution of Charles I. The limitations of seventeenth-century criticism are revealed by the fact that this book was apparently ignored by Herrick's contemporaries, and the quality of his poetry had to wait for a century and a half till it received adequate recognition.

In the reign of James I, Donne developed from the wild and brilliant bohemian rake of the early poems into a devout Anglican and one of the most impassioned of English preachers. But before reaching that goal he had to pass through an agony of doubt and scepticism, well illustrated by the famous lines in 'An Anatomie of the World. The first Anniversarie', which express the temper of many Englishmen in that age of reaction after the ardours of the Elizabethan period, when it seemed that the new knowledge of the Renaissance had brought nothing to mankind but moral and social chaos:

> ... *new Philosophy calls all in doubt,*
> *The Element of fire is quite put out;*
> *The Sun is lost, and th' earth, and no man's wit*
> *Can well direct him where to looke for it.*
> *And freely men confesse that this world's spent,*
> *When in the Planets, and the Firmament*
> *They seeke so many new; they see that this*
> *Is crumbled out again to his Atomies.*
> *'Tis all in peeces, all cohaerance gone;*

> *All just supply, and all Relation:*
> *Prince, Subject, Father, Sonne, are things forgot,*
> *For every man alone thinkes he has got*
> *To be a Phoenix, . . .*

An Anatomie of the World is a title (like the title of the *Anatomy of Melancholy* by Robert Burton, Donne's contemporary) that epitomizes the spirit of the age, with its intense desire to explore and to dissect, its passion for spiritual and intellectual experiment. The Frenchman, Montaigne, whose *Essays* were published in Florio's English translation in 1603, was one of the great prophets of this seventeenth-century England, and his introspection and endless sceptical questioning helped to create the 'climate of opinion' that produced its 'metaphysical poets', its Burtons and its Brownes.

It was indeed as J. B. Leishman has written, an 'age of lonely and divided souls'. It was also a religious age. The personal experience of religion seemed to many to be the one valid truth in this welter of conflicting creeds and opinions. It was this experience that produced the great poetry of Donne's last years, his hymns to Christ and to God the Father, and the gorgeous prose poetry of his sermons. He founded the great school of 'metaphysical' religious poetry, the only important religious poetry which England has produced. The greatest of his followers was George Herbert, who united a passionate religious experience with the fragrance of a singularly beautiful and saintly character, the finest flower of the Church of Laud and Charles I, reflected equally in his poems, his prose work, *The Country Parson*, and Walton's biography. Even the Puritan Baxter wrote that 'Herbert speaks *to* God like one that *really believeth a God* . . . *Heart-work* and *Heaven-work* make up his Books.' In the poetry of one of Herbert's disciples, Richard Crashaw, a convert to Romanism, the exotic cults of the counter-Reformation find a single dazzling expression in English poetry. Another disciple of Herbert, Henry Vaughan, and his younger contemporary, Thomas Traherne, wrote 'divine contemplations' in which English poetry passes into that world of mystical vision which it did not enter again till the age of Blake and Wordsworth. The characteristic quality of the whole school of 'metaphysical' religious poets is to be found, not so much in their 'conceits', their pursuit of the 'unexpected and surprising' which Dr Johnson described so well in his *Life of Cowley*, but rather in their abandonment of the Arcadian conventions of early Renaissance poetry in favour of the direct and unflinching expression of personal experience.

> *Her pure, and eloquent blood*
> *Spoke in her cheekes, and so distinctly wrought,*
> *That one might almost say, her body thought;*

Such a fusion of intellect and passion as that which Donne describes in these lines is the distinguishing mark of their best work. It is found in Shakespeare's later plays and sometimes in those of the other dramatists, but it faded out of English poetry towards the middle of the seventeenth century, and, as T. S. Eliot has pointed out, there is hardly a trace of it in the 'pure, colourless diction' of Philip Massinger, the last eminent dramatist of the old school.

Francis Bacon, like Montaigne, exerted an influence which pervades almost every corner of seventeenth-century thought. If religious experience was the sheet anchor of the 'metaphysical' poets, there seemed to be another inviting path to truth and salvation in the revived attitude towards Nature of which Bacon is the supreme herald and prophet. Ever since the conversion of Europe to Christianity the study of Nature had been under a cloud. The physical universe was regarded as accursed, the dwelling place of Satan, and those evil spirits formerly worshipped as Gods and Goddesses by the pagans. The study of natural phenomena was popularly regarded as the Black Art, and the few daring spirits like Roger Bacon, the thirteenth-century friar, who attempted it, were considered to be magicians. The myth of Doctor Faustus shows that this was still the popular view of the matter in the sixteenth century. But the Renaissance scholars had gone back behind Christianity, and revealed the glories of a civilization that regarded Nature in an entirely different way, either with religious and poetic feeling in its myths or as a subject for scientific inquiry in writers like Lucretius and his forerunners among the early Greek thinkers. By the end of the sixteenth century it was beginning to be felt by some minds that this was an attitude which ought to be recovered, and that man had now a greater need for the kind of truth that was to be found in things than for the kind that was to be found in religion and metaphysics. Bacon, with his encyclopaedic mind (early in life he wrote 'I have taken all knowledge to be my province') and his incomparable literary gift, made himself the evangelist of the new gospel of natural science—'*buccinator novi temporis*'. Although he was no great scientist himself, he had the power of indicating in language of imperishable quality the lines along which scientific inquiry should advance and the defects of the medieval attitude:

> The philosophy we principally received ... must be acknowledged puerile, or rather talkative than generative—as being fruitful in controversies, but barren of effects....
>
> Our method is continually to dwell among things soberly ... to establish a true and legitimate union between the experimental and rational faculty....
>
> This kind of degenerate learning did chiefly reign among the schoolmen: who having sharp and strong wits, and abundance of leisure, ... as their persons were shut up in the cells of monasteries and colleges ... did out of no great quantity of matter and infinite agitation of wit spin out unto us those laborious webs of learning which are extant in their books....
>
> Nothing parcel of the world is denied to man's inquiry and invention.

Bacon himself had a strong sense of the value of metaphysics, and also genuine religious convictions, but he believed that God had given two books to mankind, the Book of Revelation and the Book of Nature. Hitherto, man had neglected the second, and the time had now come, not for the rejection of metaphysical and religious truths, but for the assertion of the claims of the kind of truth to be found in Nature. It should be noted that Bacon's 'Nature' was neither mechanical nor abstract. His attitude towards it, as Basil Willey has pointed out, is more like that of Wordsworth than that of the scientists. It is this reverent, almost religious feeling for Nature that gives so much of his work its high imaginative quality.

The scientists who followed Bacon lost this reverence and this poetic feeling for Nature, but it became a permanent part of the English heritage. There is a touch of it in Milton, and it was to reappear later in the work of the great romantic poets. Bacon's *New Atlantis* is a sketch of an imaginary commonwealth in the unknown West, which forms a curious contrast with More's Utopia. Its most prominent feature is a college of scientific research called Salomon's House, which suggested to the English scientists of the mid-seventeenth century the plan of the Royal Society.

Of the prose writers after Bacon the most interesting are Sir Thomas Browne and Izaak Walton. The *Religio Medici* of Browne, a provincial physician, is one of the most delightful and characteristic books of the period. Browne stands, as it were, midway between the religious attitude of the later Donne and George Herbert and the sceptical and experimental moods of Montaigne and Bacon. He can rejoice in 'wingy mysteries in Divinity' and loves to lose himself 'in an O Altitudo', while, on the other hand he speaks in Baconian fashion of Nature as the 'universal and publick Manuscript' of God which all men should study and in his *Christian Morals* exhorts his readers not to 'fly only upon the wings of Imagination' but to 'joyn Sense unto Reason, and Experiment unto Speculation'. Browne was what he himself called the 'great and true amphibium', and was able to live at once in the old world of spirit and imagination and the new world of science, so that, when he attempted to write an antiquarian tract on some funeral urns discovered in Norfolk, he produced one of the most sublime prose poems in the English language. Walton shares with Herrick and Herbert a peculiar fragrance that belongs to certain retired writers of this period. His *Lives* are one of the first great experiments in English biography. They might be described as Lives of the Anglican saints, Hooker, Donne, Herbert, Wotton and Sanderson. His *Compleat Angler* is a prose idyll with a charm and a freshness that recall Herrick's best poems.

The most influential prose work of this age, and indeed in the whole of English literature, was the great Authorized English version of the Bible published in 1611. The translation was the work of a committee of divines who made excellent use of the older versions of Tyndale, Coverdale and others. The result of their labours was to place in the hands of every Englishman a work that is unrivalled for its combination of dignity, simplicity and poetic feeling. The English Bible has been to the English people what the Homeric epics were to the Greeks or rather something more, because it was not only a literary masterpiece, but the sacred book of a religion which, in spite of its numerous varieties, was passionately believed in by nearly the whole nation. In the seventeenth century almost every non-Romanist Englishman and Englishwoman from Quaker to High Anglican was an ardent Bible reader, and the Bible of all the sects was the version of 1611.

The drama after Shakespeare ceased to be national in character, and became an amusement of the court and the literary circles under its patronage. The Puritans were in a large degree responsible for this change. The Elizabethan drama had never claimed to be anything more than a 'pastime', and for such 'pastimes' there was no room in the Puritan scheme of things, which aimed at the entire domination of human life by religion. Humanistic Puritans like Milton and Peter Sterry, who read and admired Shakespeare, were a small minority. William Prynne was voicing the opinions of the vast majority of his party in his enormous, ill-tempered and pedantic book *Histriomastix* (published in 1633) when he proved to his own satisfaction by means of copious quotations from early Christian writers that 'all popular and common Stage-Playes, whether Comicall, Satyricall, Mimicall, or mixt of either . . . are altogether unseemely and unlawfull unto Christians'. The drama thus became what it was to be for a very long time, the entertainment, not of the whole nation, but of a small section with a veneer of courtly culture, but little serious aesthetic appreciation of the theatre, while the dramatists were forced to become showmen for an audience in which the frivolous and heartless elements predominated. Beaumont and Fletcher were fashionable dramatists of the period, brilliant versifiers, masters of stagecraft, clever imitators of Shakespeare, but writers who substitute sentimentality for Shakespeare's high imagination and who are entirely lacking in his intellectual power and sense of significant and organic form. Middleton, Webster and Ford, their contemporaries, were men with a higher conception of dramatic art, poets who often come close to the 'metaphysical writers' in the intensity and power of their language. In the plays of Massinger and Shirley the glow of poetry is fading and we are conscious of the transition to a new kind of drama which, except for certain formal elements, has little in common with the drama of the age of Shakespeare. When the Civil War broke out the triumphant Puritans closed the London theatres. Clandestine performances appear to have taken place, but it was not until the last years of the Protectorate that Cromwell, who was not nearly so strait-laced as most of his supporters, allowed some semi-public performances to be organized by Sir William Davenant, Shakespeare's godson.

The most important of the younger poets of this period, John Milton, was neither a 'metaphysical', nor a courtier of the tribe of Ben, nor a dramatist of the school of Fletcher. He was the son of a substantial citizen of Elizabethan London who had some ability as a musician and writer of verse. The household of John Milton the elder was apparently Puritan, Anglican, tolerant, and humanistic, an unusual but not an impossible combination in the reign of James I. The young Milton was originally designed for the Church, but at an early age dedicated himself to the production of the great English Poem with the fervour of a young Hannibal consecrating his life to the overthrow of Rome. It speaks volumes for the civilization of early seventeenth-century England that the elder Milton, a quiet, undistinguished citizen, should not merely have acquiesced in this plan, but willingly provided the necessary funds for its accomplishment. After leaving Cambridge Milton spent seven years in studious retirement in Buckinghamshire, acquiring a truly immense erudition. He crowned this magnificent education by a 'Grand Tour' in France, Switzerland and Italy. He was designing to visit Sicily and Greece when the Civil War threatened to break out and he returned to England, because he 'thought it base to be travelling for amusement abroad' when his 'fellow citizens were fighting for liberty at home'. His early poems (first collected in 1645) are a series of brilliant experiments in English, Latin and Italian verse, which he wrote with almost equal facility. In the English poems there are only slight traces of 'metaphysical' influence. The young Milton's tendency is to go back behind Donne to Spenser and the Elizabethans, to the Italians and to the classics. In *L'Allegro* and *Il Penseroso* the exquisite taste and culture of a scholar-courtier are combined with a freshness and a fragrance that recall Herrick and Walton. *Comus* is a Caroline masque (the form of entertainment that Jonson had popularized at the courts of the first two Stuart kings), transformed almost out of recognition by the high seriousness of the poet and the loftiness of his style. In *Lycidas*, the most highly wrought of his early poems, Milton combines in a single dazzling fabric reminiscences of Greek, Latin, Italian and Elizabethan poetry, and achieves a technique that raises English verse for a moment to the level of Sophocles and Virgil. But *Lycidas* is not merely a triumph of technique. It represents a turning-point in the history of the English mind. For a moment the poet looks back with regret to the life of passion, the life of the court:

> *Were it not better don as others use,*
> *To sport with* Amaryllis *in the shade,*
> *Or with the tangles of* Neæra's *hair?*

But in the bitter invective against the High Church clergy, the 'blind mouthes' (one of whom, we may remember, was George Herbert!), he puts aside the courtly ideal that meant so much to him in his youth and sets his face towards the road that led to the Puritan revolution:

> *But that two-handed engine at the door,*
> *Stands ready to smite once, and smite no more.*

Abandoning for the time being his great design for a national epic (which was originally to have dealt with an Arthurian theme) Milton shut English poetry, except for the writing of occasional sonnets, out of his life for about twenty years after the composition of *Lycidas*. He became at first a free-lance pamphleteer on the Puritan side, and later Secretary for Foreign Tongues and official propagandist to the Protectorate. During this period he moved from Puritan Anglicanism to Presbyterianism, and from Presbyterianism to an Independency of the left wing which ended in something very like pantheistic deism. In the great passages in his prose writings in English and in Latin he achieves in a way the prophetic poem 'doctrinal to a nation', of which he had dreamed in his youth. Milton is the fountain-head of the prophetic tradition in English literature, the tradition of Blake, of Wordsworth, of Ruskin and D. H. Lawrence.* His Latin prose writings were valuable weapons for the Protectorate in its propagandist campaign on the Continent, and gave their author a European reputation such as no English writer since the Middle Ages except More and Bacon had hitherto achieved.

* See *Milton and Wordsworth* by Sir Herbert Grierson, 1937.

RESTORATION THOUGHT AND LITERATURE

If Montaigne and Bacon were the most powerful influences on English thought in the first half of the seventeenth century, the 'climate of opinion' in the second half was conditioned largely by the work of another Frenchman and another Englishman, Réné Descartes and Thomas Hobbes. It is highly significant that both these philosophers were mathematicians. The latter part of the seventeenth century is the age of the triumph of mathematical thought throughout Europe. It may be noted that mathematics practically assumed their modern form in this period, when logarithms and the calculus were invented. Descartes' philosophy starts with complete scepticism, both with regard to traditional ideas and with regard to sense impressions. Looking for a 'truth' in which he could believe he found it, not in religious experience like Donne, or in 'Nature' like Bacon, but in the act of thinking: *'cogito ergo sum'*. From this proof of his own existence as an imperfect being he deduces the existence of God as the perfect being, and from these two certainties he deduces the rest of the universe. The details of Descartes' philosophy do not matter so much as his method and spirit. Fontenelle, a French writer of the end of the century, wrote that Descartes's 'method of reasoning' was 'more estimable than his philosophy itself'. This method was the geometrical method. Descartes dealt only with 'clear ideas', the only ideas that seemed valid to him. 'I will assuredly reach truth', he writes, 'if I fix my attention sufficiently on all the things I conceive perfectly, and separate them from others I conceive more confused and obscurely.' Descartes's 'truth' is founded neither on emotion nor on sense-perception, but on intellectual abstraction. His philosophy is a dualism which distinguishes 'thought' from 'extension', or in other words, mind from matter. Matter is controlled by wholly mechanical laws, and mind is only connected with it in man though the intervention of God. The Cartesian spirit was to affect literature profoundly during the 'neo-classic' periods in France and England. It was one of the forces that led to that 'dissociation of sensibility' which T. S. Eliot has noted as a characteristic of English poetry after the middle of the seventeenth century. In Shakespeare, Donne and Browne thinking and feeling are blended together in a single process. As the seventeenth century went on, and the influence of Descartes began to be felt, this kind of writing became impossible, and 'judgment' and 'reason', sharply distinguished from 'imagination' and 'fancy', were held to be the only means by which 'truth' could be apprehended. Thomas Hobbes of Malmesbury, mathematical tutor to Charles II, had a powerful, limited, positive mind and a genius for simplification. He revived the doctrine of materialism. For him

> the world, . . . that is the whole mass of all things that are, is corporeal, that is to say body, and hath the dimensions of magnitude . . . that which is not body is no part of the universe; and, because the universe is all, that which is no part of it is 'nothing', and consequently 'nowhere'.

Hobbes although he disguises his thought by the use of orthodox phraseology, believed that nothing existed except matter and motion. The terms 'soul', 'spirit', and 'mind' were mere words used to frighten people 'as men fright birds from the corn with an empty doublet, a hat, and a crooked stick'. Thought and perception are purely mechanical processes and can be accounted for by purely material causes: '*conceptions* and *apparitions* are nothing *really* but *motion* in some internal substance of the *head*'. Imagination is simply 'decaying sense', or the remains of impressions made in the past on the human brain by other pieces of matter: 'This obscure conception is what we call *phantasy* or *imagination*.' 'Good' and 'evil' are mere convenient terms with no permanent meaning, and no divine authority behind them. 'Whatsoever is the object of any man's appetite, or desire, that is it which he for his part calleth "good", and the object of hate, or aversion "evil".' Persons who condemn the pleasures of sense are the priests and teachers who have a vested interest in illusions inherited from the ages of monkery, 'the kingdom of darkness' of the medieval church, for which Hobbes had a supreme contempt. His *Leviathan* (which gives its name to his chief book published in 1651), or ideal state, is all powerful, founded on a contract between rulers and ruled, which remains eternally valid. It was the moral and religious aspects of Hobbes's teaching that alarmed the churchmen, and delighted the young courtiers of the Restoration. The Cambridge Platonists tried to answer him by demonstrating the existence of 'mind' or 'spirit' and its superiority over matter, while other Anglicans, such as Bishop Bramhall, showed quite truly that his arguments led to atheism.

Another current of thought which affected literature in the Restoration period as much as the philosophies of Descartes and Hobbes was that of the scientists who were carrying out the programme of Bacon and beginning that thorough investigation of 'Nature' which he recommended. The Royal Society, the first organized body of English scientific investigators, grew out of a group of Oxford thinkers who used to meet at the lodgings of Dr Wilkins, the Warden of Wadham College, in the last years of the Protectorate. It moved to London after the Restoration and was granted a Charter by Charles II, who became its Founder and Patron and took a keen interest in its proceedings. Among the distinguished men who were its original Fellows was Robert Boyle, author of the *Sceptical Chymist* (1662), and one of the founders of modern chemistry. According to Thomas Sprat, the first historian of the Society, its members tried 'to separate the Knowledge of *Nature* from the Colours of *Rhetorick*, the Device of *Fancy*, or the delightful Deceit of *Fables*', so that by it 'Mankind may obtain a Dominion over *Things*'. In their writings Sprat tells us they

> extracted from all their members, a close, naked, natural way of speaking, positive expressions, clear senses, a native

easiness, bringing all things as near the Mathematical plainness as they can, and preferring the language of Artizans, Countrymen, and Merchants, before that of Wits or Scholars.*

The philosophies of Descartes and Hobbes and the 'experimental knowledge' of the Royal Society might have been expected to kill poetry altogether. Boileau the contemporary French poet, is said to have remarked that 'la philosophie de Descartes avait coupé la gorge à la poésie'. Poetry, after all, depended largely on the 'decaying sense' despised by Hobbes, and on 'the Devices of *Fancy*' and 'delightful Deceit of *Fables*' scorned by the Royal Society. But the poetical tradition in England was far too strong to be quenched by the new rationalism and materialism, and Englishmen even if they are rationalists and materialists, are incurably poetical. What actually happened was that the neo-classic manner first attempted by Jonson and his followers, a manner peculiarly well suited for the forcible expression of clear thoughts dear to this mathematical age, replaced the metaphysical manner as the orthodox poetic style. Far from disappearing, poetry was much written and highly prized, but its subject matter became limited, while its diction lost that aura of suggestion that had been the glory of the older English poetry, though it acquired in its place a new perspicuity and energy. The poets could deal with realistic subject matter, with intellectual argument, or with satire. The first of these subjects represents the 'real' bodily world of Hobbes, the second, Descartes's world of pure thought, and the third, the contrast between the ideals of the individual and the world of actuality seen in the dry light of reason. The notion was also gaining ground that languages develop until they reach a point of perfection, an 'Augustan' age, and that this point ought soon to be reached by the English language. 'The English language seems at this time (1667)', writes

* Thomas Sprat, *The History of the Royal Society*, London 1667, pp. 62, 113.

Sprat, 'to require some such aid to bring it to its last perfection.' The aid to which he alludes is a projected English Academy like the newly-erected French Academy. Such an academy was planned in the reign of James I, and again by Cowley at the Restoration. It never came into existence, but its place was taken in some degree by the 'wits' of Charles II's court. The beginning of the new poetry is to be found in the middle of the century. It is mingled with frigid survivals of 'metaphysical wit' in Cowley and Davenant, and with the old Jonsonian court poetry in Waller and Denham. The 'merry gang' among the courtiers of Charles II carried the process a stage further, and they were not unaffected by the parallel movement in contemporary France. These young men were typical of the 'post-war' period in their intellectual brilliance, their insolence, their scorn of the older generation, and their affectation of hardness. Clarendon wrote that among them 'the tenderness of bowels, which is the quintessence of justice and compassion, the very mention of good nature was laughed at, and looked upon as the mark and character of a fool: and a roughness of manners or hardheartedness and cruelty was affected'. Among the new 'Mob of Gentlemen who wrote with ease', Sir Charles Sedley wrote some exquisite songs and Lord Buckhurst some sparkling vers-de-société, but the one member of the group who was a poet of real power and significance was John Wilmot, Earl of Rochester, the son of a cavalier general and a Puritan lady. A few of his love songs have a passion and a tenderness that were not to be recovered in the English lyric till the days of Burns, but his most important and characteristic work is to be found in his satires and realistic poems. In some of these he paints vivid, ironic pictures of the fops, cuckolds and courtesans of Restoration London. In the greatest, his *Satyr against Mankind* he attacks Reason itself, the naked rationality that he had formerly worshipped:

> *Reason, which Fifty times for One does err,*
> *Reason, an* Ignis fatuus *of the Mind,*

Which leaves the Light of Nature, Sense, behind.
Pathless, and dang'rous, wand'ring ways, it takes,
Through Error's fenny Bogs, and thorny Brakes:
While the misguided Follower climbs with Pain,
Mountains of Whimsies, heapt in his own Brain:
Stumbling from Thought to Thought, falls headlong down
Into Doubt's boundless Sea, . . .

Rochester is the last great courtier-poet of the Renaissance. With his work and that of his friends the great line that began with Sir Thomas Wyatt ends. The new centre of literary culture after the Revolution was no longer the court but the 'Town', the society of the coffee-houses and the taverns that was already flourishing in the reign of Charles II. Rochester's conversion, during his last illness in 1680, by Gilbert Burnet, the latitudinarian divine, is as significant in its way as his poetry. It prefigures the alliance between liberal Christianity and rationalistic philosophy that was to be characteristic of the next century.

Living aloof in contemptuous isolation from the court and the 'town', the blind John Milton, greatest of the fallen Independents, completed the heroic poem of which he had dreamed in the reign of Charles I. The tragic majesty of his situation can only be adequately described in his own words:

Standing on Earth, not rapt above the Pole,
More safe I sing with mortal voice, unchang'd
To hoarce or mute, though fall'n on evil dayes,
On evil dayes though fall'n and evil tongues;
In darkness, and with dangers compast round,
And solitude.

After much meditation he had chosen as his subject the Biblical story of the Fall of Man instead of a tale from the Arthurian cycle. This story, moving before a vast background of Heaven, Earth and Hell, was well adapted to a mind with a cosmic quality like that of Milton. It also suited the Puritan mentality with its strong sense of sin, its intense belief in the importance of the personal relationship between God and Man, and its idealization of marriage. For Milton himself it had a profound personal significance, for it symbolized the tragedy of his own situation with peculiar force. With consummate skill he overcame the difficulty of adapting this bare Hebrew myth to the vast and complicated framework of the classical epic, and produced the great poem which represents the Protestant humanism of the Renaissance as completely as Dante's Divine Comedy represents the Catholic scholasticism of the Middle Ages. Among the many attempts made in the seventeenth century in France and England to produce an epic or 'heroic' poem, it is the only success, perhaps because Milton was the only man among those who attempted the task with the necessary combination of sublimity of character, leisure, immense erudition, adequate technical skill, variety and intensity of experience, and depth of poetic feeling. *Paradise Lost* has been called the last great Elizabethan poem, and there is something Elizabethan in the richness and profusion of its imagery, in the atmosphere of sea and strange lands felt in the numerous allusions to travel, and in the use of exotic geographical names:

> *Damasco*, or *Marocco*, or *Trebisond*,
> . . . . . .
> *Mombaza*, and *Quiloa*, and *Melind*
> . . . . . .
> *Guiana*, whose great Citie *Geryons* Sons
> Call *El Dorado*.

But it is also essentially a poem of the neo-classic period in its firm outlines, its Latinized diction (the source of much of that of the Augustan age), its perfectly organized design and, above all, in the dualism of its thought, which is as significant as the philosophic dualism of Descartes. In Milton's hands the primitive Hebrew myth is transformed into a symbol of the consciousness of his own age. The tremendous figure of Satan (who does not even appear in Genesis) comes to represent in *Paradise Lost* the untamed and passionate will of the individual in revolt against a God who is no longer the personal deity of the Hebrews, but the abstract Reason or First Cause of philosophy:

> *Boundless the Deep, because I am who fill*
> *Infinitude....*
> *Necessitie and Chance*
> *Approach not mee, and what I will is Fate.*

'It is', as Lascelles Abercrombie has written, 'in the figure of Satan that the imperishable significance of *Paradise Lost* is centred.' All the indomitable heroism of the Puritan armies finds expression in his defiance:

> *What though the field be lost?*
> *All is not lost; the unconquerable Will,*
> *And study of revenge, immortal hate,*
> *And courage never to submit or yield:*
> *And what is else not to be overcome?*

But it is more than the tragedy of Milton and his friends that is expressed in *Paradise Lost*. It is the tragedy of the modern world, the conflict of the individual will in revolt against the determinism of an inexorable fate. Milton expressed that conflict, but the nature of the mythology to which he was bound prevented him from resolving it, at any rate, on the poetic plane, though he attempted to do so on the plane of argument by means of the elaborate pantheistic system of his Latin *De Doctrinâ Christianâ*. Blake's words remain the profoundest comment on the antinomy that troubles every thoughtful reader of *Paradise Lost*, however much he may admire the splendour of its art:

> ... The reason Milton wrote in fetters when he wrote of Angels & God, and at liberty when of Devils & Hell, is because he was a true Poet and of the Devil's party without knowing it.

The metre of *Paradise Lost* closes an era in English versification and begins a new one. It is the old blank verse of the dramatists hardened and strengthened into an epic metre by a great architect of language. Its example overshadowed all English poetry that aimed at epic sublimity for two hundred years. *Paradise Regained* is not so much a sequel to *Paradise Lost* as an experiment in a different kind of epic, modelled on the Book of Job, and moving on the plane of discussion instead of that of action. The subject, the Temptation in the Wilderness, is treated in a much more austere manner than that of *Paradise Lost*. The central figure is the Puritan Christ, a Stoic hero with little enough of the tenderness of the Gospels. The poem is a triumph of technique conceived in a rarefied intellectual atmosphere, and only appealing to that 'fit audience though few' which Milton desired for his work. In *Samson Agonistes*, the third great work of his later years, Milton again takes a great Hebrew legend and charges it with the force of his own tremendous personality and experience. Although there is no overt allusion to contemporary events, the Samson of this classic tragedy, the most successful of all attempts to reproduce the pure Greek model in English, is a transparent disguise for the blind old poet in the reign of Charles II,

> *Eyeless in Gaza at the Mill with slaves.*

The heroic faith of the long-suffering Puritans in the coming of a day of deliverance inspires its magnificent lyrics, in some ways the summit of Milton's technical achievement:

> *Oh how comely it is and how reviving*
> *To the Spirits of just men long opprest!*
> *When God into the hands of their deliverer*
> *Puts invincible might*
> *To quell the mighty of the Earth, th' oppressour,*
> *The brute and boist'rous force of violent men . . .*
> *He all their Ammunition*
> *And feats of War defeats*
> *With plain Heroic magnitude of mind. . . .*

John Dryden was a man as different from John Milton (whom he sincerely admired) as Charles II was from Oliver

THE SEVENTEENTH CENTURY

Cromwell. Throughout his long literary career he had to write to earn a living, and was never at liberty to move in lofty regions of the imagination. He became the most admired poet of the younger generation, the dictator of the literary society of the 'town' that met in the coffee-houses and taverns of Covent Garden. Dryden's poetry completes the development of the neo-classic tradition that began with Jonson. His early work in The *Heroick Stanzas* on Cromwell's death and *Annus Mirabilis* is encumbered by frigid remnants of 'metaphysical wit', which had little life in it after Cowley, and by a pedantic display of erudition, but he gradually purified his diction from these encumbrances and evolved a magnificent poetic style perfectly adapted to an age dominated by the thought of Descartes and Hobbes. He himself summed up that style in an early essay as 'the art of clothing and adorning... thought... in apt, significant and sounding words'.

Perspicuity and energy are the great merits of his verse and he can combine them with dignity and passion or with wit and humour. His production was immense, and covered over forty years. He was known as a poet before the end of the Protectorate, and his last work was published in 1700. The secret of his success was that of the modern journalist. He knew what his public wanted, and gave it willingly, for his tastes were the tastes of the average man. He was always abreast of contemporary literary fashion, but rarely in advance of it. His versatility was remarkable and is almost unparalleled in English literature. He wrote comedies, tragedies, operas, complimentary verses, narrative poems, verse satires, translations from the classics, songs, odes, epistles, prologues and epilogues and a great body of critical prefaces in prose. His voluminous works may be said to have established the chief kinds of imaginative writing that came to be recognized as orthodox in the eighteenth century, with the single exception of the novel. His most excellent and enduring work is to be found in his verse satires, his poems of argument and controversy, his epistles and complimentary poems, and his prose criticism. In *Absalom and Achitophel*, his attack on Shaftesbury and the Whigs, written, is is said, at the request of Charles II, he raises political satire, which had been a coarse though powerful instrument in the hands of writers like Butler and Marvell, to an epic grandeur. Indeed a poem in which such lines as the character of Achitophel (Shaftesbury) occur might more properly be called an ironic epic than a satire:

> *Of these the false Achitophel was first;*
> *A name to all succeeding ages curst:*
> *For close designs and crooked counsels fit;*
> *Sagacious, bold and turbulent of wit;*
> *Restless, unfix'd in principles and place;*
> *In power unpleas'd, impatient of disgrace:*
> *A fiery soul, which working out its way,*
> *Fretted the pigmy body to decay,*
> *And o'er-inform'd the tenement of clay.*

In Dryden's hands poetry, which had been intimately personal with the 'metaphysicals', becomes a public art, the expression of the mind of a society. It is significant that he dreamed all his life of an epic on the Black Prince or King Arthur and was never able to write it. The 'town' did not really want epics, although it might pay lip-service to Virgil and Homer. It wanted poems dealing with contemporary human life and contemporary thought. The greatness of Dryden can be measured by the fact that he succeeds again and again in turning this difficult material into fine poetry. His courage and magnanimity can prevail even over such stubborn subject-matter as political satire and theological argument. Never have wit and magnificence been more admirably combined in English poetry than in his attack on democracy in *The Medal*:

> *Almighty crowd, thou shorten'st all dispute;*
> *Power is thy essence, with thy attribute:*
> *Nor faith nor reason make thee at a stay,*
> *Thou leap'st o'er all eternal truths in thy Pindaric Way.*

The fame of Dryden's satires has obscured the excellence of much of his other poetry. Its range includes the splendour (often mingled with irony) of the 'heroic plays', the passion and dignity of *All for Love*, the noble, melancholy music of the elegy on Oldham, and the invigorating, metallic quality of his best lyrics, such as his farewell to the seventeenth century in the *Secular Masque:*

> *All, all of a piece throughout:*
> *Thy chase had a Beast in View;*
> *Thy wars brought nothing about;*
> *Thy lovers were all untrue.*
> *'Tis well an Old Age is out,*
> *And time to begin a New.*

Dryden may be said to have brought poetry down to earth, but it was necessary for poetry to be brought down to earth at that time, just as it was necessary at the beginning of the twentieth century, when the romantic manner had become outworn and threadbare.

The Restoration period was the age in which modern English prose came into existence. Milton's prose works embody all the faults as well as all the splendours of early seventeenth-century prose. It would be difficult to find in English anything more splendid and imaginative than the great poetical passages in them, or anything more cumbrous and involved than the less inspired portions. The new English prose banished splendour and clumsiness alike. The Royal Society's demand for a 'close, naked, natural way of speaking' has already been quoted. Beside it may be placed Hobbes's contemptuous reference in *Leviathan* to the 'frequencie of insignificant speech', and Burnet's account in the *History of His Own Times* (I, 191), of the insistence of Charles II on a plain style in sermons. As in poetry, French influence counted for something, but it only reinforced a development that would have certainly taken place even if there had been no intercourse between the two countries. All the chief types of modern English prose composition have their roots in this period. It was particularly rich in diaries, memoirs, histories of contemporary events, in biographies and character studies of contemporary figures, and in prose comedies, from the delicate airy sketches of Etherege to the coarse, powerful realism of Shadwell and the savage satire of Wycherley. English writers in this period seem suddenly to acquire the power of observing their contemporaries and recording their observations, just as the scientists observed and experimented upon natural phenomena. The incomparably vivid journal of Pepys, the decorous, gentlemanly memoirs of Evelyn, Clarendon's majestic *History of the Great Rebellion*, and his more personal and intimate *Autobiography*, Burnet's fresh and vigorous *History of His Own Times*, Aubrey's inspired jottings and sketches in his *Brief Lives*, and the biographies called *The Lives of the Norths* contain such a wealth of shrewd observation of life and character expressed in direct, racy language as can hardly be paralleled in English literature. The critical essay as understood in modern times was created by Dryden in his Prefaces, where he achieves a style that is at once cool, lucid, familiar and dignified. It remained the standard of English prose for a century. The personal essay or causerie was written with delicacy and a new ease and familiarity by Cowley and Sir William Temple. Among the many political pamphleteers Halifax, the 'Trimmer', is pre-eminent for the purity and vigour of his English. Religious and philosophic prose is to be found at its best in the Cambridge Platonists, Whichcote, Smith, Cudworth, and More and in some of their successors such as Joseph Glanville and Archbishop Tillotson. The *pensée* or aphorism, so fashionable in France at this time, appears in English in Halifax's *Political and Moral Thoughts and Reflections*, in Whichcote's *Moral and Religious Aphorisms*, and in *Some Fruits of Solitude* by William Penn, the Quaker leader. The most interesting type of drama produced for the revived theatre of the Restoration was the prose comedy of manners, which began with the three sparkling plays of Sir George Etherege, the friend of Rochester and Sedley, acquired weight and energy in the powerful dramatic satires of Wycherley, and finally flowered at the end of the century in the four great works of William Congreve.

Apart from their innumerable sermons and bible commentaries, the Puritans and Quakers also made a curious and characteristic contribution to this new prose literature. This contribution arose from that intense interest in personal morality and the condition of the individual soul which led them to write introspective records of psychological experience. The Journals of George Fox, the Quaker, of Richard Baxter, the Presbyterian and, above all, the *Grace Abounding to the Chief of Sinners* of John Bunyan, the Baptist, are the most notable books of this kind. As Professor Grierson has pointed out, these books are the forerunners of the realistic and psychological novel, of *Pamela* and *Clarissa*, *David Copperfield*, *Wuthering Heights*, and *A Portrait of the Artist as a Young Man*. Bunyan is the one great author who sprang from the Puritans of the artisan class, and it is instructive to compare his work with that of Milton, the aristocratic and humanistic Puritan. His *Pilgrim's Progress* (1678-84) is at once an allegory of real imaginative power and a striking realistic picture of the life of the countryside in Restoration England. The Pilgrimage of Christian was the journey through life of thousands of simple Puritan souls, but the future lay with Mr Worldly Wiseman, who might be a prophetic portrait of Daniel Defoe, and Mr Facing Both-ways who is a caricature of the Latitudinarians. Bunyan, the last of the old heroic Puritans, died in 1688. In the previous year a Fellow of the Royal Society called Isaac Newton had published his *Philosophiae Naturalis Principia Mathematica*, a work that completed the revolution begun by Descartes and firmly established that mechanico-materialistic view of the universe which dominated European thought for the next two centuries.

CHAPTER IV

LITERATURE AND MUSIC

By BRUCE PATTISON

Professor of Education in the University of London

THE association of music and literature is based on the fact that the human voice is both the instrument of speech and a musical instrument. When it sings it usually speaks too: it is not like man-made musical instruments, because self-expression is more natural in speech, and melody and rhythm therefore become more expressive if accompanied by linguistic conventions. The forms of music and what is expressed in language vary, however, and so the relationships between vocal music and its texts are always changing. In the period with which this volume is concerned music and poetry were particularly conscious of each other; there was a lively sense that they had 'ever been considered brothers', and each influenced the other. There were historical and social reasons for this, and it was assisted by much traditional and new theory.

There was plenty of both amateur and professional music in the everyday lives of Elizabethan Englishmen of all classes. Labour-saving machinery was comparatively primitive and automation not even conceivable in the imagination. Physical exertion was sweetened and concerted effort directed by rhythmical song.

> And hence it is that manual labourers, and Mechanical Artificers of all sorts keepe such a chaunting and singing in their shoppes, the tailor on his bulk, the shomaker at his last, the mason at his wall, the shipboy at his oar, the tinker at his pan, and the tiler on the house-top.*

Seasonal and religious festivals brought relief from work

* John Case, *Praise of Musicke* (1588), p. 44.

LITERATURE AND MUSIC

and opportunities for recreation, and a popular pastime with all classes was dancing. Queen Elizabeth herself was very fond of it. At the other end of the social scale the countryman enjoyed his humbler measures just as much. 'Sunday he esteemes a day to make merry in, and thinkes a Bagpipe as essentiall to it as Evening-Prayer where he walkes very solemnly after the service with his hands coupled behinde him and censures the dauncing of his parish.'* The pipe and tabor often accompanied dancing, and Will Kemp, the most famous comedian of the day, took a taborer with him when he danced a morris all the way from London to Norwich, a nine-days' wonder that attracted all the publicity he no doubt wanted, for he was not only greeted with friendly interest everywhere but a number of people danced short distances with him. Besides the pipe and tabor, the fiddle was a common accompaniment for popular dancing, and professional fiddlers were nearly always readily available. 'London is so full of unprofitable Pipers and Fiddlers,' complains a Puritan writer, 'that a man can no soner enter a taverne, but two or three caste of them hang at his heeles, to give him a dance before he departe.'†

New dance tunes were played in the theatres. Words were fitted to them, as to older tunes, and they were printed on single sheets of paper embellished with crude woodcuts. These 'broadsides' or ballads dealt with the matters that are now the staples of 'pop' songs and Sunday newspapers. There were London journalists who made a livelihood by writing them: William Elderton, Thomas Deloney and Martin Parker were notorious authors of them. Amateurs produced ballads too. In *A Midsummer Night's Dream* Bottom says he will get Peter Quince to write about his adventures in the wood. Falstaff threatened to pay back those who had played a trick on him by having ballads about them sung to 'scurvy tunes' (presumably tunes associated with disreputable verses). In *The Return from Parnassus*, a Cambridge play

* J. Earle, *Microcosmographie* (1628), ed. G. Murphy, p. 36.
† S. Gosson, *An Apologie for the Schoole of Abuse* (1579), ed. Arber, p. 70.

(1606), a character says: 'I thinke there be never an Ale-house in England nor yet so base a Maypole on a country greene, but sets forth some poets petternels or demilances to the paper warres in Paules Churchyard' (i.e. the current controversies, St Paul's churchyard being a meeting-place and a sort of Hyde Park Corner of the period). Ballad singers sold broadsides at fairs and wherever there were crowds. Nightingale in *Bartholomew Fair* and Autolycus in *A Winter's Tale* are typical representatives of the trade.

The state of more serious music is obscured rather than revealed by a profusion of statements attributable to the respected position music occupied in sixteenth century philosophy, psychology and political theory. A garbled version of Greek speculations, which had filtered down to the Middle Ages, largely through the sixth century philosopher Boethius, was given a new importance in the sixteenth century by the revival of classical studies. Greek scientists had been intrigued to discover that intervals in their modes or scales resulted from stopping the monochord at various points so that the two parts into which the string was thus divided had proportions expressible in whole numbers. As whole numbers were usually thought more satisfactory than fractions, being in tune could be identified with a greater degree of approximation to a mathematical perfection. Numbers had a prestige based on their order of abstraction from crude reality. Moreover, because the number of notes in a mode happened to correspond to the number of spheres round the earth in the Ptolemaic system of astronomy (both had the magic number seven), the legend of the music of the spheres was evolved: each sphere was supposed to have a siren going round with it and singing a single note. The heavenly bodies were thought to influence human temperament, and the imitation of their tone system in terrestrial music could affect the hearer powerfully. The harmony or ordered relationship of notes in a tune gave him an experience of heavenly harmony; his feelings were ruled by the system governing the universe.

As music developed in the course of centuries the meaning

LITERATURE AND MUSIC

of the theory changed without anybody's realizing it. It was forgotten that the Greeks had known only monodic music. Their term 'harmony' was applied to part-music. Their cosmology and psychology became entangled with notions about natural order—in the heavens, among all kinds of life and in human society and individual psychology. So, according to Castiglione, 'it hath beene the opinion of most wise Philosophers, that the worlde is made of musike, and the heavens in their moving make a melodie, and our soule is framed after the verie same sort and therefore lifteth up it selfe, and (as it were) reviveth the virtues of it selfe with Musicke.'*
But Sir Thomas Elyot goes further and considers music necessary 'for the better attayning the knowledge of a publike weale: whiche is made of an ordre of astates and degrees, and, by reason thereof, conteineth in it a perfect harmony.'†

To be told that

> *The man that hath no music in himself,*
> *Nor is not moved with concord of sweet sounds,*
> *Is fit for treasons, stratagems and spoils*‡

was certainly an inducement to pretend to like music. An amateurish interest in it is recommended in all the courtesy books throughout the period. The nobility inherited a tradition of generosity to minstrels. The Court maintained a considerable establishment of professional musicians, and the secular part of it increased in size under the Tudors. The great houses emulated the Court, though on a smaller scale. An important nobleman would have his trumpeters. A few had chapels with men and boy singers. More would have bands, each consisting of four instrumentalists in their patron's livery and owing certain obligations to him but also available for engagement by others. London and the larger cities kept professional players called waits, who could also

---

* *The Boke of the Courtyer*, trans. T. Hoby (1561), Everyman ed., pp. 75-6.
† *The Boke Named the Governour*, Everyman ed., p. 28.
‡ *The Merchant of Venice*, V i.

be hired privately when not occupied with civic ceremonial. Kemp praises the Norwich waits who took part in his public welcome at the conclusion of his morris dance from London. They apparently could sing as well as play wind and stringed instruments.

Ability to sing and play an instrument, though only very amateurishly, is required by all the manuals of behaviour intended to instruct ladies and gentlemen of the new type coming into fashion under Italian influence during the first half of the sixteenth century. Henry VIII, who seemed on his accession to be the very model of the Renaissance ruler, composed songs and played several instruments. His sister Margaret and her future husband, James IV of Scotland, played the lute and the virginals to each other during her progress to his kingdom. Henry's daughter Mary entertained some French visitors in 1520 by playing on the virginals, and her half-sister Elizabeth, much later when she was Queen, allowed Sir James Melville to hear her perform on the same instrument. As the sixteenth century advanced it became increasingly customary for gentlemen's families to have music teachers living with them to instruct the children and sometimes the lady of the house too. The lute, which established itself as the chief domestic instrument during the sixteenth century, was, like the guitar, which has become popular in recent years, admirable for amateurs to accompany their own singing and for transcriptions of part-music originally intended for several voices or for instrumental consorts. Young men with agreeable voices and ability to strum on the lute attracted the favour of noble patrons.

Singing was popular, and in some circles part-singing was a regular recreation. Henry VIII used to call on Sir Peter Carew to join him in a 'freeman's song' or 'three men's song' —it is not certain which is the correct term. This kind of composition, which retained its popularity throughout the century, may have consisted of the improvization of additional parts at fixed intervals to a well-known tune. But Henry could read a part at sight, and there must have been

LITERATURE AND MUSIC

others who could do so, because Sagudino, the secretary of the Venetian ambassador, tried to get from Italy 'a few new *frottole*' in exchange for English songs (*frottole* were part-songs).* The extent of musical literacy, however, increased greatly and far beyond the Court circle during the three or four decades after Henry VIII's death. A book for teaching French, published in 1573,† consists of a series of everyday situations, and one of them deals with the entertainment of a guest. After supper music books are brought out and members of the host's family sing a four-part unaccompanied song by Richard Edwards, Master of the Children of the Queen's Chapel until his death seven years before the book's publication. In the eighties 'a great number of Gentlemen and Merchants of good accompt (as well of this realme as of forreine nations)' used to gather at the City house of Nicholas Yonge, who imported part-songs from Italy and elsewhere for them to sing together.‡ The dearth of English songs was remedied during the next decade by the publication of many volumes of madrigals, unaccompanied part-songs in the Italian manner.

The rise to favour of the viols in the middle of the century also opened new possibilities for amateur music-making. The consort of these soft-toned strings was excellent for the domestic circle. The string fantasy retained its popularity until after the Restoration, when new styles from the Continent came into fashion with the brighter and fuller tone of the violins.

Domestic music-making, then, became steadily more widespread and accomplished from the middle of the sixteenth century onwards and reached its highest standard during the Commonwealth. Roger North gives a Royalist explanation of this which cannot be accepted as objective, but he concedes that music flourished while his enemies were in power.

---

* *Four Years at the Court of Henry VIII: A Selection of Despatches written by the Venetian Ambassador*, trans. Rawdon Brown (1854).

† C. Holyband, *The French Schoole maister*.

‡ *Musica Transalpina* (1588).

> When most other arts languished, [he says] musick held up her head, but in private society, for many chose rather to fidle at home, then to goe out & be knockt on the head abroad; and the entertainement was very much courted & made use of not only in country but in citty familys, in wch many of the Ladys were good consortiers.*

In fact, many of the leading Puritans, including Cromwell, were very fond of music. Music publishing, which began late in England (there was very little before 1590, nearly a century after it had become quite common in Italy), received a new impetus in the middle of the seventeenth century. Private music-making continued to be popular after the Restoration. Pepys reports that when householders evacuated their furniture by river during the Great Fire of London in 1666 one boat in three had virginals in it. But in the seventies the first public concerts were organized in London, first by J. Banister in the Whitefriars, near the Temple, and then by Thomas Britton. About 1680 a concert room was specially constructed in York Buildings for the Music Meeting.

In the early part of the period with which we are concerned music was either incidental to another activity or made by a person for himself or with his family and friends: people did not often gather together specially to listen to it, though the waits did play in the open air sometimes rather as military bands do at holiday resorts to-day. It was one element in the ceremonial at Court, for example. The pageantry of royal progresses was accompanied by impressive instrumental and choral music, and often verses of welcome would be sung by soloists or small groups of singers. Music was played during banquets. It had a variety of functions in the more elaborate 'revels'. An evening's entertainment might include an 'interlude' acted by the Gentlemen of the Chapel Royal, a 'disguising' with ingenious machinery and richly costumed mythological or grotesque figures, and a general dance in which the whole company participated.

* *The Musicall Gramarian*, ed. H. Andrews (1925), pp. 18-19.

The term 'masque', first applied to a 'disguising' on Twelfth Night, 1512, became a general description of increasingly stylized entertainments with one or two constant features. A party or procession in various disguises 'visited' the company in hall, danced and perhaps performed symbolic actions, and, before retiring, chose partners from among the spectators and danced with them. Fixed scenery tended later to replace the decorated chariots of the early 'disguisings'; a narrator often recited explanations, and a slight plot, presented through dialogue and song, filled out the central theme; but the end was always the masked ball, so that the performers did not keep the distance from the audience that is necessary for the illusion appropriate to drama. Music, both vocal and instrumental, was an essential element in the masque. In Italy the masque led the way towards opera. In the early seventeenth century Ben Jonson made the text more important and more poetic, and at the same time the whole structure more dramatic, adding an antimasque with grotesque characters as a deliberate foil to the symbolic characters of the main action. This movement towards drama might have been assisted by Italian example. Drama cannot be conveyed entirely by songs and choruses; some kind of 'speaking in music' is necessary. Jonson's musical collaborators, Alfonso Ferrabosco and Nicholas Lanier, did develop a declamatory style intended to serve the same functions as the recitative of the Italians. But Jonson's differences of opinion with his scene designer, Inigo Jones, show that the masque could not become drama without so complete a transformation as to unfit it for the social context in which it flourished. It was only when court pageantry had been almost eliminated by the Commonwealth government that Sir William Davenant produced the first English opera, *The Siege of Rhodes*. But French influence proved stronger than Italian. The operas of the Restoration period were really romantic plays with plenty of incidental music. Shadwell and Locke imitated the *comédies-ballets* of Molière and Lully in *Psyche* (1664). Dryden and Purcell collaborated in *King*

Arthur (1691), an ingenious succession of dramatic and musical episodes. The only true operas were small-scale experiments privately performed—John Blow's *Venus and Adonis* (1685) and Purcell's exquisite *Dido and Aeneas* (1689).

The choir of the Chapel Royal in the early Tudor period was drawn into plays as well as masques. There was a tradition of school plays, usually in Latin, and so it was not surprising that the boys of the choir should act by themselves, and some of their masters wrote as well as produced plays. The St Paul's choir-boys, too, enjoyed favour at Court as actors. In 1576, the year Burbage opened the first public theatre, Richard Farrant, a Gentleman of the Chapel Royal, took a lease on some of the old priory buildings at Blackfriars and began to give public performances with the Chapel Royal children. Though the venture foundered in 1584, children's companies continued to attract attention from time to time. There is a reference in *Hamlet* to 'an aery of children, little eyases', which was apparently a serious rival even to Shakespeare's company. Musicians were naturally apt to be associated with these companies, which exploited boys' singing to make up for their limitations as actors. The lutanists John Daniel, Robert Jones and Philip Rosseter were all connected with such ventures in the reign of James I. Perhaps because of the early Court interest in boy players, these companies also relied on spectacle, insofar as they could afford it. In Peele's *Araygnement of Paris*, produced before the Queen by the Chapel Royal boys in 1584, there is choral singing off-stage, and at the end the three Fates make complimentary speeches and Diana presents a golden ball to the Queen. All this is reminiscent of the masque and is not surprising in a Court play. The children's companies tried to maintain this tradition. They performed in private theatres, so called because they suggested the atmosphere of a private house, being smaller and more expensive than the public theatres and lighted artificially. From 1608 Shakespeare's company ran such a threatre at Blackfriars as well as its public theatre, the Globe, and music and masque are given more prominence in Jacobean and Caroline plays than they had been in Elizabethan, no doubt to some extent because of the competition of private theatres, for the children's companies were not the only ones in private theatres who employed music and spectacle modelled on those of the Court and special occasions in large private households.

The greater use of music by the private, in contrast to the public, theatres, however, was due merely to their different resources. A public theatre always employed a band of musicians, who sat in a balcony above the stage. The London waits played in the theatres when not otherwise engaged. It is probable that a normal band consisted of treble and bass viols, bass recorder, lute, cittern and pandora. Trumpets, cornets and drums would be available for special effects, such as military scenes and royal entries. The instruments were all easily portable. The band had sometimes to move to another position or to appear on the stage when a 'noise' of musicians was required in the play. The acting company itself might include singers. Actors were expected to be versatile. The English companies who toured on the Continent, where they were very popular, sang and danced as well as acted: no doubt frequent breaks were necessary in plays in a language foreign to the audience, which had to rely on the actions rather than the speech to follow the plot. Two of the actors who went into the Lord Chamberlain's company when it was founded in 1594 had been members of the Earl of Leicester's company of musicians, and the leading clowns in the new company could always sing. Shakespeare took advantage of the fact, and when Robert Armin became the chief comedian the amount of singing given to the leading clown's part was increased. Feste in *Twelfth Night* has a number of songs and is not only expected to break into song briefly, as a less accomplished clown would customarily do. At that time, or a little later, there was also a boy singer capable of taking leading female parts, and so Ophelia and Desdemona are both given songs.

No sharp distinction can be drawn between Court and

popular drama. Shakespeare's company performed at Court. When he could he exploited music and spectacle. *Love's Labour's Lost* and *A Midsummer Night's Dream* bear some resemblance to masques, and there are masque-like interludes in the later plays—in *A Winter's Tale* and *The Tempest*, for example. Shakespeare differs from his contemporaries only in his capacity to integrate music and masque into his drama. Even when he had available only a singer able to take a minor part, such as Amiens in *As You Like It*, he made his songs serve a dramatic purpose.

There was, then, a great demand for all kinds of music, both vocal and instrumental, for everyday life, for special occasions, for ceremonial and pageantry, for the theatres and for domestic entertainment. Until the middle of the seventeenth century the demand was probably greatest for vocal music. Dance tunes nearly always had words fitted to them, as they always have had and as they still do to-day. People wanted to sing. 'We doe daily observe,' says Campion, 'that when any shall sing a Treble to an Instrument, the standers by wil be offring at an inward part out of their own nature; and true or false, out it must, though to the perverting of the whole harmonie.'* Part-songs provided an outlet for this desire to sing. Even the growing popularity of the string consort did not affect the demand for vocal music. People liked to play on instruments versions of songs they knew. Part-songs were published with the recommendation that they were 'apt for viols or voices'.

The people who enjoyed part-songs and were musically literate enough to read their parts and learn fairly complicated music (and madrigals were not easy to sing) were, of course, the people who were interested in the other arts, particularly literature. Texts were provided for a great variety of vocal music from dance tunes to madrigals, and the most sophisticated singers would prefer something with greater literary merit than 'pop' lyrics, especially as the best craftsmanship of the day went into the music: the madrigal

* *Two Bookes of Ayres.*

attracted all the most eminent composers. The vogue of the short poem inspired by Petrarch's vernacular works produced the right kind of texts and so, during the sixteenth and early seventeenth centuries, brought music and poetry closer together than they had been for some time or were ever to be again.

Petrarch's prestige was due to his leading part in the revival of classical studies, but his vernacular poetry was in a medieval tradition in which poetry and music had been closely related. Traces of that fact persisted even in the later stages of the tradition. When it was discovered that an intimate association of the two arts had also characterized the Greek lyric in its freshest period, a conscious effort to bring the two together again was thought to be the best way of improving both.

When literature is intended to be heard rather than read privately, verse predominates, and the metre of verse comes from the regular patterns of music. Most stanza forms originally corresponded to tune forms. Very often dance forms in their turn lie behind tune forms, so that several medieval poetic forms were derived ultimately from round dances, in which a ring of dancers moved round while singing a refrain and marked time as a leader sang different lines. The roundel, the ballade and the carol all originally came from dances of this type. The carol was perhaps the most important of them in England and was practised as a literary form right up to the beginning of the sixteenth century, long after its dance origins had been forgotten.

The earliest constellation in the poetic tradition to which Petrarch's vernacular works belonged was the troubadours of twelfth century Provence. These aristocratic amateurs composed both poems and the melodies for solo voice to which they were sung. Their forms and styles and their theme of courtly love spread throughout Western Europe. By the time they had reached Italy in the thirteenth century they had already become largely literary conventions, but in the following century Dante still talks of poetry as intended for music. 'Every stanza,' he says, 'is set for the reception of a certain Ode' (i.e. a melody in a certain form).* The musical origin of fixed stanza forms had not been forgotten, and poems written in them were expected to be set to music and sung.

The poet by that time no longer usually composed the music for his own verses. The development of polyphony made composition very much an affair for experts working in the courts which maintained large staffs of performers, such as those of the Dukes of Burgundy and the Italian city states. There were other forces producing men of letters. Chaucer is not known to have been musical at all. Nevertheless his French contemporary Guillaume de Machaut was equally important as a composer and as a poet. The poet-musician was a figure who persisted in the face of growing specialization.

By the fifteenth century music and poetry had to a large extent developed their own resources: poetry had come to be regarded as a province of 'rhetoric', and music was exploring the simultaneous performance of different melodies—i.e. harmony and polyphony. But verse was still cast in the moulds inherited from musical forms—ballade, rondeau, carol, etc. The repetition of lines in Chaucer's roundels achieves no literary effect but is merely a reminiscence of the alternation of two themes in the original musical form. Composers, for their part, set their texts line by line and with regard to the form of the poetry. A carol would be set as a carol, even in the early sixteenth century: verse and refrain would still be clear, but the composer might assert his independence by varying or repeating either, just as he might treat the melody set to any line of text so freely as to obscure the line's function in the original metrical pattern.

Though contrapuntal music had become too elaborate for most amateurs, and poetry had its own conventions, yet singing poetry was still quite usual. At Court poetry, singing and dancing all mingled in the ritual of courtly love. 'The baudy

* *De Vulgari Eloquentia*, trans. A. G. Ferrers Howell (1890).

balades of lecherous love that commonly are indited and song of idle courtyers in princes and noblemens houses'* scandalized some moralists, who wrote more edifying poems to their tunes, and sometimes even moralized the tunes too, making them like psalm tunes, so that only echoes of the original song are left in the text. Several 'balets' by Wyatt and his contemporaries were moralized, from which it can be inferred that they were sung to tunes popular in their circles. The collection of poems by Wyatt and Surrey published by Richard Tottel in 1557 did not mention any tunes, but some of the poems have been found elsewhere with indications of tunes to which they might be sung. These would not necessarily be the tunes to which they were written or originally sung. *The Paradise of daynty devises* (1576), an imitation of Tottel's collection, claims that its 'ditties . . . are both pithy and pleasant, as well for the invention as meter, and wyll yeelde a farre greater delight, being as they are so aptly made to be set to any song in .5. partes, or song to instrument'. Many of the poems in the volume are by Richard Edwards, who wrote court plays in which there were solo songs to string quartet accompaniment. That explains the reference to songs 'in .5. partes'. But most of the tunes recommended for poems in the series of miscellanies, beginning with Tottel's and running up to the end of the century, are ballad tunes. It was evidently customary to sing short strophic poems to any tunes that would fit them. Poetry had a social function to a much greater extent than it has to-day. It not only provided matter for individual silent reading but could be drawn upon for gallantry at Court, entertainment of friends, private music-making and other occasions, and when playing a role in social intercourse the poems in the miscellanies most frequently became songs.

Writing verses to existing tunes was as common as fitting tunes to verses and continued to be so throughout the whole period. Ballads were generally written to popular tunes, often dance tunes, as has already been mentioned. A marked

* W. Baldwin, *Canticles or Balades of Salamon* (1549).

change in dance fashions could have indirect effects on poetry. The greater liveliness of seventeenth, as opposed to sixteenth century dances partly accounts for a continuous increase in liveliness and in the use of triple rhythms in seventeenth century verse. Apart from the galliard or cinquepace (so called from its five drum-beats in triple time), the sixteenth century court dances were all rather stately four-square movements in duple or common time. But the new dances of the seventeenth century—the corranto, the volta and the saraband—were vivacious and in triple time. It is more than a coincidence that triple measures then begin to loosen up the iambic regularity of Elizabethan verse.

It is not only ballads that were written to tunes. Sir Philip Sidney wrote several poems to Neapolitan *villanelle*, one to a Spanish song and one to *Wilhelmus van Nassau*, the tune that has become the Dutch national anthem. Lord Herbert of Cherbury wrote poems to Italian tunes. Lovelace and Waller both wrote attractive sarabands. The boundary between courtly and popular is hard to draw. Suckling's Ballad upon a Wedding and Lovelace's 'When Love with unconfined wing' both gave their names to tunes to which other poems were set.

The ancient custom of reciting narrative to the harp persisted throughout the sixteenth century. Sidney heard the old song of Percy and Douglas sung by a blind harper, and Puttenham mentions tales of King Arthur sung to the harp. The harp had been a favourite instrument of medieval English kings, and there was still a harper at Court in the early part of Queen Elizabeth's reign—William More, who did not die until 1564. This kind of performance, however, was losing its better educated audiences. That it should have survived at all makes it less surprising that the singing of other types of verse should have survived too.

It was short poems, 'songs and sonnets', that were usually sung in sophisticated circles. These were influenced by current literary fashions, those with greatest prestige during the sixteenth century coming from Italy, but this did not affect the practice of singing such poetry. Wyatt, who was regarded by the Elizabethans as the pioneer of a new Italianate poetry, must have known that the Italian verse he imitated was usually sung. There was a school of *improvisatori* who sang to the lute poems composed in the Italian courts and produced four-part, simply harmonized settings of them. Various fixed poetic forms were so treated, including even the sonnet, though it was never very satisfactory as a text for music, despite its name: they were all collectively called *frottole* after the form predominant among them. The musical settings of *frottole* must have been known to some of Henry VIII's courtiers, because, as has already been mentioned, the secretary of the Venetian ambassador sent for some to exchange for English songs. Wyatt was perhaps too busy with diplomatic business during his visit to Italy to devote much time to poetry, and he had probably been influenced by Italian poetry before that, but he must have heard some *frottole* when he was there.

Not only were the poems Wyatt and his contemporaries admired usually sung: the notion spread from Italy that poetry ought to be sung. Information about the Greek choral ode and the Greek lyric were responsible for it. They were the proper models to imitate just because they were Greek. At their best both had been sung. The choral ode superficially seemed comparable to contemporary vocal music: it was forgotten that Greek music had been monodic. Nor was it realized that the term lyric was a late one and that the lyre had been by no means essential to solo performance. The lyre was identified with the lute. In Castiglione's *Courtier*, the authoritative handbook on the Renaissance gentleman, Sir Frederick thought part-songs 'a faire musicke. . . . But to sing to the lute is much better.' Ronsard took pride in having restored the lyre to poetry and tuned the lute to his Odes.* Whatever the particular merits of one voice singing to lute accompaniment, some sort of setting to music at least was thought necessary. Sidney describes the poet

* *Œuvres*, ed. Vagaray, III, 68-9.

as a creator of 'words set in delightful proportion, either accompanied with or prepared for the well inchaunting skill of Musicke',[*] and Ronsard goes so far as to say that poetry is not pleasing unless sung by a soloist with instrumental accompaniment or by several voices, any more than instruments are satisfactory without a singer.[†]

The increased interest in short, elegant poems, in 'songs and sonnets', found the Greek lyric easy to imitate in its character of verse intended to be sung. Lyrics had long been sung to popular or improvised tunes, and the voice was commonly supported by the lute, which was the favourite instrument for domestic music. But the theory of the intimate relationship of the two arts, the notion that they were sisters and 'one god is god of both, as poets feign', had further implications. They needed each other, and therefore in any particular instance of their co-operation each should reinforce the effect of the other; the total result should be more powerful than either could have achieved separately. They should be adapted to each other from their first conception. Such ideas caused poets to be more conscious than they would otherwise have been of the effect of their verses when sung. As poetry usually came first and then was set to music—and this was so even in a period when writing poems to tunes was fairly common—the influence of these speculations on music was even more obvious. Great trouble was taken by composers to suit their music to the texts they were setting.

Medieval music was too preoccupied with counterpoint, the distinctive European contribution to the art of music, to pay much attention to the text, except perhaps to make sure each voice could sing its lines. There was certainly little attempt to express the sentiment or mood of the text. There could scarcely be when the conception was predominantly contrapuntal. The parts were thought of as separate melodies in harmonious relationships with each other. In the *motet*, a very characteristic medieval form, the voices actually all

[*] Gregory Smith, *Elizabethan Critical Essays*, I, 172.
[†] *Abrégé de l'art Poétique*.

sang different texts, often texts of completely different characters: no one text could be expressed by the total effect of the music. The form of the music was based on a *canto firmo*, a piece of plain-song or a song melody. Round that the other parts were woven, but its rhythm was often changed. Any added part might have long runs on any syllable with little regard for the original verbal rhythm or phrasing. Even if all the voices sang the same words, the total effect aimed at was largely sensuous, and it was sufficient if it was appropriate to the text only in a very general sense—for example, that jubilation was different from intercession. During the fifteenth century, however, interest in canon and the fugal principle opened possibilities of developing the basic song melody itself, its verbal rhythm being preserved and its characteristic features, particularly the beginning of each phrase, being taken up by all voices in turn. Closer attention to the harmony produced at various points in the movement of the separate parts also foreshadowed note-against-note counterpoint, thinking in terms of chords and the harmonization of a single melody rather than the addition of other melodies to it.

Early sixteenth century English music had reached this stage. There were two main styles, a simple and an ornate. In the former the tune was harmonized in fairly plain chords. In the latter the text was set line by line, a note for each syllable, the voices often entering with a point of imitation, and at the end of each line the voices broke into wordless runs, the time often changing from duple to triple. The voices may have been doubled by instruments, and the runs may have been instrumental interludes covering the gaps between the lines.

In the middle of the century the development of the consort of viols led to solo songs accompanied by string quartet. The voice part is usually second, or even third, highest but is for a treble. These songs were principally for choir-boy plays. The text is set rather stiffly, a note to a syllable, except perhaps at the end or where an important word needed to be given prominence. The songs are strophic, and the final couplet of each stanza is repeated to the same music. They are a sort of extension or a choir-boys' equivalent of the rhetorical speeches characteristic of early Elizabethan plays. Death-songs, like dying speeches, were very common, and catch-phrases such as 'I die' are often repeated. The accompaniment is contrapuntal, with delayed entries imitating each other and anticipating the beginnings of the lines in the voice part. William Byrd wrote a number of songs in this style, but by the time he published them in 1588 Italian part-songs had become fashionable, and so, although the songs had been 'originally made for Instruments to expresse the harmonie, and voyce to pronounce the dittie', he tried to make them look like Italian madrigals by arranging them 'in all parts for voyces to sing the same' [words].

The transition from the English tradition represented by Byrd's 1588 volume to the Italian madrigal, the secular form with greatest prestige throughout Europe at that time, was easy, since both owed a great deal to the Netherlands school of composers of the late fifteenth and early sixteenth centuries. Netherlanders occupied many of the most important musical posts in Italy. Their very elaborate contrapuntal art, which found its freest scope in church music but was also applied to a limited extent in secular *chansons* with French texts, did not suit the exaggerated and often frivolous court poetry of the late fifteenth century, which was usually set in a cruder and more homophonic style. But the Petrarchan movement, which was gathering strength during the first three decades of the sixteenth century, called for more serious and sophisticated music. The Netherlanders gradually filled out the simple outlines of the *frottola* and brought a higher standard of artistry to the part writing. The fourteenth century term madrigal was revived to describe the new compositions. They were based on song melodies to non-strophic poems of seven to eleven lines of varying lengths. The various voices enter with a point of imitation at the beginning of each line, and the words are repeated as often as is necessary to bring in all the voices required in that phase of the composition. For variety short homophonic sections may occur here and there. The musical phrases are designed to give the impression of corresponding to the speech rhythms of the text. Indeed, the distinctive characteristic of the madrigal is its consistent striving 'to applie the notes to the wordes', as Thomas Morley, the first thoroughly Italianate English composer, put it. There was a continuous attempt at 'word-painting,' at the illustration of the text in as much detail as possible. This was assisted by the stereotyped themes and imagery of the Petrarchan poetic convention, to which madrigal texts always belonged. It was essentially 'a kinde of musicke made upon songs and sonnets, such as *Petrarcha* and many Poets of our time [i.e. the sixteenth century] have excelled in.'* All the situations and attitudes in the convention had their musical representations, and composers displayed great ingenuity in handling them in original ways. To compose a successful madrigal, says Morley,

> you must possesse your selfe with an amorus humor (for in no composition shal you prove admirable except you put on and possesse yourselfe wholy with vaine wherin you compose) so that you must in your musicke be wavering like the wind, sometime wanton, sometime drooping, sometime grave and staide, or herwhile effeminat.†

There was a prolific school of madrigal composers in England from the 1590's to the 1620's. Though the madrigal was a very literary kind of music, its interest was primarily musical. It did not affect the long-established habit of singing verses to simple tunes, often with lute accompaniment. Indeed, contemporary with the madrigal a school of song writers was very active in the production of what were called 'airs'. These composers were mainly lutanists, though there were others who produced both madrigals and airs. The

---

* Thomas Morley, *A Plaine and Easie Introduction to Practicall Musicke* (1597), p. 180.
† ib.

most distinguished of them, John Dowland, was a famous virtuoso on the lute. Another accomplished composer of airs was Thomas Campion, a medical practitioner who set his own poems. The air was obviously attractive to the literary amateur, but the accompaniments of the best composers, John Dowland and John Daniel, showed great musical ability and were much more than adequate to support the tune, which is all that can be said for those of the simplest airs. There were, indeed, airs at all stages of artistic development from the tune with improvized accompaniment that was its foundation. The popularity of part-singing caused airs generally to be set as songs for four voices as well as solos accompanied by the lute. Whereas in the madrigal all the voices were of equal melodic importance and interest, the air was primarily a tune or a setting of words for a solo voice. When other voices were added they usually supported the tune, which was treated as the highest part, with harmony, though Dowland did sometimes introduce contrapuntal writing into his accompaniment, whether it was for lute or voices.

Unlike the madrigal, the air was strophic: the same tune served for more than one stanza. The madrigal technique did influence airs a little, however—or perhaps it would be fairer to say the two forms occasionally used similar technical devices. The contrapuntal texture of some of Dowland's accompaniments, which has just been mentioned, is one respect in which this is so, and another is the occasional abandonment of the strophic form by Dowland and Daniel. But these two composers are not typical of the school: with them the air became a much more powerful and technically accomplished form than the attractive, simply harmonized tune it is in the hands of most of their contemporaries. They are both major song writers of much more than historical interest.

If poets considered the possibility of their works being set to music, it was the air they thought of rather than the madrigal, which influenced poetry only by introducing a few Italian metres and rhythms, since it always remained an essentially Italian form. Many short poems of the period, and not only those in the books of airs, have careful correspondences in the stanzas that bring to mind the strophic character of the air. In Elizabethan poetry the play of wit and rapid changes of mood are restrained by the need to communicate when words are difficult to hear because they are sung. Speech rhythm is subordinated to a metrical regularity similar to that which is to some extent necessary in music.

> Our poeticall proportion [says George Puttenham, the Elizabethan critic] holdeth of the Musical, because, as we sayd before, Poesie is a skill to speake and write harmonically: and verses be a kind of Musicall utterance, by reason of a certaine congruitie in sounds pleasing the eare, though not perchance so exquisitely as the harmonicall concents of the artificiall Musicke, consisting in strained tunes, as is the vocall Musike or that of melodious instruments, as Lutes, Harpes, Regals, Records, and such like.*

Campion 'chiefly aimed to couple Words and Notes lovingly together', as was natural for one who had 'power over both'. Composers did not hesitate to alter the verse they chose to set, but did not always achieve as satisfactory results as Campion's. His aim, however, was the one generally approved by a period when it was believed the two arts would both benefit from an intimate relationship between them: even if it was not always realized, it was an objective seldom forgotten.

Despite its efforts to illustrate and express the text, the madrigal eventually incurred criticism from theorists. They could not see how several voices entering at different times and with contrasting rhythms audible together could represent the voice of the poet. The rhythmic difficulty was brought to notice by the consideration of classical metres as a source of new forms for poetry that wished to break with its immediate past and learn from an earlier civilization. It was suspected that music, in which the duration of notes was important, could help to solve the problems of quantitative

* Gregory Smith, *Elizabethan Critical Essays*, II, 68-9.

verse in languages with significant stress. In France the Académie de Musique et de Poésie, founded in 1571 by the poet Jean-Antoine de Baif and the lutanist Thibaut de Courville, and a later Académie du Palais, in which Claude Lejeune and Jacques Maudit were the chief musicians, set quantitative verse with exact time values, either in homophonic four-part versions (there could be no question of counterpoint, since all the voices had to have the same metrical pattern) or as solos accompanied on the lute. These experiments had some influence in England. Campion thought 'the Lyricke Poets among the Greekes and Latines were first inventers of Ayres, tying themselves strictly to the number, and value of their sillables'.* He wrote a treatise on quantitative metres in English. Though only one of his airs is in strict quantitative metre, his musical settings often show an appreciation of syllable length as one element, along with stress, in the rhythmic effect of English verse.

A more radical attack on counterpoint came from a Camarata meeting in the house of Count Bardi in Florence from about 1570. The members were chiefly concerned with the effect of music on the hearer. They asked themselves why modern music lacked the power Greek music was reported to have had. They decided that it was because music at its best was a blend of words, rhythm and harmony. Contemporary music was instrumental in its conception. It aimed at sensuous effect, not at expressing the intellectual concepts coloured by emotion that the poet intended to convey in his verse. Let the words be heard, instead of obscured by the cross-rhythms of counterpoint, and the poetry will make its own effect. The Camarata perceived that rhythm was a good deal more complex than metre and did not trouble about classical metres. It was more interested in choosing voices appropriate to the character and situation portrayed and reproducing in melody the contours of emotionally charged speech. Caccini, one of the first to succeed in putting its ideas into practice, referred to his work as talking in music ('quasi

* Preface to Rosseter's *Booke of Ayres* (1601).

in musica favellare). The whole approach was dramatic, and it was the recitative of opera that was the enduring result of the theories of the Camarata.

Campion levels at the madrigal's 'word-painting' much the same criticism as the Camarata, that it

> is long, intricate, bated with fuge, chaind with sincopation, and ... the nature of everie word is precisely exprest in the Note, like the old exploded action in Comedies, when if they did pronounce *Memini*, they would point to the hinder part of their heads, if *Video*, put their finger in their eye. But such childish observing of words is altogether ridiculous, and we ought to maintaine as well in Notes, as in action a manly cariage, gracing no word, but that which is eminent, and emphaticall.*

Dowland has a few declamatory passages in some of his later airs. He was in Florence in 1595, when the declamatory style of the Camarata's disciples was being tried out, and four declamatory songs, two of them by Caccini, were included by Dowland's son Robert in *A Musicall Banquet* (1610). Angelo Notari, an Italian lutanist, was in the service of Prince Henry and published declamatory airs in his *Prime Musiche Nuove* (1613). But Italian influence in England was slight. The lutanist air was little affected by it. In England as in Italy it was drama that impelled a movement towards a solo song giving the illusion of impassioned speech. Alfonso Ferrabosco, the son of Italian immigrants but himself quite English, used a declamatory style for his songs in Jonson's masques, and Lanier, who succeeded as collaborator with Jonson, continued the development by simplifying the accompaniment, spacing out the chords into sustained or slowly changing harmonies, except where reiterated chords were required for a special effect. As has already been said, one further development in the masque or dramatic entertainment was a kind of recitative for the speech carrying the action forward; but the lyrics were set to tunes, though with a rather declamatory

* ib.

underlay of the text. Poems by Carew, Suckling and other Cavalier poets were set in this way as chamber music by Henry and William Lawes. The theorbo lute was the usual accompanying instrument. The tunes are often very attractive, especially those in triple time, which suggest dances, but the music is definitely subservient to the verse. Henry Lawes must have been flattered when it was said of his airs

> All may be *Sung* or *Read*, which thou hast drest,
> Both are the same, save that the *Singing*'s best.*

Poetry was bound to be the dominant partner when the rhythms of impassioned speech were the centre of interest to musicians. Dramatic verse had taught poets their effectiveness, too. They were already exploited by Donne in the 1590's. The incantatory chant of serious, and the metrical drum-taps of more sportive, Elizabethan verse gave way to dramatic speech in the first half of the seventeenth century. The metaphysical conceit pays little attention to possible musical setting. Yet so strong was tradition that Donne, exclaiming

> *I am two fooles, I know,*
> *For loving, and for saying so*
> *In whining Poetry,*

adds

> *... When I have done so*
> *Some man, his art and voice to show,*
> *Doth Set and sing my paine,*
> *And, by delighting many, frees againe*
> *Griefe, which verse did restraine.*†

Poems were still set to music, but it was up to the composer to present the poetry and to be careful not to get in the poet's way. Only a minor composer could be content with such a subordinate role.

The Lawes brothers look very pedantic and trivial beside

* John Cobb in *Ayres and Dialogues* (1653).
† 'The Triple Foole' in *Songs and Sonets*.

Henry Purcell, the dominating figure of Restoration music. He had a wonderful gift for the setting of English speech. Though he often illustrates at length some detail of the text, he always fits with music the contours of the phrase as a whole. But he always imposes a musical structure, using repetition of melodic and rhythmical patterns for that purpose and not merely as suggested by the text.

Jonson introduced English versions of the classical ode, and Cowley wrote a whole set of *Pindarique Odes* (1656). The ode was essentially choral, and in the last two decades of the century it was the form chosen for annual events such as the King's birthday, New Year's Day and St Cecilia's Day. It was set in choruses, solos and duets, with instrumental interludes by strings or a mixed consort that already foreshadowed the eighteenth century orchestra. It was indeed almost a cantata. Larger musical forms were emerging. Music was finding its own principles of structure and becoming essentially instrumental. The voice would henceforth be treated as a musical instrument rather than the medium of speech. Poetry would provide only slight texts to be handled according to the composer's musical intentions. The *da capo* aria, in which the text is entirely submerged in a purely musical form, was establishing itself in Italy by the end of the century. The arrival of Handel with Italian opera in the early years of the next century, at a time when there was no comparable English composer to succeed Purcell, accelerated the divergence between music and poetry. It was inevitable, however, that they should follow their own separate lines of development and that these should take them ever further away from each other. The close relations and mutual influence of music and poetry during the sixteenth and seventeenth centuries was due to the stage both had reached in their European histories. While they lasted they produced interesting results. It is impossible to appreciate the shorter poems of the period properly without reference to the music with which they were associated or the vocal music without awareness of the literary pressures upon it.

STUDENTS' GUIDE TO READING

STUDENTS' GUIDE TO READING

THIS guide has been compiled with the object of indicating to the student some of the most significant books of the period, the chief editions in which they have been published, and the most important biographical and critical works that can be consulted as helps to the understanding of them. The limited space at the disposal of the compiler has made it impossible to print complete lists of the works of some of the authors, but such omissions have been indicated in the text, and reference has been made to fuller bibliographies wherever these are available. An attempt has been made to indicate very briefly the nature of the contents of certain books, and the relative values of some of the editions and critical works. The judgments implied have no claim to represent anything except a personal opinion. It has only been possible to cite the full titles and imprints of some of the most important books; only 'short titles' of other books are generally given. Certain technical bibliographical terms are used to indicate the size of books. In a *folio* each of the sheets of paper used to make the book is folded twice so as to give two large *leaves* or four *pages*. In a *quarto* (4to) the sheets are folded four times, in an *octavo* (8vo, the usual modern size) eight times, and in a *duodecimo* (12mo), which is a very small book, twelve times. Folios are large volumes; they are rarely produced now, but were commonly used in the sixteenth and seventeenth centuries for important works. The quarto was the normal size of pamphlets containing short works such as plays or sermons.

The Guide is divided into twenty sections represented by roman numerals. Some of them deal with single important authors such as Milton and Shakespeare, and others with groups of authors. These sections are arranged in three main divisions, corresponding to the first three chapters of the Introduction. Each of the twenty sections is subdivided under various appropriate headings. In the sections dealing with groups of writers, general studies of the whole group, collections and anthologies (if these exist) come first, and then individual authors. The sections dealing with single authors begin with collective editions; accounts of MSS. (if these exist) follow, and then edd. of individual works, biographies, criticism and works of reference. Dates of publication are given, where known, and places, if outside the United Kingdom.

GUIDE TO READING

LIST OF ABBREVIATIONS

acc.—according to
Adams—*Chief Pre-Shakespearian Dramas*, ed. J. Q. Adams (Boston, 1924)
Add. MS.—Additional Manuscript
App.—Appendix
attrib.—attributed to
B.C.S.—British Council Series
B.L.—Belles Lettres Series
B.M.—British Museum
Bang—*Materialien zur Kunde des älteren englischen Dramas*, ed. W. Bang (Louvain, 1902-14); New Series (N.S.), ed H. de Vocht (1928-)
Bodl.—Bodleian
Bib. Soc.—Bibliographical Society
Br. Ac.—British Academy
C.H.E.L.—*The Cambridge History of English Literature*, ed. A. Ward and A. R. Waller (14 vols., 1908-16)
C.Q.—*Critical Quarterly* (Bangor, and Hull, 1959-)
C.P.T.—Cambridge Plain Texts
C.S.E.—*Columbia Studies in English*
Chalmers—*The Works of the English Poets*, ed. A. Chalmers (21 vols., 1810)
chap.—chapter
Diss.—Dissertation
D.N.B.—*The Dictionary of National Biography* (21 vols., 1885-1909)
E.A.—The English Association
E.C.—*Essays in Criticism* (Oxford, 1951-)
E.E.T.S.—The Early English Text Society
E.H.R.—*The English Historical Review*
E.L.H.—*A Journal of English Literary History*
E.M.—*The English Miscellany* (Rome, 1949-)
E.M.L.—*English Men of Letters Series*
E.S.—*Englische Studien*
E.S.M.E.A.—*Essays and Studies by Members of the English Association*

ed.—edition, edited by
edd.—editions
enl.—enlarged
Eng. St.—*English Studies*
Ev. Lib.—Everyman's Library
facs.—facsimile
G.T.—Golden Treasury Series
H.L.B.—*Huntington Library Bulletin*
H.L.Q.—*Huntington Library Quarterly*
H.U.L.—Home University Library
introd.—introduction, introduced by
J.E.G.P.—*The Journal of English and Germanic Philology*
K.C.—The King's Classics
M.L.—The Muses' Library
M.L.N.—*Modern Language Notes*
M.L.R.—*The Modern Language Review*
M.P.—*Modern Philology*
M.S.R.—*The Malone Society Reprints*, ed. W. W. Greg (1907-1963)
M.U.L.—Morley's Universal Library
McIlwraith—*Five Elizabethan Comedies*, ed. A. K. McIlwraith (W.C., 1934)
Manly—*Specimens of Pre-Shakesperian Drama*, ed. J. M. Manly (2 vols., Boston, 1900-03)
N.C.—North Carolina
n.d.—no date
N.J.—New Jersey
N.S.—New Series
N.Y.—New York
Neilson—*The Chief Elizabethan Dramatists*, ed. W. A. Neilson (Boston, 1911)
O.B.S.—*The Oxford Bibliographical Society's Proceedings and Papers*
O.E.P.—*A Collection of Old English Plays*, ed. A. H. Bullen (4 vols., 1882-85)
O.H.E.L.—*The Oxford History of English Literature* (1945-   )
O.P.T.—Oxford Plain Texts
op. cit.—work cited above
orig.—original, originally
P.B.—paper-back edition
P.G.E.L.—*Pelican Guides to English Literature*, ed. B. Ford (6 vols., 1954-58)

P.M.L.A.—*Publications of the Modern Language Society of America* (N.Y., 1935-)
Pollard—*English Miracle Plays*, ed. A. W. Pollard (1914)
prob.—probably
pub.—published, published by, publication
R.E.C.—*Representative English Comedies*, ed. C. M. Gayley and A. Thaler (4 vols., N.Y., 1903-36)
R.E.L.—*A Review of English Literature* (1960-)
R.E.S.—*The Review of English Studies*
R.M.S.—*Renaissance and Modern Studies* (Nottingham, 1957-)
R.S.L.—The Royal Society of Literature
re-ed.—re-edited by
rev.—revised, revised by
S.C.—South Carolina
S.P.—*Studies in Philology*
S.P.E.—*Society for Pure English*
S.P.C.K.—*Society for Promoting Christian Knowledge*
Sh. Jb.—*Jahrbuch der Deutschen Shakespeare-Gesellschaft* (Berlin, 1865-)
Sh. S.—*Shakespeare Survey* (Cambridge, 1948-)
Soc.—Society
St.—Studies
T.C.—The Temple Classics
T.D.—The Temple Dramatists
T.L.S.—*The Times Literary Supplement*
tr.—translated by, translation
U.M.P.—University of Michigan publications
Univ.—University
vol.—volume
W.C.—The World's Classics
Y.S.E.—Yale Studies in English
Y.U.S.—Yale University Studies
Y.W.E.S.—*The Year's Work in English Studies* (1919-)

RENAISSANCE AND REFORMATION

(For general historical background see J. D. Mackie, *The Early Tudors* [1952], G. R. Elton, *England under the Tudors* [1955], and S. T. Bindoff, *Tudor England* [P.B.]; for social history G. M. Trevelyan, *English Social History*, chaps. IV and V. For economic conditions R. H. Tawney, *Religion and the Rise of Capitalism* [P.B.] is invaluable. The lives of Henry VII by A. F. Pollard and *Thomas More* by R. W. Chambers can be profitably consulted. For the intellectual background reference should be made to R. R. Bolgar, *The Classical Heritage and its Beneficiaries* [1954], and F. Caspari, *Humanism and the Social Order in Tudor England* [Chicago, 1954].)

CONTENTS

CHAPTER		PAGE
I	THE HUMANISTS	141
II	THE NEW POETRY UP TO THE ACCESSION OF ELIZABETH	148
III	THE PROTESTANT REFORMERS	156

CHAPTER I
THE HUMANISTS

GENERAL STUDIES

A USEFUL popular study of the early English humanists is *The Oxford Reformers of 1498* by F. Seebohm (Ev. Lib.), containing essays on Colet, Erasmus and More with extracts from their writings and discussion from the liberal Anglican viewpoint. The famous parody of medieval pedantry, *Epistolae Obscurorum Virorum*, was ed. with tr. by F. G. Stokes (1925). The works of Erasmus are essential for a serious study of the period. His Letters (those up to 1518 available in a good tr. by F. M. Nichols, 3 vols., 1901-18, complete Latin text, ed. P. S. and H. M. Allen and H. W. Garrod, 11 vols., 1901-47), his *Colloquia* (ed. E. Johnson, 3 vols., 1900, selection tr. R. Lestrange, Abbey Classics, 1924) and his *Encomium Moriae* or *Praise of Folly* (tr. by T. Challoner, 1549, ed. J. E. Ashbee, 1901, tr. by J. Wilson, 1668, ed. P. S. Allen, 1913) are particularly recommended. The best modern study of Erasmus is *Erasmus, A Study of his Life, Ideals and Place in History* by Preserved Smith (1924). See also J. Huizinga, *Erasmus* (1924) and Margaret Phillips, *Erasmus and the Northern Renaissance* (1949). P. S. Allen's British Academy Lecture, *Erasmus's Services to Learning* (1923) is of the highest value. H. A. Mason, *Humanism and Poetry in the Early Tudor Period* (1959) is stimulating and suggestive.

INDIVIDUAL AUTHORS

SIR (SAINT) THOMAS MORE (1478-1535)
Utopia and Latin Works

The original Latin text of More's famous philosophic romance, *Utopia*, was first printed in four editions on the continent: Louvain, November 1516; Paris, 1517; Bâle, March and November

1518. The English tr. by Raphe Robinson first appeared in 1551, (second, rev. ed., 1556). The best ed. of the Latin text is that by Marie Delcourt (Paris, 1936). There are many modern rpts. of Robinson's tr. The best modern ed. is that of P. E. Hallett (1937). The other important English tr. is by Gilbert Burnet, Bishop of Salisbury, pub. 1684. The definitive modern ed. of *Utopia* is that of J. H. Lupton, containing the Latin text and Robinson's translation with a very full and valuable intro. See also H. W. Donner's useful *Introduction to Utopia* (Uppsala, 1945).

More's other Latin works entitled *Thomae Mori Lucubrationes* were printed at Bâle in 1563.

English Works

More's translation of the Latin Life of Pico della Mirandola, the Italian humanist, entitled *The Lyfe of Johan Picus, Erle of Myrandula*, was printed about 1510, and his short humorous poem, *How a Sergeaunt wolde lerne to be a frere*, about 1516. Various other English works were printed in his lifetime by his nephew William Rastell. They include controversial pamphlets against Tyndale and other reformers, pub. between 1529 and 1533, and the two dialogues entitled *The debellacyon of Salem and Byzance* (1533) and *A dialogue of comfort again tribulacion* (written 1534, pub. 1553). Rastell collected all his English works (including the notable *History of Richard III* and extant letters) and printed them in a folio in 1557.

A sumptuous modern ed. of *The English Works of Sir Thomas More* is in course of publication. The editor is W. E. Campbell, and there are introd. and notes by A. W. Reed, R. W. Chambers and W. A. G. Doyle Davidson. The text of 1557 is reproduced in facs. together with a modernized version. Vols. I and II have appeared.

St Thomas More, A Preliminary Bibliography of his Works and of Moreana up to 1750, compiled by R. W. Gibson, was pub. at Yale in 1962 and is announced as 'the forerunner of The Yale edition of the Complete Works and Selected Letters'.

There is an annotated ed. (with omissions) by J. R. Lumby of More's *History of Richard III*.

A very useful selection from *The English Works of Sir Thomas More* (ed. P. S. Allen), with extracts from Erasmus and Roper, is included in the Clarendon Series (1924).

Selected Letters of St Thomas More, ed. Elizabeth F. Rogers (New Haven), appeared in 1962.

Biography and Criticism

The earliest biography of More is the *Life* by his son-in-law, William Roper, which was not printed till 1626. The standard modern ed. is that of Miss E. V. Hitchcock (E.E.T.S., 1935). Nicholas Harpsfield (1519-75), Archdeacon of Canterbury under Mary I, wrote a valuable *Life of Sir Thomas More*, which was first printed in 1932 for the E.E.T.S. by Miss E. V. Hitchcock, with historical notes by Professor R. W. Chambers.

Of the *Life of Sir Thomas More* written by William Rastell, his nephew, only some MS. fragments remain. They are in the B.M. Thomas Stapleton's Latin *Vita Thomae Mori*, in his book called *Tres Thomae*, was pub. at Douai in 1588. There is an English version by P. Hallet entitled *The Life and Illustrious Martyrdom of Sir Thomas More* (Burns and Oates, 1928). *A Life of Sir Thomas More* by his great-grandson Cresacre More was pub. in 1626. It was rptd. in 1828. The standard modern biography was by T. E. Bridgett's *The Life of Blessed Thomas More* (1891) until the appearance of Professor R. W. Chambers' monumental *Sir Thomas More* (Jonathan Cape) in 1935. This book is both a biography and a critical monograph. It is indispensable for the study of the whole period. *Saint Thomas More*, by the Rev. J. R. O'Connell (1935) and Algernon Cecil's *Portrait of Sir Thomas More* (1937) are recent studies by Roman Catholic authors. Among critical works mention may be made of Karl Kautsky's *Thomas More und seine Utopia* (Stuttgart, 1888), English tr. by H. J. Stenning (1927). The anonymous Elizabethan play of *Sir Thomas More*, in which Shakespeare is said to have had a hand, was first printed from a MS. by A. Dyce in 1844. The most easily accessible modern ed. is in *The Shakespeare Apocrypha*, ed. C. F. Tucker Brooke (see p. 257). There is a valuable handbook of *Moreana 1478-1945* by F. and M. P. Sullivan (Kansas City, 1946). *Sir Thomas More* by E. E. Reynolds (B.C.S., 1965) is a useful short study with a bibliography.

(SAINT) JOHN FISHER (1469-1535)

English sermons by Fisher were pub. in 1508, 1509, 1521, 1525-26 and 1532. His Latin works (*Opera Omnia*) were pub. at Wurzburg in 1597. Part I of his *English Works* (all issued) were ed. by

J. E. B. Mayor in 1876 and the anon. *Life* (c. 1576) by R. Bayne in 1921, both for the E.E.T.S. The standard ed. of the *Life* is that of Fr. Van Ortroy in *Analecta Bollandiana*, X (1891) and XII (1893). There is a good modernized ed. by P. Hughes (1935). The standard biography remains T. E. Bridgett, *The Life of Blessed John Fisher* (1888). E. E. Reynolds, *Saint John Fisher* (1955), adds much new matter. J. Delcourt, *Deux Saints anglais: Fisher et More* (Paris, 1935), is a notable French study.

JOHN COLET, DEAN OF ST PAUL'S (1467-1519)

Works

Colet's writings are mostly in Latin. These include his expositions of some of St Paul's Epistles, treatises on the Hierarchies of the Pseudo-Dionysius, and the remarkable *Letters to Radulphus* on the Mosaic Account of the Creation, where it is contended that the opening chapters of Genesis must be considered as poetry rather than as records of fact. These Latin works remained in MS. until they were pub. J. H. Lupton between 1867 and 1876. The statutes of St Paul's school and the catechism for the boys written by Colet in English are printed by Lupton in an app. to his *Life of Colet*. The *Convocation Sermon* of 1512 was delivered in Latin, but an English tr. (probably by Thomas Lupset) was pub. prob. in 1530. It was rptd. in 1661 and several times later. F. Seebohm quotes in full in his *Oxford Reformers*. In 1534 a little treatise of Christian morality by Colet appeared. It is called *A ryght fruteful monycion, concerning the ordre of a good crysten mannes lyfe*. It passed through many edd., the latest of which appeared in 1772. It is rptd. in full in an app. to Lupton's *Life of Colet*.

Life

The standard *Life of Colet* is that of J. H. Lupton (2nd ed. George Bell, 1909). This contains all the extant English works in an app. A more recent biography by Sir J. A. R. Marriott appeared in 1933. There is a particularly interesting account of Colet with extracts from his writings in Seebohm's *The Oxford Reformers*. For more recent views see E. W. Hunt, *Dean Colet and his Teaching* (S.P.C.K., 1956), and L. Miles, *John Colet and the Platonic Tradition* (La Salle, Ill., 1962).

SIR THOMAS ELYOT (1490-1546)

Works

Elyot's chief work, *The Boke named the Governour*, was first pub. in 1531, and passed through seven edd. by 1580. The standard modern ed. is that of H. H. S. Croft (1880). This contains a very complete biographical introd., a commentary and a glossary. A useful ed. of *The Governour* with an introd. by Foster Watson is pub. in Ev. Lib. Elyot's other works include moral dialogues, trs. from St Cyprian, Pico della Mirandula, Isocrates and Plutarch, a medical work called *The Castel of Helth* (1534), a collection of sayings from the Fathers called *The Bankett of Sapience*; *The Image of Governance*, said to be tr. from a Greek MS., and a Latin English Dictionary. There is no complete ed. of Elyot's writings.

The Castel of Helth (1541 ed.) has been repd. with an Introduction by S. A. Tannenbaum (N.Y., 1937).

THOMAS STARKEY (?1499-1538)

Thomas Starkey's *A Dialogue between Reginald Pole and Thomas Lupset* has some literary merit and is of great historical interest. It was first printed in *England in Henry VIII's Time* (E.E.T.S., 1871-78) with Life and Letters, ed. J. M. Cooper and S. R. Heritage. Another ed. by K. M. Burton with Preface by E. M. Tillyard was pub. in 1948.

SIR JOHN CHEKE, Professor of Greek at Cambridge, (1514-57)

Cheke's works consist chiefly of trs. from Greek into Latin. They include, however, an English tr. of the Gospel of St Matthew and part of the first chapter of the Gospel of St Mark written in Cheke's own system of phonetic spelling. The trs. were pub. with seven letters of Cheke by Goodwin in 1843. A little political pamphlet called *The hurt of sedicion howe grevous it is to a commune welth* was pub. in 1549, and a very interesting letter to Sir Thomas Hoby on the English language prefixed to Hoby's tr. of Baldassare Castiglione's *The Courtier* (1561). There is a valuable diss. by W. L. Nathan, *Sir John Cheke und der englische Humanismus* (Bonn, 1928).

THOMAS WILSON (1525-81)

Works

Wilson's two famous books are *The Arte of logike sette forthe in Englische* (1551) and *The Arte of Rhetorique* (1533, 2nd ed. 1560). His other works include a scholarly tr. of *the Three Orations of Demosthenes chiefe orator among the Grecians, in favour of the Olynthians, ... with those his fower Orations titled expressely & by name against King Philip of Macedonie* (1571). This version of the Olynthiacs and Philippics had a political purpose and was directed against Philip of Spain.

There is a good modern ed. of the *Arte of Rhetorique* by G. H. Mair in the *Tudor and Stuart Library* (1909) with a valuable introd. His interesting *Discourse upon Usurye* (1572) was ed. R. H. Tawney (1925).

ROGER ASCHAM (1515-68)

Works and Life

Toxophilus was the only work of Ascham printed in his lifetime. The first ed. was pub. E. Whitechurch in 1545. It had been ed. by E. Arber (1868) in *Arber's English Reprints* (Constable). The *Report and Discourse of the Affairs and State of Germany*, written in 1553, was pub. J. Daye prob. about 1570. *The Scholemaster* was printed by Daye in 1570. There is a rpt. in *Arber's English Reprints* (1869) and an ed. by J. E. B. Mayor (1863). Ascham's Latin Letters were collected and pub. E. Grant, together with a Latin oration on the author's life by the editor in 1576. The fourth ed. of this book with considerable additions, including Ascham's Latin and Greek poems was pub. in 1590. His reputation as a scholar on the continent is attested by three other edd. of the Latin works which were pub. in Germany in 1602, 1610, 1611 respectively. A handsome ed. of the Latin correspondence ed. Elstob was pub. at Oxford in 1703. The first collected ed. of Ascham's English works was pub. James Bennet (4to, London, 1761). The actual editor was almost certainly Dr Johnson. It includes the *Life of Ascham* by Dr Johnson rptd. in collected edd. of Johnson's works. Another ed. of the English works appeared in 1815; it includes six letters of Ascham to Sir William Cecil which had not been printed before. The standard modern ed. of Ascham is that of Giles (4 vols. 1865). It includes all Ascham's extant works in English, Latin and Greek, and contains a valuable biographical introd. There is a useful rpt. of *The English Works* ed. by W. Aldis Wright in *The Cambridge English Classics* (1964). In this ed. the orig. Tudor spelling is retained. The fullest study of Ascham is A. Katterfeld's *Roger Ascham, sein Leben und seine Werke* (Strassburg, 1789). There is a *Concise Bibliography* by S. A. and D. R. Tannenbaum (N.Y., 1946).

CHAPTER II

THE NEW POETRY UP TO THE ACCESSION OF ELIZABETH (1558)

GENERAL STUDIES

CHAPTERS xxxvii and xxxviii of *The History of English Poetry* by Thomas Warton (1774-81) contain accounts of Surrey and Wyatt. Warton's historical details are often incorrect. He wrote before modern research had revealed the facts concerning Wyatt and Surrey. For instance he regards them as exact contemporaries, and he accepts the apocryphal legend of Surrey's love for the Fair Geraldine as historical fact. But much of his criticism of their poetry is penetrating and of permanent value. *A History of English Poetry* by W. J. Courthope (Vol. II, i-vi, 1897) gives a critical account of this phase of English poetry which is still valuable. J. M. Berdan, *Early Tudor Poetry* (N.Y., 1920) is a most useful and scholarly introduction not only to the poetry but to the whole literature and intellectual background of Tudor England. Indispensable is C. S. Lewis's brilliant and stimulating *English Literature in the Sixteenth Century excluding Drama* (O.H.E.L.). M. Evans, *English Poetry in the Sixteenth Century* (Hutchinson, 1953), is a good short, up-to-date introduction. V. L. Rubel, *Poetic Diction in the English Renaissance* (N.Y., 1941), can also be profitably consulted.

MANUSCRIPT COLLECTIONS

The most important MS. collections of the court poetry of the reign of Henry VIII are in the B.M.

Egerton MS. 2711 (sometimes called E) was Wyatt's own property. Most of the poems in it were written out by a scribe, but many were corrected by Wyatt himself and signed by him. Besides many lyrics of Wyatt and his satires and

Psalms the book includes one of Surrey's sonnets in praise of Wyatt, Sir John Harington's version of some psalms and some other pieces in English, Latin and French. It once belonged to Sir John Harington.

The Devonshire MS., B.M. Add. 17492 (sometimes called D) is a small quarto vol. containing many lyrics by Wyatt and others. Sixty-three of the poems signed by Wyatt in this book are found in no other collection. It contains Surrey's fine lyric *A Ladys lament for her Lover Overseas* and poems by several other courtiers. It is believed to have belonged to Surrey and then to have passed into the hands of the Duke and Duchess of Richmond. 'Unpublished Poems in the Devonshire MS' were ed. by K. Muir in *The Proceedings* of the Leeds Philos. and Lit. Soc., Lit. and Hist. Sect., IV, iv (1943).

Add. MS. 36529 (sometimes called P) is a transcript of the late sixteenth century including twenty-eight poems by Surrey and nine by Wyatt. For a description of these and less important MSS. see A. K. Foxwell's *Sir Thomas Wyatt's Poems* (1911, unreliable) and Ruth Hughey's important 'The Harington Manuscript at Arundel Castle and Related Documents', *The Library*, 4th Ser., xv (1934-5), pp. 388-444. The Blage MS. in Trinity College, Dublin, Library is an anthology of poems written between 1530 and 1550, containing poems by Wyatt and Surrey. A selection from it entitled *Unpublished Poems from the Blage MS.* ed. K. Muir was pub. at Liverpool in 1961.

EARLY PRINTED COLLECTIONS

(i) *The Courte of Venus* was an anthology of verse, the first ed. of which may have been printed about 1537-39, and a second probably about 1547-49. Only three small fragments of it are known to survive. One, formerly in the Bright and Britwell collections, is now in the Folger Shakespeare Library, Washington, a second is in the Bodleian (Douce, g. 3), and a third in the Stark collection in the Library of the University of Texas. A meticulous ed. of *The Courte*, ed. Russell A. Fraser, was pub. at Durham, N.C. in 1955. See also Sir E. K. Chambers, *Sir Thomas Wyatt and Some Other Collected Studies* (1933).

(ii) *Tottel's Miscellany*. The first ed. of this famous book appeared on June 5th, 1557. Its title is *Songes and Sonettes written by the ryght honorable Lorde Henry Haward late Earle of Surrey, and other*. Only one copy of this ed. survives. It is in the Bodleian, and contains 271 poems of which 40 are ascribed to Surrey, 96 to Wyatt, 40 to Nicholas Grimald and 94 to uncertain authors. This first ed. must have been withdrawn soon after publication. On June 31st, 1557, a second rev. ed. appeared of which two copies survive, one being now in the B.M. and one in the Henry Huntington Library in California. The number of poems is increased to 280; 30 poems by Grimald are dropped, and 39 new poems by uncertain authors are inserted instead. The ten remaining poems by Grimald are transferred to the end of the text and the initials N. G. are replaced by Grimald's full name at the end of the poems. Of a second setting of this ed. three copies are known. Two more edd. appeared in 1559, and others in 1565, 1567, 1574, 1585 and 1587. It is not unlikely that there were other Elizabethan edd. no copies of which have survived. After 1587 no rpt. appeared till 1717, when a very incorrect ed. was printed for W. Meares and J. Brown. The editor was George Sewell. Then came two abortive attempts to produce better edd. Bishop Percy had planned one as early as 1673. It was to form the first vol. of a collection of sixteenth-century poetry. The work was interrupted, but resumed, possibly with the help of George Steevens. The printing was almost completed in 1808, when the whole impression was destroyed by fire, except for a few copies, one of which is in the Grenville collection in the B.M. Another important unpublished ed. is also said to have been destroyed by fire, having been printed at Bristol in 1812 acc. the B.M. Catalogue. Four incomplete copies survive in the B.M. and are ascribed in the Catalogue to Dr John Nott of Bristol, but H. J. Byrom in his

'Tottel's Miscellany, 1717-1817', R.E.S. III, 1927, pp. 47-53, has shown conclusively that the real editor was George Frederic Nott, the scholar who produced edd. of the poems of Wyatt and Surrey in 1815-16. There is a useful ed. by E. Arber in his *English Reprints* (1870). The standard modern ed. is that of H. E. Rollins (2 vols., Harvard, 1928-29) with valuable introd. and commentary. See also H. E. Rollins 'Marginalia in two Elizabethan Miscellanies' in *Joseph Quincy Adams Memorial Studies* (Washington, 1948) and G. Sherburn, 'Songs and Sonnettes', T.L.S. 24, July, 1930.

MODERN COLLECTIONS

1. *The Surrey and Wyatt Anthology* ed. E. Arber (in the British Anthologies Series). This anthology covers Skelton, Lord Vaux and others in modernized spelling.

2. *Early Sixteenth Century Lyrics* ed. F. M. Padelford (B.L.). A valuable collection including lyrics by Wyatt and Surrey together with poems by Henry VIII in the orig. spelling, many of which are transcribed from the D and E MSS. There is a useful introd. and commentary in which Italian sources and parallels are carefully noted.

3. *The Silver Poets of the Sixteenth Century* ed. G. Bullett (Ev. Lib.) contains poems by Wyatt, Surrey (excluding tr. of the *Aeneid*), Sidney, Ralegh and Sir J. Davies).

INDIVIDUAL AUTHORS

SIR THOMAS WYATT (ALSO SPELT WYAT AND WIAT) (1503-42)

Works

The only poems of Wyatt which are known to have been pub. before the nineteenth century are those contained in *Tottel's Miscellany* (97 in all), the pieces in *The Courte of Venus* and his tr. of the *Penitential Psalms* (imitated from the Italian version of Aretino) printed in 1549. Two copies of the 1549 ed. of the *Psalms* is known to survive. A considerable body of other poems remained in the MSS. described on pp. 148-9. These MS. versions show that Tottel or his editor made considerable alterations in order to regularize the metre, and remove strange words and constructions.

The first editor of Wyatt to make use of these MSS. was G. F. Nott, whose important ed. of *The Works of Henry Howard, Earl of Surrey, and Sir Thomas Wyatt* appeared in 1816. In this ed. Nott prints for the first time texts of the D and E MSS. with a biography, critical study and elaborate notes. R. Bell's ed. of *The Poetical Works of Sir Thomas Wyatt* (1854) is of less importance. The first attempt at a complete modern ed. of Wyatt's poetry was that of A. K. Foxwell (2 vols., 1913). It includes specimens of Wyatt's prose. It has been superseded by *The Collected Poems of Sir Thomas Wyatt*, ed. K. Muir (M.L.) which is the most reliable and up-to-date ed. A very valuable contribution to the study of Wyatt is E. M. W. Tillyard's *The Poetry of Sir Thomas Wyatt a Selection and a Study* (1949). This selection contains the best of Wyatt's poetry in modernized spelling but in the texts of the MSS. with an excellent critical introd. and notes. Wyatt's prose tr. of *Plutarch's Quyete of Mynde* made at the command of Catherine of Aragon was prob. pub. in 1528. A single undated copy is extant in the Huntington Library in California. A facs. ed. with an introd. by C. R. Baskervill has been pub. at Harvard in 1931.

Biography and Criticism

G. F. Nott's ed. of Wyatt's poems (1816) contains an elaborate memoir. There is a useful article in the D.N.B. by Sir Sidney Lee giving the principal sources of information. Miss Foxwell planned a *Life and Letters of Wyatt* that has never been pub. The Introductions to the edd. of Muir and Tillyard are both valuable. Reference should also be made to the essay on Wyatt by Sir E. K. Chambers in his *Sir Thomas Wyatt and Other Studies* (op. cit.). The best modern short study is *Sir Thomas Wyatt* by Sergio Baldi (B.C.S., 1961). See also the important monograph in Italian by the same author, *La Poesia di Sir Thomas Wyatt* (Firenze, 1953), Hallett Smith, 'The Art of Wyatt' in H.L.Q., ix, 1946, D. W. Harding, 'The Rhythmical Intention of Wyatt's Poetry', *Scrutiny*, xiv, 1947, and E. D. Mackerness, 'The Transitional Nature of Wyatt's Poetry', *English*, vii, 1948. See also the study of

Wyatt in H. A. Mason, *Humanism and Poetry in the Early Tudor Period* (1959).

HENRY HOWARD, EARL OF SURREY (1517-47)

Shorter Poems

The earliest poem by Surrey to be printed seems to have been his epitaph on Wyatt in the undated *An Excellent Epitaffe of syr Thomas Wyat*. See H. E. Rollins, *Marginalia* (op. cit.), p. 464. Forty lyrics are ascribed to him in Tottel, and his was the only author's name to appear on the title-page. Two of the anonymous poems in Tottel are attrib. to him in *Englands Helicon* (1600) and two more are admitted into Padelford's ed. on rather dubious evidence. Five other short orig. poems survive, four in the MS. collections now in the B.M., and one, the sonnet on his squire Clere, which was first printed in *Remains Concerning Britain* by William Camden, the Elizabethan antiquary, in 1605. It was also quoted by John Aubrey in his *History of Surrey* (written about 1673). There are extant also nine verse trs. from the Bible (*Ecclesiastes and Psalms*) by Surrey in the B.M. MSS. These MS. poems are all in the hands of scribes. No autograph MS. poem by Surrey is known to be extant. The 1717 ed. of *Tottel's Miscellany* is called *The Poems of Henry Howard, Earl Surrey*, but the first separate ed. of his poems is that of G. F. Nott (1815-18). This was also the first pub. ed. to make use of the MSS., though these had been used by the editors of the abortive edd. of *Tottel's Miscellany* ii 1808 and 1814 (see p. 150). Nineteenth-century edd. appeared in the Aldine Series (1830), Bell's annotated poets (1854), and ed. by Gilfillan with Shakespeare's *Poems* (1856). A complete critical ed. of Surrey's *Poems* was pub. by F. M. Padelford in 1920 as Vol. I of the University of Washington's Publications, 2nd rev. ed. 1928. The best modern ed. of the *Poems* is that of Emrys Jones with introd., notes and glossary (1964).

Translation of the Aeneid

Three sixteenth-century versions of Surrey's blank verse trs. from the *Aeneid* survive. Of these two are printed and one is MS. Up till the twentieth century the only known printed text was that pub. Tottel in 1557 entitled *Certain Bokes of Virgiles Aeneis turned into English meter, by Henry Earle of Surrey*. This version contains

Surrey's trs. of the Second and Fourth Books of the *Aeneid*. A single copy of another early ed. printed by John Day for William Owen came to light when the Britwell Court Library was sold. Day's ed. is undated, and it contains only the Fourth Book. Its title is *The fourth Boke of Virgill, intreating of the love between Aeneas and Dido translated into English and drawne into a strange meter by Henrye Howard Earl of Surrey worthy to be embrased*. Gladys D. Willcocks in an article in the *Modern Language Review* (July 1919) brought forward evidence to show that Day's ed. was printed in 1554. The MS. version is in a sixteenth-century collection in the B.M. (Hargrave 205) written probably early in Elizabeth's reign. Like Day's ed. it contains the Fourth Book only, but its text differs both from Tottel's and Day's, and is probably nearer to Surrey's orig. version than either (see F. M. Padelford's notes in his ed.).

A modern rpt. of the Day-Owen ed. of *Surrey's Fourth Boke of Virgill*, ed. H. Hartman, was pub. in a limited ed. in 1933.

Biography and Criticism

The story of Surrey's love for the Fair Geraldine and his romantic journey to Italy is a fabrication due apparently to Thomas Nashe, the Elizabethan author, in whose novel *Jack Wilton or the Unfortunate Traveller*, it first appeared. It was accepted as a historical record by Anthony à Wood, T. Warton (in his *History of English Poetry*), and even by G. F. Nott in his ed. of Surrey's poems. Drayton, the Elizabethan poet, included an epistle from Surrey to the Fair Geraldine in his *England's Heroical Epistles* (see p. 212).

E. Bapst in his *Deux Gentilshommes Poètes de la Cour de Henry VIII* (Paris, 1891) gave the first reliable account of Surrey's life. There is a detailed biography by Sir S. Lee in the D.N.B. and a monograph by E. Casady (P.M.L.A., 1938). The reviews of his poetry in Courthope's *History of English Poetry* and Berdan's *Early Tudor Poetry* are valuable. G. D. Willcocks discusses Surrey's tr. of the fourth book of the *Aeneid* in M.L.R. xiv, 1919, xv, 1920, and xvii, 1922. See also A. Oras, 'Surrey's Triumphs', T.L.S., 18 Jan., 1947, and R. Chapman, 'Surrey in France', T.L.S 7 Mar., 1952.

NICHOLAS GRIMALD OR GRIMOALD (1519-62)

Grimald's extant English poems include the forty pub. Tottel in the first ed. of *Songs and Sonnettes* and one (with three Latin poems) printed in William Turner's *Preservative or Tryacle agaynst the Poyson of Pelagius* (1551). His English prose tr. of Cicero's *De Officiis* was pub. about 1553. A second ed. appeared in 1556 and five more up to and including that of 1600. He wrote much in Latin including two plays of some merit, *Christus Redivivus* (Cologne, 1543) and *Archipropheta, Tragedia* (Cologne, 1548). John Bale in his Latin *Catalogue of English writers* (Bale, 1557) gives a long list of works of Grimald in Latin and English, most of which have disappeared. It is interesting to notice that it includes an English verse tr. of the *Georgics* of Virgil, no copy of which has survived. There is a valuable modern ed. of Grimald's extant poems in English and Latin (including the two plays with English trs.) by L. R. Merrill (Y.S.E., No. LXIX, 1925).

THOMAS VAUX, LORD VAUX (1510-56).

At least two poems by Lord Vaux and probably a third are included in *Tottel's Miscellany*. Thirteen other pieces are signed by him in *A Paradyse of Dayntie Devices* (1576; see p. 169). A fourteenth was added in the 1578 ed., and another poem in the *Paradyse* was assigned to him in the same ed. but not in the first. On the other hand two poems attrib. to him in the 1576 ed. were assigned to William Hunnis in later edd., and one more poem may be by John Harington. The verses sung by the First Gravedigger in Hamlet are a perversion of one of Vaux's contributions to Tottel. All his undoubted poems are included by Grosart in his *Fuller Worthies Library Miscellanies* Vol. iv (1872). There is a Life of Lord Vaux by Sir Sidney Lee in the D.N.B.

CHAPTER III
THE PROTESTANT REFORMERS

GENERAL WORKS

THE *Actes and Monuments* of John Foxe (1516-87), commonly known as *The Book of Martyrs*, is an elaborate Protestant propagandist history of the English Reformation with lives of the early Reformers and lurid accounts of their martyrdoms. It was pub. orig. in a Latin form at Strassburg in 1554, then at Basle (considerably enl. ed.) in 1559-63 and in English in 1563. It was very popular and went through five edd. by the end of the sixteenth century; the best modern ed. is that of S. R. Cattley, rev. J. Pratt (8 vols., 1877). See the valuable *John Foxe and his Book* by J. F. Mozley (S.P.C.K., 1940). Fuller's *Church History of Britain* (1655) and Burnet's History of the Reformation (1679) give seventeenth century Anglican views. The most complete modern studies are R. W. Dixon, *History of the Church of England* (6 vols., 1878-1902) and P. Hughes, *The Reformation in England* (3 vols., 1950-54). See also *The Reign of Henry VIII*, ed. J. Gairdner (2 vols., 1884) and H. M. Smith, *Henry VIII and the Tudor Reformation* (1948), and for Roman Catholic views F. A. Gasquet, *Henry VIII and the English Monasteries* (2 vols., 1885-87), and H. Belloc, *History of England* (4 vols., 1925-31). T. M. Parker, *The English Reformation to 1558* (Harvard, 1950), is a good short introd.

See also *Tudor Books of Saints and Martyrs* by Helen C. White (Madison, 1963).

COLLECTIONS

The Parker Society's Publications (Cambridge, 1841-55) in fifty-five vols. include all the chief works of 'The Fathers and Early Writers of the Reformed English Church'. The *British Reformers* (2 vols., Religious Tract Society, London, 1831) is a small collection containing works of Edward VI and Lady Jane Grey as well as those of Cranmer and others.

INDIVIDUAL AUTHORS

SIMON FISH (d. 1531)

Works and Life

The famous pamphlet against the clergy called *A Supplicacyon for the Beggars* was pub. anonymously in an undated ed. which probably appeared in 1529 at Antwerp. The authorship of it was attributed to Fish by Sir Thomas More and by Foxe, and there can be little doubt that this attribution is correct. It was followed by two other anonymous *Supplicacyons* which appeared in 1544 and 1546 respectively. These are not by Fish, who died in 1531. J. M. Cowper attributed them to Henry Brinklow. All three pamphlets were ed. F. J. Furnival and J. M. Cowper with an introd. for the E.E.T.S. (Extra Series No. XIII, 1871) There is another ed. by E. Arber in The English Scholars' Library. There is also a rpt. in *Tracts and Pamphlets* ed. W. C. Ward (W.C.). A Life of Fish is prefixed to Furnivall's ed. and the article in the D.N.B. is by Bishop Creighton.

WILLIAM TYNDALE (c. 1490-1536)

Works

Tyndale's works consist mainly of his controversial writings and his Bible trs. His early tr. of Erasmus's *Enchiridion* is prob. that pub. anon. in 1533 as *A Booke called . . . the Manuell of the Christian Knight*. The controversial writings are numerous and no complete bibliography of them exists. The earliest seems to have been *The Parable . . . of the Wicked Mammon* printed at Marburg in May 1528. The most important is *The Obedience . . . of a Christen Man and how Christen rulers ought to governe*, also pub. at Marburg in October of the same year. In 1530 appeared *The Practyse of Prelates* in which he attacked the Roman Catholic hierarchy (2nd ed., London, 1548) and in 1531 at Antwerp his *Answere unto Sir Thomas More's dialoge* written in reply to More's *Dyalogue* against heresy which had appeared in 1529. More replied to the *Answere* in a *Confutacyon* and other works.

The sheets of Tyndale's English tr. of part of the New Testament, with which he escaped from Cologne in 1525, were perhaps pub. at Worms and a fragment of them is preserved in the Grenville Library in the B.M. It consists only of St Matthew's Gospel up to the 12th verse of the 22nd chapter. A complete ed. of Tyndale's New Testament also appeared at Worms in 1525. Two copies survive, one in the Baptist College at Bristol and one in St Paul's Cathedral Library in London. Tyndale's rev. ed. appeared at Antwerp in 1534, and numerous others followed in Antwerp and London. His version of the Pentateuch appeared in an undated ed. at Marburg (part of it is dated January 17th, 1530; 2nd ed. 1534). His version of the Book of Jonah was issued at Antwerp in 1531 and nearly all his Bible trs. including some hitherto unpublished versions from the O.T., were included in 'Matthew's Bible' of 1537. [For the printing of Tyndale's Bible translations see M. E. Kronenberg, 'Notes on English Printing in the Low Countries (Early Sixteenth Century)', *The Library*, 4th ser., ix (1928-29).]

The complete text of Tyndale's N.T. tr. is given in the *English Hexapla* (S. Bagster, 1841) with parallel texts of other important English trs. An excellent modern ed. of Tyndale's New Testament was pub. in 1938 for R.S.L. ed. N. Hardy Wallis with introd. by Isaac Foot. There is a facs. ed. of the B.M. copy of the orig. fragmentary New Testament of Tyndale (printed at Cologne in 1525) with an introd. A. W. Pollard (1926).

The Whole Works of W. Tyndale, John Frith and Dr Barnes with a preface by John Foxe were pub. in a folio by J. Daye in 1572-73. A modern ed. of Tyndale's works is included in *The Parker Society's Publications*, and there is an ed. of *The Obedience of a Christian Man* by R. Lovett in the Christian Classics Series (1886).

Biography

There are numerous Lives of Tyndale. An early account of him was given by John Foxe in his *Acts and Monuments*. The *Life* by R. Demaus (Religious Tract Society, 1871 rev. R. Lovett (1886)) is a sound, scholarly work. It has now, however, been superseded in a large measure by the important study *William Tyndale* by J. F. Mozley (S.P.C.K., 1937). The articles in various periodicals on the fourth centenary of his death in 1936 should also be consulted.

HUGH LATIMER (?1492-1555)

Latimer's earliest printed English sermon is the famous *Sermon on the Ploughers*, which appeared in 1548 under the title of *A Notable Sermō of ye reverende father Maister Hughe Latimer*. Two more vols. of sermons which he preached before Edward VI appeared in 1549. In 1562 John Daye printed twenty-seven of his sermons. A second enl. ed. of this collection called *Frutefull Sermons . . . Newly Imprinted* appeared in 1571-72. This ed. contains also an English tr. of the Latin sermon preached by Latimer before Convocation in 1537. His complete Remains and Sermons are included in the Parker Society's publications. There are rpts. of the *Sermon on the Ploughers* and of *Seven Sermons before Edward VI* in Arber's *English Reprints*, and a useful ed. of selected sermons by Latimer ed. H. C. Beeching in Ev. Lib. (1906).

The best *Life of Latimer* is that of R. Demaus (Religious Tract Society, rev. ed., 1881). A recent standard work is *Hugh Latimer, Apostle to the English* (Pennsylvania, 1954). See also H. S. Darby, *Hugh Latimer* (1953).

MILES COVERDALE (1488-1568)

Works

Coverdale's important literary work is his contribution to the tr. of the Bible. His first version appeared in a folio in 1535, dedicated to Henry VIII. There are two copies of it in the B.M., one of which is imperfect. In all about fifty copies are extant. It was the first complete English Bible to be printed. Another complete English Bible based on Coverdale's and Tyndale's was published by John Rogers in 1537. It was attributed on the title page to a person called 'Thomas Matthew', apparently a fictitious name, and hence was known as 'Matthew's Bible'. It was on the basis of this tr. that the famous 'Great Bible' of 1539 was compiled by Coverdale under the patronage of Thomas Cromwell. Coverdale was also the reviser of the second ed. of Cranmer's 'Great Bible' of 1540 (so called from the author of its Preface); which became the official version, and was placed in the churches (see p. 26). Coverdale also ed. a rev. version of the New Testament in Latin and English, which was pub. in 1538. His version of 1535 is rptd. by Bagster (1838 and 1847). His tr. of the Psalms was included in the Prayer Books of Edward VI, and has been retained as the 'Prayer Book version' ever since. Coverdale's other works include theological writings mostly tr. from the German; *A shorte Recapitulation of Erasmus's Enchiridion* (1545), an abbreviated version of the anon. English tr. prob. by Tyndale (1533) (see above under 'William Tyndale'), and *Goostly Psalmes and Spirituall Songs drawne out of Holy Scripture*, pub. in an undated 4to, one copy of which survives at Queen's College, Oxford. The *Goostly Psalmes* (which are mostly tr. from German Hymn Books) are interesting examples of early English Protestant hymnology. They are discussed by C. H. Herford in his *Studies in the Literary Relations between England and Germany in the Sixteenth Century*, and by E. Althoff in his diss. *Myles Coverdale's 'Goostly Psalmes and Spirituall Songs' und das Deutsche Kirchenlied* (Bochum, 1935). Coverdale's *Writings and Remains* were ed. G. Pearson for the Parker Society (1842-46).

Life

Memorials of Myles Coverdale with Dyvers Matters relating to the Promulgation of the Byble in the Reign of Henry VIII was pub. in 1838. It includes a bibliography. The Parker Society's ed. includes a biographical sketch, and there is a *Life* by H. R. Tedder in the D.N.B.

J. F. Mozley, *Coverdale and his Bibles* (1953) is a standard work.

THOMAS CRANMER, ARCHBISHOP OF CANTERBURY (1489-1556)

Works

Cranmer's English Works (apart from his share in the Prayer Books of Edward VI) include his so-called *Catechism* (a tr. from the Latin of Justus Jonas) entitled *A shorte Instruction into Christian Religion for the synguler commoditie and profyte of childre and yong people*, prefaces to the English Bible, and the Book of Common Prayer, the first *Book of Homilies* of 1547, an answer to the Devonshire Rebels, and some controversial works on the sacrament of the Lord's Supper. The standard ed. is that of H. Jenkyns (Oxford, 1833) which includes Cranmer's extant letters in English and Latin and specimens of his handwriting. There is another ed. by J. E. Cox in the Parker Society's publications (2 vols. Cambridge 1844-46).

Life

There are numerous *Lives* of Cranmer. The best modern study is that of A. F. Pollard: *Cranmer and the English Reformation* (1904). For a Roman Catholic view see Hilaire Belloc's *Cranmer* (1931). F. E. Hutchinson's *Cranmer and the English Reformation* (1951) is an excellent introd.

The Book of Common Prayer

The first Prayer Book of Edward VI was printed by Edward Whitchurch in March 1549 and entitled *The Booke of the Common Prayer and administracion of the Sacramentes, and other Rites and Ceremonies of the Churche after the Use of the Churche of England*. The exact shares of the various divines in its composition are unknown, but there is no doubt that Cranmer was the controlling influence, and he was probably the author of a large part of the book. The services are mostly tr. and altered from the old Latin service books (especially the Sarum Breviary, Missal and Manual). The Psalms are from Coverdale's tr. The second Prayer Book of Edward VI was a revision of the first with alterations, which gave it a distinctly more Protestant character. It was printed by Whitchurch in 1552. The first Prayer Book of Elizabeth, printed by Richard Grafton, appeared in 1559. It is a rev. ed. of the Second Book of Edward VI. There have been various subsequent revisions, among which that of 1662 was specially important. These subsequent revisions have all tended in a Catholic direction. This was specially noticeable in the Book Proposed of 1927, which was rejected by Parliament.

The Two Liturgies of Edward VI, ed. J. Ketley, and the *Liturgies and Occasional Forms of Prayer set forth in the Reign of Queen Elizabeth*, are included in the Parker Society's publications. J. H. Blunt's *Annotated Book of Common Prayer* (rev. ed., 1895) is the standard modern annotated ed. There is a useful rpt. of the *First and Second Prayer Books of Edward VI* in Ev. Lib., ed. by E. C. S. Gibson. The standard critical works are J. Dowden's *The Workmanship of the Prayer Book* (1899), *A New History of the Book of Common Prayer* by Procter and Frere (1902), and *English Prayer Books: An Introduction to the Literature of Christian Worship* by S. Morrison (1943; 3rd rev. ed., 1949).

THE ELIZABETHANS

(For historical background, in addition to works recommended on p. 139, J. B. Black, *The Reign of Elizabeth* [1936], and J. E. Neale, *Queen Elizabeth*, should be consulted. For social background, see *Shakespeare's England*, ed. C. T. Onions [2 vols, 1916], M. St Clair Byrne, *The Elizabethan Home* [1930], and Louis B. Wright, *Middle Class Culture in Elizabethan England* [N. C. 1935]; for intellectual background, E. M. W. Tillyard's short but very valuable *The Elizabethan World Picture* [1943], A. O. Lovejoy, *The Great Chain of Being* [Harvard, 1936], Hardin Craig, *The Enchanted Glass: the Elizabethan Mind in Literature* [N.Y., 1936], and C. Morris, *Political Thought in England: Tyndale to Hooker* [H.U.L.]; for Elizabethan psychological theories, J. B. Bamborough, *The Little World of Man* [1952]; for general studies of Elizabethan literature, C. S. Lewis, *English Literature in the Sixteenth Century*, op. cit., Bk. III, F. P. Wilson, *Elizabethan and Jacobean* [1945], T. S. Eliot, *Elizabethan Essays* [1934], *The Age of Shakespeare*, ed. B. Ford [P.G.E.L.], and Helen Morris's useful short introduction, *Elizabethan Literature* [Harvard, 1958]; for the musical background P. Warlock, *The English Ayre* [1926], and Bruce Pattison's indispensable *Music and Poetry of the English Renaissance* [1948]; for pictorial art, E. K. Waterhouse, *Painting in Britain, 1530-1790*, and C. Winter, *Elizabethan Miniatures* [P.B., 1943].)

CONTENTS

CHAPTER		PAGE
IV	EARLY ELIZABETHAN POETRY	165
V	THE TRANSLATORS	177
VI	CHRONICLES, ANTIQUARIAN WORKS AND VOYAGES	193
VII	LATER ELIZABETHAN POETRY	202
VIII	TUDOR DRAMA UP TO SHAKESPEARE	219
IX	ELIZABETHAN SECULAR PROSE	236
X	WILLIAM SHAKESPEARE	248
XI	ELIZABETHAN DIVINES	270

CHAPTER IV

EARLY ELIZABETHAN POETRY

A MIRROR FOR MAGISTRATES

Texts

THIS famous book was designed originally as a continuation of Lydgate's *Falls of Princes* (an English verse paraphrase of Boccacio's Latin *De Casibus Virorum Illustrium*). Whitchurch, the printer of the Edward VI prayer books, planned an ed. of *The Falls of Princes* in Edward VI's reign and he was advised by 'many both honourable and worshipful' to have it continued up to his own day. He commissioned William Baldwin (see p. 170) to produce the continuations, but Baldwin, finding the work beyond his powers, called in 'divers learned men' to help him. The chief of these collaborators seems to have been George Ferrers. When Edward VI died and Mary came to the throne, Whitchurch, a zealous Protestant, went out of business and sold his stock (including, presumably, the unfinished ed. of *The Falls of Princes*) to two other printers, Tottel and Wayland, both of whom pub. edd. of Lydgate's poem in Queen Mary's reign. Wayland also seems to have intended to pub. with his ed. of 1554 the continuation by Baldwin and his associates and actually printed it. In some extant copies the following title page appears as folio xl of this ed.: *A memorial of suche Princes, as since the tyme of King Richard the Seconde, have been unfortunate in the Realme of England. Londini In Aedibus Johannis Waylandi*. On the verso of this title page is his licence to print the book dated October 20, 1553. The continuation, however, was not pub. with this ed. as permission was withheld by Mary's Lord Chancellor, Stephen Gardiner. In 1559, after Elizabeth's accession, permission was obtained through the influence of Lord Stafford to pub. the printed (but hitherto unpublished) English continuation of *The Falls of Princes*, and it now appeared under the title of *A Myrroure for Magistrates. Wherein may be seen by example of Other, with howe gevous plages vices are punished; and howe frayle and unstable worldly prosperitie is founde, even of those, whom Fortune seemeth most highly to favour.* This book was printed by Thomas Marsh, Wayland having now retired. It contains nineteen legends from English history beginning with that of Robert Tressillian, Chancellor to Richard II, and ending with that of Edward IV. Four of these legends are by Baldwin, three by Ferrers, and one each by Cavyll, Chaloner and Phaer. Eight are by unknown authors, and the last (that of Edward IV) Baldwin declares that 'Maister Skelton made' and that he repeated it from memory. The legends are joined by prose links, where Baldwin in his own phrase usurps 'Bochas rome'. In 1563 Marsh printed a new and enl. ed. containing eight more legends (including that of Jane Shore by Thomas Churchyard) and the famous *Induction* by Thomas Sackville (see p. 47), by far the best poem in the collection. One of the added legends (that of the Duke of Buckingham) is also by Sackville. Thus it appears that Sackville joined Baldwin's committee after the publication of the ed. of 1559 and proposed to remodel the whole work. Another ed. of the Baldwin–Sackville *Mirror* of 1563 appeared in 1571. In 1574 Marsh printed *The First parte of the Mirour for Magistrates containing the falles of the first infortunate Princes of this lande: From the comming of Brute to the incarnation of our saviour and redeemer Jesu Christe*. This new collection was the work of John Higgins. It includes an Induction written in imitation of Sackville's and sixteen legends dealing with heroes and heroines of Ancient British history from Albanact to Nennius. In 1578 another printer called Richard Webster pub. a collection called *The seconde part of the Mirrour for Magistrates* containing twelve legends of early British and Saxon characters by Richard Blennerhassett. In 1587 Marsh pub. an important ed. called *The Mirour for Magistrates ... Newly imprinted and with the addition of divers Tragedies enlarged*. This book was ed. by Higgins and contains both his own previously pub. work (enl. by the addition of many new legends), and the Baldwin–Sackville *Mirror* also enlarged by legends that bring it down to Cardinal Wolsey. The last attempt to remodel *The Mirror* was that of Robert Niccols who pub. in 1610 *A Mirour for Magistrates: Being a true chronicle historie of the untimely falles of such unfortunate Princes and men of note, as have happened since the first entrance of Brute into this Iland untill this our latter Age. Newly enlarged with a last part, called A Winter night's Vision, being an addition of such Tragedies, especially famous, as are exempted in the former, Historie, with a Poem annexed, called Englands Eliza.* This vol. is a piece of book-making that includes the matter ed. by Higgins, Blennerhassett and Baldwin, much altered by the new editor, who omits all the intermediate matter between the legends whether in prose or verse, and takes many liberties with the text. He places Sackville's induction at the beginning of Baldwin's Part II, placing Higgins's induction at the beginning of Part I and supplying one of his own for Part II. He also adds many legends of his own composition and one (that of Thomas Cromwell) by Drayton, omitting some of the legends of his predecessors. The popularity of *The Mirror* had passed away by the time of James I, and Niccols's ed. did not sell. It was re-issued under fresh titles in 1619, 1620 and 1621. No other text appeared till 1815 when Joseph Haslewood pub. his fine scholarly ed. based on that of 1587 with collections from the other ed. and Niccols's supplement together with a valuable introd. The definitive modern edition is that of Lily B. Campbell in two vols., *The Mirror for Magistrates* (1938) containing the *Mirror* of 1559 with the additions of 1563, 1578 and 1587, and *Parts added to the Mirror for Magistrates* (1946) containing the Higgins-Blennerhassett version with subsequent additions. Both vols. include valuable introductions and critical apparatus.

Criticism

The most complete study of *A Mirror for Magistrates* is that of W. F. Trench (privately printed, 1898). There is a very valuable Chapter on the *Mirror* by J. W. Cunliffe in

C.H.E.L. (Chapter IX, Vol. III) with a useful bibliography. Lily B. Campbell attacked certain conclusions of Trench's in H.L.B., 6 (1934). An article by Fitzroy Pyle in T.L.S., December 28th, 1935, contains an answer to Lily Campbell's arguments. See also A. L. Rowse, 'Mirror for Magistrates', T.L.S., April 15th, 1939, and A. Thaler, 'Literary Criticism in *A Mirror for Magistrates*', J.E.G.P., XLIX, 1950.

EARLY ELIZABETHAN POETICAL MISCELLANIES

A Handeful of pleasant delites

The earliest known Elizabethan poetical miscellany appears to have been pub. in 1566. No complete copy of this ed. survives; it is only known from an entry in the *Stationers' Register* under the date 1566 (ed. Arber, I. 313) and a single leaf preserved in the B.M. (643. M. g. 83) with the running-head, *Sonnets and Histories, to sundrie new tunes*. This fragment is supposed to belong to the first ed. of *A Handeful of pleasant delites*, a miscellany pub. in 1584 which may be regarded as a second, enl. ed. of the earliest Elizabethan miscellany. Its full title is *A Handeful of pleasant delites, containing sundrie new Sonets and delectable Histories in divers kindes of Meeter. Newly devised to the newest tunes that are now in use, to be sung: everie Sonet orderly pointed to his proper Tune. With new additions of certain Songs, to verie late devised Notes, not commonly knowen, nor used heretofore, By Clement Robinson, and divers others. At London Printed by Richard Ihones: . . . 1584.* Only one copy of this book survives. It is now in the B.M. As its title page implies, it is a collection of popular songs for music. It includes the famous song of *Greensleeves* and the flower song ('A Nosegaie Alwaies Sweet'), part of which is sung by Ophelia in *Hamlet*. Some of the songs are signed. The contributors besides Robinson himself include Thomas Richardson, J. Tomson and George Mannington. It is not rptd. till 1871, when James Crossley edited it for the Spenser Society. Another ed. Edward Arber appeared in *The English Scholar's Library* in 1878. There is a scholarly ed. by H. E. Rollins (Harvard, 1924) and another by Arnold Kershaw (1926).

The Paradise of daynty devises

The most popular of the early Elizabethan poetical miscellanies was *The Paradise of daynty devises, aptly furnished, with sundry pithie, and learned inventions: devised and written for the most part, by M. Edwards, sometimes of her Maiesties Chappel: the rest by sundry learned Gentlemen, both of honor, and woorshippe . . . Imprinted at London . . . 1576.*

Richard Edwards, the editor of this collection, was a poet and dramatist of some repute (see p. 226 for his work in the drama). The other contributors include Lord Vaux, the Earl of Oxford, Thomas Churchyard, Jasper Heywood, George Whetstone, Francis Kinwelmersh and others. Attempts have been made to prove that the collection contains poems by Fulke Greville, Walter Ralegh and Edwin Sandys. There is no evidence, however, to support these attributions. A second, enl. ed. appeared in 1578 and others in 1580, 1585, 1596, 1600 and 1606. Sir Egerton Brydges produced the first modern ed. in 1810. It is based on a transcript of the 1576 ed. made by George Steevens. The standard modern ed. is that of H. E. Rollins (Harvard, 1927).

A gorgious Gallery of gallant Inventions

The Paradise of daynty devises was followed in 1578 by another miscellany entitled: *A gorgious Gallery of gallant Inventions. Garnished and decked with divers dayntie devises, right delicate and delightful to recreate each modest minde with all. First framed and fashioned in sundrie formes, by divers worthy workemen of late dayes: and now, ionyed together and builded up by T. P. Imprinted at London, 1578.* 'T.P.' the editor of this vol., is Thomas Proctor, who contributed some pieces to it himself. Other poems are by Owen Roydon, who may have been the orig. editor. There are also poems by Churchyard, Howell,

Clement Robinson, Jasper Heywood and others 'joyned together and builded up' by Proctor probably without the permission of their authors. Proctor borrows from previous miscellanies and, perhaps, makes alterations in the poems that he appropriates.

A gorgious Gallery was not so successful or popular as *The Paradise of daynty devises*; no second ed. of it appeared in the Elizabethan period. It was not rptd. until the appearance of Thomas Park's *Heliconia* of 1814 (see below). Another rpt. was included in the fifty-third vol. of the publications of the Roxburghe Society (1844) entitled *Three Collections of English Poetry of the Latter Part of the Sixteenth Century*. The standard modern ed. is that of H. E. Rollins (Harvard, 1926).

Later Collections

Heliconia. Comprising a Selection of English Poetry of the Elizabethan Age edited by Thomas Park in three vols. appeared in 1815. It includes rpts. of *A gorgious Gallery of gallant Inventions* and a *Handeful of pleasant delites*, as well as poems by Whetstone, Constable, Burnes, Churchyard and others. Park also rptd. in the third vol. of *Heliconia* the later miscellany, *England's Parnassus*. The fifty-third vol. of the Roxburghe Society's Publications (1844), *Three Collections of English Poetry of the Latter Part of the Century*, includes *A gorgious Gallery of gallant Inventions* and two other collections called *A poore Knight his Pallace of Private pleasures* (*1579*) and *A speciall remedy against the furious force of lawless Love* (*1579*). J. P. Collier's *Seven English Poetical Miscellanies printed between 1557 and 1602* (1867) includes *Tottel's Miscellany*, *The Paradise of daynty devises*, *The Gorgious gallery*, *The Phoenix Nest*, *England's Helicon*, *England's Parnassus* and *Davison's Poetical Rhapsody*. The text is not very accurate.

INDIVIDUAL AUTHORS

WILLIAM BALDWIN (fl. 1547-60)

William Baldwin, the first editor of *The Mirrour for Magistrates*, pub. in 1549 *The Canticles or Balades of Salomon phraselyke declared in English Metres*. This rare quarto printed by Baldwin himself contains some lyrics of considerable charm. His *Funeralles of Edward the Sixt*, a series of elegies in verse, appeared in 1560 and his anti-Catholic prose satire, *A Marvellous Hystory intitulede, Beware the Cat.*, in 1571. He also pub. in 1547 a prose work entitled *A Treatise of Morall Phylosophie*. All Baldwin's books are very rare, and none have been rptd. except *A Mirrour for Magistrates*. Two of his poems are included by Norman Ault in his *Elizabethan Lyrics*. There is a biography by A. H. Bullen in the D.N.B.

THOMAS CHURCHYARD (? 1520-1604)

This voluminous but dull writer began his literary career under Edward VI and finished it under James I. His legend of *Shore's Wife* pub. in the 1563 ed. of *The Mirror for Magistrates* was written in the reign of Edward VI. Churchyard is said to have contributed to *Tottel's Miscellany* as well as to *The Mirrour for Magistrates*. He also pub. numerous elegies, epitaphs, epistles and other works in verse which are mostly mere hack-work. *His Worthiness of Wales*, pub. in 1587, is a long 'chorographical' poem containing much valuable antiquarian and historical information. It may have suggested to Drayton the plan of *Poly-Olbion*. It was rptd. in 1776 and by the Spenser Society in 1871. Spenser's description of Churchyard in Colin Clout's *Come Home Again* as Palemon 'that sung so long untill quite hoarse he grew' is well deserved. There is an article on Churchyard by A. H. Bullen in the D.N.B.

GEORGE GASCOIGNE (? 1539-77)

Works

The first ed. of Gascoigne's works is anonymous. It appeared in 1573 and is entitled *A Hundreth sundrie Flowres bounde up in one small Poesie Gathered partely (by translation) in the fyne outlandish Gardins of Euripides, Ovid, Petrarke, Ariosto and others, and partly by invention out of our owne fruitefull Orchardes in England. . . . At London, imprinted for Richard Smith*. The book is undated, but certain references show that it appeared in 1573. It contains a miscellaneous collection of verse and prose including Gascoigne's prose tr. of Ariosto's comedy *The Supposes*, which had been acted at Gray's Inn in 1566, a free verse tr. or rather imitation of *The Phoenissae of Euripides* (from the Italian version of Dolce) made in collaboration with Francis Kinwelmersh called *The Wofull tragedie of Iocasta*, an extant MS. of which is dated 1568 (it was acted at Gray's Inn in 1566), a number of lyrics and other pieces in verse, a prose tale and an unfinished sequence of autobiographical poems entitled *The Delectable history of Dan Bartholomew of Bath*. Gascoigne pub. a second enl. ed. of this book under his own name in 1575 entitled *The Posies of George Gascoigne, Esquire. Corrected, perfected, and augmented by the Authour, 1575*. Among the pieces added in this ed. is the important critical essay entitled *Certayne notes of Instruction concerning the making of verse or ryme in English, written at the request of Master Eduardo Donati*. In 1575 also appeared Gascoigne's orig. prose play called *The Glasse of Government*, and in 1576 his satire in blank verse called *The Steele Glas*, with an elegy called *The complaynt of Phylomene*. He pub. two moralizing prose tracts in 1576, called *The Droomme of Doomes day* and *A delicate Diet for daintie mouthde Droonkardes*. In the same year also appeared *The Princelye pleasures at the Courte at Kenelwoorthe*, which included *The copies of all such verses, Proses, or Poetrical inventions and other Devices of pleasure, as were then devised, and presented by sundry gentlemen before the Queenes Majestie* (see p. 35). The contributors to this vol. include Gascoigne, George Ferrers and others. The last known copy of the 1576 ed. of *The Princelye pleasures* was destroyed by fire at Birmingham, but a rpt. made at Chiswick in 1821 survives. It was rptd. in full in the 1587 ed. of Gascoigne's works. Another work by Gascoigne written in honour of the Queen survives in a MS. in the B.M. (Royal MS. 18, A, xlviii). It is a prose story in English, Latin, Italian and French called *The Tale of Hemetes the Heremyte pronownced before the Q. Majestie at Woodstocke, 1575*. To this MS. is prefixed the famous drawing of Gascoigne kneeling before the Queen and presenting her with his book. *Hemetes the Heremyte* was printed with *A Paradoxe*, a tr. by A. Fleming from Synesius, in 1579 and also in a quarto vol. that appeared in 1585, known from its running title as *The Queenes Maiesties Entertainment at Woodstock* (the unique copy in B.M. has lost its first four pages, including title-page). A series of elegies by Gascoigne called *The Grief of Joye* also survives in the Royal MS. (18, A, lxi) at the B.M. The tract called *The Spoyle of Antwerpe Faithfully reported by an Englishman who was present at the same*, pub. anonymously in November 1576, has been attributed to Gascoigne. He prefixed complimentary poems to several contemporary books. His poem, *The Arraignment of a Lover* appeared as a broadside ballad in 1581. He ed. Sir Humphrey Gilbert's *A Discourse of a Discoverie for a New Passage to Cataia* in 1576 (see p. 200). In 1587 Abel Jeffes pub. *The Plesauntest workes of George Gascoigne Esquire*, which included most of his writings in prose and verse but not *The Glasse of Government, The Droomme of Doomes day*, or *A Delicate Diet*. Chalmers's *English Poets* (1810) contain a comprehensive selection from Gascoigne's poems. W. C. Hazlitt ed. his *Complete Poems* for the Roxburghe Society (1869-70). The only complete modern ed. is that of J. W. Cunliffe (*Cambridge English Classics*, 2 vols., 1907-10) which includes both the verse and prose. *The Supposes* and *Jocasta* were edited in B.L. by J. W. Cunliffe (1906), *The Steele Glas* and *The complaynt of Phylomene* by E. Arber in his *English Rpts.*, *The Glasse of Government* by J. S. Farmer in his *Tudor Facs. Texts*, and *The Queenes Majesties Entertainment* by A. W. Pollard (1903 and 10) and by J. W. Cunliffe (P.M.L.A., xxvi, 1911). The best ed. of *A Hundreth Sundrie Floures* is that of C. T. Prouty (Columbia, Missouri, 1942).

Biography and Criticism

The earliest biography of Gascoigne is by his friend George Whetstone: *A remembraunce of the wel imployed Life and godly end of George Gaskoyne Esquire* (1577, rptd. Arber with *The Steele Glas* etc.). W. C. Hazlitt wrote a memoir which is prefixed to his ed. of Gascoigne's works. There is a study of *The Life and Writings of George Gascoigne with three poems heretofore not reprinted* by F. E. Schelling included in the *Publications of the University of Pennsylvania* (Vol. II, No. 4, 1893). J. W. Cunliffe contributed an important article on Gascoigne to the C.H.E.L. (III, x), and Sir Sidney Lee's biography in the D.N.B. is very full. There are studies of *The Glasse of Government* by C. H. Herford in E.S. (ix. 201-9), and of 'Gascoigne's *Jocasta*: a Translation from the Italian' by M. T. W. Förster in M.P. (ii, 147-50).

An exhaustive monograph by C. T. Prouty entitled *George Gascoigne, Elizabethan Courtier, Soldier and Poet* was pub. at N.Y. in 1942.

There is a *Concise Bibliography* by S. A. Tannenbaum (N.Y., 1942).

BARNABE GOOGE (1540-94)

Barnabe Googe's orig. poetry is to be found in his *Eglogs, Epytaphes and Sonnettes*, pub. on March 15th, 1563. Edwin Arber ed. this collection for his *English Rpts* (1895). Googe's other works include trs. of *The Zodiake of Life*, a Latin poem by Marcellus Palingenius Stellatus and *The Popish Kingdome*, another Renaissance Latin poem by Thomas Naogeorgus.

JOHN HARINGTON THE ELDER (d. 1562)

Some poems by the father of Sir John Harington, the Elizabethan courtier and writer, were preserved in MS. and printed by the Rev. Henry Harington in his *Nugae Antiquae* (1769, later edd. 1792 and 1804). Some of the MSS. are now in the B.M. These poems include the famous lines addressed to Isabella Markham, dated 1564:

> *Whence comes my love, O hearte disclose*
> *'Twas from cheeks that shame the rose.*

Three of the poems ascribed to the elder Harington are included in Ault's *Elizabethan Lyrics*.

THOMAS HOWELL (fl. c. 1568)

Howell pub. three books of verse: *The Arbor of Amitie*, 1568; *New Sonnets and pretie Pamphlets*, undated but licensed 1567-68, and *H. His Devises, for his owne exercise, and his Friends pleasure* (1581). Only one copy of each of these three books survives. *The Newe Sonets* is at Cambridge and the other two in the Bodleian. All three were rptd. by A. B. Grosart in his *Occasional Issues*, 1879. The *Devises* is the most important of the three vols.: it includes some pieces from the earlier books corrected and rev. It was rptd. in 1906, with a valuable introd. by Sir W. Raleigh.

THOMAS SACKVILLE (1536-1608)

Sackville's extant works consist of his two contributions to *The Mirrour for Magistrates* (see p. 166), his share in *Ferrex and Porrex* (see p. 225), and a single sonnet prefixed to Sir Thomas Hoby's tr. of *The Courtyer* of Castiglione (see p. 188). He appears to have written other poems that have not survived. Jasper Heywood in his tr. of Seneca's *Thyestes* (1560) refers to 'sonnets' by Sackville. His extant works were rptd. in Chalmers's *English Poets*, and separately by C. Chapple (1820), R. Bell (1854), and Reginald Sackville-West (1859), and Sackville-West's ed. contains a valuable memoir including Sackville's extant correspondence. See also D. Davie, 'Sixteenth Century Poetry and the Common Reader: the Case of Thomas Sackville', E.C., April, 1951.

GEORGE TURBERVILLE (? 1540-? 1598)

Most of Turberville's poetry appeared in his *Epitaphes, Epigrams, Songs and Sonets* (1567, ed. J. P. Collier, 1870). He accompanied T. Randolph's embassy to Russia in 1568, and, according to A. à Wood, he pub. in that year *The Places and Manners of the Country and People of Russia*. No copy of this work survives, but three verse epistles written by Turberville to his friends from Russia were printed in his *Tragical Tales* and again by Hakluyt in his *Voyages* (see below, pp. 198-9). Turberville also pub. verse trs. of *The Heroycall Epistles* of Ovid (1567, ed. F. S. Boas, 1928) and *The Eglogs of the Poet Mantuan* (1567; facs. rpt. ed. D. Bush, N.Y., 1937). His principal prose work was the tr. of a collection of *novelle* called *Tragical Tales* (1587), for which, see below, p. 188. He also tr. from Mancinus *A plaine Path to perfect Vertue* (1568) and from the French *The Book of Faulconrie or Hauking* (1575) and *The Noble Art of Venerie* (1575, rptd. as *The Booke of Hunting*, 1908). His poems are rptd. in Chalmers, Vol. II, with a short biography. The fullest account of Turberville is J. E. Hankins, *The Life and Works of George Turberville* (Kansas, 1940). See also H. E. Rollins, 'New Facts about George Turberville', M.P., XV, 1918, and M. P. Pruvost, 'The Source of the *Tragical Tales*', R.E.S., X, 1934.

THOMAS TUSSER (? 1524-80)

Richard Tottel printed for this Suffolk farmer *A Hundreth good points of husbandrie*, in 1557. It was followed by *A Hundreth good points of husbandrie lately married unto a hundrethe good points of Huswifery newly corrected in 1571*. Tusser enl. this book into *Five Hundreth points of good husbandry united to as many of good huswiferie . . . now lately augmented*, pub. in 1573, second ed. 1577. An enl. and rev. ed. of the *Five Hundred Points* appeared in 1580. In 1710 a selection from Tusser was pub., and in 1846 *The last will and testament of Thomas Tusser with a Metrical Autobiography*. The Dialect

Society pub. in 1878 an ed. of *The Five Hundred Points* by Messrs W. Payne and S. J. Heritage. The text is that of the ed. of 1580 collated with those of 1573 and 1577, and the book includes also a rpt. of the first ed. of *A Hundreth good pointes of husbandrie*. There is a delightfully illustrated and produced modern ed. of *Thomas Tusser His Good Points of Husbandry* by Dorothy Hartley (Country Life, 1931).

CHAPTER V

THE TRANSLATORS

COLLECTIONS, GENERAL STUDY AND BIBLIOGRAPHY

THE standard collections are the two series of *Tudor Translations*. The first series (44 vols.) was pub. between 1892 and 1909 by David Nutt under the general editorship of W. E. Henley, the second (14 vols.) between 1924 and 1927 by Constable (London) and Knopf (N.Y.), general editor, Charles Whibley. Various works included in these collections are recorded below under the appropriate headings. Both series are now out of print. The best general study of the trs. is that of Charles Whibley in C.H.E.L. (Vol. III, ch. i). A bibliography containing many errors is appended to this article. *Tudor Translations An Anthology* ed. Clements (Blackwell) is a useful selection, and F. O. Matthiesen's *Translation An Elizabethan Art* (Harvard, 1931) is an excellent critical survey of the most important Elizabethan prose trs.

The standard bibliography of Elizabethan and early Stuart trs. from the classics is the *List of English Editions and Translations of the Greek and Latin Classics* compiled by H. R. Palmer and pub. by the Bib. Soc. in 1911 with an introd. by V. Scholderer.

TRANSLATIONS FROM THE CLASSICS

Pre-Elizabethan versions of Greek Works

The earliest English tr. of a Greek author seems to have been John Skelton's version of the *Bibliotheca Historica* of Diodorus Siculus. This was first pub. from the unique MS. at Corpus Christi College, Cambridge, in two vols. ed. F. M. Salter and H. L. R. Edwards for E.E.T.S. in 1956-57. Sir Thomas Elyot's versions from Isocrates and Plutarch, which appeared in the reign of Henry VIII, were the first English trs. from the Greek to be printed. His English version of the Oration of Isocrates to Nicocles was printed by Berthelet in 1534 under the title of *The Doctrinall of Princes made by the noble oratour Isocrates, and translated out of Greke into English*. About 1535 Berthelet also printed Elyot's tr. of Plutarch's *The Education or bringing up of Children* and *Howe one may take profit out of one's enemyes*.

In 1532 the same publisher printed Gentian Hervet's tr. of *Xenophon's Economicus, or Treatise of Household*, a popular work that was often rptd.

English versions from Aristotle and Thucydides appeared in the reign of Edward VI. John Wilkinson's *The Ethiques of Aristotle* was printed by Richard Grafton in 1547 and *The hystory writtone by Thucidides the Athenyan*, tr. Thomas Nicolls a citizen and goldsmith of London, appeared in 1550. Niether of these books were tr. directly from the Greek, Wilkinson tr. from an Italian version and Nicolls from a French.

The Greek Poets

In the Elizabethan period the chief trs. from the Greek were from Homer, Plutarch, the historians and the authors of the late Greek prose romances. The dramatists, the lyric poets and the philosophers received little attention.

The only Greek plays of which trs. are known to have been made in the Elizabethan and early Stuart periods are *The Phoenissae* of Euripides of which Gascoigne and Kinwhelmersh made a version not from the orig. but from the Italian paraphrase of Dolce (see p. 172) and the *Iphigenia in Aulis* tr. from the Greek by Lady Lumley into English prose. Her MS. version now in the B.M. (Reg. 15. A. ix) was ed. H. H. Child in M.S.R., no. 11, 1909, and by G. Becker in Sh. Jb., xlvi, 1910. No versions from Aeschylus, Sophocles or Pindar appear to have been made. The first English tr. of Homer (except for a few lines quoted by Elyot and Ascham in their works) was Arthur Hall's *Ten Bookes of Homers Iliades*, tr. out of the French, pub. in 1581. George Chapman began his work on Homer with an English version of *Seaven bookes of the Iliades*, pub. in 1598 and *Achilles Shield* from the eighteenth book in the same year. In 1610 he pub. his tr. of the first twelve books of the Iliad, and in 1611 the first complete English Iliad entitled *The Iliads of Homer Prince of Poets. Never before in any language truly translated* ... The first twelve books of Chapman's tr. of the Odyssey appeared in 1614 and the whole twenty-four in the following year: Chapman completed his Homeric trs. by pub. in 1624 *The Crowne of all Homers Workes Batrachomyomachia Or the Battaile of the Frogs and Mice. His Hymns and Epigrams*. There are modern rpts. of Chapman's Iliad and Odyssey in *The Library of Old Authors* (1856), of the Iliad in M.U.L. (1883), of also the Homeric trs. in R. H. Shepherd's ed. of Chapman's works (1874-75), in T.C. (1897) and Newnes's Pocket Classics (1904). The standard modern ed. is *Chapman's Homer* ed. Allardyce Nicoll (2 vols., N.Y., 1956). Chapman's trs. from the Greek include also *The Georgicks of Hesiod* (1618) with commendatory verses by Ben Jonson and the late Greek poem ascribed to Musaeus on Hero and Leander, which he pub. in 1616 under the title of *The divine poem of Musaeus. First of all Bookes*. This version is not to be confused with Chapman's continuation of Marlowe's *Hero and Leander*. Neither Marlowe's poem nor Chapman's continuation can be described as trs. from the Greek.

The only other notable Elizabethan tr. of Greek poetry is *Sixe Idillia* of Theocritus tr. into English verse and pub. anonymously at Oxford in 1588. This version was rptd. by A. H. Bullen in his *Longer Elizabethan Poems* (English Garner).

Greek Prose Works

The most important Elizabethan tr. of a Greek prose classic was *The Lives of the noble Grecians and Romanes* tr. by Sir Thomas North (? 1535-? 1602) from the French version of Jacques Amyot. This book was the main source of Shakespeare's Roman plays. The first ed. was a folio printed in 1579. A second ed. appeared in 1595 and a third in 1603 with fifteen extra lives not by Plutarch, but, if we are to believe the title page, tr. by North. A fourth ed. appeared in 1612, a fifth in 1631 and a sixth in 1656-67 with twenty additional lives. These were all pub. in London. A seventh ed. was printed at Cambridge in 1676. This was the last of the old edd. North's version was then supplanted by other trs. and not rptd. till 1895 when G. Wyndham edited it with a valuable introd. for *The Tudor Translations* (first series). Other complete modern edd. are pub. in T.C. (ed. Rouse) (1898-99) by The Shakespeare Head Press (1928), and by the Nonesuch Press (1929-30). There are many modern edd. of North's Translations of the *Lives* used by Shakespeare. The best is C. F. Tucker Brooke's *Shakespeare's Plutarch* in the *Shakespeare Library* ed. Gollancz, which has a valuable introd. Plutarch's *Moralia* was tr. Philemon Holland (1552-1637), called by Fuller 'The Translatour Generall of his Age'. His version appeared in 1603. Holland, unlike North, tr. from the Greek text. There are modern edd. of this tr. by Joseph Jacobs (1888), F. B. Jevons (1892) and E. H. Blakeney (in Ev. Lib.).

Among the Greek historians the first two books of Herodotus were tr. by a certain B. R. under the title of *The Famous History of Herodotus* (1584). Andrew Lang ed. B. R.'s version of the book called *Euterpe* in 1888 and the whole tr. was ed. for the second series of *The Tudor Translations* by Leonard Whibley (1924). After Nicolls's version (see p. 178) no tr. of Thucydides appeared till the publication of Thomas Hobbes's excellent version of the first eight books made from the orig. Greek in 1629. Hobbes's complete tr. of Thucydides appeared in 1650. Polybius's *History* tr. by Christopher Watson appeared in 1568 and *The Works of Josephus* tr. Thomas Lodge from Latin and French versions in 1602. Xenophon's *Cyropaedia* was englished by W. Barkar or Bercker (? 1560, 2nd ed. 1567) and again by Philemon Holland (1632). A version of the *Anabasis* by John Bingham under the title of *The Historie of Xenophon* appeared in 1623.

Thomas Wilson englished *The Olynthiacs* and *Philippics of*

Demosthenes (1570) (see p. 146) and a certain T. G. pub. a version of the first *Philippic* in 1623.

The three chief Greek prose romances were all englished before the end of the sixteenth century, the *Aethiopian History of Heliodorus* by Thomas Underdowne in an undated ed. (probably 1569), the *Daphnis and Chloe* of Longus by Angel Day in 1587, and *The most delectable and plesant historye of Clitophon and Leucippe* of Achilles Tatius by W. Burton in an undated ed. licensed in 1597. Underdowne's *Aethiopian History* was ed. Charles Whibley for the first series of *The Tudor Translations* and Angel Day's *Daphnis and Chloe* was rptd. with an introd. by Joseph Jacobs in 1890.

Among philosophical and scientific works tr. from the Greek mention may be made of *Aristotle's Politiques or Discourses of Government* tr. by J. D. from a French version (1598), *Marcus Aurelius Antoninus the Roman Emperor his Meditations* tr. from the orig. Greek by Meric Casaubon (1634). *The Manuell of Epictetus* tr. from the French by J. Sanford (1567) are *Epictetus his Manuall* by J. Healey tr. from the orig. Greek (1610), *Certaine Workes of Galen* by Thomas Gale (1586), *The Aphorismes of Hippocrates* by Humfry Lloyd (? 1550), *The Presages of Divine Hippocrates* by Peter Lowe (1597), and *The Elements of Euclid* by R. Candish (? 1560) and again by H. Billingsley (1570).

From Plato no tr. seems to have been made, unless we can count a version of the pseudo-Platonic dialogue called *The Axiochus* which was published in 1592, and is ascribed on the title page to 'Edw. Spenser'. It has commonly been supposed that it is by Edmund Spenser the poet. There is a modern ed. with introd. by F. M. Padelford (Baltimore, 1934).

The Latin Poets

Surrey's English verse tr. from the *Aeneid* (see above, p. 153) marked the beginning of a new era in English verse tr. from the Classics. It should be noted that Surrey's shorter poems also include verse trs. from Horace and Martial.

Thomas Phaer pub. *The Seven First Bookes of the Eneidos of Virgil* in English fourteeners in 1558 and *The Nyne fyrst Bookes of the Eneidos* in 1526. His tr. was completed by Thomas Twyne who pub. the complete *Aeneid* in English verse in 1573. The Phaer-Twyne *Aeneid* was rptd. in 1584, 1596, 1600, 1607 and 1620. Richard Stanyhurst's version of the first four books of the *Aeneid* in 'English Heroical verse' (i.e., hexameters) was pub. at Leyden in Holland in 1582 and at London in 1583. It was rptd. with an introd. by E. Arber in his *English Scholars' Library*.

Early seventeenth-century versions from the *Aeneid* include a complete version by J. Vicars (1632), trs of the first book by G. Sandys (1632), of the second book by Sir T. Wroth (1620), and Sir J. Denham (with part of Book IV, 1636), and of the fourth book by an anonymous author (1622) and Robert Stapylton (1634). Sir Richard Fanshawe's noble version of the Fourth Book of the *Aeneid*, '*On the loves of Dido and Aeneas*' pub. in 1647 with his tr. of Guarini's *Il Pastor Fido*, is the only seventeenth-century version in the Spenserian stanza. It was rptd. with the Latin text and a preface by A. L. Irvine in 1924. Versions of the Eclogues were pub. by G. Turberville (1567), Abraham Fleming (1575), John Brinsley (1620) and John Bidle (1634). No complete English Virgil appeared till 1649, when John Ogilby's tr. was pub. This pedestrian work was replaced by Dryden's great version of 1697. See L. Proudfoot's valuable study, *Dryden's Aeneid and its Seventeenth Century Predecessors* (1960).

Three versions from Ovid appeared early in Elizabeth's reign, *The Fable of Ovid treting of Narcissus* by T. Howell (1560), *The pleasant fable of Hermaphroditus and Salmacis* by T. Peend (1565) and George Turberville's *The Heroycall Epistles of . . . Ovidius Naso in Englishe Verse* in 1567. Arthur Golding pub. his tr. of the first four books of the *Metamorphoses* in 1565 and of the whole fifteen books in 1567. This version was certainly used by Shakespeare. It was rptd. in 1575, 1584, 1587, 1593 (twice) and 1612. There is a modern ed. ed. W. H. D. Rouse in The King's Library. The *Meta-*

morphoses was tr. again by John Brinsley (1618) and George Sandys (first five books 1621, complete version 1626. An elaborate rev. ed. of this popular tr. with commentary appeared in 1632. It reached a 4th ed. in 1656.) For the influence of Sandys's Ovid and his other trs. on English verse and diction see C.H.E.L. VII, iii and G. Tillotson *On the Poetry of Pope* (1938), Chap. III. Thomas Underdowne's version of the *Ibis* appeared in 1569 and Thomas Churchyard's of the first books of the *Tristia* in 1572. Christopher Marlowe's fine version of the *Amores* was probably first printed in 1590 at Middleburgh in Holland and again in 1597 and 1600. An anonymous English version of the *De Arte Amandi* also appeared at Middleburgh probably in 1600, and another of *The Remedie of Love* at London in the same year.

Horace did not appeal to the Elizabethans like Ovid. Ascham's friend Thomas Drant tr. two books of the *Satires* and pub. them under the title of *A Medicinable Morall* in 1566, and in 1567 a complete version of the *Epistles* and *Satires* called *Horace His Arte of Poetrie, Pistles and Satyrs Englished*. Ben Jonson's verse tr. of *Q. Horatius Flaccus: His Art of Poetry* appeared in 1640. Some isolated odes were tr. or adapted by the Elizabethans. The best of these versions are perhaps Campion's of Odes I, 22, 'The man of life upright', and Ben Jonson's of IX, 3, 'Whilst *Lydia*, I was loved of thee'. Many trs. of the *Odes* appeared in the seventeenth century. John Ashmore's *Certain Selected Odes of Horace* of 1621 is the earliest and one of the worst collections. Sir Thomas Hawkins's *Odes of Horace the best of lyric poets* (1625) and Henry Rider's *All the Odes and Epodes of Horace* are not without merit. Sir John Beaumont's *Bosworth Field with a Taste of the Variety of other Poems* (1629) and Sir Richard Fanshawe's *Selected Parts of Horace . . . with a piece of Ausonius and another out of Virgil* (1652) contain some excellent versions. Famous trs. of individual odes were made by Milton, Herrick, Cowley, Sedley and others.

Both Ben Jonson and Campion produced free trs. of Catullus, V. (*Vivamus, mea Lesbia, atque amemus*). Jonson's version is in *Volpone* (III, v.) and Campion's in *A Book of Ayres* (1601).

Marlowe's line for line version of the first book of Lucan's *Pharsalia* in blank verse appeared in 1600. The first complete English version of the *Pharsalia* was that of Sir Arthur Gorges (1614). Thomas May's version of the first three books appeared in 1626 and of the whole poem in 1627. The earliest English version of *Lucretius* is a tr. of the First Book of the *De Rerum Natura* by John Evelyn in 1656. A complete version by T. Creech appeared in 1682. Leonard Digges's *The Rape of Proserpine: Translated out of Claudian* was printed in 1617.

Latin Drama

An undated fragment of an ed. of the *Andria* of Terence with an English tr. by Maurice Kyffin is preserved in the B.M. It is called *Terens in Englysh* and was pub. John Rastell perhaps about 1520. Kyffin's tr. of the *Andria* was rptd. in 1588. Nicholas Udall (see p. 225) pub. a selection from Terence with an English tr. called *Floures for Latine Speaking* about 1533. It was rptd. with additions in 1560, 1575 and 1581. R. Bernard's tr. of all Terence's Plays appeared in 1598 and passed through five edd. by 1643. The only Tudor tr. from Plautus was William Warner's *Menaechmi* of 1595. It was rptd. by J. Nichols in *Six Old Plays* (1779) and in Hazlitt's *Shakespeare's Library* (1875).

Jasper Heywood (1535-98), younger son of John Heywood the dramatist, pub. early in Elizabeth's reign versions of three of the Latin tragedies attributed to Seneca: *Troas* (1559), *Thyestes* (1560) and *Hercules Furens* (1561) (all three ed. de Vocht, Bang, xli, 1913). Alexander Nevyle's version of the *Oedipus* appeared in 1563, John Studley's *Agamemnon* and *Medea* in 1566 (ed. Spearing, Bang, xxxviii, 1913) and T. Nuce's *Octavia* at an unknown date. In 1581 rpts. of these versions were combined with trs. of the *Hippolytus* and *Hercules Oetaeus* by Studley, and the *Thebais* by T. Newton form a complete version called *Seneca his Tenne Tragedies*. The book was rptd. by the Spenser Society in 1887 and again with an important introd. by T. S. Eliot in *The Tudor Translations* (second series). See E. M. Spearing in M.L.R., XV, 1920.

A tr. of a choral passage from *Hercules Oetaeus* in verse was made by Queen Elizabeth and is extant in MS. It is printed in *Anglia*, XIV (1892).

Latin Prose Works

Nearly all the works of the chief classical Latin prose writers were tr. into English during the Tudor period, besides a number of Christian authors. Only some of the most notable of these trs. can be mentioned here. The earliest English version of a Latin prose classic was probably the tr. of Cicero's *De Amicitia* and *De Senectute* by John Tiptoft, Earl of Worcester, printed by Caxton in 1481. In the reign of Henry VIII Robert Whittington pub. versions of *Tullyes Offyces* (i.e., Cicero *De Officiis*) (1533) and *De Senectute* (? 1535). Nicholas Grimald (see p. 154) pub. a version of the *De Officiis* in 1553 and John Dolman of the *Quaestiones Tusculanae* in 1561.

Much attention was paid to the Latin historians. Anthony Cope englished from Livy *The History of Two of the moste noble capitaines of the worlde, Anniball and Scipio* (1544), while Thomas Wilson prefixed to his version of the Olynthiacs of Demosthenes (1570) *The Hystorie of P. Sulpicius Consull according to Titus Livius*. The great Elizabethan Livy, however, is Philemon Holland's complete version of *The Romane History written by T. Livius of Padua*, which appeared in 1600. It was rptd. in 1659 and a selection from it called *Hannibal in Italy* is included in *Blackie's English School Texts* (1905). A complete modern ed. is needed. Holland also tr. *The Roman Historie* of Ammianus Marcellinus (1609) and Suetonius's *The Historie of Twelve Caesars* (1606). The latter was ed. with an introd. by Charles Whibley for *The Tudor Translations*, First Series (1899). There is also a fine rpt. by the Haslewood Press (1931). Alexander Barclay made a version of Sallust's *Jugurtha* which was printed by Richard Pynson about 1520. A much better tr. of the *Two most worthy and Notable Histories* of Sallust by Thomas Heywood appeared in 1608. Sir Henry Savile, the great Elizabethan scholar tr. *Fower bookes of the Histories of C. Tacitus* with the *Agricola* (1598), and in the same year Richard Greneway pub. his version of the *Annals of C. Tacitus* with *the Description of Germany*. An English version of *Iulius Caesars commentaryes* was printed with the Latin text (perhaps by Rastell) as early as 1530. Arthur Golding's tr. of the *Gallic Wars* was first printed in 1565 and was reissued in 1578 and 1590.

The prose works of Seneca appealed to the Elizabethans no less than the tragedies ascribed to him. Robert Whittington's version of the *De Remediis Fortuitorum* appeared in 1547 and Arthur Golding's of the *De Beneficiis* in 1577. Thomas Lodge's complete version of *The Workes of Lucius Annaeus Seneca* first appeared in a folio dated 1614 which was rptd. with corrections in 1720. A tr. from Pliny's *Natural History* called *A Summary of the Antiquities and wonders of the world* made by J. A. (? John Alday) from the French appeared in 1566, and in a slightly abridged version entitled *The Secrets and Wonders of the World* in 1585 and 1587. It was supplanted by Philemon Holland's noble complete version of *The Historie of the World. Commonly called, The Naturall Historie of C. Plinius Secundus* (1601). Apuleius's *The Golden Ass* was excellently englished by William Adlington whose version first appeared in 1566 and was rptd. in 1571, 1582, 1596, 1600 and 1639. There are many modern edd. of this tr. Among them is that of Charles Whibley in the *Tudor Translations*, First Series (1893), another by T. Seccombe (1913), one in the *Abbey Classics* (1922) and a rev. text by S. Gaselee with the Latin orig. in the *Loeb Classics*.

Among trs. of Latin works by Christian authors mention may be made of John Healey's version of St Augustine's *Of the Citie of God* (1610), Sir Tobie Matthew's of *The Confessions* (1620), Thomas Stapleton's of Bede's *The History of the Church of Englande* (1565), Thomas Paynell's of Erasmus's *The Complaint of Peace* (1559), Sir Thomas Chaloner's of the same author's *The Praise of Folly* (1549), Richard Tavener's of *The Proverbes or Adagies* of Eramus (1550), John Bradford's of *The Private Prayers* of Ludovicus Vives, the Spanish humanist (1559) and his *Godly Meditations* (1562), Thomas Paynell's of Vives's *The office and duetie of a husband* (1553), and Philemon Holland's of William Camden's *Britannia*, pub. under the title of *Britain or a Chorographicall description of the most flourishing Kingdomes, Scotland, Ireland* (1610).

TRANSLATIONS OF WORKS IN MODERN EUROPEAN LANGUAGES

Italian Novelle (short stories)

The first English collection of *novelle* tr. from Italian (and other languages) was *The Palace of Pleasure* of William Painter, the first vol. of which containing sixty stories was printed by William Jones in 1566. A second vol. containing thirty-four stories appeared in 1567, followed by another enl. ed. of the first vol. in 1569. A second ed. of the whole work now consisting of one hundred tales appeared in a second ed. of 1575. The complete *Palace of Pleasure* includes stories from classical, Italian, Spanish and French sources. Herodotus, Aelian and Plutarch provide three each. Six are from Livy, one from Tacitus, thirteen from Aulus Gellius, three from Quintus Curtius, sixteen from Boccacio, twenty-six from Bandello (some through French versions), two from Cinthio, two from Ser Giovanni Florentino, one each from Pedro Mexia, Straparola and Masuccio, two from Guevara and sixteen from the Heptameron of Margaret of Navarre. Among the famous stories in this collection are those of Romeo and Juliet, the Duchess of Malfi, and Giletta of Narbonne (the source of Shakespeare's *All's Well that Ends Well*). The whole collection was rptd. by Joseph Haslewood in 1813, by Joseph Jacobs in 1890, and by the Cresset Press in 1929. There is a good modern selection ed. by P. Haworth called *An Elizabethan Story Book* (1928). In 1567 Sir Geoffrey Fenton pub. *Certaine Tragicall Discourses written oute of Frenche and Latin.*

This collection contains thirteen stories of Bandello tr. from the French version of Belleforest. It was included in the first series of *The Tudor Translations* with an introd. by R. L. Douglas. This is probably the book that is strongly condemned by Roger Ascham in Book I of *The Scholemaster*. *The French Bandello: a Selection—the Original Text of Four of Belleforêt's Histoires Tragiques*. Tr. Geoffrey Fenton and William Painter ed. F. S. Hook was pub. in Missouri Univ. Studies, xxii, 1948. George Turberville's *Tragical Tales ... translated ... out of sundry Italians* (1587, rptd. 1837) is a collection of ten stories, six of which are from Boccacio, two from Bandello and two from unknown sources. George Whetstone's *An Heptameron of Civill Discourses* is divided into seven 'Days' and one 'Night'. The stories in it are mainly drawn from the *Hecatommithi* of Giraldi Cinthio. The story of Promos and Cassandra in the 'Fourth Dayes Exercise' is the source of Shakespeare's *Measure for Measure*. It was rptd. in Collier and Hazlitt's *Shakespeare's Library* (I, iii.).

A version of the *Philocopo* of Boccacio by H. Grantham appeared in 1566, and one of his *Amorous Fiammetta* by Bartholomew Young in 1587. It was not till 1620 that the first complete English version of the Decameron appeared. It was anonymous and was entitled *The Decameron, containing an hundred pleasant novels*, rptd. 1625 and 1634 (Vol. I only), *The Model of Wit, Mirth, Eloquence, and Conversation*. It was included in the first series of *Tudor Translations* with an introd. by E. Hilton in 1909.

Other Italian Prose Works

Besides the novelle the other works tr. by the Elizabethans from the Italian dealt chiefly with ethics and conduct. The greatest of the 'courtesy books', Baldassare Castiglione's *Il Cortegiano*, was excellently englished as *The Courtyer* by Sir Thomas Hoby (1561, later edd. 1577, 1588 and 1603). It was rptd. as no. 23 of the first series of *The Tudor Translations* with an introd. by Sir W. Raleigh. A rpt. is now also available in Ev. Lib. with an introd. by W. B. Drayton Henderson. A version of Stephen Guazzo's *The Civile Conversation* appeared in 1586. The first three books are tr. by George Pettie and the fourth by Bartholomew Young. Baptista Giraldo's *A Discourse of Civill Life* was englished by Spenser's friend Lodowick Bryskett. His version was pub. in 1606, but it had been made some time before. Sir Thomas North tr. from the Italian a collection of fables of Indian origin called *The Morall Philosophie of Doni* (1570, rptd. with a valuable introd. by Joseph Jacobs as *The Fables of Bidpai*, 1888). Machiavelli's *The Arte of Warre*, tr. by Peter Whitehorne, appeared in 1560, and Thomas Bedinfield's version of *The Florentine History* in 1593. The earliest English tr. of *The Prince* to be printed was that of E. Dacres, pub. 1640, rptd. with introd. by W. E. C. Baynes, 1929. There were, however, at least three Elizabethan versions which survive in manuscript. Attention was drawn to two of these by N. Orsini in his *Studii nel Renascimento Italiano in Inghilterra* (Florence, 1937). A third came to light at Queen's College, Oxford, after the pub. of Orsini's book. One of these MS. versions, now in a private collection in Los Angeles, is possibly in the handwriting of Thomas Kyd. It was ed. with a valuable introd. by Hardin Craig (Chapel Hill, 1944.)

Italian Poetry

Ariosto's *Orlando Furioso* was first englished by Sir John Harington (1561-1612). His version appeared in 1591. It was rptd. in 1697 and 1634. Robert Tofte's version of the first three books of Boiardo's *Orlando Innamorato* was pub. in 1598. The first attempt to translate Tasso's epic into English was Richard Carew's *Godfrey of Bulloigne* (1594). This was superseded by the much better tr. of Edward Fairfax *Godfrey of Boulogne or the Recoverie of Jerusalem* (1600, rptd. 1624, 1687, 1726 and 1749). There is a modern ed. in M.U.L. (1894). Many Tudor lyrics and sonnets are imitated from the Italian and especially from Petrarch. A MS. version of the *Trionfi* by Henry Parker, Lord Morley, has been preserved and was printed by the Roxburghe Club in 1887. Guarini's *Il Pastor*

Fido was tr. by Edward Dymock (1602). A far superior version of Sir Richard Fanshawe appeared in 1647 and was rptd. in 1664, 1676 and 1692.

Translations from the Spanish

Some notable prose narratives were tr. from the Spanish during this period. As early as 1557 Sir Thomas North pub. *The Diall of Princes*, a version of the *Libro Aureo*, a kind of historical romance by Antonio Guevara, Bishop of Guadix. Pedro Mexia's *The Forest or collection of historyes*, englished by T. Fortescue (1571), was used by Marlowe for his *Tamburlaine*. The famous picaresque novel, *The pleasant history of Lazarillo de Tormez*, ascribed to Diego Hurtado de Mendoza, was tr. by D. Rowland (1571). This version has been ed. with an introd. by J. E. V. Crofts in the Percy Reprints. Anthony Munday tr. two Spanish romances of chivalry, *Palmerin d'Oliva* (1588) and *Amadis de Gaule* (1589). James Mabbe made some notable versions from the Spanish in the seventeenth century. His fine tr. of Rojas's *Celestina* appeared under the title of *The Spanish Bawd* in 1631. It was rptd. in *The Tudor Translations*, first series, with an introd. by J. Fitzmaurice Kelly in 1894, and also in Routledge's *Library of Early Novelists* (1908). He also tr. *The Rogue or the Life of Don Guzman Alfarache* of Mateo Aleman (1623). This is rptd. in the second series of *The Tudor Translations* with an introd. by J. Fitzmaurice Kelly. His version of *The Exemplary Novels* of Cervantes called *Delight in Several Shapes* appeared in 1740. The first English tr. from Cervantes was, however, Thomas Shelton's notable version of *The History of the Valorous and Witty Knight Errant Don Quixote of la Mancha* (first ed. 1612, rptd. 1620). Shelton's *Don Quixote* was rptd. in the first series of *The Tudor Translations* with an introd. by S. Fitzmaurice Kelly.

In 1598 Bartholomew Young pub. his tr. of the pastoral romance *Diana Enamorada* written in Spanish by the Portuguese Jorge Montemayor and the Spaniards Alonzo Perez and Gaspar Gil Polo.

Translations from the French

There was an old tradition of tr. from French into English going back to the Middle Ages. The trs. of John Bourchier Lord Berners made in the reign of Henry VIII belong rather to the medieval than to the Renaissance type of tr., but they had a very great influence during the whole of the Tudor period. Berners probably began by translating a French romance, *The hystory of Arthur of lyttel Brytayne* (earliest extant ed. about 1560, later ed. 1589, rptd. 1812). His great work of tr. was however his version of *The Chronicles of Froissart* (1523-25). This has been rptd. in 1812; in the Globe Series with an introd. by G. C. Macaulay; and in a sumptuous form by the Shakespeare Head Press (1927). His version of the romance of *Huon of Bordeaux* (in which Oberon makes his first appearance in English literature) was printed in 1534 and again in 1570 and 1601. The first ed. was rptd. by the E.E.T.S. in 1883-85 with an introd. by Sir S. Lee Berners, also tr. two Spanish works, probably both from French versions. They are *The Castell of Love* by Don de San Pedro and *The Golden Boke of Marcus Aurelius* from a French version of the *Libro Aureo* of Antonio Guevara, later englished by Sir T. North (see p. 190). There is a selection from Berners's works ed. with an introd. by V. de S. Pinto (1937).

Among Elizabethan trs. from French prose special mention may be made of Thomas Danett's version of *The Historie of Philip de Commines* (1596), rptd. in *The Tudor Translations* first series, with an introd. by Charles Whibley in 1897, and John Florio's classic version of Montaigne's *Essayes* (1603, rptd. 1613 and 1632). There are many modern rpts. of Florio's *Montaigne*. They were ed. by George Saintsbury for the first series of *The Tudor Translations* and are available in T.C., W.C. and Ev. Lib. Florio also tr. from an Italian version Jacques Cartier's narrative of his *Two Navigations* (1580).

English notions of Machiavelli were largely derived from Innocent Gentillet's attack on *The Prince* called *A discourse upon the meanes of well governing and maintaining in good peace a*

Kingdome, or other principalitie, tr. by Simon Patrick (1602). The most considerable French work in verse tr. into English during this period is the *Devine Weekes and Workes* of Du Bartas, the Protestant poet, englished by Joshua Sylvester (first collective ed. 1605-6, later edd., 1608, 1611, 1613, 1633 and 1641). This was a very popular and influential work. For its influence on 'poetic diction' see *On the Poetry of Pope* by G. Tillotson (1938), Chap. III. Many sonnets and lyrics by the French poets of the Pléiade (Ronsard, Du Bellay, Desportes, De Bäif and others) were paraphrased and imitated by Elizabethan poets.

CHAPTER VI

CHRONICLES, ANTIQUARIAN WORKS AND VOYAGES

CHRONICLES

GENERAL STUDIES

THERE are remarks on the Tudor Chronicles in Edmund Bolton's *Hypercritica* (1618; rptd. Spingarn in *Seventeenth Century Critical Essays*, I. 83). The vol. *England* in the series called *The Early Chronicles of Europe*, 1883) by James Gairdner, gives an account of the English Chronicles of the Tudor period. There is a valuable chapter on *Chronicles and Antiquaries* by Charles Whibley in C.H.E.L. (III, xv.)

INDIVIDUAL AUTHORS

ROBERT FABYAN (d. 1513)

Robert Fabyan 'was the first of the citizen chroniclers of London who conceived the design of expanding his diary into a general history' (D.N.B.). The first ed. of his work, *The New Chronicles of England and France*, was printed by Pynson in 1516, again by Rastell in 1533, and again in 1542 and 1559. The standard modern ed. is that of Sir H. Ellis (1811) with biographical and literary preface.

EDWARD HALL (d. 1547)

Hall's *Chronicle* is a much more important work than Fabyan's and a valuable authority for the reigns of Henry VII and Henry VIII. Subsequent chroniclers such as Holinshed and Stow borrowed much from it. It is called *The Union of the two noble and illustrate famelies of Lancastre & Yorke*, the first ed. printed by Berthelet in 1542. A second was printed by R. Grafton in 1548, and the same printer produced a more complete version in 1550. Hall left his work unfinished at his death, breaking off the *Chronicle* at the year 1532. Grafton in his last ed. claimed to have printed his notes for a continuation. It was one of the books prohibited by Mary in 1555, and copies of the early edd. are very rare. There is a standard modern ed. by Sir H. Ellis (1809) and also an excellent ed. of the part dealing with *The Triumphant Reign of King Henry VIII*, with an introd. by Charles Whibley (1904).

GEORGE CAVENDISH (1500-61)

The Life of Cardinal Wolsey, by George Cavendish, may be grouped with the work of the Tudor Chroniclers. Cavendish was gentleman-usher to Wolsey and his biography of his master is one of the most vivid English prose narratives of the Tudor period. It remained in MS. for a long period, though it was fairly well known to writers, and was used by Stow, who printed extracts from it in his *Annales*. A garbled version of it was printed in 1641, and rptd. several times in the seventeenth and eighteenth centuries. It was ed. from the MSS. by Bishop Wordsworth in his *Ecclesiastical Biography* (1810), and more completely with Cavendish's 'metrical visions' by S. W. Singer in 1825. Singer's text was rptd. by H. Morley in M.U.L. (1885). There are many modern edd., including one by F. S. Ellis in T.C.

RAPHAEL HOLINSHED (d. 1580)

The great Elizabethan chronicle called *Holinshed's Chronicle* was the final result of a plan formed early in Elizabeth's reign by a London printer called Reginald Wolfe to publish a universal history and cosmography. Wolfe had inherited the notes of John Leland, the antiquary (see p. 197). Raphael Holinshed, a Cambridge graduate, worked under Wolfe's direction at the English, Scottish and Irish parts of the scheme. Wolfe died in 1573, and three publishers, George Bishop, John Harrison and Luke Harrison, employed Holinshed to continue the histories and descriptions of England, Scotland and Ireland. William Harrison was appointed to help with the descriptive parts of the work, and Richard Stanyhurst (see p. 182) with the history of Ireland, which Holinshed had started with the help of the notes of Edmund Campion, the Jesuit. The work was completed in 1578 and licensed for publication on July 1st. It appeared in that year in two large folio vols., the first of which bears the date 1577. In this work the history of England is carried up to 1575. The first ed. is very rare. A few passages offended the Queen and her council and were excised. These passages have been inserted in a copy of the expurgated ed. in the B.M. (G. 6006, 6007) from a copy of the unexpurgated orig. *The Description of England* is by William Harrison. Holinshed himself wrote *The Historie of England*, drawing freely on the work of previous chroniclers. *The Description of Scotland* is tr. by Harrison from the Latin of Hector Boece, and Holinshed compiled *The Historie of Scotland* from Boece and other Latin writers. *The Description of Ireland* was by Stanyhurst, who used Campion's material, and Richard Hooker supplied the *Historie of Ireland* by translating Giraldus Cambrensis. John Hooker ed. a second ed. with many additions, bringing the history up to 1586. This ed. appeared in January 1586-87. Elizabeth's Council took offence at many passages in it, and it was heavily expurgated, especially in the parts dealing with recent events. Unexpurgated copies are very rare. In February 1722-23 some London booksellers printed a thin folio containing the expurgated portions. This chronicle was the great source for Shakespeare's historical plays and for other Elizabethan dramas. It was rptd. in six vols. in 1807-08. Harrison's *Description of England* from the first two vols. was ed. F. S. Furnivall for the New Shakespeare Society in 1867. In 1896 W. G. Boswell Stone pub. his valuable ed. of *Shakespeare's Holinshed the Chronicle and the Historical Plays Compared*, containing an ed. of the parts of Holinshed's Chronicle used by Shakespeare with notes and parallel passages from the plays. Since then many other rpts. of extracts from Holinshed have appeared. *Holinshed's Chronicle as used in Shakespeare's Historical Plays*, ed. by Allardyce and Josephine Nicoll in Ev. Lib. is particularly useful.

JOHN STOW (? 1525-1605)

John Stow, a London tailor, was a member of the Society of Antiquaries founded by Archbishop Parker, who encouraged his early work. His ed. of Chaucer appeared in 1561, and in 1565 he pub. a chronological epitome of English history called *A Summary of English Chronicles*. He ed. with Parker's aid a number of medieval English chronicles, and in 1580 pub. his own historical work, *The Chronicles of England from Brute ... unto the present Yeare of Christ 1580*. In 1594 it was rptd. as *The Annales of England ... from the first inhabitation ... untill 1592*. His other great work was *A*

Survey of London, pub. in 1598, 'an exhaustive and invaluable record of Elizabethan London' (D.N.B.). Stow pub. a second, enl. ed. of the *Survey* in 1603. Other enl. edd. appeared after his death in 1618 and 1633. It was expanded by Strype in 1720 and 1754. W. J. Thomas pub. a rpt. of the ed. of 1603 in 1842, and Henry Morley another in 1830. The standard modern ed. is that of C. L. Kingsford (Text of 1603 with introd., 1908). There is also a useful rpt. in Ev. Lib.

JOHN SPEED (1552-1629)

John Speed, like Stow, was originally a tailor, but he became a cartographer and antiquary and made various maps and genealogies in the latter part of Elizabeth's reign. In 1611 he pub. a collection of maps called *The Theatre of the Empire of Great Britain*. He was a member of the Society of Antiquaries, where he met Camden, Cotton and other scholars. Encouraged by them he turned to the writing of history and in 1611 pub. as a continuation of *Theatre, the Historie of Great Britaine under the Conquests of ye Romans, Saxons, Danes and Normans ... from Julius Caesar ... to King James*. A second ed. appeared in 1623 (rev. edd. 1625 and 1627), a third in 1632, a rev. ed. in 1650, and an epitome in 1656.

RICHARD GRAFTON (d? 1672)

Richard Grafton was a zealous Protestant, who had been official printer to Edward VI. He printed the second ed. of Hall's *Chronicle* (1548) and wrote an *Abridgment of the Chronicles of England* (pub. 1562), which was intended to expose the inaccuracies of Stow's *Summarie of English Chronicles*. In 1569 he pub. his *Chronicle at large & meere historye of the affayres of Englande*. This book is for the most part a compilation from previous chroniclers and especially from Hall.

ANTIQUARIAN WORKS

MATTHEW PARKER, ARCHBISHOP OF CANTERBURY (1504-75)

Parker, appointed by Elizabeth Archbishop of Canterbury in 1559, was a patron of antiquarian studies, and was himself a great antiquary. He founded the first English Society of Antiquaries in 1572. This society lasted till 1606, when it was dissolved by James

I. Its proceedings were pub. Thomas Hearne in 1720 under the title of *A Collection of Curious Discourses written by eminent antiquaries*. Parker's own chief work was in Latin, a folio entitled *De Antiquitate et Privilegiis Ecclesiae Cantuarensis cum Archepiscopis ejus dem 70*, privately printed at Lambeth in 1572, and perhaps the first book to be privately printed in England. With the help of John Stow he produced the first edd. of the medieval English chroniclers, Gildas, Asser, Florence of Worcester and Matthew Paris. The chief authority for Parker's life is Strype's *The Life and Acts of Matthew Parker, Archbishop of Canterbury* (1711).

JOHN LELAND (? 1506-52)

John Leland, antiquary and writer of Latin verse, pub. little in his lifetime, but left a large number of valuable MSS., some of which are now in the Bodleian. His most interesting Latin poem is his *Naeniae in Mortem Thomae Viati equitis incomparabilis*, an elegy on Sir Thomas Wyatt dedicated to the Earl of Surrey. His great antiquarian work was his *Itinerary*, the MS. of which is in the Bodleian. It was first printed at Oxford in 1710. Later edd. appeared in 1745 and 1770. The standard modern ed. is that of Miss Toulmin Smith (1906-08). Holinshed, Stow and Harrison made extensive use of Leland's *Collectanea* or Antiquarian notes.

WILLIAM CAMDEN (1551-1623)

The chief works of William Camden, the greatest of the Elizabethan antiquaries, are his *Britannia* (1586) and his *Annales* (1615-25). Both are in Latin. *Britannia* is 'a Chorographical description of England, Scotland and Ireland', and the *Annales* is a history of English and Irish affairs in the reign of Elizabeth. The *Britannia* was tr. into English by Philemon Holland, apparently under Camden's own direction. Two edd. of this tr. appeared in 1610 and 1637 respectively. Other trs. are those of R. Gibson (1695) and R. Gough (1789). The *Annales* were originally pub. at Leyden, the first vol. in 1615 and the second in 1625. Later edd. were issued at Leyden, the first vol. in 1639 and 1677. A French tr. of the first vol. appeared in London in 1642, and another of both vols. in Paris in 1627. Abraham Darcy's English tr. of the first part of this French version appeared in 1625, and Thomas Browne's of the second part in 1632. Later English versions appeared in 1635, 1675 and 1688. The whole work is included in White Kennet's

Complete History of 1676. Modern edd. of Camden's works are badly needed. There are important Lives of Camden in Wood's *Athenae Oxonienses*, *Biographia Britannica*, and by Sir E. Maunde-Thompson in the D.N.B.

VOYAGES

GENERAL STUDIES

J. A. Froude's *English Seamen of the Sixteenth Century* (1895) gives a vivid and picturesque account of the great Elizabethan mariners. Sir Walter Raleigh's *The English Voyagers of the Sixteenth Century* is a brilliant study first pub. as an introd. to the Hakluyt Society's ed. of Hakluyt's *Principal Navigations* and afterwards separately in a rev. ed. in 1905. There are two valuable chapters on the subject in C.H.E.L. by Commander C. N. Robinson and John Leyland (IV. iv. and v.) with a useful bibliography.

COLLECTIONS

The Hakluyt Society's publications form the standard English collection of rpts. of accounts of voyages. Its *First Series* consists of 100 vols., its *Second Series* of 73, and its *Extra Series* of 33. These publications include excellent edd. of most of the important contemporary accounts of the voyages of English and foreign travellers in the sixteenth and seventeenth centuries. The valuable prospectus of the Society pub. in 1934 contains a complete list of its publications.

INDIVIDUAL AUTHORS

(The following are only a very few of the numerous writers who dealt with voyages and discoveries during this period.)

RICHARD HAKLUYT (? 1552-1616)

Works

Richard Hakluyt, author of 'the prose epic of the Modern English Nation' (Froude) was a Student of Christ Church, Oxford, and an omnivorous reader of accounts of voyages in

Greek, Latin, Italian, Spanish, Portuguese, French and English. His first publication was *Divers voyages Touching the Discoverie of America* (1582). In 1584 he wrote *A Particular Discourse Concerning Western Discoveries*, which was not pub. till 1887. He tr. the *Journal* of the Frenchman Laudonnière and pub. his version in 1587 as *A Notable Historie concerning fowre Voyages made by certain French captains unto Florida* (1587). In the same year he pub. in Paris a rev. ed. of the Latin *Decades* of Peter Martyr, the Spanish historian of the discovery of the New World. In 1588 he pub. an illustrated account of Virginia. In 1589 appeared the first and shorter version of his great work for which he had been amassing material for years. This version was in one folio vol. entitled *The Principal Navigations, Voiages and Discoveries of the English Nation*. He expanded this book into his masterpiece *The Principal Voyages, Traffiques & Discoveries of the English Nation* in three vols. (1598-1600). Modern edd. appeared in 1809, 1884 and 1903-05. The last is the fine ed. of the Hakluyt Soc., to which Sir Walter Ralegh's essay on *The English Voyages of the Sixteenth Century* was originally contributed as an introd. There is a complete rpt. in Ev. Lib. in 9 vols., with a preface by John Masefield. There are numerous modern selections and rpts. of parts of *The Principal Voyages*. Particular mention may be made of that ed. by E. J. Payne in 2 vols. under the title *Voyages of the Elizabethan Seamen* (1893, rev. ed. by C. R. Beazley, 1907). See also *The Original Writings and Correspondence of the two Richard Hakluyts* ed. C. G. R. Taylor (2 vols. 1935), S. C. Chew, *The Crescent and the Rose* (N.Y., 1937) and R. R. Cawley, *The Voyagers and the Elizabethan Drama* (Boston, Mass., 1938).

Biography and Criticism

There is a biographical and critical study of Hakluyt by Foster Watson in The Pioneers of Progress Series, pub. the Sheldon Press (1924). A lecture on Richard Hakluyt's *Life and Work* given by Sir Clements Markham to the Hakluyt Society was printed in 1896. G. B. Parks's *Richard Hakluyt and The English Voyages* is an elaborate study with many illustrations pub. the American Geographical Society (1928), p. 201.

SAMUEL PURCHAS (? 1576-1626)

Purchas is inferior as a writer to Hakluyt. His works are (1) *Purchas His Pilgrimage* (1617); (2) *Purchas His Pilgrim* (1619);

(3) *Hakluytus Posthumus or Purchas his Pilgrimes* (1625). The last-named book was based partly on Hakluyt's MS. notes, and has been rptd. by the Hakluyt Society in 20 vols. (1905-7)

RICHARD EDEN (? 1521-76) and RICHARD WILLES (fl. 1558-73)

Richard Eden, secretary to Sir William Cecil, was a pioneer in the English literature of discovery and navigations. His works are all tr. His first book was a tr. from the Latin of the German writer Sebasian Münster: *Universal Cosmography. A Treatyse of the Newe India with other newe founde landes and islands* (1553). In 1555 appeared his chief work, a tr. of *The Decades*, which Peter Martyr a Spanish writer had written in Latin concerning the discovery of America: *The Decades of the Newe Worlde or West India, conteyning the Navigations and Conquests of the Spaniards* (1555). Richard Willes pub. a new ed. of this work in 1577 with considerable additions.

SIR HUMPHREY GILBERT (? 1539-? 83)

Sir Humphrey Gilbert's *A Discourse of a Discoverie for a new Passage to Cataia* (1576) is an examination of the arguments in favour of the existence of a north-west passage round America to 'Cataia' or China written in the form of a letter to his brother Sir John Gilbert. It was printed in 1576 (apparently without the author's consent) by George Gascoigne, to whom he lent the MS. (see p. 173) and rptd. in 1940 in *The Voyages of Sir Humphrey Gilbert* ed. D. B. Quinn (Hakluyt Soc.).

SIR JOHN HAWKINS (1532-95), and SIR RICHARD HAWKINS (? 1562-1622)

The elder Hawkins (Sir John) pub. in 1569 *A True Declaration of the troublesome Voyage of M. John Haukins to the Partes of Guynea and the West Indies In the Yeares of Our Lord 1567 and 1568*. A more elaborate work full of interest for students of early navigation is the book by his son Sir Richard Hawkins, *The Observations of Sir Richard Hawkins Knight, in his Voiage into the South Sea, Anno Domini, 1593* (1622).

The Hawkins Voyages have been rptd. by the Hakluyt Society. There is also a fine modern ed. of Sir Richard's *Observations* by A. Williamson (1933).

PHILIP NICHOLS and FRANCIS FLETCHER

These two men, both preachers, seem to have been responsible for the two chief accounts of Drake's voyages. A work called *Sir Francis Drake Revived*, by Nichols, giving an account of Drake's voyages of 1572 and 1573, and according to the title page reviewed by Drake himself appeared in 1628. Francis Fletcher, who was Drake's chaplain, pub. an account of Drake's circumnavigation of the world in his tract called *The World Encompassed* (1628 rptd. 1652). There are modern rpts. by the Hakluyt Society and in the useful vol. called *Three Voyages of Drake*, ed. Lipscott (1936). Fletcher's *The World Encompassed* is also obtainable in a cheap ed. in Blackie's English Texts ed. W. H. D. Rouse.

THOMAS HARIOT (1560-1621)

Thomas Hariot, the distinguished Elizabethan astronomer and mathematician, wrote *A Brief and True Report of the new-found Land of Virginia*, which he pub. in 1588 after his return from a visit to Virginia undertaken at the request of Sir Walter Ralegh. The first ed. of Hariot's book is very rare. It was rptd. by De Bry at Frankfort in 1590, and Hakluyt included it in the third vol. of his Voyages, A facs. ed. by G. Adams was pub. at Ann Arbor in 1931. It is also rptd. in S. Lorant's *The New World* (N.Y., 1946). There is a study of Hariot by Henry Stevens (1900).

SIR WALTER RALEGH (1552-1618)

For Sir Walter Ralegh's writings on voyages, etc., see p. 243.

JOHN SMITH (1580-1631)

Captain John Smith, the famous Virginian pioneer, pub. several works on the colony of Virginia. The most important is *The Generall Historie of Virginia, New England and The Summer Isles* (1624). Smith's works were ed. by Edward Arber in his English Scholars' Library (1884).

CHAPTER VII
LATER ELIZABETHAN POETRY

GENERAL STUDIES

IN addition to the works mentioned on p. 148 see Hallett Smith, *Elizabethan Poetry* (Cambridge, Mass, 1952), C. Ing, *Elizabethan Lyrics* (1951) and M. C. Bradbrook's stimulating and suggestive *Shakespeare and Elizabethan Poetry* (1951). In spite of its title H. J. C. Grierson's *Cross Currents in the English Literature of the Seventeenth Century* (1929) contains valuable criticism of Elizabethan poetry. R. Tuve, *Elizabethan and Metaphysical Poetry* (1947), D. Bush, *Mythology and the Renaissance Tradition in English Poetry* (1932), and J. F. Danby, *Poets on Fortune's Hill* (1952), are valuable studies of special aspects of the subject. For the Elizabethan sonnet, see Janet G. Scott, *Les Sonnets élisabéthains* (Paris, 1929), L. C. John, *The Elizabethan Sonnet* (N.Y., 1938), and J. W. Lever's illuminating study, *The Elizabethan Love Sonnet* (1956).

COLLECTIONS AND MODERN ANTHOLOGIES

Rpts. of many of the Elizabethan poetry books were pub. Edward Arber in *The English Garner* between 1877 and 1896. This work contains a collection of rpts. in prose and verse belonging to different periods. It was re-ed. and the rpts. arranged by subjects by T. Seccombe. This ed. was pub. in 12 vols. in 1903. In this ed. each of the sections contains an introd. by an authority on the particular subject. The relevant vols. are *Some Longer English Poems*, ed. A. H. Bullen, *Some Shorter English Poems*, ed. A. H. Bullen, *Elizabethan Sonnets*, ed. Sidney Lee (2 vols.). The Spenser Society pub. a series of rpts. of the works of Elizabethan poets between 1866 and 1894. A list of the Society's publications was issued with its final report in 1894.

The Poetry of the English Renaissance 1509-1660, ed. J. W. Hebbel and H. H. Hudson (N.Y. 1929) is a useful compendium of Tudor and early Stuart poetry. Modern anthologies are numerous. Among the best are *Elizabethan Lyrics*, ed. Norman Ault (1925), *The Oxford Book of Sixteenth Century Verse*, ed. Sir E. K. Chambers (1932), *A Sixteenth Century Anthology*, ed. A. Symons (1905, rev. ed. 1925), *The Silver Poets of the Sixteenth Century* ed. G. Bullett (Ev. Lib.) and *Elizabethan Lyrics* ed. K. Muir (with valuable introd.). For popular poetry see *The Common Muse* ed. V. de S. Pinto and A. E. Rodway (1957).

LATER ELIZABETHAN MISCELLANIES

The first of the later miscellanies of the Elizabethan period was *The Phoenix Nest . . . set foorth by R.S. of the Inner Temple* (1593). It was rptd. in Park's *Heliconia* (1815), by Collier in his *Seven English Poetical Miscellanies* (1876), by F. Etchells and H. Macdonald as one of *Haslewood Reprints* (1926), and in a scholarly ed. by H. E. Rollins (1931). John Bodenham's *Belvedere or the Garden of the Muses* (1600) is a series of short extracts. It was rptd. in 1610 and for the Spenser Society in 1875. In 1600 *England's Helicon*, one of the finest of the miscellanies, appeared. It includes poems by Breton, Barnfield, Sidney, Spenser, Drayton and others, and contains the earliest text of Marlowe's famous lyric, 'Come live with me and be my love'. A second ed. appeared in 1614. There are modern edd. by A. H. Bullen (1887), Etchells and Macdonald (1925), H. E. Rollins (1935), and H. Macdonald (M.L., 1950). *England's Parnassus* also pub. in 1600 is a poorly ed. collection of snippets from contemporary authors, but contains some notable poetry. Among modern edd. mention may be made of that of E. Arber in *The English Garner* and that of C. Crawford (1913). The last and perhaps the richest of the important Elizabethan miscellanies was *A Poetical Rhapsody containing, diverse sonnets, odes, elegies, madrigalls and other poesies, both in rime and measured verse* (1602), usually known as Davison's *Poetical Rhapsody* from the name of the editor, Francis Davison. Some of the best poems in the collection are by him or his brother Walter. A fourth rev. ed. appeared in 1621. The best modern edd. are those of A. H. Bullen (1890-91) and H. E. Rollins (1932). There is a *Bibliography of English Miscellanies 1521-1750* by A. E. Case (Bib. Soc., 1935).

ELIZABETHAN SONG-BOOKS

A great deal of Elizabethan poetry was pub. in the numerous books of 'ayres', 'madrigals', 'ballets', 'canzonets', etc., which were the result of the great English musical revival of the later sixteenth century. The words printed with the music in these books consists sometimes of stanzas from well-known poems, lyrics, either borrowed or specially written for the occasion, and even sonnets or prose passages. Some of the poetry is of inferior quality, but there is a large quantity of lyrical verse of great delicacy and beauty, mostly by unknown authors. Campion is the most notable poet among the contributors to the song-books, but some of the anonymous contributions are not inferior to his best work. The Elizabethan song-book poetry can best be studied in the following collections: A. H. Bullen's *Lyrics from the Song-Books of the Elizabethan Age* (1887) and *More Lyrics from the Song-Books of the Elizabethan Age* (1889) (rev. ed. 1889, 1891, pocket ed., a selection from the two books, 1913), C. K. Scott's *Euterpe, a Collection of Madrigals and Other Vocal Music of the 16th and 17th Centuries* (Oriana Madrigal Society, 1905 rev. ed. 1925, words and music), and the best modern collection, E. H. Fellowes' *English Madrigal Verse 1588-1632. Edited from the Original Song books* (1920). This work contains a valuable introd. and bibliographical data. *English Madrigal Composers* also by E. H. Fellowes (1921) is the standard modern work on the subject. Editions of the Books of Ayres by Dowland, Campion and other lutanists, with the music, were issued by E. H. Fellowes from 1921; and an excellent selection was made by

Frederick Keel, and issued as *Elizabethan Love Songs* in two parts, 1919. Fellowes gives the lute version of the music, as well as an adaptation for the piano. *La Chanson en Angleterre au temps d'Elizabeth* by Germaine Bontoux (Paris, 1938) is a valuable and exhaustive study. See also Bruce Pattison, *Music and Poetry of the English Renaissance* (op. cit., p. 163) and P. Warlock and P. Wilson, *English Ayres* (6 vols. 1927-31).

INDIVIDUAL AUTHORS

SIR PHILIP SIDNEY (1554-86)

Works

Sidney, greatest of all the poet-courtiers, and, with Spenser, the pioneer of the new poetry of the later Elizabethan period, authorized the publication of none of his works during his lifetime. They circulated, however, in MS. Sidney left three important works: The great sonnet sequence *Astrophel and Stella*, the long prose romance sprinkled with verses called *The Arcadia*, and the famous critical essay called *The Apologie for Poetrie or The Defence of Poesie*. *Astrophel and Stella* was probably begun in 1580, but finished some time after 1581. It was not pub. till 1591, when it appeared with an epistle by T. Nashe, probably the editor. *The Apologie* was probably begun in 1579-80 and finished in 1583-4. It was a reply to a Puritan attack on poetry and the drama by Stephen Gosson called *The Schoole of Abuse*, and was first printed for Henry Olney with the title *An Apologie for Poetrie* in 1595, and again in the same year for William Ponsonby with the title *The Defence of Poesie*. For later edd. see p. 246. The *Arcadia* was written in its orig. form 'in loose sheetes of paper' to amuse Sidney's sister, the Countess of Pembroke, about 1580-2, but was afterwards recast and considerably enl. This rev. version was pub. in 1590 by William Ponsonby. This publisher issued a corrected ed. from MS. material provided by the Countess of Pembroke in 1593 and a third ed. in 1598 with *Astrophel and Stella, The Apologie for Poetrie*, the masque called *The Lady of the May*, and other poems of Sidney. This book was regarded as the definitive ed. of Sidney's works and was often rptd. An ed. of 1621 incorporated a supplement to the third book of the *Arcadia* by Sir William Alexander and an ed. of 1627 includes a sixth book by R. Beling. The orig.

quarto ed. of the *Arcadia* pub. in 1590 was ed. in photographic facs. with a bibliographical introd. by H. Oskar Sommer in 1891. A. Feuillerat in his collective ed. of Sidney's works (1926), printed for the first time the first version of the *Arcadia* which survived in six MS. copies. The same ed. also includes a rpt. of the 1590-93 edd. A tr. of the Psalms by Sidney and his sister was circulated in MS., but not printed till 1821, when it was pub. S. W. Singer. Ruskin included an ed. of it in his *Bibliotheca Pastorum* (1877).

Sidney's *Works*, actually rpts. of the 1598 ed. of the *Arcadia*, etc., were first issued as such in the fourteenth ed. of 1724-5. The standard modern collective ed. is that of A. Feuillerat (4 vols., 1912-6). There are a number of modern edd. of the lyrics and sonnets, including the one vol. ed. of the Poems ed. John Drinkwater (M.L., 1910). There is a good selection in G. Bullett's *The Silver Poets of the Sixteenth Century* (Ev. Lib.).

Biography and Criticism

The earliest life of Sidney was written by his friend Fulke Greville, Lord Brooke, pub. in 1652, rptd. by Sir S. E. Brydges in 1816, and ed. for the Tudor and Stuart Library by Nowell Smith (1907). There are several good modern biographies. The fullest is, perhaps, that of H. R. Fox-Bourne (1862) rptd. in the Heroes of the Nations Series (1891). A useful monograph by M. W. Wallace was pub. in 1915, and another by Mona Wilson in 1931. More recent studies are E. J. M. Buxton's valuable *Sir Philip Sidney and the English Renaissance* (1954) and F. S. Boas, *Sidney his Life and Writings* (1955). See also the excellent French study *Sidney: le chevalier poète élisabéthain* (Lille, 1948).

Critical works are very numerous. A useful bibliography is included in M. S. Goldman's *Sir Philip Sidney and the Arcadia* (Vol. 17 *Illinois Studies in Language and Literature*). R. W. Zandvoort in his valuable work, *Sidney's Arcadia. A Comparison between the two Versions* (Amsterdam, 1928), gives an account of dissertations on Sidney. There is a *Concise Bibliography* by S. A. Tannenbaum (N.Y., 1941).

THOMAS WATSON (1557-92)

Thomas Watson, a poet of no originality but with considerable skill as an imitator of Petrarch and other foreign models, was the first of the Elizabethan poets to make a name as a sonneteer. His first book of verse ῾Ἑκατομπαθία *or Passionate Centurie of Love* appeared in 1582. It consists of a hundred poems described as 'sonnets', though each contains eighteen lines. They are a cento of trs. from Petrarch and other Italian and French writers. Watson acknowledges his borrowing in footnotes. ῾Ἑκατομπαθία was very popular and was much imitated. It was rptd. by the Spenser Society in 1869. In 1590 Watson pub. a tr. of Italian songs called *The First Sett of Italian Madrigalls Englished*, and in 1593 his second sonnet sequence *The Tears of Fancie, or Love disdained*. These sonnets are in the usual fourteen line form, and contain poetry of some merit. They were rptd. in Sidney Lee's *Elizabethan Sonnets* (English Garner, 1904, see p. 202). Watson also pub. a number of Latin poems including a free tr. of the *Aminta* of Tasso, which was tr. into English hexameters by Abraham Fraunce. Watson's English poems, excluding the madrigals, were rptd. by Aber in his *English Reprints* (1870, reissued, 1895).

Accounts of Watson's Life are to be found in the D.N.B. (art. by Sir S. Lee), and in Aber's introd. to his ed. There is an article by Janet G. Scott on *The Source of Watson's 'Tears of Fancie'* in M.L.R., Vol. XXI, 1936. See also M. Eccles, *Marlowe in London* (Harvard, 1934).

EDMUND SPENSER (1552-99)

Works

Spenser's earliest writings to be pub. probably appeared in 1569, when he was still at Merchant Taylors' School. They are some verse trs. from Marot and Du Bellay printed in a little vol. called *A Theatre wherein be represented as wel the miseries & calamities that follow the voluptuous Worldlings, As also the great ioyes and plesures which the faithfull do enioye*. Rev. versions of some of the poems in this collection were included by Spenser in his *Complaints* of 1591. W. J. B. Pienaar contributed a discussion of this vol. to Eng. St., VIII, 1926. Spenser's first great work, the book that marks his appearance before the public as the 'new Poete', was *The Shepheardes Calender, Conteyning twelve Aeglogues proportionable to the Twelve monethes* which appeared in 1579 with the famous prefatory epistle to Gabriel Harvey and commentary by E. K. A second ed. appeared in 1581, and a third in 1586. Its popularity is shown by the fact that it continued to be rptd. up to 1597.

There are many modern edd. Among the best are the photographic facs. pub. for the Spenser Society in 1890, ed. H. Oskar Sommer; the valuable ed. of C. H. Herford (1895) and W. L. Renwick's excellent ed. (1930). J. J. Higgonson contributed a *Study of Spenser's Shepherd's Calendar in relation to Contemporary Affairs* to C.S.E. (1912). The first part of Spenser's great unfinished epic, *The Faerie Queene*, consists of the first three books pub. W. Ponsonbie in 1590. In 1596 Ponsonbie pub. a second ed. of this vol. and also *The Second Part of the Faerie Queene containing the fourth, fifth and sixth bookes*. In 1609 a folio ed. was pub. containing Books I–VI and the noble fragment of Book VII called *Two Cantos of Mutabilitie*, which now appeared for the first time. No other separate ed. of *The Faerie Queene* appeared till 1751. There have been numerous rpts. since then. The standard modern text is that ed. J. C. Smith (2 vols.). Spenser pub. six other vols. of verse. They are (1) *Daphnaida an Elegie upon the death of the Noble and Vertuous Douglas Howard* (1591); (2) *Complaints containing sundrie small Poemes of the World's Vanitie* also pub. in 1591; this vol. includes *The Ruines of Time*, *The Teares of the Muses*, the charming *Virgils Gnat* and *Muiopotmos* (with title page dated 1590) and the verse satire *Mother Hubberd's Tale*; (3) the record of his intercourse with Ralegh and his visit to London in 1589-90 called *Colin Clouts Come Home Againe* (1595). With this poem Spenser also pub. a collection of elegies on his friend Sidney including his own *Astrophill*; (4) the sequence of love sonnets called *Amoretti* with *Epithalamion*, the great ode on his own wedding (1595); (5) the philosophic poems called *Foure Hymnes* (1596); (6) the marriage ode for the ladies Elizabeth and Katherine Somerset called *Prothalamion* (1596). Among modern edd. of these works mention may be made of W. L. Renwick's annotated edd. of *Daphnaida and other Poems* (1929), *Complaints* (1928). There is a Noel Douglas Replica of *Amoretti and Epithalamion* and a useful ed. of *The Foure Hymnes* by Lilian Winstanley with extracts from Ficino, etc. (1907). H. Stein pub. *Studies in Spenser's Complaints* (1934). Spenser's powerful prose tract called *A Veue of the Present State of Ireland* was entered at Stationers' Hall in 1598 but not pub. till 1633. There is a valuable modern ed. (based on the MSS. in the Bodleian and at Caius College, Cambridge) by W. L. Renwick (1934).

Matthew Lownes pub. the first collected ed. of Spenser's works in a folio vol., between 1611 and 1617. Another collected ed. in folio was pub. by J. Edwin in 1679. The first attempt at a critical ed. was that of John Hughes with an interesting and significant introd., pub. in 1715. Among the many subsequent edd. mention may be made of those of H. J. Todd ('Variorum ed.', 1805), F. J. Child (Boston, Mass., 1855), J. Payne Collier (1862), R. Morris and J. W. Hales (1869), the excellent one vol. Oxford ed. by E. de Sélincourt and J. C. Smith with valuable introd. (1912), the Shakespeare Head ed. W. L. Renwick (1930-43). The great variorum ed. of E. Greenlaw, C. G. Osgood, F. M. Padelford and others (10 vols., Baltimore, 1932-49) is a monumental work and indispensable for serious study of the poet. There is a selection ed. W. B. Yeats with a notable introd. for the Golden Poets Series (1906), and another, scholarly selection ed. W. L. Renwick for the Clarendon Series (1923).

Biography and Criticism

A vast literature has grown up round Spenser's life and writings. Much of it is to be found in contributions to periodicals. Guides to it will be found in *A Critical Bibliography of the Works of Edmund Spenser printed before 1700* by F. R. Johnson (1933); *A Reference Guide to Edmund Spenser* by F. I. Carpenter (1923); *A Critical Bibliography of Spenser from 1923-1928* by Alice Parrott (S.P., XXV, 1928); *Edmund Spenser. A Bibliographical Supplement* by D. F. Atkinson (1937); and in the useful *Spenser Handbook* by H. S. V. Jones (N.Y., 1930). Among separate monographs special mention may be made of the following: *Spenser* by R. W. Church (E.M.L.), *Edmund Spenser* by E. Legouis (English tr. 1923), the very able and illuminating study called *Edmund Spenser an Essay in Renaissance Poetry* by W. L. Renwick (1925), *Edmund Spenser a Critical Study* by B. E. C. Davis (1933), E. B. Fowler, *Spenser and Courtly Love* (Kentucky, 1934), E. Greenlaw's valuable *Studies in Spenser's Historical Allegory* (Johns Hopkins Monographs), *That Soveraine light . . . Essays in Honour of Spenser* ed. W. R. Mueller and D. C. Allen (Baltimore, 1952), and the brilliant pages on Spenser's allegory and his conceptions of love and marriage in C. S. Lewis's *The Allegory of Love* (1936). The best biography is *The Life of Edmund Spenser* by A. C. Judson included in the Variorum ed. (1945). See also V. Kostić, 'Spenser's *Amoretti* and Tasso's Lyrical Poetry', R.M.S. III, 1959.

SIR WALTER RALEGH (? 1552-1618)

Ralegh, poet, courtier, explorer, captain of the Queen's guard and historian of the world, was the author of a considerable body of works in verse and prose. His poems appeared casually as commendatory verses in other men's books and in miscellanies. It is extremely difficult to establish either a canon of his authentic verse or a correct text. He contributed commendatory verses to Gascoigne's *Steele Glas* (1576) and a noble sonnet of his was appended with other commendatory poems to the 1590 ed. of the *Faerie Queene*. Other poems by him were certainly printed in *England's Helicon* (1600, see p. 203). They were signed Ignoto, but poems by other authors also appear over this signature, and Warton in his *History of English Poetry* wrongly ascribes them all to Ralegh. He was followed by Sir S. E. Brydges in the first separate ed. of Ralegh's poems pub. in 1829. The poems ascribed to Ralegh by Brydges with other were included in the 1829 ed. of Ralegh's *Works*. In 1845, J. Hannah pub. his ed. of *Poems by Sir Henry Wotton, Sir Walter Ralegh and others* in which, after a careful examination, he ascribes 44 poems to Ralegh. Ralegh's poem on Queen Elizabeth entitled *Cynthia* was long thought to be entirely lost. Hannah, however, discovered a fragment of the 'Twenty-First and Last Book' of it at Hatfield and pub. it in his *Courtly Poets from Ralegh to Montrose* (1870, 1875). The standard modern ed. of Ralegh's poems is that of Agnes M. C. Latham (M.L., 1951).

For Ralegh's prose works and biography and criticism see p. 243.

ROBERT SOUTHWELL (1561-95)

Robert Southwell, the Jesuit martyr, wrote most of his poetry while he was in prison. In 1595 after his execution there appeared two vols. of his verse, *Saint Peter's Complaint* written in the same metre as Shakespeare's *Venus and Adonis* and intended as a counterblast to such profane poems, and *Maeoniae*, a collection of 'excellent poems and spirituall hymnes'. In 1606 appeared *A Foure-Fould Meditation of the foure last things . . . composed in a divine poeme*, by R. S. Of this a unique fragment survives in the B.M. This work which was rptd. by C. Edmonds in 1895 is, however, ascribed to P. Howard, Earl of Arundel, by modern critics.

A collected ed. of Southwell's poems appeared in 1616, *S*.

Peters Complaint and Saint Mary Magdalens Funerall Teares with sundry other selected and devout poems. Modern edd. by W. B. Turnbull appeared in 1856, by A. B. Grosart in 1872 re-issued by D. Stewart in 1876. There are selections by W. Jarold (Hull, 1905), and by C. B. M. Hood, *The Book of Robert Southwell* (1926). There are numerous lives of Southwell mostly written from the religious viewpoint. The best studies are those of M. Bastian, *Robert Southwell* (Geneva, 1931), and the very comprehensive and scholarly work of P. Janelle, *Robert Southwell the Writer* (1935), which contains a complete bibliography.

SAMUEL DANIEL (1562-1619)

Daniel was called by his contemporaries 'well-languaged' and was praised by Coleridge for the purity of his style. His first poems to be pub. were twenty-eight sonnets, which were included in the 1591 ed. of Sidney's *Astrophel and Stella*. In 1592 he pub. his sonnet sequence *Delia* with the monologue called *The Complaint of Rosamond*. The third ed. of this book contains a very much enl. version of the *Complaint* and the fine Senecan tragedy *Cleopatra*. *Delia* has been rptd. in Lee's *Elizabethan Sonnets* (op. cit.) and by Arundell Esdaile in his *Daniel's Delia and Drayton's Idea* (1908). Daniel's most ambitious work was his historical poem on the Wars of the Roses. The first instalment appeared in 1595 as *The First Foure Bookes of the Civile Wars*; a fifth book followed in the same year, a sixth in 1601 and the complete work in 1609. In 1605 he pub. *Certaine Small Poems . . . with the Tragedie of Philotas*. This vol. contains his best known lyric *Ulisses and the Syren*. He also pub. various masques and complimentary poems. His famous prose essay, *A defence of Ryme*, appeared in 1603 and his *Whole Works in Poetry* in 1623. His complete works ed. A. B. Grosart appeared in 1885-96. There is a selection of the poetry of Samuel Daniel and Michael Drayton, ed. H. C. Beeching (1899) and Daniel's *Poems* with *A defence of Ryme* were ed. A. C. Sprague (Harvard, 1930, reissued London, 1950). *The Tragedy of Philotas* ed. L. Michel was pub. in 1949.

Biography and Criticism

There is an article by Sir S. Lee on Daniel in the D.N.B., and half a chapter by H. Child in C.H.E.L. A bibliography by A. Sellers has been pub. in O.B.S., II, 1927-30.

Two American dissertations have been pub. in abstract; they are *Samuel Daniel a Critical Study* by G. K. Brady (Urbana, 1926) and *Samuel Daniel's relation to the Histories and Histocrial Poetry of the Sixteenth Century* by J. H. Roberts (University of Chicago Abstracts of Theses, 1923-4). There is a full bibliography (including letters) by H. Sellers (O.B.S., 1928) and a *Concise Bibliography* by S. A. Tannenbaum (N.Y., 1942).

MICHAEL DRAYTON (1563-1631)

Drayton was one of the most industrious and also one of the most unequal of Elizabethan poets. His long literary career covered forty years, and during that period he attempted nearly all the chief types of non-dramatic poetry used in the Elizabethan age. His first work was a collection of rather dull religious poems called *The Harmonie of the Church* (1691). He then turned his attention to the writing of historical 'legends' in the manner of *A Mirror for Magistrates* (see pp. 165-7) and produced *Piers Gaveston, Earl of Cornwall* and *Matilda the faire and chaste daughter of Lord R. Fitzwater* (1594). These were rptd. in 1596 with *The Tragical Legend of Robert Duke of Normandy*. In 1594 Drayton had also pub. his famous sonnet sequence, *Ideas Mirrour*, containing fifty-one sonnets. This collection was very popular: it went through 11 edd. by 1631. Drayton constantly revised it by dropping some sonnets and adding new ones. Some of the best appear for the first time in the ed. of 1619. These include the famous sixty-first, 'Since there's no helpe, Come let us kisse and part'. In 1596 Drayton produced his historical epic, *Mortimeriados the lamentable Civill Wars of Edward the Seconde and the Barons*. Later he rewrote it expanding his seven line (rime royal) stanzas to ottava rima, and pub. the new version with his historical verse epistles called *England's Heroicall Epistles* in 1603. *England's Heroicall Epistles* was one of the most successful works. It passed through many edd. and continued to be rptd. down to the eighteenth century. Among his later vols. of verse the most important are (1) *Poems Lyrick and Pastorall, Odes, Eglogs, the Man in the Moone* of 1605 containing some of his best lyrics such as *To the Virginian Voyage* and *The Ballad of Agincourt*. (2) *Poly-Olbion, a Chorographicall Description of the Tracts, Rivers, Mountains . . . of this renowned Isle of Great Britaine* (1612), Drayton's famous topographical poem, inspired largely by Camden's *Britannia* (see

p. 197); a second enl. ed. appeared in 1622. (3) *The Battaile of Agincourt* (not to be confused with Drayton's ballad on the same subject) pub. with the delightful fairy poem, *Nimphidia* and the lovely pastoral, *The Shepheards Sirena* containing the lyric, 'Neare to the Silver Trent, Sirena dwelleth', in 1627. Drayton pub. several edd. of his collected works. The first appeared in 1605, others in 1608, 1610, 1613, 1619, 1630 and 1637. Robert Dodsley pub. an ed. in folio in 1748 (2nd ed. 1753). The best modern ed. is that of the complete works, started in 1931 by J. W. Hebel, and completed in 1941 by Kathleen Tillotson and Bernard H. Newdigate (5 vols.). Selections were pub. A. H. Bullen (1883) and H. C. Beeching (1899). *The Minor Poems*, ed. C. Brett (1907), is a convenient small ed. There are many rpts. of separate works. Vol. 47 of M.U.L. included *The Baron's Wars, England's Heroicall Epistles*, and *Nimphidia*. The Spenser Society pub. a facs. of Poly-Olbion and edd. of *The Muses Elisium* and the *Poems* of 1605. Arundell Esdaile's ed. of Daniel's *Delia* and Drayton's *Idea* (1907) is of great value. *Poems* ed. J. Buxton, 2 vols. (M.L., 1953), is a full and valuable selection.

Biography and Criticism

The best critical study of Drayton is Oliver Elton's, first pub. the Spenser Society in 1895 as an *Introduction to Michael Drayton*, and in a rev. ed. in 1905 under the title *Michael Drayton*. There is a chapter in C.H.E.L. by H. Child, a short article in the D.N.B. by A. H. Bullen, and a valuable monograph by B. H. Newdigate entitled *Michael Drayton and his Circle* (1941). See also *Drayton's Secondary Modes: a Critical Study* by G. P. Haskell (Urbana, 1936) and 'Drayton' by M. Praz in Eng. St., xxviii, 1947. There is a *Concise Bibliography* by S. A. Tannenbaum (N.Y., 1948).

WILLIAM DRUMMOND OF HAWTHORNDEN (1585-1649)

William Drummond was the most notable Scottish poet of the later Renaissance. In 1612 he pub. *Teares on the Death of Meliades*, a vol. of elegies on the death of Prince Henry, rptd. 1613, 1614, and in 1616 in a vol. with other verses called *Poems: Amorous, Funerall, Divine, Pastorall in Sonnets, Songs, Sextains, Madrigals*. In 1617 he celebrated the visit of King James to Scotland in the courtly poem called *Forth Feasting*. His religious poems *Floures of*

Sion with the fine prose essay *A Cypress Grove* appeared in 1623. It is significant in view of the Miltonic quality of much of Drummond's work that the first collective ed. of his poems was pub. Milton's nephew Edward Phillips in 1656. The best modern ed. of Drummond's Works is that of L. E. Kastner (Manchester, 1913).

When Ben Jonson visited Drummond in 1619, the Scottish poet made copious and extremely interesting notes of his conversation. Drummond's orig. MS. of the 'conversations' has perished, but a transcript was made by Sir R. Sibbald at the beginning of the eighteenth century and first printed in 1833 by D. Laing in *Archaelogia Scotica*. The best modern ed. is that of Herford and Simpson in their ed. of *The Works of Ben Jonson* (I, 128-178).

The best modern study of Drummond is F. R. Fogle, *A Critical Study of Drummond* (N.Y., 1952).

GILES FLETCHER THE YOUNGER (1588-1623), and PHINEAS FLETCHER (1582-1650)

These two Cambridge poets were among the principal disciples of Spenser and their work forms a link between Spenser and Milton. Giles's chief poem was the religious epic *Christ's Victorie and Triumph in Heaven, and Earth, over and after Death* (1610). Phineas's most notable work was his allegorical poem, *The Purple Island or the Isle of Man*, pub. in 1633 with his 'piscatorie eclogs'. The best modern ed. of the works of Giles and Phineas Fletcher is that of F. S. Boas (1908). Phineas Fletcher's *Venus and Anchises* (*Brittain's Ida*) is also available in an ed. by E. Seaton. An ed. of Giles Fletcher's *Complete Poems* ed. D. C. Sheldon was pub. at Madison in 1938.

FULKE GREVILLE, LORD BROOKE (1554-1628)

Fulke Greville, the friend of Sidney, and the poet admired by Charles Lamb, pub. during his lifetime a few poems in the miscellanies, and his *Tragedy of Mustapha* in 1609. In 1633 appeared *Certaine learned and elegant works by the Right Honorable Fulke Greville, Lord Brooke*, containing his two tragedies *Mustapha* and *Alaham*, and other poems, including the sonnet seqeunce *Caelica*. In 1652 his *Life of Sidney* was pub. and in 1670 a vol. of his *Remains*. A. B. Grosart's ed. of Fulke Greville's works in his *Fuller's Worthies Library* is a most unsatisfactory production. The standard modern ed. is *Poems and Dramas of Fulke Greville First Lord Brooke* ed. G. Bullough (2 vols., 1939). An ed. of *Caelica* by U. Ellis Fermor was pub. by the Gregynog Press in 1936. There is a University of Pennsylvania dissertation on his works by Morris W. Croll (1903), an article in M.L.R. by Geoffrey Bullough (Vol. XXVIII, 1933) and an important essay on 'Religion et raison d'état dans l'œuvre de Greville', by J. Jacquot in *Études anglaises*, V, 1952.

CHRISTOPHER MARLOWE (1564-93)

Marlowe's most important non-dramatic poem is the fragment of *Hero and Leander*, of which he completed two 'sestiads', entered for publication in 1593, but not printed till 1598, when they appeared in two edd., in one separately and in the other with Chapman's continuation (see below). The famous lyric called *The passionate Shepherd to his love* was first printed in its complete form in *England's Helicon* (1600); a garbled version had appeared in 1599 in *The Passionate Pilgrim* (see p. 256). Izaak Walton, who quotes it in his *Compleat Angler* (1653) calls it 'the smooth song which was made by Kit Marlowe, now at least fifty years ago'. There is also an interesting MS. version in the Thornborough Commonplace Book. The fragment of twenty-four lines in ottava rima, ascribed to Marlowe in *England's Parnassus* and included in all the modern edd. of his poems, was shown by John Crow in an article contributed to T.L.S., January 4th, 1947, to be an extract from a poem called *Devereux* by Jervis Markham pub. in 1597. For Marlowe's trs. from Ovid and Lucan see pp. 183-4 and for his plays, and biography and criticism see below, pp. 228-30. Marlowe's poems are included in Tucker Brooke's one vol. ed. of his works (1910). The best separate ed. is that of L. C. Martin in the Methuen Marlowe (1931). There is a selection of the Poems ed. F. Marnam (1948).

GEORGE CHAPMAN (c. 1560-1634)

Chapman was a powerful, though difficult and recondite poet as well as a dramatist and translator. In some respects his poetry anticipates that of the 'Metaphysical school' (see p. 293). His chief original poems are Σκιὰ Νυκτός. *The Shadow of Night: containing two Poeticall Hymnes* (1594), *Ovids Banquet of Sense. A Coronet for his Mistresse Philosophie, and his amorous Zodiacke* (1595) and *Euthymiae Raptus; or the Teares of Peace* (1609). All these are rptd. in *Shakespeare and the Rival Poet* by A. Acheson (1903). Chapman ed. Marlowe's *Hero and Leander* and completed it by adding four 'sestiads' to Marlowe's original two. Chapman's continuation is a notable poem, but it lacks the clarity and music of Marlowe's work. Chapman's poems are included in R. H. Shepherd's ed. of his *Works* (1874-75). A separate ed. of *The Poems of George Chapman* ed. Phyllis B. Bartlett was pub. 1938 (P.M.L.A.). For Chapman's trs. from Greek poets see pp. 178, 179. For his plays, and biography and criticism see pp. 309-10.

BEN JONSON (1572-1637)

For Ben Jonson's non-dramatic poems see p. 306.

THOMAS CAMPION (1577-1620)

Thomas Campion, physician, musician, critic, and one of the most exquisite lyric poets of the Elizabethan age, seems to have been forgotten from the time of his death, until he was rediscovered by A. H. Bullen in the latter part of the nineteenth century. Most of his poetry appeared in a series of song books: *A Book of Ayres Set foorth to be song to the Lute, Orpherian and Base Violl*, by P. Rosseter (1601), *Two Bookes of Ayres* (1613), and the *Third and Fourth Books of Ayres . . . composed by Thomas Campian* (? 1617). Both words and music in the last two vols. are by Campion. *Songs of Mourning* on the death of Prince Henry (1613) contains words by Campion and music by John Coprario. His *Observations on the Arte of English Poesie* (see p. 246) appeared in 1602. It contains, among examples of unrimed lyric, the famous song, 'Rose cheekt, Laura come'. Campion also pub. a beautiful masque in honour of the marriage of Lord Hayes (1607) and other similar court entertainments. His works were first collected and pub. A. H. Bullen in 1889. The best modern edd. are those of S. P. Vivian (small ed. in M.L., 1907, and larger and more scholarly ed., 1909).

There is a biographical introd. to Vivian's edd. and a chapter on him by the same writer in C.H.E.L., IV, viii. There is a critical study by T. Macdonagh entitled *Thomas Campion and the Art of English Poetry* (Dublin, 1913). See also M. M. Kastendieck, *England's Musical Poet, Campion* (N.Y., 1938) and the notable critical survey of Campion's poetry in C. S. Lewis, *English Literature in the Sixteenth Century*, op. cit., pp. 552-57.

WILLIAM BROWNE OF TAVISTOCK (1591-1643)

William Browne of Tavistock was a Spenserian poet who kept the late-Elizabethan literary tradition alive in the early seventeenth century. He began his literary career with an elegy on Prince Henry pub. in 1613. The first book of his best-known work *Britannia's Pastorals* was pub. in 1613 and the second in 1616. In 1925 the two books appeared in one vol. A third book remained unpublished till the MS. was discovered in the library of Salisbury Cathedral in the nineteenth century. It was printed for the Percy Society in 1852, and was included in W. C. Hazlitt's ed. of Browne's works. Browne contributed seven eclogues to the collection called *The Shepherd's Pipe*, pub. 1614. He also composed an *Inner Temple Masque* performed on January 13th, 1614-15. A number of his shorter poems are preserved in the Lansdowne MSS. They include sonnets to Caelica, Visions modelled on Du Bellay, Epistles, Elegies and Epitaphs. One of the epitaphs is the famous poem on the Countess of Pembroke, Sidney's sister, 'Underneath this sable hearse', which has been attributed to Ben Jonson and others, but is almost certainly by Browne. The poems in the Lansdowne MS. were first printed by Sir Egerton Brydges in 1815. In 1772 T. Davies pub. a collection of Browne's work in 3 vols. W. C. Hazlitt's ed. (2 vols, 1868-9) includes a memoir. There is a useful modern ed. by Gordon Goodwin (M.L., 2 vols., 1894) with a valuable introd. by A. H. Bullen, who also contributed an article on Browne to the D.N.B. F. W. Moorman's *William Browne, his Britannia's Pastorals and the Pastoral Poetry of the Elizabethan Age*, a doctoral dissertation pub. at Strassburg in 1897, is an illuminating study, which should be rptd. Both Milton and Keats studied *Britannia's Pastorals* carefully, and owe something to Browne. See also the articles by J. Grundy on 'Tasso, Fairfax and Browne' in R.E.S., N.S., iii, 1952, and 'Browne and Italian Pastoral', ibid., iv, 1953.

BALLADS

Popular ballad poetry was a prominent feature of English life both in town and country throughout the sixteenth and seventeenth centuries. Printed 'broadside' ballads, such as those hawked by Shakespeare's Autolycus, survive in large numbers. There are important collections in the B.M., at the Library of the Society of Antiquaries and at Magdalene College, Cambridge. This popular poetry of the Tudor and Stuart periods may be studied in *The Roxburgh Ballads* (9 vols., The Ballad Society, 1869-99), *The Shirburn Ballads* ed. A. Clark, and *A Pepysian Garland* and *Old English Ballads* both ed. H. E. Rollins. See also A. Esdaile, *Autolycus's Pack* (1940), and V. de S. Pinto and A. E. Rodway, *The Common Muse* (1957).

CHAPTER VIII
TUDOR DRAMA UP TO SHAKESPEARE

GENERAL STUDIES

(This section includes General Studies for Chapter XIV.)

THE standard works for the history of the drama during the period are F. E. Schelling, *The Elizabethan Drama, 1558-1642*, 2 vols. (Boston, 1908), and W. Creizenach, *The English Drama in the Age of Shakespeare*, 5 vols. (Eng. tr. 1916). Useful shorter studies are F. S. Boas, *An Introduction to Tudor Drama* (1933) and *An Introduction to Stuart Drama* (1946), A. W. Reed, *Early Tudor Drama* (1926), U. Ellis Fermor, *Jacobean Drama, an Interpretation* (1936), A. Harbage, *Cavalier Drama* (1936), F. T. Bowers, *Elizabethan Revenge Tragedy, 1587-1642* (Princeton, 1940), M. C. Bradbrook, *Themes and Conventions of Elizabethan Tragedy* (1935) and *The Growth and Structure of Elizabethan Comedy* (1956), Willard Farnham, *The Medieval Heritage of Elizabethan Tragedy* (Berkeley, California, 1937), A. P. Rossiter, *English Drama from Early Times to the Elizabethans* (1950), and P. Simpson, *Studies in Elizabethan Drama* (1955). For valuable and stimulating criticism see also T. S. Eliot, *Elizabethan Essays* (1936). Bibliographical information will be found in W. W. Greg's invaluable *A List of English Plays written before 1643 and published before 1700*, 4 vols. (Bib. Soc., 1900) and the supplement containing *A List of Masques, Pageants etc.* (1902), and in A. Harbage, *Annals of English Drama, 975-1700* (Philadelphia, 1940).

The standard works on the history of the theatre are E. K. Chambers, *The Medieval Stage*, 2 vols. (1903) and *The Elizabethan Stage*, 4 vols. (1923), and for later period G. E. Bentley, *The Jacobean and Caroline Stage*, 5 vols. (1941-56). See also A. H. Thorndike, *Shakespeare's Theater* (N.Y., 1916), J. Q. Adams, *Shakespearean Playhouses* (Boston, 1917), W. J. Lawrence, *Pre-Restoration Stage Studies* (Boston, Mass., 1927),

M. C. Bradbrook, *Elizabethan Stage Conditions* (1932), J. Isaacs, *Production and Management at the Globe Theatre* (Shakesp. Assoc., 1933), C. W. Hodges, 'Unworthy Scaffolds ... Elizabethan Playhouses' in *Shakespeare Survey*, 3 (1950), J. le G. Brereton, 'The Elizabethan Playhouse' in his *Writings on Elizabethan Drama* ed. R. G. Howarth (Melbourne, 1948) and B. L. Joseph, *Elizabethan Acting* (1951). *Henslowe's Diary* (1904-8) and *Henslowe Papers* (1907), both ed. W. W. Greg, are valuable records of the activities of Philip Henslowe, one of the chief Elizabethan theatrical managers, containing much information about plays, actors and playwrights. Equally important for theatrical information is *Dramatic Documents from Elizabethan Playhouses* ed. W. W. Greg, 2 vols. (1931). See also C. J. Sisson, *The Lost Plays of Shakespeare's Age* (1936) and *Essays on Shakespeare and the Elizabethan Drama in Honor of Hardin Craig* ed. R. Hosley (Missouri, 1962).

COLLECTIONS AND ANTHOLOGIES

There are many old and modern collections of plays. The oldest is that of R. Dodsley, orig. pub. 1744 in 12 vols. and re-ed. three times; by I. Reed in 1780 (12 vols.); by I. Reed and J. P. Collier (1825-27, 12 vols.); and by W. C. Hazlitt (1874-76, 15 vols.). None of the edd. of Dodsley provides reliable texts. Richard Simpson's *The School of Shakespeare* (3 vols.) appeared in 1878, and A. H. Bullen's *Collection of Old English Plays* in 1882-85 (4 vols.). The series of Temple Dramatists consisting of single plays by various authors was pub. between 1896 and 1905. J. M. Manly's *Specimens of Pre-Shakespearian Drama* (1897) is an extremely valuable collection. Professor W. Bang of Louvain began in 1902 the publication of his scholarly series of edd. of English Tudor and Stuart plays called *Materialien zur Kunde des älteren englischen Dramas*. This publication continued till 1914 when 44 vols. had appeared. The series was continued and completed by Professor H. de Vocht in a new issue begun in 1927. The *Malone Society's Reprints*, started in 1907 under the general editorship of W. W. Greg is a valuable series of scholarly edd. of plays of the sixteenth and seventeenth centuries. A series of photographic facs. of single plays ed. S. S. Farmer, called *Tudor Facsimile Texts*, appeared between 1907 and 1914. *Representative English Comedies* is a useful and scholarly selection in 4 vols., containing representative plays with monographs: vol. 1, *Pre-Shakespearian Comedies* ed. C. M. Gayley; vols. 2 and 3, *Comedies of the Late Sixteenth and Early Seventeenth Centuries* ed. C. M. Gayley; vol. 4, *Restoration Comedies* ed. Gayley and Thaler. Among modern 1-vol. collections are *The Chief Elizabethan Dramatists excluding Shakespeare* ed. W. J. Neilson, the very useful *Pre-Shakespearian Dramas* ed. J. Q. Adams, *Elizabethan Tragedy* ed. G. H. Rylands, *Five Elizabethan Comedies* ed. McIlwraith (W.C.), *Five Pre-Shakespearean Comedies* ed. F. S. Boas (W.C.), *Early Plays from the Italian*, ed. R. Warwick Bond (1911), *Early English Classical Tragedies*, ed. J. W. Cunliffe (1912), and the two useful vols in Ev. Lib. *Minor Elizabethan Drama, Tragedies* and *Comedies*, ed. Thorndike. The most famous anthology of extracts from the plays is Charles Lamb's *Specimens of the English Dramatic Poets* (orig. ed. 1808, modern ed. by E. V. Lucas), a collection notable not only for the fine taste with which extracts are chosen, but also for the notes which contain some of Lamb's best criticism. A. W. Pollard's *English Miracle Plays* (1914) includes useful annotated selections from the Tudor Interludes.

INDIVIDUAL AUTHORS AND PLAYS

The Tudor Interlude

There is no sharp line of demarcation between the 'moralities' of the fifteenth century and the 'interludes' of the early Tudor period. Both terms were applied at an early date to allegorical plays. In the early Tudor period the word 'interlude' came to be used more and more for shorter plays composed for production at court or in the halls of great houses. For the derivation and use of 'interlude' see Chambers's *Medieval Stage*, ii, 181-3. The circumstances in which the typical interlude was performed are well illustrated by the fourth act of the Elizabethan play *Sir Thomas More* (see below p. 259).

A feature of the early Tudor interludes is the disappearance of the religious element that characterized the late medieval moralities; it is often replaced by attempts at intellectual edification reflecting the new desire for secular learning. A whole group of interludes are affected by humanistic influences. The earliest are those of Henry Medwall, chaplain to Cardinal Morton, in whose household Sir T. More was brought up. Medwall's two extant plays are *Nature* and *Fulgens and Lucres*, both probably written in the reign of Henry VII. He is also said to have written a play called *The Fynding of Truth*. *Nature* is simply a morality adapted to the new educational interests. A single copy of an undated ed. is in the B.M. There is a facs. by J. S. Farmer. *Fulgens and Lucres*, a much more interesting work, is founded on an Italian story in humanistic Latin, and is the earliest example of a purely secular English play. A single copy of an ed. printed between 1513 and 1519 was discovered in 1919 and is now in the Henry Huntington Library. There is a fragment of another copy in the B.M. It has been carefully ed. by F. S. Boas and A. W. Reed (1926) and is included in *Five Pre-Shakespearean Comedies* ed. F. S. Boas. John Rastell, brother-in-law of Sir T. More, was author of *The Nature of the Four Elements*, printed by Rastell himself in 1520. It is definitely of an educational character and refers to the voyages of Vespucci and Cabot. There is a facs. by J. S. Farmer and it is included in Hazlitt's *Dodsley*.

John Redford's *Wyt and Science*, another educational interlude, remained in MS. till it was printed by J. O. Halliwell-Phillipps in 1848. There are edd. in Hazlitt's *Dodsley*, Farmer's '*Lost*' *Tudor Plays* (1907), and Adams. *The World and the Child* (first printed 1522) shows the use of the old morality plot for entirely new purposes. It was rptd. in Hazlitt's *Dodsley*, in Manly and facs. by Farmer.

The interludes were also used as propagandist weapons in

the religious and political controversies of the reign of Henry VIII. Among the propagandist plays mention may be made of *Hycke Scorner* (printed by Wynkyn de Worde, n.d.), a Romanist play, ed. Hazlitt's *Dodsley* and facs, by Farmer, and *Lusty Juventus*, an anti-popish play with two fine songs (three early edd. all undated, ed. Hazlitt's *Dodsley*, facs. by Farmer; there is an interesting adaptation of this interlude in the Elizabethan play of *Sir Thomas More*).

Later propagandist plays are the five interludes by John Bale, Bishop of Ossory (1495-1563), anti-popish works, the most interesting of which is *Kynge Johan*, not an early chronicle play as might be expected, but an interlude in which quasi-historical material is used for anti-catholic propaganda (MS. at Chatsworth, edd. in Bang and Manly, selection in Pollard). See J. W. Harris, *Bale: A Study in the Minor Literature of the Reformation* (Urbana, 1940), and W. T. Davies, *A Bibliography of Bale* (O.B.S., 1939 and 1947).

John Skelton, the poet (? 1460-1529) was the author of several plays of which only one survives. This is *Magnyfycence*, a political allegory probably referring to Wolsey. The orig. ed. was printed by J. Rastell about 1533. It has been rptd. by the E.E.T.S. (1908), facs. by Farmer and selection in Pollard. A fragment of another morality by Skelton called *Good Order* was ed. G. L. Frost and R. Nash in S.P. XLI, 1944, and rptd. in Collections, IV, of the Malone Soc., 1956.

The most famous author of interludes and the most interesting English dramatist of the early Tudor period was John Heywood (? 1497-1580), who married Sir T. More's niece and was a prominent member of More's circle. It is possible that More had a hand in Heywood's plays, Heywood's simplest and probably his earliest plays are mere dialogues in the style of the medieval *débats*, such as *Wytty and Wytless* (MS. in the B.M., facs. by Farmer) and *A Play of Love* (printed by W. Rastell, 1534, facs. by Farmer). His characteristic works, however, are four brilliant little plays which combine something of the old allegory with a great deal of vivid realism and owe much to Chaucer and to the French farces. They are *A mery Play between Johan, Johan the husbande Tyb his wyfe and Sir John the preest* (printed by W. Rastell, 1533, ed. by A. W. Pollard in R.E.C. Vol. i, and rptd. in Adams, facs. by Farmer); *A mery Play betweene the pardoner and the frere, the curate and neybour Pratte* (printed by W. Rastell, 1533, rptd. Hazlitt's *Dodsley*, facs. by J. S. Farmer); *A new and very mery enterlude of all maner wethers* (usually called the *Play of the Weather*), printed by W. Rastell, 1533, ed. A. W. Pollard in R.E.C. Vol. i, and rptd. in Adams; *The playe called the foure PP. A newe and very mery interlude of A palmer, A pardoner, A potycary, A pedlar* (early edd. 1545, 1555, 1569, rptd. in all edd. of *Dodsley*, in Manly and Adams, facs, by Farmer).

A complete ed. of Heywood's plays (in modernized spelling) by J. S. Farmer was pub. in 1905. Critical works on Heywood include Wilhelm Swoboda's *John Heywood als Dramatiker* (in *Wiener Beiträge*, 1888); Karl Young's *Influence of French Farce in the plays of John Heywood* (M.P. II, 1904); A. W. Pollard's introd. to his ed. of *The Play of the Weather* in R.E.C. vol. i; A. W. Reed's articles on *John Heywood and his Friends* and *The Canon of John Heywood's Plays* in *The Library*, 1917 and 1918, R. W. Bolwell's *The Life and Works of John Heywood* (C.S.E.); and the most recent studies, R. de la Bère's *John Heywood, Entertainer* (1937), and Ian Maxwell's *French Farce and John Heywood* (Melbourne, 1946). There is a *Concise Bibliography* of Heywood's writings by S. A. and D. R. Tannenbaum (N.Y., 1947).

Interludes continued to be written up to the beginning of the seventeenth century. These later interludes have little literary value; specimens will be found in Hazlitt's *Dodsley*, Manly, Farmer's *Tudor Facsimile Texts* and M.S.R.

EARLY ACADEMIC AND COURT PLAYS

The vernacular drama begins to be affected by the comedies of Plautus and Terence about the middle of the sixteenth century. The play which shows the influence of Latin comedy in its most elementary form is *Jack Jugeler*, 'a new Enterlued for Chyldren to playe' (licensed for publication and printed 1562, but probably written at least a decade before, facs. by Farmer and Malone Society, ed. W. H. Williams (C.U.P.). This play is only a single scene derived from the *Amphitryon* of Plautus, but cleverly adapted to contemporary life. Nicholas Udall, a master at Eton from 1534 to 1541, was author of the first orig. English play constructed on the model of Latin comedy, *Ralph Roister Doister* (entered for publication 1577, a single copy of an early ed. without title page preserved at Eton College, rptd. in Hazlitt's *Dodsley*, Manly and Adams). The other famous early English classical comedy is *Gammer Gurton's Needle* by *Mr S., Mr. of Art;* a Cambridge play pub. 1575 and said to have been recently acted at Christ's College. It was rptd. in 1661, in all edd. of *Dodsley*, in Manly, R.E.C. Vol. I. (ed. Bradley), and facs. by J. S. Farmer and ed. H. F. Brett Smith (1920).

Just as Eton and Cambridge produced the first English classical comedies, so the Inns of Court, the great London Law colleges, produced the first attempts to imitate classical tragedy in the vernacular. The models were the rhetorical Latin tragedies attributed to Seneca. The first English trs. of these plays appeared between 1559 and 1566 (see above p. 184). In January 1561-62 *Ferrex and Porrex or The Tragedie of Gorboduc* was acted before Elizabeth at Whitehall. It was by two members of the Inner Temple, Thomas Norton and Thomas Sackville. It was the first of a series of Inns of Court plays built on the model of Senecan tragedy and also affected by contemporary Italian drama. It was first printed in a pirated text in 1565: the authorized text appeared c. 1570 with the title *The Tragedie of Ferrex and Porrex*. It is rptd. in all edd. of *Dodsley*, in Manly and Adams, facs. by Farmer. Other Inns of Court tragedies are *Jocasta*, the tragedy adapted from an Italian version of the *Phoenissae* by G. Gascoigne and F. Kinwelmersh (see p. 178), which bears a considerable resemblance to *Ferrex and Porrex*; *Gismond of Salerne*, a play by R. Wilmot and others, acted before the Queen by gentlemen of the Inner Temple in 1567-68 (rptd. in 1591 as *The Tragedie*

of *Tancred and Gismond*); and *The Misfortunes of Arthur* by
T. Hughes and others, acted before the Queen by members
of Gray's Inn in 1587 (first printed in *Certain devises and shewes
presented to her Maiestie*, 1587). Cunliffe's *Early English Classical
Tragedies* (see above, p. 221) includes *Gorboduc*, *Jocasta*,
Gismond of Salerne, and *The Misfortunes of Arthur*.

From this point onwards the Senecan tradition is continued in two directions. On the one hand it produces plays
by cultured dilettantes not intended for public performance,
such as the plays of the Countess of Pembroke, Sir William
Alexander and Fulke Greville, on the other it contributes
powerfully through the work of such men as Kyd and Marlowe to the development of popular tragedy. See *The Growth
of the Senecan Tradition in Renaissance Tragedy* by H. B. Charlton
(introd. to vol. I of *The Poetical Works of Sir William Alexander,
Earl of Stirling*, ed. L. E. Kastner and H. B. Charlton [1921-29]). Apart from the Senecan dramas there were certain plays
presented at court and elsewhere in the early part of Elizabeth's reign, which retained the form and style of the old
interlude but used themes from classical history and legend.
A foreshadowing of this type of 'transitional interlude' is seen
in *Thersites*, which was probably composed about 1537
(printed after 1561, rptd. in Pollard's *English Miracle Plays*).
The most interesting writer of the courtly interlude dealing
with classical themes is Richard Edwards (?1523-66), master
of the Children of the Chapel Royal, who composed a number of plays for his pupils to act at court. The only one that
survives is *Damon and Pithias* (two early edd. 1561 and 1582
rptd. in Hazlitt's *Dodsley*, Manly, and Adams).

EARLY ELIZABETHAN POPULAR PLAYS

One of the most interesting of these, as showing popular
taste in tragedy in the early part of Elizabeth's reign, is
Thomas Preston's *A lamentable Tragedie mixed full of plesant
mirth, containing the life of Cambyses, King of Percia* (?1570, rptd.
in Hazlitt's Dodsley, Vol. iv). Preston was probably an actor-playwright, and the play is 'designed for a troupe of pro-

fessional actors to be acted on a bare platform stage' (J. Q. Adams). Shakespeare parodied it in M.N.D., and probably acted in it himself in his youth. Rough popular dramatizations of heroic stories seem to have existed as early as the fifteenth century. A fragment of a play on Robin Hood written probably about 1475 is extant. It is printed in Manly and Adams, and ed. with facs. by W. W. Greg in the Malone Society's publications. Another short play on the Robin Hood story was printed with one of the Robin Hood ballads between 1553 and 1569. It is rptd. in Manly and Adams, and ed. in the Malone Society's publications by W. W. Greg. Later in Elizabeth's reign more elaborate dramatizations of heroic stories from history and legend were made for the rapidly developing professional troupes. They were the forerunners of the chronicle plays and heroic tragedies of the age of Shakespeare. One of the most interesting extant examples is the rough but vigorous and racy old play called *The Famous Victories of Henry the Fift* (printed 1598, but certainly written before 1588). Shakespeare certainly took hints from it for his chronicle plays on Henry IV and Henry V. It is rptd. in Adams. Other early popular heroic plays by anonymous authors are the old play on King Lear, *The Chronicle History of King Leir and his Three Daughters* (printed 1594, rptd. by W. C. Hazlitt in *Shakespeare's Library* and by Sir S. Lee in *Shakespeare Classics*) and the old play on King John called *The Troublesome Raigne of King John* (printed 1591, rptd. in *Shakespeare's Library* and *The Shakespeare Classics*).

INDIVIDUAL AUTHORS AND PLAYS

JOHN LYLY (?1554-1606)

Lyly became assistant master at St Paul's Choir School in 1585, and his plays were written for performance at court by the choristers. He was a pioneer in psychological and courtly comedy and in the use of prose and of the lyric for dramatic purposes. His two earliest plays, *A most excellent Comedie of Alexander, Campaspe and Diogenes* (called in later edd. *Campaspe*) and *Sapho and Phao* were both pub. anonymously in 1584. Campaspe has often been rptd. It is in Manly, Adams, R.E.C. and McIlwraith. *Endimion, the Man in the Moone*, an elaborate court allegory, appeared in 1591. There is an ed. with introd. by A. P. Baker (1894). It was followed by *Gallathea* and *Midas* (both 1592, both rptd. O.E.P.). Lyly's realistic comedy, *Mother Bombie*, appeared in 1594 (rptd. O.E.P. and ed. K. M. Lea and D. Nichol Smith in M.S.R.). All these plays were pub. anonymously, but Lyly's name appeared on the title page of the delicate phantasy in blank verse called *The Woman in the Moone* (1597). His last play, *Love's Metamorphosis*, a pastoral, was pub. in 1601. An anonymous play, *The Maydes Metamorphosis*, has also been ascribed to him; it is rptd. in facs. by Farmer.

A collection of Lyly's plays, entitled *Six Court Comedies Often presented and acted before Queen Elizabeth*, was pub. by E. Blunt in 1632. There are modern edd. by F. W. Fairholt, *The Dramatic Works of John Lyly* (1858), and in *The Complete Works of John Lyly*, ed. R. W. Bond (3 vols., 1902). For his novels, see p. 237.

Criticism and Biography

There is a valuable biographical and critical introd. to Bond's ed. of the Works. The best studies are *John Lyly, contribution à l'histoire de la Renaissance en Angleterre*, by A. Feuillerat (1910), J. Dover Wilson, *John Lyly* (1905), and G. K. Hunter, *John Lyly, The Humanist as Courtier* (1962). There is a *Concise Bibliography* by S. A. Tannenbaum (N.Y., 1940).

CHRISTOPHER MARLOWE (1564-93)

Marlowe's first dramatic work to be acted and pub. was almost certainly *Tanburlaine the Great*. The two parts were probably acted in 1587 and 1588 respectively. They were both pub. together in an octavo entered at Stationers' Hall in 1590, rptd. 1593, 1597 and 1605. All these early edd. were anonymous, but modern scholarship has established Marlowe's claim to their authorship beyond any doubt. There are valuable modern edd. by A. Wagner in *Englische Sprach-und Literaturdenkmäler* (1885), in the M.S.R. and in Methuen's complete Marlowe, ed. U. M. Ellis Fermor with an excellent introd. Marlowe's second great play, *The Tragicall History of Doctor Faustus*, was first acted not later than 1590 and was entered for publication in 1600-01. No copy of a 1601 ed. exists. The oldest extant ed. is that of 1604. Other edd. appeared in 1609, 1611, 1616, 1619, 1620, 1624, 1631, and 1663. There is no doubt that in all the extant edd. the text is very corrupt. On Nov. 22, 1602, Henslowe paid W. Bird and S. Rowley £4 for 'additions' which they made to the play. A very full and penetrating discussion of the difficult problems connected with the text are to be found in P. Simpson's essay on *The 1604 Text of Marlowe's Faustus* (E.S.M.E.A. VII, 1921). There are modern edd. by W. Wagner (1877), by I. Gollancz in T.D. (1897) and by F. S. Boas in the Methuen Marlowe. *The Jew of Malta* is known from Henslowe's Diary to have been acted on February 26, 1591-2. It was then, however, an old play and had probably been first produced in 1590. It was entered for publication in 1594, and was probably printed then, but the earliest extant text is that of an ed. of 1633 pub. under the supervision of Thomas Heywood, who probably altered the orig. for a revival in that year. There are modern edd. by A. Wagner (1889), and by H. S. Bennett in Methuen's complete Marlowe, and a discussion of the text by C. Brennan and J. le Gay Brereton in *Anglia Beiblatt*, 1905, 205-8. The first ed. of Marlowe's historical play, *Edward II*, appeared in 1594. It was probably first acted in 1591 or 1592. The text of this play is the best of any of Marlowe's extant dramatic works. There are edd. in all issues of Dodsley, by W. D. Briggs (1914), by A. W. Verity in T.D., in M.S.R. by Tancock, and by H. B. Charlton in the Methuen Marlowe. There is a German dissertation by C. T. Tzchaschel, *Marlowe's Edward II und seine Quellen* (Halle, 1902). *The Tragedie of Dido Queen of Carthage*, a play of considerable lyrical beauty was pub. in 1594 and ascribed on its title page of Christopher Marlowe and Thomas Nashe. It is not clear what Nashe's connection with the play was. Marlowe's manner is apparent on every page of it. Possibly Nashe prepared it for publication. There are edd. in McKerrow's ed. of Nashe, facs. by Farmer, and by C. F. Tucker Brooke in the Methuen Marlowe. The crude and obviously hastily-written play called *The Massacre at Paris with the death of Guise* (n.d.), dealing with contemporary events in France was probably Marlowe's last dramatic work. It was marked by Henslowe as a new play on January 30th, 1593, and was probably written shortly before that date. There are edd. in M.S.R. and by H. S. Bennett in the Methuen Marlowe.

For Marlowe's poems and trs. see above, pp. 183, 184, 215.

The first collected Marlowe was a poor ed. by G. Robinson, pub. in 1826. The first scholarly ed. is that of A. Dyce (1850). There are many modern collective edd. The best are the single vol. ed. of C. F. Tucker Brooke (1910) and Methuen's ed. in 6 vols., general editor, R. H. Case (1930-33, rev. ed. 1955, separate vols. recorded under the different plays and poems above). The Mermaid ed. has a valuable introd. by J. Havelock Ellis, and there are texts in Ev. Lib. and W.C.

Biography and Criticism

J. H. Ingram's *Christopher Marlowe and his Associates* (1904) contains some useful material, but is now rather out of date. U. M. Ellis Fermor's *Christopher Marlowe* (1927) is valuable for its criticism. Works of modern research which have thrown much light on Marlowe's biography are L. J. Hotson's *The Death of Christopher Marlowe* (1925) and M. Eccles's *Christopher Marlowe in London* (1934). C. F. Tucker Brooke's Life in the Methuen ed. is valuable, and there is an important paper by the same author on the *Marlowe Canon* in P.M.L.A., Vol. 37, 1922. F. S. Boas's *Marlowe and His Circle* (1929) is a useful summary of authentic biographical information. *The Tragicall History of Christopher Marlowe* by J. Bakeless (1942) is an exhaustive American study. T. S. Eliot's *Notes on the Blank Verse of Christopher Marlowe* (in the *Sacred Wood*, 1920) should also be consulted. See also F. S. Boas, *Marlowe, a Biographical and Critical Study* (1940), B. Cellini, *La Vita e Il Carattere di Marlowe* (Rome, 1937), M. Poirier, *Marlowe* (1951) and H. Levin, *The Overreacher* (1954).

There is a *Concise Bibliography* by S. A. Tannenbaum (N.Y., 1937, Supplement, 1947).

ROBERT GREENE (1558-92)

Greene's earliest plays are crude imitations of Marlowe. *The Comical History of Alphonsus King of Aragon* (printed 1599), *The Historie of Orlando Furioso* (printed 1594), and *A Looking Glasse for London and England* (with Lodge, printed 1594). This last includes interesting realistic scenes in prose. Greene's really important work is to be found in his romantic comedies, *The Honourable Historie of Frier Bacon and Frier Bungay* (1594) and the *Scottish Historie of James the fourth, slaine at Flodden* (1598), a play notable for the fact that in it Oberon, King of the Fairies, makes his first appearance on the English stage. *Friar Bacon and Friar Bungay* has often been rptd. separately. It is ed. A. W. Ward (1901), facs. by Farmer (1914), in M.S.R., the Fortune Play-books ed. Harrison, McIlwraith, and ed. B. Cellini (Florence, 1953). *James IV* has been rptd in M.S.R. The pleasant anonymous play of English country life called *A Pleasant Conceited Comedie of George a Green the Pinner of Wakefield* has also been ascribed to Greene on the strength of a note scribbled on the title page of the first ed., and some internal evidence. It is in Reed and Collier's Dodsley, Adam and M.S.R. The ranting tragedy called *The Tragical Reign of Selimus* has also been ascribed to Greene. It was rptd. in M.S.R.

Greene's *Dramatic Works* were first collected by A. Dyce in 1831. In 1861 the same editor pub. the *Dramatic and Poetical Works of Robert Greene and George Peele*. The *Complete Works in Prose and Verse* were pub. A. B. Grosart in 1881-86. The best modern ed. is *The Plays and Poems* ed. J. Churton Collins. There is an ed. of the plays by C. H. Dickinson in the Mermaid Series. For Greene's pamphlets, see p. 238.

Biography and Criticism

There are biographical and critical introd. to all the edd. mentioned above. The best modern study is the doctoral dissertation, *Robert Greene*, by J. C. Jordan (Columbia, 1909).

There is a *Concise Bibliography* by S. A. Tannenbaum (N.Y., 1939, Supplement, 1945).

THOMAS KYD (1558-95)

Thomas Kyd, no great poet like Marlowe, but a most able dramatist, was the author of one very important play, *The Spanish Tragedie*, probably acted in 1587 or 1588, and entered for publication in 1592. The earliest extant text is a single undated quarto, probably a second ed., pub. in 1592. It was rptd. in 1594 and its popularity is shown by the fact that 10 edd. appeared by 1633. An ed. pub. in 1602 contains for the first time famous additional scenes, powerful and brilliant interpolations by another hand. According to entries in Henslowe's Diary these additions were written by Ben Jonson. *The Spanish Tragedie* is rptd. in the first three edd. of Dodsley and there are modern edd. by J. Schick in T.D., by J. de Smeet (Brussels, 1925), by Sir W. W. Greg and

D. Nichol Smith in M.S.R., and L. T. Prouty (N.Y., 1952), as well as in various modern collections such as Thorndike's *Minor Elizabethan Drama* (Ev. Lib.)

The only other play that appeared with Kyd's name on the title page is *Cornelia* (1594), a tr. from the French of Garnier. *The Tragedy of Solyman and Perseda* (n.d. ?1592) is an anonymous play almost certainly by Kyd. Henslowe refers to some kind of humorous introductory play by Kyd, sometimes performed before *The Spanish Tragedie*. It is doubtful whether this is the crude piece called *The First Part of Ieronimo*, pub. 1605. Other plays have been assigned to Kyd on conjectural grounds. F. S. Boas in his ed. of the Works tried to show that he was the author of the old play of *Hamlet*, on which Shakespeare founded his tragedy. This play is not extant and Boas based his reasoning mainly on an obscure reference in Nashe's prefatory epistle to *Menaphon*. His conclusions have, however, been by no means generally accepted. It has also been suggested that Kyd was the author of *Arden of Feversham* (see p. 257).

Besides his plays, Kyd pub. a prose tr. from Tasso called *The Householders Philosophie* (1588).

The only collected ed. is that of F. S. Boas with biographical and critical introd. (1901).

Biography and Criticism

G. Sarrazin's *Thomas Kyd und Sein Kreis* (Berlin, 1892) has to a large extent been superseded by the Introd. to Boas's ed. and by H. Baker, *Induction to Tragedy* (Baton Rouge, 1939), and F. Carrière, *Le Théâtre de Kyd* (Toulouse, 1951). There are important critical articles by W. Bang (E.S., xxviii, 1900), F. W. Moorman (M.L.R., I, 1906) and J. C. Maxwell, 'Kyd's Spanish Tragedy' (P.Q. XXX, 1951).

There is a *Concise Bibliography* by S. A. Tannenbaum (N.Y., 1951).

GEORGE PEELE (1558-96)

Peele was a lyrical poet of a high order and a pioneer in poetical drama. His first work, the lovely little mask-like pastoral called *The Araygnement of Paris*, appeared anonymously in 1584. There are modern edd. by O. Smeaton, in T.D. (1905) and in M.S.R. He wrote a second pastoral play, apparently of the same type, called *The Hunting of Cupid*. This work was entered for publication in 1591, but no copy is known to exist. There are quotations from it, however, in *England's Parnassus* and *England's Helicon* (see p. 203). Peele's single English Chronicle play, *Edward I* (1593) is a poor affair, and the *Battle of Alcazar* (1594) a worthless imitation of Marlowe. Both are ed. in M.S.R. *The Old Wives' Tale* (1595), however, is one of the most delicate and charming of Elizabethan dramatic idylls. There are modern edd. by F. Gummere in R.E.C. with a valuable introd., in M.S.R., and in McIlwraith. Some of Peele's finest work is to be found in his last play, *The Love of King David and the Faire Bethsabe. With the Tragedie of Absalom* (1599), one of the few Elizabethan plays dealing with a scriptural subject. It is rptd. in Manley and in M.S.R. Other plays have been assigned to Peele on conjectural grounds. Peele wrote some notable non-dramatic poetry including *A Farewell* to Drake and Norris in 1593 and the beautiful *Polyhymnia* of 1590 on the retirement of Sir Henry Lee from his office of the Queen's Champion.

Peele's works were first collected by A. Dyce and pub. in 1828. The same editor pub. a combined ed. of Greene and Peele in 1861 (see p. 231). There is a useful little ed. of some of the plays and poems in M.U.L. (1887), and a complete ed. by A. H. Bullen (1888). Vol. I of the *Life and Works of Peele*, gen. ed. C. T. Prouty, ed. D. H. Horne was pub. at New Haven in 1952. The second volume of a projected Yale ed. in 3 vols. of Peele's *Dramatic Works* ed. F. S. Hook and J. Yaklovich appeared in 1962.

Biography and Criticism

There are biographical and critical introds. to the edd. of Dyce and Bullen. There are monographs on Peele by F. A. R. Lämmerhirt (Rostock, 1882), and P. H. Cheffaud (Paris, 1913). Three important articles by T. Larsen in M.P., (xxvi 1928; xxviii, 1930; and xxx, 1932) may also be consulted; and by the same author *A Bibliography of the Writings of George Peele* in M.P., XXXII, 1934, and *The Early Years of George Peele Dramatist* in *The Transactions of the Royal Society of Canada*, XXII, 1928. See also H. Jenkins, 'Peele's *Old Wives Tale*', M.L.R., xxxiv, 1939.

There is a *Concise Bibliography* by S. A. Tannenbaum (N.Y., 1940).

THOMAS LODGE (c. 1558-1625)

Lodge is notable as a lyrical poet and a writer of prose. His dramatic work is the least important part of his numerous and varied writings. The only play for which he is known to have been wholly responsible is an early and rather crude attempt at a Roman historical tragedy called *The Wounds of Civill Warr, Lively set forth in the True Tragedies of Marius and Scilla* (1594). It was rptd. in Collier's and Hazlitt's *Dodsleys*, and in M.S.R., ed. J. Dover Wilson. Lodge also collaborated with Greene in *A Looking Glasse for London and England* (see p. 230). It has been conjectured that Lodge had a hand in other extant and lost plays.

There is a collective ed. of Lodge's Works (except trs.), ed. Sir E. Gosse for the Hunterian Club (Glasgow), with an Introd. A new ed. by A. Walker is in preparation. For biography and criticism see N. B. Paradise, *Thomas Lodge* (1931), C. J. Sisson, *Thomas Lodge and Other Elizabethans* (Cambridge, U.S.A., 1933) and A. Walker in R.E.S. ix, X, 1933-4. There is a *Concise Bibliography* by S. A. Tannenbaum (N.Y., 1940).

THOMAS NASHE (1567-1601)

Apart from his somewhat shadowy connection with Marlowe's *Tragedy of Dido* (see p. 229), Nashe was certainly author of at least two plays, one of which is extant. It is the pretty lyrical drama entitled *A pleasant comedie called Summer's last will and Testament* (acted at Croydon in 1592 but not pub. till 1600). It is rptd. in Collier's and Hazlitt's *Dodsley*, and there is a modern critical ed. in McKerrow's *Works of Thomas Nashe* (see p. 239). Nashe's lost play was a comedy called *The Isle of Dogs*. For his other works, see p. 239. There is a *Concise Bibliography* by S. A. Tannenbaum (N.Y., 1941).

ANTHONY MUNDAY (1553-1633)

Anthony Munday was an industrious popular dramatist of the last decade of Elizabeth's reign, and an imitator of Greene in romantic comedy. His earliest extant play, *John a Kent and John a Cumber*, is preserved in an MS. dated December 1595. It has been printed by Collier in 1851 and in the M.S.R. in 1923. Munday attempted a dramatic treatment of the Robin Hood legends in two plays, *The Downfall of Robert, Earl of Huntington* (acted 1598), rev. by H. Chettle, and *The Death of Robert, Earl of*

Huntingdon, in which Chettle and Munday collaborated. The plays were pub. together in 1591 and rptd. in Hazlitt's *Dodsley* and Farmer's *Tudor Facsimile Texts*. Munday collaborated with Michael Drayton, Richard Hathaway and Robert Wilson, in the *First Part of the true and honourable Historie of Sir John Oldcastle*, pub. anonymously in 1600 and fraudulently ascribed to Shakespeare in an ed. pub. in 1619, wrongly dated 1600 (see p. 253). *Sir John Oldcastle* has been ed. for M.S.R. by P. Simpson and there is a facs. by Farmer. Munday was certainly the author of other plays which are lost. He probably had a hand in the anonymous play of *Sir Thomas More* (see p. 259), the MS. of which appears to be mainly in his handwriting. In the latter part of his life he was employed to write Lord Mayors' Pageants. There is no collected ed. of his works. There is a valuable series of articles on him by M. St C. Byrne in *The Library* (1918-1921-1923), and a monograph by Celeste Wright (née Turner) in the University of California's Publications in English, Vol. II, No. 1. There is a *Concise Bibliography* by S. A. Tannenbaum (N.Y., 1942).

LATER ACADEMIC PLAYS

A full account of these will be found in F. S. Boas's *University Drama in the Tudor Age*. Special mention may be made of the interesting 'Parnassus' trilogy, three plays in English acted at St John's College, Cambridge, between 1597 and 1601, called *The Pilgrimage to Parnassus, The Return from Parnassus*, Pt. I (both in MS. in the Bodleian) and the second part of the 'Return', called *The Returne from Parnassus: Or the Scourge of Simony*, pub. in 1606. The Trilogy was first printed in full by W. D. Macray in 1886. The best modern ed. is *The Three Parnassus Plays* ed. J. B. Leishman (1949). The 'Parnassus' plays are full of topical allusions and contain important references to Shakespeare.

CHAPTER IX
ELIZABETHAN SECULAR PROSE

PROSE FICTION
GENERAL STUDIES

THE most exhaustive account of Elizabethan prose fiction is to be found in A. E. Baker's *The History of the English Novel* Vol. II (1929). Sir Walter Raleigh's *The English Novel* (1904) contains a brief but brilliant survey. J. J. Jusserand's *The English Novel in the Time of Shakespeare* (Eng. tr. by E. Lee, 1899), is a valuable work though some of it is now out of date. Foreign influences are discussed in J. G. Underhill's *Spanish Literature in the England of the Tudors* (N.Y. 1905); S. L. Wolff's *The Greek Romances in Elizabethan Prose Fiction* (1912); M. A. Scott's *Elizabethan Translations from the Italian* (Vassar Semi-Centennial Series, 1916) and R. Pruvost, *Bandello and Elizabethan Fiction* (Paris, 1937). For the literature of roguery see F. W. Chandler's *Romances of Roguery* (1899) and *The Literature of Roguery* (1907), which contains a bibliography, and F. Aydelotte's *Elizabethan Rogues and Vagabonds* (1913). The most complete bibliography is Arundell Esdaile's *A List of English Tales and Prose Romances printed before 1640*. (Bib. Soc. 1912.)

COLLECTIONS

The first two volumes of the anthology called *Shorter Novels* (Ev. Lib.) contain a selection of prose stories by Elizabethan, Jacobean and Restoration authors with introductions by G. Saintsbury and P. Henderson. *Elizabethan Fiction* ed. R. Ashley and E. M. Moseley (N.Y., 1953) is a useful collection.

TRANSLATIONS FROM THE ITALIAN NOVELLE

The starting point of much Elizabethan prose fiction is to be found in the Italian short stories of the school of Boccaccio and Bandello. For English versions of these stories, see p. 187.

INDIVIDUAL AUTHORS

GEORGE PETTIE (1548-89)

George Pettie, a graduate of Christ Church, Oxford, pub. in 1576 a collection of twelve tales called *A Petite Pallace of Pettie his Pleasure*. He was indebted for his title and also for the groundwork of a number of his stories to William Painter's *The Palace of Pleasure* (see p. 187). Other stories in the *Petite Palace* were derived from Ovid and other sources. The most remarkable feature of Pettie's book is its curiously wrought style which anticipates most of the characteristics of the 'Euphuism' of John Lyly. There is a useful modern rpt. of the *Petite Palace*, ed. Gollancz, in the K.C., and a scholarly ed. by H. Hartman (1938).

JOHN LYLY (?1554-1606)

John Lyly's two stories, *Euphues: The Anatomy of Wyt* (1578) and its sequel, *Euphues and his England* (1580), are notable both for their curiously elaborate style and for the way in which the author combines elements from the Italian novella with a peculiarly English vein of moralizing. Lyly did not invent 'Euphuism' (a term which should be confined strictly to this peculiar type of Elizabethan prose and should not be used vaguely as an equivalent to affectation or bombast), but in his two stories it is found in its most highly developed form. They were immensely popular, and each of them passed through at least nine edd. before 1600. In 1617 they were printed together. There are modern edd. by E. Arber in his *English Reprints* (1886, later ed. 1895) and by M. W. Croll and H. Clemens (N.Y., 1916); also in *Elizabethan Fiction*, ed. R. Ashley and E. M. Moseley (see above). For Lyly's dramatic works and biographical and critical studies, see pp. 227-8.

SIR PHILIP SIDNEY (1554-86)

Sidney's famous romance *Arcadia* (for the different versions and edd., see p. 205), represents an entirely different tradition in European prose fiction from that of the Italian novelle. It is at once a pastoral and a heroic romance influenced by the late Greek prose romances of Longus and Heliodorus and by the Spanish *Diana Enamorada* of Montemayor. It won instant popularity and exerted a great influence on succeeding writers.

ROBERT GREENE (1558-92)

Greene was an industrious writer of romantic fiction as well as a dramatist, and he imitated both Lyly's *Euphues* and Sidney's *Arcadia*. His chief stories are *Pandosto the Triumph of Time* (1588), containing the story of Dorastus and Fawnia used by Shakespeare in *The Winter's Tale*. The title of this book was changed in later edd. to *Dorastus and Fawnia*. There is a modern ed. by P. G. Thomas in *The Shakespeare Library* (1907). *Perimedes the Blacksmith*, a shorter story, was also pub. in 1588. The only modern ed. is that by J. P. Collier (1870). *Menaphon*, first pub. in 1589, exhibits in its title pages Greene's debts to his contemporaries. In the first ed. it is significantly called *Menaphon, Camilla's Alarum to slumbering Euphues*, in the second (1599) this title is changed to *Greene's Arcadia or Menaphon*. There are modern edd. by E. Arber (1880) and by G. B. Harrison (with Lodge's *A Margarite*, 1927).

Greene's other prose writings can be conveniently mentioned here, though they are only partly fiction. They include a series of semi-autobiographical pamphlets and a series of vivid studies of contemporary low life in London. To the first class belong *Greene's Mourning Garment* (1590), *Greene's Never Too Late*, with its second part, *Francisco's Fortunes* (1590), *Greene's Groatsworth of Witte bought with a million of repentance*, and *The Repentance of Robert Greene* (both 1592). There is a rpt. of *Greene's Groatsworth*, ed. R. M. Hewitt (1919), and of all the pamphlets, ed. G. B. Harrison *Bodley Head Quarto* No. 6 (1923). The second class includes the famous 'cony-catching pamphlets' in which Greene anticipates Defoe as a reporter of the London underworld. These pamphlets are (1) *A Notable Discovery of Coosnage* (1591), (2) *The second and last part of conny catching* (1592), (3) *The Thirde and last part of conny-catching* (1592), (4) *A Disputation, betweene a Hee conny-catcher*, *and a Shee conny-catcher* (1592, rptd. in *Three Elizabethan Pamphlets* ed. G. R. Hibbard, 1951), (5) *The Blacke Bookes Messenger* (1592), an anticipation of 'The Black Book' or list of London Rogues which Greene threatened to pub. All these pamphlets are rptd. by G. B. Harrison in *The Bodley Head Quartos* (1923-24). For Greene's other works and biographical and critical studies see pp. 230-1. The best account of Greene's prose works is to be found in R. Pruvost, *Robert Greene et ses Romans* (Paris, 1938).

THOMAS LODGE (c. 1558-1625)

Lodge, like Greene, attempted to make capital out of the success of *Euphues*. His first notable story *Rosalynde* is called on the title page *Euphues Golden Legacy: found after his death in his cell at Silexeda* (1590). This pretty story interspersed with lyrics is one of the sources of *As You Like It*. It was rptd. often and there are numerous modern edd., the best being that of W. W. Greg in The Shakespeare Library (1907; new ed. 1931). Lodge also wrote quasi-historical romances such as *The Famous True and Historicall Life of Robert Second Duke of Normandy, surnamed Robert the Divell* (1591) and *The Life and Death of William Long-beard* (1593). *A Margarite of America* (1595) is, perhaps, his best story. There is a modern ed. by G. B. Harrison (1927). For Lodge's other works and biographical and critical studies, see p. 234.

THOMAS NASHE (1567-1601)

Nashe only wrote one story, but his numerous pamphlets contain studies of contemporary manners which anticipate the methods of prose fiction. The most important are (1) *The Anatomie of Absurditie* (1589), (2) *Pierce Penniless his Supplication to the Divell* (1592, rpt. in *Bodley Head Quartos*, 1934, and in *Three Elizabethan Pamphlets* ed. G. R. Hibbard (1951)), (3) *Christ's Tears over Jerusalem* (1593), (4) *The Terrors of the Night, or, a discourse of Apparitions* (1593), (5) *Nashe's Lentern stuffe containing the description and the full procreation and increase of the Towne of Great Yarmouth* (1599). His one 'novel' is the famous picaresque story called *The Unfortunate Traveller or the Life of Iacke Wilton* (1594). There are modern edd. by E. Gosse (1892), H. F. Brett Smith (1920), S. C. Chew (1926) and P. Henderson (1930). The standard ed. of Nashe's Works is that of R. B. McKerrow (6 vols, 1904-10), rev. ed. by F. P. Wilson (5 vols., 1958). See also p. 234. The best account of Nashe is *Thomas Nashe* by G. R. Hibbard (1962). There is a *Concise Bibliography* by S. A. Tannenbaum (N.Y., 1941).

THOMAS DELONEY (? 1543-1600)

Deloney, like Bunyan, was a popular writer whose merits were ignored by academic critics for a long time. Unlike Bunyan's, however, his works had no religious interest to appeal to a large audience in succeeding centuries. His stories, however, are now recognized as among the best written during the Elizabethan period. It is interesting to notice that he was a writer of popular ballads as well as of popular stories in prose. His tales provide invaluable pictures of Elizabethan middle-class life. They are (1) *The Pleasant history of John Winchcomb, in his younger yeares called Iack of Newberie* (licensed 1597, now only extant in the 8th ed. of 1619). There are modern edd. by R. Sievers in *Palaestra*, no. 36, 1904, and *Blackie's English Texts*, 1920. This book is written in honour of the Clothiers. (2) *The Gentle Craft. A Discourse containing many matters of delight* (licensed 1597, but only extant in an ed. of 1637). A second part, licensed 1633 is extant in an ed. of 1639. Numerous later edd. appeared in the seventeenth century. There is a modern ed. by A. Lange in *Palaestra* no. 18 (1903), and by W. J. Halliday (Part I only, 1928). This novel celebrates the Shoemakers. (3) Deloney's third and last story is the quasi-historical *Thomas of Reading. Or, the Sixe worthy yeomen of the West* (licensed 1602, extant in the fourth ed. of 1612). There are modern edd. by W. J. Thomas in *Early English Prose Romances*, Vol. i, 1858, by F. D. Senior in *Some Old English Worthies* (1912) and in Blackie's *English Texts* (1920).

The standard modern ed. of Deloney's *Works* is that of F. O. Mann with a valuable introd. (O.U.P., 1912). *Jack of Newberie* and *Thomas of Reading* are rptd. in *Shorter Novels* (Ev. Lib.) Vol. I. There is also a valuable French dissertation by A. Chevalley, *Thomas Deloney le roman des métiers au temps de Shakespeare* (Paris, 1926). See also E. D. Mackerness, 'Deloney and the Virtuous Proletariat', *Cambridge Journal*, V, 1951.

EMMANUEL FORDE (fl. c. 1607)

Forde was a very popular writer of romances. His works are (1) *The Most Pleasant History of Ornatus and Artesia* (? 1598, rptd. 1607, 1619, 1634, etc.), (2) His greatest success, *Parismus, the*

Renowned Prince of Bohemia (1598) with its sequel *Parismenos* (1599) which continued to be rptd. right down to the middle of the eighteenth century, (3) *The Famous Historie of Montelyon Knight of the Oracle* (earliest known ed. 1633) another very popular book, the latest ed. of which appeared in 1761. There is a rpt. of *Ornatus and Artesia* in *Shorter Novels* (Ev. Lib.) Vol II. The D.N.B. contains an article on Forde by Sir S. Lee. See also P. Henderson's criticism in the Introduction to *Shorter Novels*, Vol. II.

ANTHONY MUNDAY (1553-1633)

Munday was another popular romance-writer as well as a dramatist. He began his career as an author of prose fiction with a euphuistic 'novel' *Zelanto, the Fountaine of Fame* (1580), but his most popular works were his versions of the late Spanish romances of chivalry such as *Palmerin of England* (1596), *Palladin of England* (1588), *Palmerin d'Oliva* (1588), *The First Book of Amadis of Gaule* (1590), *The Second Part of Amadis* (1595), etc. These were the books read by Ralph, the grocer's apprentice in *The Knight of the Burning Pestle* (see p. 307). For Munday's plays, see p. 234. See C. Turner, *Anthony Munday, An Elizabethan Man of Letters* (California, 1928).

PAMPHLETS AND MISCELLANEOUS PROSE

GENERAL WORKS

The list of works cited at the beginning of the previous section will be found useful for this section also. In particular F. W. Chandler, *The Literature of Roguery*, 1907, F. Aydelotte, *Elizabethan Rogues and Vagabonds*, 1915, and A. E. Baker, *The History of the English Novel*, Vol. II, 1929, may be mentioned.

COLLECTIONS

Useful collections of Elizabethan tracts and pamphlets are A. V. Judges, *The Elizabethan Underworld* (1930), G. Orwell and H. Reynolds *British Pamphleteers I: Sixteenth Century* (1948) and G. R. Hibbard, *Three Elizabethan Pamphlets* (1951).

INDIVIDUAL WRITERS

THOMAS DEKKER (c. 1572-1632)

Dekker was a very industrious and popular writer of prose tracts, which give a lively picture of contemporary manners.

In 1603 he pub. *The Wonderful Yeare wherein is shewed the picture of London, lying sicke of the Plague*. There is a modern ed. of this vigorous work with other pamphlets on the same subject entitled *The Plague Pamphlets of Thomas Dekker*, ed. F. P. Wilson, 1925. *The Wonderful Yeare* is also rptd. in the *Bodley Head Quartos* ed. G. B. Harrison and in *Three Elizabethan Pamphlets* ed. Hibbard. In the same year appeared Dekker's adaptation of the famous fifteenth-century satire *Les Quinze Joyes de Mariage* entitled *The Batchelor's Banquet*. Dekker followed Greene as a reporter of low life in London in such works as *The Seven Deadlie Sinnes of London* (1606, modern ed. by H. F. B. Brett Smith in the Percy Reprints, 1922), *Newes from Hell brought by the Devell's Carrier* (1606), *The Belman of London* (1608) and its sequel *Lanthorne and Candlelight* (1608). *The Seven Deadlie Sinnes* has been rptd. by E. Arber in the English Scholar's Library and the *Belman of London* and *Lanthorne and Candle-light* by O. Smeaton in T.C. The best known of Dekker's social studies is the lively and amusing pamphlet called *The Guls Horne Booke or Fashions 50 please all sorts of guls* (1609). It is founded on the Latin poem of Frederick Dedekind called *Grobiamus*, but is an entirely orig. work giving a vivid picture of contemporary English life. There are modern edd. by R. B. McKerrow in K.C. (1907) and by O. Smeaton in T.C. (1904).

A collected ed. of Dekker's non-dramatic works by A. B. Grosart, was pub. in 1885. For Dekker's other works, and biographical and critical studies see p. 316.

NICHOLAS BRETON (1545-1626)

Nicholas Breton was one of the best of the popular Elizabethan writers of miscellaneous prose and verse. Among his numerous works special attention may be drawn to *Wits Trenchmour in a Conference betwixt an Angler and a Scholler* (1597), a dialogue on angling which was inspired by *The Treatyse of Fyshynge* printed with Dame Juliana Berners's *Boke of Huntyng* (1496). Breton's book certainly provided a model for Walton's *Compleat Angler*.

His most attractive writing is to be found in his two collections of 'characters' which are significant both in connection with the development of the 'Theophrastan' character in the seventeenth century and also with reference to the rise of the essay on moral themes. His *Characters upon Essaies Morall and Divine* appeared in 1615 and *The Goode and the Badde: or description of the Worthies and Unworthies of this Age* in 1616 (see p. 329).

Breton's *Works in Verse and Prose* (not complete) were ed. A. B. Grosart (2 vols., 1879). A Selection in 2 vols. ed. V. Kentish Wright appeared in 1929. *Melancolike Humours* (1600) was ed. G. B. Harrison (1929). There is an ed. of *Poems* by Breton ed. J. Robertson (1952). See Nellie E. Munro *Nicholas Breton as a Pamphleteer* (Pennsylvania, 1929). There is a *Concise Bibliography* by S. A. Tannenbaum (N.Y., 1947).

SAMUEL ROWLANDS (? 1590-? 1630)

Rowlands regarded himself as the successor of Greene in the portrayal of the London underworld. His first work was a collection of stories called *Greenes Ghost Haunting Cony-catchers* (1602). His *Martin Mark-all Beadle of Bridewell* (1610) was a reply to Dekker's *Belman of London*. An anonymous pamphlet on the wiles of conjurers and gamesters called *The Art of Jugling or Legerdemaine* has been ascribed to him. He also wrote religious tracts and poems. His *Complete Works* were collected and pub. the Hunterian Club with an introd. by Sir E. Gosse (3 vols., 1880). There is an account of a dissertation on them by J. R. Bowman in the Harvard University *Summaries of Theses* (1933).

RALEGH AND BACON

SIR WALTER RALEGH (? 1552-1618)

Ralegh's earliest prose work to be printed was his account of Sir Richard Grenville's famous battle with the Spaniards off the Azores called *A Report of the Truth of the fight about the Iles of Açores this last Sommer. Betwixt the Revenge, one of her Maiesties Shippes, And an Armada of the King of Spaine* (1591). It was rptd. in Hakluyt's *Voyages* and other collections and in *Arber's English Reprints*.

In 1596 he pub. his book on Guiana, *The Discoveries of the large, rich and bewtiful Empyre of Guiana*. His famous *History of the World*, the most ambitious historical work attempted by an Englishman up to that date, was written when he was in the Tower, and licensed for pub. in 1611. It actually appeared in folio in 1614. Later edd. were pub. in 1617, 1621, 1628 and 1634. W. Oldys pub. an enl. ed. with a life in 1736. An abridgment was pub. in 1698. In 1650 there appeared *Judicious and Select Essays and Observations* by Sir Walter Ralegh and in 1651 *The Remains of Sir Walter Ralegh*.

An ed. of Ralegh's *Works* in 2 vols. with 'a new account of his Life' by T. Birch was pub. in 1751. The best collective ed. is that pub. in 8 vols. in 1829. There is a *Selection* from Ralegh's prose works ed. G. E. Hadow (1917). A bibliography by T. N. Brushfield was pub. at Exeter in 1908. Among the numerous biographies and monographs mention may be made of E. Edwards, *The Life of Sir Walter Ralegh, together with his Letters* (2 vols., 1868), W. Stebbing, *Sir Walter Ralegh* (1891), E. Ecclestone, *Sir Walter Ralegh* (P.B., 1941), E. A. Strathmann, *Ralegh, a Study in Elizabethan Scepticism* (N.Y., 1951) and P. Edwards, *Ralegh* (1953).

For Ralegh's poems, see p. 210.

FRANCIS BACON, LORD VERULAM (1561-1626)

For Bacon's philosophical works, collected edd. and biographical and critical writings on him, see pp. 281-3. His chief non-philosophical works are his essays and his historical writings.

The essays seem to have grown out of jottings in a commonplace book. Bacon borrowed the word (though not much besides) from Montaigne, whose famous *Essais* had appeared in 1580. In a draft dedication to Henry, Prince of Wales (preserved in MS. at the B.M.), Bacon describes his Essays as 'certaine breif notes, sett downe rather significantlye, then curiously, wch I have called *ESSAIES*. The word is late, but the thing is aunciently. For *Senecaes* Epistles to Lucius, yf one marke them well, are but *Essaies*,—that is dispersed Meditacons, . . .' The first ed. of Bacon's Essays appeared in 1597 and contains only ten essays together with *Meditationes Sacrae* and *Colours of Good and Evil*. This book was rptd. in 1598 and 1606. In 1612 appeared an enl. collection containing 38 essays. This was rptd. in 1624. Italian versions appeared in 1618 and 1621 and French versions in 1619 and 1621. The final English collection of 1625 contains 58 essays. Bacon's *Essays* has been one of the most popular books in the English language, and there are a very great number of old and modern edd. The best are those by R. Whateley (1856), W. Aldis Wright (G.T., 1865), E. A. Abbott (1879) and G. Grigson (W.C., 1937). There is a facs. rpt. of the 1597 ed. in *Haslewood Books* (1924). For criticism of the Essays see G. Tillotson, 'Words for Princes' in his *Essays in Criticism and Research* (1942).

Bacon's great historical work is his *History of the Reign of Henry VII*, which he composed after his fall, when he was released from the Tower in 1621. With the possible exceptions of Knolles's *History of the Turks* (1603) and Ralegh's *History of the World*, it is the most important history in English written since More's *History of Richard III* (see p. 142). Bacon also composed a fragment of a *History of the Reign of King Henry VIII*, first pub. by his secretary, Rawley, in 1629.

LITERARY CRITICISM

Literary criticism was a new 'kind' of writing introduced into England from Italy in the Elizabethan period, and re-remained something rather exotic till the days of Dryden. There are interesting critical passages in such humanist educational works as Roger Ascham's *The Scholemaster* (1570) (see p. 146), but the first real critical essays (except Gascoigne's technical 'Certayne notes . . . concerning the making of verse or ryme in English', see p. 172) seem to have been called forth by the attack on poetry and drama by the Puritan Stephen Gosson in *The Schoole of Abuse* (1579) (rptd. by E. Arber in the *English Reprints*, see W. Ringler's *Stephen Gosson, a Biographical and Critical Study* [Princeton, 1942]). The first reply to Gosson was Thomas Lodge's rather awkwardly written *A Defence of Poetry* (1579), notable, nevertheless, as the first attempt to state in English some of the arguments in favour of poetry which were the commonplaces of Italian criticism. Sir P. Sidney's far abler *Apologie for Poetrie*, probably written soon after Lodge's *Defence*, but not pub. till 1595, is of the greatest significance because it placed before the English reader for the first time in a really attractive literary form nearly all the chief doctrines of the great Italian critics such as Fracastoro, Minturno, Castelvetro and Trissino. For early edd. of Sidney's *Apologie*, see p. 205. There are modern edd. by Arber in the *English Reprints*, by E. S. Shuckburgh (1891) and J. C. Collins (1907), and a facs. ed. in the Noel Douglas Replicas. *The Apologie* is rptd. with a valuable commentary in Gregory Smith's *Elizabethan Critical Essays*.

Apart from the controversy with the Puritans most Elizabethan criticism deals with technical questions and much of it is concerned with the controversies concerning rime and the use of classical metres. The correspondence between Spenser and Gabriel Harvey (? 1550-1631), published in *Three Proper and Wittie familiar Letters . . . Touching the earthquake in April last and our English refourmed Versifying*, and *Two other very commendable Letters of the same men's writings* (both 1580), deals largely with the English hexameter. A valuable commentary on this correspondence is to be found in G. M. Young's essay on Gabriel Harvey included in *XXth Century Critical Essays* (W.C.). Harvey's own criticism is to be found in his *Letter Book* (ed. E. J. L. Scott, Camden Society, 1884), and his *Marginalia* ed. G. C. Moore Smith (1913). A later controversy on metrical questions arose out of the interesting *Observations in the Arte of English Poesie* (1602) by T. Campion, the poet, who endeavoured to sketch out a system of rimeless English verse. Campion was answered with great spirit and good sense by Samuel Daniel in his *Defence of Ryme* (1st ed. n.d. ? 1603), rptd. in *Elizabethan Critical Essays* ed. Gregory Smith and *Critical Essays XVI-XVIII Centuries* (W.C.).

There are two general Elizabethan works on English poetry. The most comprehensive is the anonymous book called *The Arte of English Poesie* (1589), which is almost certainly by George Puttenham. Both this book and *A Discourse of English Poetrie* by William Webbe (1586) were ed. by E. Arber in his *English Reprints*. There is an important modern ed. of Puttenham's work by Gladys P. Willcock and Alice Walker (1936). The most comprehensive collection of early English critical essays is *Elizabethan Critical Essays*, ed. Gregory Smith (1904). The vol. of *Critical Essays XVI–XVIII Centuries* in W.C. is also useful.

J. E. Spingarn's important *History of Literary Criticism in the Renaissance* (N.Y., 1899) relates the English critics to the chief continental critical works of the period. E. J. Sweeting's *Early Tudor Criticism* (1940) is a useful survey of the beginnings of English criticism and J. W. H. Atkins's *English Literary Criticism of the Renascence* (1946) is an exhaustive and scholarly study. See also V. Hall, *Renaissance Literary Criticism* (N.Y., 1945).

CHAPTER X

WILLIAM SHAKESPEARE (1564-1616)

COLLECTIVE EDITIONS
The Folios

THE first collective ed. of Shakespeare's plays was the 'First Folio', printed in 1623 (licensed November 8th, 1623) and ed. by John Heminge and Henry Condell, two of Shakespeare's fellow actors. The title of the book is *Mr. William Shakespeare's Comedies, Histories and Tragedies. Published according to the True Original Copies. London, Printed by Isaac Jaggard and Ed. Blount, 1623*. On the title page is the engraving called the 'Droeshout' portrait of Shakespeare. The prefatory matter includes the famous lines of Ben Jonson, 'To the memory of my beloved, The Author Mr. William Shakespeare: And what he hath left us.' The folio contains 35 plays, seventeen of which were printed here for the first time. There are believed to be about 156 copies still in existence. The original price was twenty shillings. It has been reproduced several times in facs. The standard modern facs. rpts. are those ed. by Sir Sidney Lee (1902 and 1910), and H. Kökeritz and C. T. Prouty (reduced facs., New Haven, 1954). There are studies of the First Folio in Sir S. Lee's introd. to his facs. edd., A. W. Pollard's *Shakespeare Folios and Quartos* (1909), *On The Anniversary of the First Folio* (in *Shakespeare Studies*, N.Y., 1927), and Sir W. W. Greg, *The Shakespeare First Folio* (1955).

The Second Folio is a rpt. of the First. It appeared in 1632 and in this ed. Milton's *An Epitaph on the admirable Dramaticke Poet, W. Shakespeare* is printed among the commendatory verses. There is a study by C. A. Smith on *The Differences between the First and Second Folio* (E.S. xxx, 1902), and of *The Printing and Proof-Reading of the First Folio of Shakespeare* by C. Hinman (1962).

The first issue of the Third Folio, pub. 1663, does not differ materially from the Second Folio. The second issue pub. in 1664 contains seven extra plays announced on the title page as added 'unto this impression' and 'never before printed in Folio'. They are *Pericles Prince of Tyre, The London Prodigall, The History of Thomas Ld. Cromwell, Sir John Oldcastle, Lord Cobham, The Puritan Widow, A Yorkshire Tragedy, The Tragedy of Locrine*. There is no reason to suppose that Shakespeare had a hand in any of them except *Pericles*. There is a facs. of the 1664 Folio by Methuen (1905). The Fourth Folio was printed for H. Herringman and others in 1685. It is a rpt. of the 1664 Folio, facs. by Methuen (1904). This was the last ed. of Shakespeare pub. in the seventeenth century.

Eighteenth-Century Editions

The eighteenth-century edd. of Shakespeare began with that of Nicholas Rowe, the dramatist, which appeared in 6 vols. in 1709 and included 'An Account of the Life and Writings of the Author'. A seventh vol. containing the poems; with critical essays by C. Gildon, appeared in 1710. Pope's ed. in 7 vols. appeared in 1725 and G. Sewell edited the poems in a supplementary vol. This ed. is notable chiefly for its preface. The rival ed. by Lewis Theobald 'Collated with the Oldest Copies and corrected with Notes explanatory and Critical' (6 vols, 1733; 12 vols. 1740, many later edd.) is a much more scholarly performance, the first really scholarly ed. of Shakespeare. There is an important study of the edd. of Pope and Theobald in T. R. Lounsbury's *The First Editors of Shakespeare* (1907). *Pope's Taste in Shakespeare* by J. Butt (Shakespeare Association, 1936) is an interesting essay on certain aspects of Pope's ed. Sir Thomas Hanmer's ed. (1743-44) is based chiefly on the previous eighteenth-century edd.; those of W. Warburton (8 vols. 1747) and H. Blair (8 vols. 1753) are of little importance, but Samuel Johnson's, which first appeared in 8 vols. in 1753, is valuable especially for its great critical preface and masterly notes. In the latter part of the century important work was done by the learned but erratic George Steevens, and by Edmond Malone, perhaps the greatest of Shakespearian editors. Steevens printed twenty of the plays from the pre-Restoration quartos together with the sonnets in 4 vols. in 1766, and re-issued Johnson's ed. in 10 vols. with additional notes in 1773. His ed. of 1778 in 10 vols. includes Malone's epoch-making 'Attempt to Ascertain the Order in which the Plays attributed to Shakespeare were Written', the first critical examination of the chronology of the plays. Malone pub. a supplement to this ed. in 1780, containing the first draft of his *History of the Stage*, together with Shakespeare's Poems and Doubtful Plays. Malone's own complete ed. of the *Plays and Poems* (10 vols. 1790) includes his 'Essay on the Chronological Order of the Plays', his 'Historical Account of the English Stage and other valuable critical matter.' It is, perhaps, the most important achievement of eighteenth-century Shakespearian scholarship. Other valuable late eighteenth-century edd. were those of E. Capell (10 vols., 1774) and Isaac Reed's first 'Variorum' ed. (10 vols. 1788). Before the end of the eighteenth century the first continental ed. (by A. Wagner, Brunswick, 8 vols. 1797-1801) and the first American ed. (based on Johnson's, Philadelphia, 1795-96) had appeared. There is an important account of eighteenth-century edd. in D. Nichol Smith's *Shakespeare in the Eighteenth Century* (1928).

Nineteenth and Twentieth Century Editions

It is only possible to mention a few of the most important edd. of the nineteenth and twentieth centuries. The expurgated *Family Shakespeare* of Thomas Bowdler (4 vols., Bath, 1807) has given a word to the English language. A second 'Variorum' ed. Isaac Reed appeared in 1813, and a third, the best of the 'old variorum' edd., by James Boswell, based on Malone's ed. and his own MS. collections, was pub. in 1821. J. P. Collier's ed. of 1842 contains valuable material but is not always trustworthy. A supplementary vol. containing *Notes and Emendations from Early Manuscript Corrections in a copy of the folio, 1632*, was issued by Collier in 1853. The MS.

notes were afterwards shown to be forgeries, but some of the emendations are clever and plausible. The 'Cambridge' ed. (text only 1863-68) of W. G. Clark, J. Glover and W. Aldis Wright is probably the best text of the nineteenth century, and Macmillan's one vol. Globe ed. (1st issue, 1864), founded on it, is still one of the best of its kind. The publication of the great 'New Variorum' ed. was begun at Philadelphia by two American scholars, H. H. Furness and H. H. Furness jun., in 1871. It is the fullest of all edd. of Shakespeare. Each vol. contains a single play with exhaustive textual apparatus and a large accumulation of historical and critical extracts. In the early vols. spelling is modernized, but in the later ones Elizabethan spelling is retained.

Among more recent edd. the following may be mentioned. One vol. edd. include the Oxford Shakespeare ed. W. J. Craig (1891), the Complete Works ed. P. Alexander (1951), the Complete Works ed. Hardin Craig (Chicago, 1951), both with admirable introductions, and *William Shakespeare the Complete Works* ed. C. J. Sisson (1954) with a number of valuable essays by different authors. The old Arden ed. in 37 vols. (1889-1924) is now replaced by the new Arden ed., general editors, H. F. Brooks and H. Jenkins (17 vols. have appeared up to 1962), the most fully annotated ed. of separate plays. Similarly the old Temple ed. of Sir I. Gollancz (40 vols. 1894-96) has been replaced by the new Temple ed. of M. P. Ridley (39 vols. 1934-36). The New Cambridge ed. of Sir A. Quiller Couch and J. D. Wilson (after 1944 J. D. Wilson and Alice Walker) (1921-) embodies the most recent textual discoveries. The Yale Shakespeare ed. W. L. Cross and C. F. T. Brooke and others (40 vols., New Haven, 1918-28) is the most authoritative American ed. The Penguin ed. of G. B. Harrison (35 vols.) and the corresponding American Pelican ed. of A. Harbage are handy texts for the pocket. Sumptuously produced edd. are the Stratford Town ed. (10 vols.) with essays by R. Bridges, J. Jusserand, Sir E. K. Chambers and others, the Players' Shakespeare (illustrated) with Granville Barker's introductions, and the Folio

Society's ed. (with interesting designs). The finely printed Nonesuch ed. of H. Farjeon (7 vols., 1929-34), rptd in 4 vols. (1953) with introduction by I. Brown retains original spelling and includes plays of doubtful authorship.

EARLY EDITIONS OF INDIVIDUAL PLAYS: THE QUARTOS

Before the appearance of the Folio of 1623 eighteen of the plays included in that ed. (as well as one in which Shakespeare certainly had a hand, but which was not included) had been pub. in separate edd., known from their size as the Quartos. It has been shown by A. W. Pollard that the Quartos can be divided into 'good' and 'bad' texts. The 'good' Quartos were the work of respectable printers, were generally entered at Stationers' Hall, and were often used by the editors of the First Folio. It is likely that their 'copy' was honestly obtained, and it was probably Shakespeare's MS., 'true original copies', to use the phrase of the editors of the First Folio. The following are the fourteen good Quartos: *Titus Andronicus* (1594, printed by J. Danter); *Richard II.* (1597, printed by V. Simmes for A. Wise); *Richard III.* (1597, same printer and publisher); *Love's Labour's Lost* (1598, printed by W. W. for C. Burby); *Henry IV.*, Pt. I (1598, printed by P. S. for A. Wise); *Romeo and Juliet* (1599, printed by T. Creede for C. Burby); *The Merchant of Venice* (1600, printed by J. Roberts); *Henry IV.*, Pt. II (1600, printed by V. S. for A. Wise and W. Aspley); *Much Ado about Nothing* (1600, same printer and publishers); *A Midsummer Night's Dream* (1600, printed for T. Fisher); *Hamlet* (1604, printed by I. R. for N. L.); *King Lear* (1608, printed for N. Butter); *Troilus and Cressida* (1609, printed by G. Eld for R. Bonian and H. Walley); *Othello* (1622, printed by N. O. for T. Walkley). The bad Quartos appear to have been the work of 'pirate' publishers and printers, using material dishonestly obtained, 'diverse stolne and surreptitious copies' to use the words of Heminge and Condell. They are *The First Part of the Contention betwixt the two Famous Houses of Yorke and Lancaster* (i.e., *Henry VI.*, Pt. II, in a different version from that of the Folio, 1594, printed by T. Creede for T. Millington); *The True Tragedie of Richard Duke of Yorke* (i.e., *Henry VI.*, Pt. III, in a different version from that of the Folio, 1595, printed by P.S. for T. Millington); *Romeo and Juliet* (1597, printed by John Danter); *Henry V.* (1600, printed by T. Creede for T. Millington and J. Busby); *The Merry Wives of Windsor* (1602, printed by T.C. for A. Johnson); *Hamlet* (1603, printed for N.L. and J. Trendell, the 'First Quarto' of *Hamlet*, differing in many respects from the Quarto of 1604 and the Folio text); *Pericles* (1609, printed for H. Gasson, not included in the First or Second Folios but printed in the 2nd issue of the Third Folio). To this list may be added a group of nine quarto plays by or attributed to Shakespeare, printed by W. Jaggard without a general title page and pub. in 1619, apparently an early and unauthorized attempt at a collective ed. Some of the title pages of the plays in this collection bear false dates and misled scholars till it was shown by W. W. Greg that they were all printed in 1619. They are *The Whole Contention between the Two Famous Houses, Lancaster and York* (i.e., *The First Part of the Contention* and *The True Tragedie of Richard Duke of York*, versions of Henry VI., Pts. II. and III., n.d., printed for T.P.); *Pericles* (rightly dated 1619, printed for T.P.); *A Yorkshire Tragedie* (rightly dated 1619, printed for T.P., not by Shakespeare); *Sir John Oldcastle* (wrongly dated 1600, printed for T.P., not by Shakespeare: see p. 249); *Henry V.* (wrongly dated 1608, printed for T.P.); *A Midsummer Night's Dream* (wrongly dated 1600, printed for J. Roberts); *King Lear* (wrongly dated 1608, printed for N. Butter); *The Merry Wives of Windsor* (rightly dated 1619, printed for A. Johnson). The other Quarto edd. (all recorded in A. W. Pollard's *Shakespeare Folios and Quartos*) are only rpts. of the above, except the 2nd issue of the 3rd ed. of the 'good' Quarto of *Richard II.*, pub. 1608, which contains the deposition scene, previously omitted for political reasons, and possibly the Quarto ed. of *Othello*, pub.

1630. There are two collections of facs. rpts. of the Quartos, the series of lithographic reproductions by E. W. Ashbee, ed. J. O. Halliwell-Phillipps (48 vols., 1862-76), and the photo-lithographic series by W. Gregg, ed. F. J. Furnivall (43 vols., 1880-89). There is a *Tabular View of the Quarto Editions* by F. G. Fleay in *The Transactions of the New Shakespeare Society* (1874). *A Census of Shakespeare's Plays in Quarto* by Henrietta Bartlett and A. W. Pollard (New Haven, 1916) is a record of all known copies. The most important modern studies are A. W. Pollard's *Shakespeare Folios and Quartos* (1909); *Shakespeare's Fight with the Pirates and the Problems of the Transmission of his Text* by the same author (1916); *On Certain False Dates in Shakespearian Quartos* in *The Library*, IX., 1908; *The Bibliographical Study of Shakespeare*, by P. Simpson, in *The Transactions of the Oxford Bibliographical Society*, I., i., 1923; the Textual Introd. to the *New Cambridge Shakespeare*, by J. Dover Wilson (in Vol. I., *The Tempest*, 1921), and *Shakespeare's Henry VI. and Richard III.*, by P. Alexander (1929).

THE POEMS

Collective Editions

An early attempt at a collective ed. of *Poems written by Wil. Shakespeare* appeared in 1640. It contains garbled versions of a number of the sonnets, *A Lover's Complaint*, *The Phoenix and the Turtle*, as well as some spurious pieces. About 1709 B. Lintot, the well-known publisher of Queen Anne's reign, pub. *A Collection of Poems* in 2 vols. by Shakespeare, including *Venus and Adonis*, *The Rape of Lucrece*, *The Passionate Pilgrim*, and the whole of the sonnets from the orig. ed. of 1609. In 1710 appeared a poor ed. by C. Gildon as a supplement to Rowe's ed. of the plays (see p. 249). It includes *Venus and Adonis*, *The Rape of Lucrece*, *The Passionate Pilgrim*, the garbled text of the sonnets from the 1640 ed., and some spurious pieces. This collection was ed. by Sewell as a supplementary vol. to Pope's ed. (1725). The first critical ed. of the Poems is Malone's, in his *Supplement* to Johnson's and Steevens's ed. of the *Plays* (1780, see p. 250). Numerous edd. of the Poems have been pub. in the nineteenth and twentieth centuries. Among the best are G. Wyndham's (1898) with valuable introd.; E. Dowden's (1903); C. K. Pooler's (Arden ed. 1918); and H. E. Rollins's (*New Variorum*, Philadelphia, 1938).

Venus and Adonis

This narrative poem is the first work known to have been pub. by Shakespeare. It appeared in a quarto in 1593 dedicated to H. Wriothesley, Earl of Southampton. It was very popular and went through at least 13 other edd. by 1675. There are facs. edd. by J. O. Halliwell-Phillipps (1867), A. Symons (1886), and S. Lee (1905).

The Rape of Lucrece

This fine narrative poem appeared in a quarto dated 1594 with dedication to the Earl of Southampton, signed William Shakespeare. It went through seven other edd. by 1655. There are facs. edd. by J. O. Halliwell-Phillipps (1866), F. J. Furnivall (1866), and S. Lee (1905).

The Sonnets

The Sonnets were first printed in 1609 in a small quarto entitled *Shakespeare's Sonnets Never before Imprinted*. This collection contains 154 sonnets with the narrative poem called *A Lover's Complaint*. Two of the sonnets (nos. 138 and 144) had already appeared in the piratical collection called *The Passionate Pilgrim* (1599, see below). A garbled text of 146 sonnets appeared in the 1640 ed. of the *Poems* with unauthorized titles, and was rptd. by Gildon, Sewell and other eighteenth-century editors. Lintot's *Collection* of 1709 contained all the sonnets from the 1609 ed., and Steevens rptd. the text of the 1609 Quarto in his ed. of *Twenty Plays* (1766), while Malone exposed the shortcomings of the 1640 ed. in his *Supplement* to the Johnson-Steevens ed. of 1780. Among the many modern edd. the best are G. Wyndham's in his ed. of the *Poems*, C. H. Beeching's (1904), T. G. Tucker's (1924),

C. F. Tucker Brooke's (1936), and H. E. Rollins's (2 vols., New Variorum, Philadelphia, 1944). There is a facs. of the 1609 ed. in the Noel Douglas Replicas. There are several edd. in which the sonnets have been rearranged to suit different theories. Among these may be mentioned *Shakespeare's Sonnets Reconsidered* by Samuel Butler (1899) and the edd. of C. M. Walsh (1908) and Sir Denys Bray (1925). See also J. B. Leishman's valuable study *Themes and Variations in Shakespeare's Sonnets* (1961).

A Lover's Complaint

This narrative poem of 47 stanzas of rime royal was printed with the sonnets in the 1609 ed. There is no reason to doubt that Shakespeare wrote it.

The Phoenix and the Turtle

This noble lyric signed with Shakespeare's full name appeared with a collection of poems by Marston, Chapman, Jonson and others appended to Robert Chester's *Love's Martyr or Rosalin's Complaint, Allegorically Shadowing the truth of Love, in the Constant Fate of the Phoenix and Turtle* (1601). There is every reason to believe that it is by Shakespeare. An ed. of *Love's Martyr*, by A. B. Grosart, is included in *The New Shakespeare Society's Series*, VIII., ii. The *Phoenix and Turtle* poems by Shakespeare, Marston, Chapman, Jonson and others were rptd. in the *Shakespeare Head Quartos*, ed. B. H. Newdigate (1937). Another ed. by G. Bullett was pub. in 1938. See H. Straumann, *Phönix und Taube* (Zürich, 1953).

The Passionate Pilgrim

This miscellany of sonnets and lyrics pub. under Shakespeare's name by W. Jaggard in 1599 (2nd enlarged ed., 1612) is a piece of literary piracy, an assortment of poems raked together from various sources and pub. without authorization. Shakespeare's name is omitted from the 1612 ed. It includes two sonnets and a lyric from *Love's Labour's Lost*, the two sonnets which appeared as nos. 138 and 144 in the

1609 ed., the fine lyric beginning 'Crabbed Age and Youth', which may well be Shakespare's, a sonnet on Venus and Adonis which may also be one of his early works, and a number of poems by Marlowe, Ralegh, Bartholomew, Griffin and others. There is a facs. ed. J. Q. Adams (N.Y., 1939) and another one of the 3rd ed., 1612 ed. H. E. Rollins (N.Y., 1940).

DOUBTFUL AND APOCRYPHAL PLAYS

Collections

The first collection of Shakespeare Apocrypha consists of the seven plays added in the 1664 Folio to the orig. thirty-five of Heminge and Condell. Of these *Pericles* is generally admitted to be at least partly by Shakespeare, and alone among the 'doubtful' plays has won an accepted place in the canon. The other six are *The London Prodigall*, *Thomas Lord Cromwell*, *Sir John Oldcastle*, *The Puritan Widow*, *A Yorkshire Tragedy*, *The Tragedy of Locrine*. These plays were rptd. in the 1685 Folio and in Rowe's and other eighteenth-century edd. Malone's *Supplement* to the Johnson-Steevens ed. (1780) includes *Pericles* and the six apocryphal plays. *The Doubtful Plays of Shakespeare*, ed. H. Tallis (1851) includes beside the seven plays already mentioned *Titus Andronicus*, *King Edward III.*, *The Merry Devil of Edmonton*, *Fair Em*, *Mucedorus*, *Arden of Feversham*, *The Birth of Merlin* and *The Two Noble Kinsmen*. The thirteen apocryphal plays (excluding *Pericles* and *Titus Andronicus*, both accepted in the canon) printed by Tallis, were rptd. by Warnke and Prokscholdt (Halle 1853-88) and A. F. Hopkinson (London, 1891-95). The standard modern ed. is *The Shakespeare Apocrypha*, ed. C. F. Tucker Brooke (1918) containing a valuable introd. and full bibliography. Besides the thirteen plays mentioned above it includes *Sir Thomas More* (see p. 259).

Individual Plays

The following are the most important plays among the *Shakespeare Apocrypha*:—(1) *Arden of Feversham*, a powerful realistic drama, pub. in 1592 anonymously and first attributed to Shakespeare by E. Jacob in 1660. Modern criticism tends to assign it to Kyd or one of his imitators. There are modern edd. by A. H. Bullen (1887), R. Bayne in T.D., A. Thorndike in *Pre-Shakespearian Tragedies* in Ev. Lib. and H. Macdonald in M.S. (1947).

(2) *King Edward III*, a fine historical play pub. anonymously in 1596, 2nd ed. 1599. It was first attributed to Shakespeare in a bookseller's catalogue of 1654; ed. 1760, by E. Capell, who claimed Shakespearian authorship for it. There is a good modern ed. by G. C. Moore-Smith in T.D. Tucker Brooke suggests that Peele may be the author. See also K. Muir, 'A Reconsideration of Edward III' in Sh. S., vi (1953).

(3) *A Yorkshire Tragedy*, pub. in 1608 and ascribed to Shakespeare in the first ed. A powerful realistic drama, one of the finest Elizabethan plays of its kind. Its verse is decidedly un-Shakespearian in quality, but some of the prose is worthy of Shakespeare.

(4) *The Merry Devil of Edmonton*, an excellent romantic play, first pub. in 1608 and attributed to Shakespeare by the bookseller Kirkman in the middle of the seventeenth century. There is a good ed. by H. Walker in T.D.

(5) *The Two Noble Kinsmen*. This fine play was first pub. in 1634 in a quarto where it is attributed to 'Mr John Fletcher and Mr William Shakespeare'. It was rptd. in the 1679 Folio of Beaumont and Fletcher with no allusion to Shakespeare's alleged share in the authorship. There are modern edd. by W. W. Skeat (1875), by H. Littledale in the New Shakespere Society's Series (1876), and by C. H. Herford in T.D. It has been generally agreed that the play is by two authors, one of whom was Fletcher. Lamb, Coleridge, De Quincey, Littledale and Tennyson ascribed the non-Fletcherian parts to Shakespeare, Steevens, Shelley, Hazlitt and Furnivall denied the existence of a Shakespearian element in the play. Herford suggested that the play might be based on some very late poetic fragments by Shakespeare and completed by Fletcher.

See also T. Spencer, 'The Two Noble Kinsmen', M.P., XXXVI, 1952.

(6) *Sir Thomas More*. This important and interesting play certainly belonging to the Elizabethan period, remained in MS. till 1844. This MS. (B.M. Harl. 7368) is said to be in five different hands. The play was submitted to Sir E. Tilney, Master of the Revels, and in order to meet certain objections of his was recast and certain passages were added. It was first transcribed and ed. for the New Shakespere Society by W. Dyce in 1844, and was rptd. privately by E. M. Hopkinson in 1892. The standard modern ed. is by W. W. Greg in M.S.R. R. Simpson and J. Spedding were the first to claim that part, at any rate, of the additions to the original draft were by Shakespeare; and it is generally agreed that the 'insurrection scene' inserted in Act I. is of Shakespearian quality. Powerful support to this theory has been given by Sir E. Maunde Thompson in his *Shakespeare's Handwriting* (1916). The whole question is discussed in detail in *Shakespeare's Hand in the Play of Sir Thomas More*, by A. W. Pollard, W. W. Greg. Sir E. M. Thompson, J. D. Wilson and R. W. Chambers (1923). See also J. D. Wilson's Textual Introd. to the *New Cambridge Shakespeare* in Vol. I. (*The Tempest*). There are edd. of the play by J. Shirley (1938) and H. Jenkins in *The Complete Works of Shakespeare* ed. C. J. Sisson (1954).

SHAKESPEARE'S LIFE AND PERSONALITY

Biographies

The earliest attempt to record biographical details of Shakespeare (with the exception of a few brief earlier memoranda) is to be found in John Aubrey's jottings made between 1669 and 1690 and printed in his *Brief Lives*, ed. Clark (II, 225-227). Nicholas Rowe's *Account of the Life and Writings of the Author*, is a slight sketch pub. with his ed. of 1709 (see p. 249). The first really competent and critical Life was that of E. Malone, first pub. in the Boswell-Malone Variorum ed.

of 1821. Many other biographies appeared in the nineteenth and twentieth centuries. Special mention may be made of those by F. G. Fleay (1886), S. Lee (1890, rev. ed. 1925), and J. Quincy Adams (N.Y., 1923). The standard modern biography is *William Shakespeare, A Study of Facts and Problems*, by Sir E. K. Chambers (2 vols., 1930). The first vol. contains the most complete account of Shakespeare's life now available with an authoritative study of the conditions under which his plays were produced; the second vol. consists of app. including a very complete collection of all records, allusions, documents, etc. There is an abridged ed. of Chambers's work by C. Williams (1933). Among the many short biographies mention may be made of E. G. Lamborn and G. B. Harrison, *Shakespeare, the Man and his Stage* (1923) and J. S. Smart, *Shakespeare, Truth and Tradition* (1928), a very valuable and acute examination of the data on which our knowledge of Shakespeare's life is based. More recent studies which combine biography with criticism are P. Alexander's masterly *Shakespeare's Life and Art* (1938), E. I. Fripp's *Shakespeare, Man and Artist* (2 vols., 1938), H. Spencer's *The Art and Life of Shakespeare* (N.Y., 1940) and I. Brown's *Shakespeare, a Biography and an Interpretation* (1949). The chief collections of documents bearing on Shakespeare's life are D. H. Lambert's *Cartae Shakespearianae* (1904), C. F. Tucker Brooke's *Shakespeare of Stratford* (1926), and the second vol. of Sir E. K. Chambers's *William Shakespeare*.

Studies of Shakespeare's Personality and Interests

These are very numerous. Among the best are W. Bagehot's essay, 'Shakespeare' in his *Literary Studies* (1879), A. C. Bradley's 'Shakespeare the Man' in *Oxford Lectures on Poetry* (1909), H. C. Beeching's *The Character of Shakespeare* (Br. Ac., 1917), J. Middleton Murry's *Shakespeare* (1936), and *The Voyage to Illyria*, by K. Muir and S. O'Loughlin (1937). Among the many works dealing with Shakespeare's interests mention may be made of R. W. Chambers's essays, 'The Expression of Ideas, particularly Political Ideas, in the Three

Pages and in Shakespeare' in *Shakespeare's Hand in The Play of Sir Thomas More*, op. cit., and 'The Elizabethan and Jacobean Shakespeare' in his *Man's Unconquerable Mind* (1939); H. C. Beeching's study of 'The Religion of Shakespeare' (in the Stratford Town ed. of Shakespeare's Works, 1907 see p. 251); D. H. Madden's *The Diary of Master William Silence, A Study of Shakespeare and Elizabethan Sport*, and C. H. Herford's *The Normality of Shakespeare illustrated in his Treatment of Love and Marriage* (E.A., 1920). The standard work on his handwriting is *Shakespeare's Handwriting*, by Sir E. Maunde Thompson (1917). The general background of his life and work can be studied in *Shakespeare's England* (2 vols., 1916), and *Life in Shakespeare's England*, ed. J. Dover Wilson (1911). *Amazing Monument: a Short History of the Shakespeare Industry* (1939) by Ivor Brown and George Fearon is an ironic and salutary survey of bardolatry.

GENERAL CRITICISM

History of Shakespearian Criticism

Accounts of the development of Shakespearian criticism will be found in *Shakespeare as a Dramatic Artist with an Account of his Reputation at Different Periods*, by T. R. Lounsbury (N.Y., 1901), and *A History of Shakespearian Criticism*, by A. J. Ralli (2 vols., 1932). Nichol Smith's *Shakespeare Criticism* and A. Bradby's *Shakespeare Criticism 1919–33* (both W.C.) are useful anthologies containing some of the chief critical essays on Shakespeare.

Shakespearian Criticism in the Seventeenth and Eighteenth Centuries

All the early critical allusions to Shakespeare will be found in *The Shakespeare Allusion Book* (rev. ed. by E. K. Chambers, 2 vols., 1932). Serious Shakespearian criticism begins with Dryden's 'character' of Shakespeare in his *Essay of Dramatic Poesy* (1668) and other passages in his critical writings (see W. P. Ker's ed. of Dryden's *Essays*). For Thomas Rymer's adverse criticisms, see Spingarn's *Critical Essays of the Seventeenth Century* (II. 181-255). Early eighteenth-century views of Shakespeare will be found in Pope's preface to his ed. (1725) and in the essays of Steele and Addison (*Tatler*, 35, 47, 188; *Spectator*, 40, 44, 235, 592). Dr Johnson's earliest Shakespearian criticism is to be found in his *Miscellaneous Observations on the Tragedy of Macbeth* (1745) and *Proposals for Printing the Dramatick Works of William Shakespeare* (1756). His most valuable Shakespearian criticism is to be found in the great *Preface to Shakespeare* (1765) and notes to his ed. A good selection from his Shakespearian criticism is to be found in *Johnson on Shakespeare* ed. Sir W. Raleigh. Among the most notable critical essays of the later eighteenth century are M. Morgann's *Essay on the Dramatic Character of Falstaff* (1777, rptd, 1912) and W. Whiter's *Specimen of a Commentary on Shakespeare* (1794). There is a useful collection of eighteenth-century criticisms of Shakespeare in *Eighteenth Century Critical Essays on Shakespeare*, ed. D. Nichol Smith (1903). See also D. Nichol Smith, *Shakespeare in the Eighteenth Century* (1928) and D. Lovett, *Shakespeare's Characters in Eighteenth Century Criticism* (Baltimore, 1935).

Nineteenth and Twentieth Centuries

S. T. Coleridge's *Notes and Lectures on Shakespeare* contain the most important Shakespearian criticism of the romantic period. They are collected in the vol. called *Lectures on Shakespeare*, ed. T. Ashe (Bohn's Library), and in the modern standard ed., *Coleridge's Shakespeare Criticism*, ed. Raysor (2 vols., 1935). W. Hazlitt, *Characters of Shakespeare's Plays*, still one of the best books of its kind, appeared in 1817 and is now available in W.C. C. Lamb's contributions to Shakespearian criticism are to be found in his essay on *The Tragedies of Shakespeare considered with Reference to their Fitness for Stage Representation* (1811), and various passages in his *Miscellaneous Prose* (see *The Works of Charles and Mary Lamb*, ed. E. V. Lucas, Vol. I). Among the most important critical works of the later nineteenth century were E. Dowden, *Shakespeare, his Mind and Art* (1894) and A. C. Swinburne, *A Study of Shakespeare* (1880). R. G. Moulton, *Shakespeare as a Dramatic Artist* (1885) is an interesting study of the structure of the plays, and there are stimulating remarks in Bernard Shaw's *Dramatic Opinions and Essays* (1906). The most notable critical studies of the twentieth century include A. C. Bradley, *Shakespearian Tragedy* (1904) and his other Shakespearian essays in *Oxford Lectures on Poetry* and *A Miscellany*, Sir Walter Raleigh, *Shakespeare* (E.M.L., 1907); J. Masefield, *Shakespeare* (H.U.L., 1911); Sir A. T. Quiller Couch, *Shakespeare's Workmanship* (1918); G. Wilson Knight, *The Wheel of Fire* (1930, enl. ed., 1948), *The Imperial Theme* (1941), *The Sovereign Flower* (1958); J. D. Wilson, *The Essential Shakespeare* (1932); E. E. Stoll, *Art and Artifice in Shakespeare* (1933); *Aspects of Shakespeare* (British Academy Lectures by various authors, 1933); H. Granville Barker, *Prefaces to Shakespeare* (5 vols., 1933-46); J. Middleton Murry, *Shakespeare* (1936); K. Muir and S. O. Loughlin, *The Voyage to Illyria* (1937); B. Traversi, *Approach to Shakespeare* (1938, enl. ed., 1957); R. W. Chambers, *Man's Unconquerable Mind* (1939); G. B. Harrison, *Introducing Shakespeare* (P. B., 1939); T. Spencer, *Shakespeare and the Nature of Man* (1943); S. L. Bethell, *Shakespeare and the Popular Dramatic Tradition* (1944); L. C. Knights, *Explorations* (1946) and *Further Explorations* (1965), *Some Shakespearian Themes* (1959); U. Ellis Fermor, *The Study of Shakespeare* (1948); H. Fluchère, *Shakespeare* (Marseilles, 1948, Engl. tr., 1953); F. P. Wilson, *Marlowe and the Early Shakespeare* (1950); A. Sewell, *Character and Society in Shakespeare* (1951); D. G. James, *The Dream of Learning* (1951); J. F. Danby, *Poets on Fortune's Hill* (1951); F. R. Leavis, *The Common Pursuit* (1952); P. Cruttwell, *The Shakespearian Moment* (1954); D. Bush, *Shakespeare and the Natural Condition* (1956). Useful general guides are *A Companion to Shakespeare* ed. H. Granville Barker and G. B. Harrison (1935), F. E. Halliday, *A Shakespeare Companion 1550–1950* (1952), G. I. Duthie, *Shakespeare* (1951) and T. M. Parrott, William Shakespeare, a Handbook (1944).

Shakespeare's Theatre and Audience

The theatrical aspect of Shakespeare's art is discussed in A. C. Bradley's 'Shakespeare's Theatre and Audience' in his *Oxford Lectures on Poetry*; in C. J. Sisson's *Le goût public et le théâtre élisabethian jusqu'à la mort de Shakespeare* (Dijon, 1922); in R. Bridges's 'The Influence of the Audience on Shakespeare's Plays' in his *Collected Essays*, vol. I in three valuable Shakespeare Association Lectures (all pub. 1927): G. H. Cowling, *Shakespeare and the Elizabethan Stage*, J. Isaacs, *Shakespeare as Man of the Theatre* and G. B. Harrison, *Shakespeare's Actors*; and in M. C. Bradbrook's *Elizabethan Stage Conditions, a Study of their Place in the Interpretation of Shakespeare's Plays* (1932). See also A. C. Sprague, *Shakespeare and his Audience* (1936) and W. J. Lawrence, *Speeding up Shakespeare* (1937).

Studies of Some Special Aspects of Shakespeare's Works

Studies of Shakespeare's comedies will be found in H. B. Charlton, *Shakespearian Comedy* (1938), D. L. Stevenson, *The Love Game* (N.Y., 1946), J. Palmer, *The Comic Characters of Shakespeare* (1946), S. C. Sen Gupta, *Shakespearian Comedy* (Calcutta, 1951); of his fairies in A. Nutt, *The Fairy Mythology of Shakespeare* (1900); of his fools in Lionel Johnson, 'The Fools of Shakespeare' in his *Postlimium* (1911), and in S. Davey, 'Fools, Jesters and Comic Characters of Shakespeare' (R.S.L., XXIII, 1923); of his heroes in Wyndham Lewis, *The Lion and the Fox* (1927); of his historical plays in W. Pater, 'Shakespeare's English Kings' in his *Appreciations* (1889), E. M. W. Tillyard, *Shakespeare's History Plays* (1944, P.B., 1962), J. Palmer, *The Political Characters of Shakespeare* (1945) and Lily B. Campbell, *Shakespeare's 'Histories'* (San Marino, 1947); of his imagery in W. Whiter, *Specimen of a Commentary on Shakespeare* (1794), C. F. E. Spurgeon, *Leading Motives in the Imager of Shakespeare's Tragedies* (Shakesp. Assoc. Lecture, 1930), *Shakespeare's Iterative Imagery* (1931), *Shakespeare's Imagery* (1936) and W. Clemen, *The Development of Shakespeare's Imagery* (1951); of his last plays in D. G. James,

Scepticism and Poetry (1937), E. M. W. Tillyard, *Shakespeare's Last Plays* (1938), G. Wilson Knight, *The Crown of Life* (1947), D. A. Traversi, *Shakespeare, the Last Phase* (1954); on music in the plays in R. Noble, *Shakespeare's Use of Song* (1923) and E. W. Naylor, *Shakespeare and Music* (1931); of his poetry in F. E. Halliday, *The Poetry of Shakespeare's Plays* (1954); of his problem plays in E. M. W. Tillyard, *Shakespeare's Problem Plays* (1949); of his tragedies in A. C. Bradley, *Shakespearian Tragedy* (1904), G. Wilson Knight, *The Wheel of Fire* (1930), H. B. Charlton, *Shakespearian Tragedy* (1948), and C. Leech, *Shakespeare's Tragedies and other Studies in Seventeenth Century Drama* (1950). J. A. K. Thomson, *Shakespeare and the Classics* (1952), gives a useful account of the connections between the plays and ancient classical literature.

Studies of Individual Plays

The following are some notable studies of individual plays: P. Alexander, *Shakespeare's Henry VI and Richard III* (1929); A. C. Bradley, 'The Rejection of Falstaff' in his *Oxford Lectures on Poetry* (1919); J. D. Wilson, *The Fortunes of Falstaff* (1948); T. S. Eliot, '*Hamlet*' in *The Sacred Wood* (1920); A. J. A. Waldock, *Hamlet* (1931); J. D. Wilson, *What Happens in Hamlet* (1935, rev. ed., 1951); S. de Madariaga, *On Hamlet* (1947); J. O. Campbell, *Comicall Satyre and Shakespeare's Troilus and Cressida* (San Marino, 1938); R. W. Chambers, 'The Jacobean Shakespeare and *Measure for Measure*' (Br. Ac., 1937, rptd. in his *Man's Unconquerable Mind*); articles on *Measure for Measure* in *Scrutiny*, 1942 by F. R. Leavis, L. C. Knights and D. A. Traversi; M. Lascelles, *Shakespeare's Measure for Measure* (1953); F. R. Leavis, 'Diabolic Intellect and the Noble Hero' [study of *Othello*], *Scrutiny*, VI, 1938, rptd. in his *The Common Pursuit*; R. W. Chambers, '*King Lear*' (Glasgow, 1946); E. Muir, 'The Politics of *King Lear*' (Glasgow, 1947, rptd. in his *Essays on Literature and Society*, 1949); J. F. Danby, *Shakespeare's Doctrine of Nature*, a *Study of King Lear* (1949); A. C. Bradley, 'Shakespeare's *Antony and Cleopatra*' in his *Oxford Lectures on Poetry*; F. R. Leavis, '*Antony and Cleopatra* and *All for Love*, a *Critical Exercise*' in *Scrutiny*, V, 1937; A. C. Bradley, '*Coriolanus*' (Br. Ac., 1912, rptd. in his *A Miscellany*, 1929); D. Traversi, '*Coriolanus*' in *Scrutiny*, VI, 1938; F. C. Tinkler, '*Cymbeline*' in *Scrutiny*, VII, 1939; S. L. Bethell, '*The Winter's Tale, a Study*' (1947); C. Still, *Shakespeare's Mystery Play* [study of *The Tempest*] (1921); G. Wilson Knight, *The Shakespearian Tempest* (1932); R. G. Howarth, *Shakespeare's Tempest* (Sydney, 1936).

TEXTUAL CRITICISM AND BIBLIOGRAPHIES

The serious study of the text of Shakespeare begins with Lewis Theobald's *Shakespeare Restored* (1726, 2nd ed., 1740). Thomas Tyrrwhit and Edward Capell made useful contributions to Shakespearian textual criticism in the eighteenth century and the work of Edmond Malone in his edd. mentioned above (p. 250) is of the highest importance. The Preface to the Cambridge ed. of 1863-88 contains an account of previous work on the text. In modern times the study of Shakespeare's text has been revolutionized by the work of A. W. Pollard in his *Shakespeare Folios and Quartos* (1909), *Shakespeare's Fight with the Pirates* (1917) and other publications, by Percy Simpson's *Shakespearean Punctuation* (1911) and by Sir E. Maunde Thompson's *Shakespeare's Handwriting* (1916). Accounts of the new approach to Shakespeare's text are given in Percy Simpson's *The Bibliographical Study of Shakespeare* (Oxford Bib. Soc. i, 1923), C. H. Herford's *A Sketch of Recent Shakespearian Investigation 1893-1923* (1923) and the Textual Introd. to the New Cambridge Shakespeare by J. D. Wilson (Vol. I, *The Tempest*, 1921). The two Br. Ac. lectures, *The Foundations of Shakespeare's Text* by A. W. Pollard (1923) and *The Principals of Emendation in Shakespeare* by W. W. Greg (1928) are important. More recent valuable contributions to the study of the text are *Prolegomena for the Oxford Shakespeare* by R. B. McKerrow (1939) and *The Editorial Problem in Shakespeare* (1942).

The best general bibliographies are W. Jaggard's *Shakespeare Bibliography* (Stratford-on-Avon, 1911), and W. Ebisch and L. A. Schücking's *Shakespeare Bibliography* (1931), with *Supplement for the Years 1930-35*. Henrietta C. Bartlett's *Mr William Shakespeare. Original and Early Editions of his Quartos and Folios, his Source Books and those containing Contemporary Notices* (New Haven, Connecticut, 1922) is very full within the limits indicated by its title.

SHAKESPEARE SOCIETIES AND PERIODICALS

There is an account of *Shakespeare Societies Past and Present* by F. S. Boas in *The Shakespeare Review* (No. i, 1928). The earliest Shakespeare Society was founded in 1840 by J. P. Collier and the chief contributors to its transactions were J. P. Collier, J. O. Halliwell-Phillipps and J. N. Halpin. It issued forty-eight publications between 1840 and 1853. They included Cunningham's edd. of the *Revels Documents*, Dyce's ed. of *Sir Thomas More* and Collier's ed. of *Henslow's Diary*, besides many plays. The New Shakespeare Society was founded by F. J. Furnivall in 1874 and remained in existence till 1886. Its twenty-seven publications are of great value and include, besides numerous vols. of Transactions, edd. of *Romeo and Juliet* (parallel texts), *Henry V* (parallel texts), *Cymbeline*, and *The Two Noble Kinsmen*.

The Shakespeare Association pub. ten facs. and eighteen pamphlets between 1917 and 1934. American Societies include The New York Shakespeare Society founded in 1885, which has issued thirteen publications, and the Shakespeare Association of America founded in 1926, which publishes an *Annual Bulletin* issued at New York. The German *Shakespeare Gesellschaft* has pub. its *Shakespeare Jahrbuch* (Berlin) annually since 1865. *Shakespeare Survey, An Annual Survey of Shakespearian Study and Production* ed. A. Nicoll (1948-) is of the highest value.

COLLECTIONS OF 'SOURCES'

The first collection of Shakespearian sources to be pub. was Charlotte Lennox's *Shakespeare Illustrated* (1753-4) which includes source material for twenty-two plays. *Shakespeare's Library* ed. J. P. Collier in 2 vols. appeared in 1845. A rev. and enl. ed. of this collection in 6 vols., ed. W. C. Hazlitt (1875), contains sources of thirty-five plays. Sir I. Gollancz's *Shakespeare Classics* (1907) include notable edd. of *Shakespeare's Plutarch* by C. F. Tucker Brooke, Greene's *Pandosto or Dorastus and Fawnia* ed. P. G. Thomas and *The Sources of Hamlet* ed. I. Gollancz. The best and fullest collection is *The Narrative and Dramatic Sources of Shakespeare* ed. G. Bullough, 3 vols. (1957-60).

LINGUISTIC STUDIES

E. A. Abbott's *A Shakespearian Grammar* (1869) is still a standard work. There is a German *Shakespeare Grammatik* by Wilhelm Franz (1st ed. Halle, 1898, 2nd ed. Heidelberg, 1924). Henry Bradley's article on *Shakespeare's English* in *Shakespeare's England* (1917), and G. Gordon's *Shakespeare's English* (S.P.E. Tract No. XXXIX, 1928) are the best modern studies of Shakespeare's language. Reference should also be made to Otto Jespersen's *Growth and Structure of the English Language* (Leipzig, 1926), Owen Barfield's *History in English Words* (1926) and *Poetic Diction* by the same author (1928). Valuable works on Shakespeare's pronunciation are W. Viëtor's *Shakespeare's Pronunciation* (Marburg, 1906), and R. E. Zacchrison's *Shakespeare's Uttal* (Uppsala, 1914). See also C. Davies's *English Pronunciation from the Fifteenth to the Eighteenth Century* (1934).

SELECTIONS

William Dodds' *The Beauties of Shakespeare regularly selected from each Play* (2 vols., 1752) is an interesting selection, which was rptd. several times. The Nonesuch Press pub. a *Shakespeare Anthology* in 1936.

BOOKS OF REFERENCE

The earliest work of the concordance type seems to have been *An Index to the Remarkable Passages and Words in Shakespeare* by S. Ayscough (1790). Mary Cowden Clarke's *The Complete Concordance to Shakespeare* appeared in 1847 (rev. ed. 1870). Charles and Mary Cowden Clarke also pub. in 1880 *The Shakespeare Key forming a companion to the Concordance*. The standard modern concordance is *A New and Complete Concordance to Shakespeare* by John Bartlett (1906). The standard German lexicon is A. Schmidt's *Shakespeare-Lexicon* (Berlin, 1874-75, rev. ed. by G. Sarrazin, Berlin, 1902). There is also *A New Shakespearian Dictionary* by R. J. Cunliffe (1910). The chief glossaries are that of Alexander Dyce (1880; rev. ed. by H. Littledale, 1902) and C. T. Onions's *Shakespeare Glossary* (Oxford, 1911). W. W. Skeat's *A Glossary of Tudor and Stuart Words* (rev. ed. Oxford, 1914) may also be consulted with profit. There is an *Index to Shakespeare's Thought* by C. Arnold (1880) and *A Dictionary of the Characters and Proper Names in Shakespeare* by F. G. Stokes (1924).

CHAPTER XI

ELIZABETHAN DIVINES

GENERAL STUDIES

FOR ecclesiastical history, see R. W. Dixon, *History of the Church of England . . . to 1570*, 6 vols. (3rd ed. 1895-1902), J. Gairdner, *The English Church in the Sixteenth Century* (1905), H. N. Birt, *The Elizabethan Religious Settlement* (1907), and Sir M. Powicke, *The Reformation in England* (1941). For preaching, see E. C. Dargan, *A History of Preaching*, 2 vols. (1905-13), J. E. Kempe, *Classic Preachers of the Church of England*, 2 ser. (1877-78) and W. Fraser Mitchell, *English Pulpit Oratory* (1932). There is a useful chapter by F. E. Hutchinson in C.H.E.L. (IV, xii). For early Puritans, see J. Brown, *The English Puritans* (1910), M. M. Knappen, *Tudor Puritanism* (Chicago, 1939), and W. Haller, *The Rise of Puritanism* (N.Y., 1938, paperback ed., 1957). The last named work is particularly valuable both for this period and the early seventeenth century.

LANCELOT ANDREWES (1555-1626)

In his own day the saintly Lancelot Andrewes, Bishop successively of Chichester, Ely and Winchester, enjoyed a great reputation as a preacher, and practically all his publications issued during his lifetime were sermons. These were collected at the command of Charles I by Archbishop Laud and J. Buckeridge and pub. in 1629 with the title *XCVI Sermons*. Later rpts. appeared in 1631, 1635, 1641. *Selections from the Sermons of Lancelot Andrews* by J. S. Utterton was pub. in 1865 (re-issued 1867) and a C.P.T. ed. of *Two Sermons on the Resurrection*, delivered April 16th, 1609, and April 20th, 1617, respectively, appeared in 1932. Though an unwilling controversialist, Andrewes was called on to reply to Cardinal Bellarmine's answer to King James's *Apologie for the Oath of*

Allegiance. His reply, entitled *Tortura Torti: sive ad Matthaei Torti librum responsio* . . ., appeared in 1609. An excerpt from it, *The Limits of Royal Supremacy in the Church of England*, appeared in 1877, later ed. 1884. He was employed on the *Authorized Version* of the Bible, the tr. of the Pentateuch being allotted to him and others. The work by which Andrewes is best known to modern times was not written for publication at all. This was a devotional work of which a fragmentary version in English appeared in 1647 with the title *A Manual of the Private Devotions of Lancelot Andrewes. Translated out of a fair Greek MS. of his amanuensis by R. D. (R. Drake)*. The orig. version was pub. by John Lampshire in 1675; *Rev. Patris Lanc. Andrewes . . . Preces privatae Graece Latine*. English trs. of his work have often been printed. Among the important modern versions is that by J. H. Newman originally pub. in the *Tracts for the Times*, 1840, and several times rptd., the most recent ed. being that of 1920. Other modern edd. are those by F. Meyrick, 1865-73; P. G. Medd, 1892 (later ed. 1899); and F. E. Brightman, 1903.

Andrewes's works were ed. by J. P. Wilson and J. Bliss and pub. at Oxford in 1841-54 as part of the *Library of Anglo-Catholic Theology*, the last vol, containing an *Index of Texts*, and *General Index to Sermons*.

Lives of Andrewes have been written by R. L. Ottley (1894) and A Whyte (1896). A study by D. Macleane, *Lancelot Andrewes and the Reaction* appeared in 1910. There is a valuable essay by T. S. Eliot on *Lancelot Andrewes* (first pub. in *For Lancelot Andrewes*, 1928, rptd. in *Essays Ancient and Modern*, 1936).

JOHN JEWEL (1522-71)

Up to the time of his appointment as Bishop of Salisbury in 1559 Jewel had, in his own words, 'never set abroad in print twenty lines'. In 1559 at St Paul's Cross he preached his famous 'challenge' sermon (repeated in later sermons) against Romish practices. It was printed in 1560 with the title *The Copie of a Sermon pronounced by the Bishop of Salisburie at Paules Crosse the second Sondaye before Easter . . . 1560*. The challenge was taken up by Henry Cole and later by Thomas Harding and a number of controversial writings passed between them. In 1562 Jewel published his *Apologia pro Ecclesia Anglicana*, a methodical account of the position of the English Church. It was translated into English the same year under the direction of Archbishop Parker, but this tr. was superseded by one made by Ann Lady Bacon in 1564, *An Apologie or Aunswer in defence of the Church of England*. . . . Both the Latin orig. and the tr. were repeatedly rptd. Lady Ann Bacon's version of *The Apologie* was ed. R. W. Jelf (1859) and Extracts from it by H. L. Clarke (1925). In the following years, from 1565-70, Jewel was engaged in controversy with Harding. In 1570 he issued a reply to the Bull of 1570 excommunicating Queen Elizabeth: *A View of a Seditious Bull*. After his death his friend John Garbrand ed. a work compiled from his sermons at Salisbury, entitled *Short Treatise of Holy Scripture*, 1582. The following works were also pub. posthumously: *An Exposition upon the two Epistles to the Thessalonians*, 1583, later edd. 1584, 1594; *Certaine Sermons preached before the Queenes Maiestie and at Paules crosse* . . ., ed. 1583, later ed. 1603. Jewel's works were first ed. Fuller under the direction of Archbishop Bancroft in 1609 (later ed. 1611). Modern edd. of his works were ed. E. W. Jelf, 1848, and J. Ayre for the Parker Society, 1845-50.

A memoir of Jewel by D. Featley was included in the 1609 ed. of the works; this was based on the official *Life* by Jewel's friend Lawrence Humphrey soon after Jewel's death, *Joannis, Juelli Angli, episcopi Sarisburiensis vita et mors*, 1573. A life by Le Bas appeared in Vol. II of the *Theological Library* in 1835. Ayre's ed. of the works, 1845-50, contains a useful memoir and a useful article is contributed to the D.N.B. by Mandell Creighton.

THOMAS CARTWRIGHT (1535-1603)

Soon after the publication of the famous *Admonition to Parliament* (1572) by John Field and Thomas Wilcox, which is considered to mark the beginning of the Puritan movement in England, another work entitled *A Seconde Admonition to the Parliament* appeared. This has been attributed to Cartwright, but his latest biographer confidently rejects the attribution. Cartwright did, however, write the reply to John Whitgift's answer to these pamphlets; it was entitled, *A Replye to an Answere made of M. Doctor Whitegifte againste the Admonition to Parliament*, 1574. Cartwright had to continue his part of the controversy abroad, for a warrant was issued for his arrest and he fled the country. *The Second Replie . . . agaynst Maister Whitegiftes second answer . . .* was probably pub. Froschauer in Zürich in 1575; *The Rest of the Second Replie . . .*, 1577 was also pub. abroad. This controversy with Whitgift was one of the immediate causes of the composition of Hooker's *Of the Lawes of Ecclesiastical Polity*, a reply to which from the Puritan standpoint, *A Christian Letter of Certaine English Protestants unto Mr R. Hoo . . .*, 1599, has, without much probability, been attributed to Cartwright.

During his exile at Middleburgh he composed his learned criticisms of the Rheims version of the New Testament of 1582; these were pub. later: $\Sigma\nu\nu\ \Theta\varepsilon\tilde{\omega}\ \dot{\varepsilon}\nu\ X\rho\iota\sigma\tau\tilde{\omega}$ *The answere to the preface of the Remish Testament . . .*, 1602 and *A Confutation of the Rhemists Translation, glosses and annotations on the New Testament*, 1618; later edd. of the latter appeared in 1627, 1632, 1638, 1683. One of his interesting publications pub. after his death is an exposition of the main doctrines of the Christian religion, *A Treatise of Christian Religion or the whole Bodie and Substance of Divinitie . . .*, 1616. Cartwright also pub. commentaries on *Ecclesiastes*, *Colossians* and *Proverbs*.

A diligent but uncritical memoir of Cartwright by Benjamin Brook appeared in 1845, and J. B. Mullinger contributes a useful sketch to D.N.B. The most recent work, however, A. J. J. Pearson's scholarly *Thomas Cartwright and*

Elizabethan Puritanism, 1535-1603 (1925) contains so much new material that the older lives are entirely superseded. See also *Cartwrightiana* ed. L. H. Carlson (1951).

RICHARD HOOKER (1554?-1600)

Hooker's famous book *Of the Lawes of Ecclesiasticall Politie*, was entered at Stationers' Hall on January 29th, 1593, and submitted to Lord Burghley for approval the following March. The first four books were pub. with no date on the title page; Izaak Walton in his *Life* gives the date as 1594. This instalment bore the title *Of the Lawes of Ecclesiasticall Politie, Eyght bookes*, printed by John Windet. Book V was pub. Windet in 1597, but at the time of Hooker's premature death in 1600, three books were still unpublished. Books VI and VIII were pub. in 1648; book VII appeared for the first time in the ed. of Hooker's works pub. John Gauden in 1662. The authenticity of these three books was questioned by Izaak Walton in 1665, and has been a matter of controversy since then. As early as 1604 it was stated that the MSS. of these three books were destroyed by Hooker's wife's relatives, and it may be that our versions were put together from rough drafts. Book VI is considered the most doubtful. There have been more than thirty-five edd. of the *Ecclesiastical Polity*, besides edd. of the separate books. Following the orig. ed., books I–IV were again pub. in 1594, and books I–V in 1611. In 1617-18 another ed. appeared which included also the sermons which had been separately pub. in 1612-14. The work was then rptd. at frequent intervals. In 1648, books VI and VIII appeared for the first time. Book VII made its first appearance in the ed. of the *Works* prepared by Bishop John Gauden in 1662. Gauden's ed. included a *Life of Hooker* by Gauden himself, but in later edd. this life was replaced by that by Izaak Walton, which was originally written and pub. in 1665 as a corrective to that of Gauden. In this rev. state Gauden's ed. was rptd. in 1666 and at frequent intervals. An ed. of 1705 contained additions to this *Life* by John Strype.

In 1830 a controversial ed. by Benjamin Hanbury appeared, and this may have caused John Keble to prepare what, in its latest form, has become the standard ed. It was first pub. in 1836; a seventh ed. by R. W. Church and F. Paget was pub. in 1888. The following are the chief edd. of separate parts of the *Ecclesiastical Polity*: Book I ed. R. W. Church with introd. and glossary (O.U.P.); Book V ed. R. Bayne with Prolegomena etc. (O.U.P.); Book VIII ed. R. A. Houk (N.Y., 1931). An ed. of Books I–IV appeared in M.U.L. in 1888 and of Books I–V in the Ev. Lib. in 1907.

The other extant writings of Hooker include four noble sermons printed after his death in 1612. They contain some of the most impressive prose of the Elizabethan age. They were rptd. with *Of the Lawes of Ecclesiastical Politie* in most of the old edd. and separately in *Pocket Sacred Classics* Vol. V (1845).

Biography and Criticism

Walton's beautiful life of Hooker was first pub. in 1665 and afterwards rptd. in edd. of Hooker's works and in all edd. of Walton's *Lives*. The best modern authority is the life in Keble's ed. of the works rev. by Church and Paget, 1888. Sir Sidney Lee contributes an article to the D.N.B., which deals extensively with the question of the genuineness of Books VI–VIII. There is a valuable essay on *Hooker's Ecclesiastical Polity* by Sir James Stephen in his *Horae Sabbaticae* (1892, I. v). See also F. Paget's *Introduction to Hooker's Ecclesiastical Polity, Book V* (1899), the examination of the MS. of Book V in the Bodleian by P. Simpson in O.B.S., II, i. 1927, E. T. Davies, *The Political Ideas of Hooker* (1946), and P. Munz, *The Place of Hooker in the History of Thought* (1952).

THE MARPRELATE CONTROVERSY

'Martin Marprelate' was the name assumed by the anonymous author or authors of certain Puritan pamphlets attacking the English Bishops, which appeared between 1587 and

1589. The 'Marprelate Pamphlets' still extant are seven in number. The first two of these were written ostensibly in reply to a work by John Bridges, Dean of Sarum, *A Defence of the Government established in the Church of Englande for Ecclesiasticall Matters*, 1587, which defended the cause of the Bishops against the Puritan attacks. Martin Marprelate's first pamphlet was entitled *Oh read over D. John Bridges, for it is a worthy worke, Or an epitome of the fyrste Booke, of that right worshipfull volume . . . The Epitome is not yet published, but it shall be when the Bishops are at convenient leysure to view the same. In the meane time, let them be content with this learned Epistle . . .*, secretly printed at East Molesey, 1588. The promised *Epitome* was secretly printed at Fawsley, near Northampton, a month or so later. Both these were rptd. in J. Petheram's *Puritan Discipline Tracts*, 1860, the former also in E. Arber's, *English Scholar's Library*, No. 11, 1880, later ed. 1895.

Martin Marprelate's pamphlets were answered by Thomas Cooper, Bishop of Winchester, in *An Admonition to the People of England . . .*, three edd. of which appeared in 1589; modern rpts. in Petheram's *Puritan Discipline Tracts*, 1847, later ed. 1860 and Arber's *English Scholar's Library*, No. 15, 1882, later ed. 1895. The episcopal cause was also championed by Richard Bancroft in *A Sermon preached at Paules Crosse the 9 of Februarie*, pub. in an enl. form in March 1589. This was actually after the first Marprelate reply to Bishop Cooper's *Admonition*, which was entitled *Certain Minerall and Metaphysical Schoolpoints to be defended by the reverende Bishops . . .*, printed at Coventry and issued about February 20th. The second, more substantial reply appeared one month later with the punning title, *Hay any worke for Cooper . . .* This was later rptd. in 1641 with the title, *Reformation no enemie . . .*; a modern ed. is included in Petheram's, *Puritan Discipline Tracts*, 1845, later ed. 1860.

At this time the desertion of the Marprelate printer, Robert Waldegrave, held up 'Martin's' activities. In the interval the bishops adopted the policy, suggested by Bancroft, of employing professional writers to write their replies. Apart from the fact that John Lyly and Thomas Nashe are supposed to have been engaged in their composition these have little to recommend them and they are far inferior to Martin Marprelate's productions. The first of these, *A Whip for an Ape* . . . and *Mar-Martine* . . . have been attributed to Lyly; they are included in R. W. Bond's ed. of Lyly's works, 1902. A number of other anti-Martinist pamphlets appeared, a full list of which will be found in the bibliography, C.H.E.L. III, 537–45.

Martinist activity began again in July 1589 with the pub. of *Theses Martinianae* . . ., secretly printed by John Hodgkins at Wolston, and purporting to be by 'Martin Junior'. A sequel, by an 'elder brother, Martin Senior', entitled, *The iust censure and reproofe of Martin Junior*, appeared a week later, printed by Hodgkins at Wolston. The final Martinist tract, *The Protestatyon of Martin Marprelate* . . . appeared in October 1589 after the press had been seized and confiscated; it was probably printed by Waldegrave at the house of Job Throckmorton.

A valuable collection of documents bearing on the controversy was pub. E. Arber in the *English Scholar's Library*, *An Introductory Sketch to the Martin Marprelate Controversy*, 1880, later ed. 1895. An excellent survey by W. Pierce, entitled *An Historical Introduction to the Marprelate Tracts*, appeared in 1908. J. Dover Wilson contributed to *The Library* a series of articles on the controversy during the years 1907-12, and he is also responsible for the chapter in C.H.E.L. (III, xvii). A collected ed. of all the Marprelate tracts was pub. W. Pierce in 1911. G. Bonnard, *La Controverse de Martin Marprelate* (Geneva, 1916), gives a useful historical survey.

THE SEVENTEENTH CENTURY

(For historical background see Macaulay's *History of England*, Trevelyan's *England under the Stuarts*, the two relevant vols. in the *Oxford History of England*, *The Early Stuarts* by Godfrey Davies, and *The Later Stuarts* by G. N. Clark; C. V. Wedgwood, *Strafford* [1935], *Velvet Studies* [1946] and *The King's Peace* [1954]; and C. Hill, *The English Revolution, 1640* [1940] and *The Century of Revolution* [1961]. For social life see M. Coate, *Social Life in Stuart England* [1924], and C. Hill and M. Dell, *The Good Old Cause* [1949], and for the history of thought, *The Seventeenth Century* by G. N. Clark, *The Seventeenth Century Background* by Basil Willey, and *The Great Chain of Being* by A. O. Lovejoy [Harvard, 1942]. Other valuable general works are *Men of Letters and the English Public in the Eighteenth Century* by A. Beljame [English tr. by E. O. Lorimer, 1948]; *The First Half of the Seventeenth Century* [1906] and *Cross Currents in English Literature of the Seventeenth Century* [1925] by Sir Herbert Grierson; *Antike Renaissance and Puritanismus* by W. Schirmer [Munich, 1933]; *The Rise of Puritanism 1570-1642* by W. Haller [N.Y., 1938, P.B., 1937]; *Seventeenth-Century Studies* presented to Sir Herbert Grierson [1938], *English Literature in the Earlier Seventeenth Century 1600-1660* by D. Bush [1945], *Seventeenth Century English Literature* [H.U.L., 1950], and *Poetry and Politics under the Stuarts* [1960] both by C. V. Wedgwood.)

CONTENTS

CHAPTER		PAGE
XII	PHILOSOPHICAL WRITERS	281
XIII	METAPHYSICAL POETRY	293
XIV	THE LATER DRAMA UP TO THE CIVIL WAR	304
XV	SECULAR PROSE OF THE SEVENTEENTH CENTURY	319
XVI	RELIGIOUS PROSE OF THE SEVENTEENTH CENTURY	332
XVII	POETRY FROM CAREW TO OLDHAM	342
XVIII	JOHN MILTON	354
XIX	RESTORATION DRAMA	373
XX	JOHN DRYDEN	386

CHAPTER XII
PHILOSOPHICAL WRITERS

THE seventeenth century saw the beginning of the great age of English philosophy, and students of seventeenth-century English literature are strongly advised to pay some attention to the works of the chief philosophic writers of the period, especially those of Bacon, Hobbes and the Cambridge Platonists. They should also acquaint themselves with at least the outlines of the philosophies of Descartes (*A Discourse on Method* tr. Veitch, Ev. Lib.) and Spinoza (*Ethics etc.* tr. Boyle, Ev. Lib.). Erdmann's *History of Philosophy* Vol. 2 (Modern) and Bertrand Russell's *History of Western Philosophy* can be profitably consulted.

GENERAL STUDIES

There are valuable chapters dealing with the early English philosophical writers by W. R. Sorley in C.H.E.L. (IV, xiv, VII, xii). *A History of English Philosophy* by the same author (rev. ed. 1937), and *The Seventeenth-Century Background* by Basil Willey (1934) should also be consulted.

INDIVIDUAL AUTHORS

FRANCIS BACON (1561-1626)

Separate Works

Bacon will be considered here only as a philosophic writer. For his non-philosophic works see pp. 244–5.

All his philosophic writings are connected with his great scheme for a renewal of all the sciences to be brought about through the agency of his work called the *Magna Instauratio*, which he never lived to complete. 'I have as vast contemplative ends as I have moderate civil ends', he wrote to Burghley in about 1592, 'for I have taken all knowledge to be my province.' His earliest philosophical work to be pub. was in English, *The Two Bookes of Francis Bacon, of the Proficiencie and Advancement of Learning, divine and humane* (1605) usually known as *The Advancement of Learning*. This was a kind of preliminary sketch of the first part of the *Magna Instauratio*. It was rptd. in 1629 and 1633. The best modern ed. is that of W. A. Aldis Wright (1869, 5th ed. 1900). There is also a useful ed. by T. Case (W.C.) with *The New Atlantis* and a good introd. In 1609 Bacon pub. his curious attempt to interpret ancient mythology called *De Sapientia Veterum*, tr. by Sir A. Gorges as *The Wisdom of the Ancients* (1619) and often rptd. with the essays. The first part of the *Instauratio Magna* to be pub. was the second section with a sketch of the third, pub. in 1620 under the title *Franscisci de Verulamio . . . Instauratio Magna*. It contains the second section of the work called *Novum Organum*, the most complete statement of Bacon's philosophy, and the sketch of the third called *Parasceve ad Historiam Naturalem et Experimentalem*. Both are written in stately Latin. The best modern ed. is that of T. Fowler (1878, 2nd ed. 1889). There are English trs. by P. Shaw (1802), W. Wood (1844), G. W. Kitchin (1855) and A. Johnson (1859). The first section of the third part of the *Instauratio* called *Historica Naturales et Experimentales* appeared in 1622. An English tr. by R. G. Gent was pub. in 1653. The first part of the great work called *De Dignitate et Augmentis Scientiarum*, usually known as the *De Augmentis*, was pub. in 1623. It is partly a tr. and partly an expansion of *The Advancement of Learning*. An English version by G. Wats appeared in 1640. In 1623 there also appeared a further instalment of the third part, *Historia vitae et mortis*; English version, *The Historie of Life and Death* (1638). The last of Bacon's philosophical works to be pub. was in English, *The Sylva Sylvarum: or a Naturall Historie. In ten centuries*, pub. in 1627 with the *New Atlantis*. The 10th ed. (1676) contains an epitome of the *Novum Organum*.

In 1653, J. Gruter pub. at Amsterdam the majority of the small works and sketches connected with the *Instauratio* as *Francisci Baconi scripta in naturali et universali philosophia*.

Collective Editions

The Latin works of Bacon were first collected and ed. by J. B. Schönwetter in 1665 and again by S. J. Arnold in 1694. The first comprehensive ed. was that of J. Blackbourne (1730). The best modern ed. of the complete works is that ed. J. Spedding, R. L. Ellis and D. D. Heath (1857-74). There is a useful ed. of the *Philosophical Works* rptd. from Spedding's ed. by J. M. Robertson (1905), a selection from the *Instauratio Magna* ed. T. W. Moffett (1847) and a selection from all the works by P. E. and E. F. Matheson (1922).

Biography and Criticism

The main authority for Bacon's life is *The Life and Letters* by James Spedding (1861-74). Among shorter monographs the following may be consulted: E. A. Abbott, *Francis Bacon an Account of his Life and Works* (1885), R. W. Church, *Bacon* (E.M.L.), M. Sturt, *Francis Bacon* (1932), C. Williams, *Bacon* (1933), B. Farrington, *Bacon* (N.Y., 1949), and J. G. Crowther, *Bacon, the First Statesman of Science*, (1961).

There are studies of Bacon's philosophy by J. Nichol (1888-9) and C. D. Broad (1926). See also *Bacon and the Seventeenth Century Dissociation of Sensibility* by L. C. Knights in *Explorations* (1946).

LORD HERBERT OF CHERBURY (1583-1648)

Edward Herbert, Baron Herbert of Cherbury, elder brother of George Herbert, the poet, besides being himself a poet, was perhaps the first English thinker since the age of the Schoolmen who can be strictly described as a metaphysician; he was also the first of the English deists or believers in 'natural' as opposed to 'revealed' religion. His two important philosophical works are both in Latin. They are (1) *De Veritate* (Paris, 1624); there are many later edd. That of 1645 includes two other works, *De Causis Errorum* (Engl. tr. by M. H. Carré, 1908) and *De Religione Laici* (ed. with tr. H. R. Hutchinson, New Haven, 1944). (2) *De Religione Gentilium* (1663), one of the first essays in comparative religion, Engl. tr., *The Antient Religion of the Gentiles*, by W. Lewis (1709). See B. Willey, 'Herbert of Cherbury: a Spiritual Quixote of the Seventeenth Century', E.S.M.E.A., xxxvi, 1941, and the very valuable and exhaustive Italian study by M. M. Rossi, *La vita, le opere, i tempi di Herbert di Cherbury* (3 vols., Florence, 1947). For Lord Herbert's poems and autobiography, see pp. 297, 324.

ROBERT GREVILLE, LORD BROOKE (1608-43)

Robert Greville was the cousin and adopted son of Fulke Greville, the poet (see p. 214). A Platonist in philosophy, an independent in religion and a republican in politics, he was killed while commanding a parliamentary force at the beginning of the Civil War. He wrote one short but important philosophical treatise, *The Nature of Truth, its Union and Unity with the Soule* in 1641. His other pub. work was an attack on the episcopal system called *A Discourse, opening the Nature of that Episcopacie which is exercised in England* (1642). Milton refers to him in terms of high praise in *Areopagitica*. A modern ed. of his works is needed. See *Robert Greville, Lord Brooke* by R. E. L. Strider (Cambridge, Mass., 1958) and the account of his philosophy in W. R. Sorley, *A History of English Philosophy* (1937).

THOMAS HOBBES (1588-1679)

Separate Works

Thomas Hobbes, son of a Wiltshire parson, was the most powerful and influential English writer on philosophy after Bacon in the seventeenth century. His works are the second link in the great chain of English philosophical discussion that began with Bacon and was continued by Locke, Berkeley and Hume. Hobbes only turned to philosophy comparatively late in life. He is said to have been forty when he first came across Euclid, and was so impressed by the geometrical method that (like his great French contemporary Descartes) he adopted it for philosophic purposes. About this time he seems to have fixed on his theory of motion as the fundamental explanation of things, and he soon began to build up his social and political philosophy of absolutism on this mechanistic basis. As early as 1640 he circulated in MS. a treatise called *The Elements of law Natural and Politic* which was not printed in full till 1889 when it was ed. from the MS. by F. Tönnies (later ed. 1928). His *Elementorum philosophiae sectio tertia de cive* appeared at Amsterdam in 1647. This treatise usually known as the *De Cive* was a development of the *Elements of law Natural and Politic* and was tr. into English under the title *Philosophicall Rudiments concerning Government*. Two parts of the *Elements* entitled *Humane Nature or the Fundamentall Elements of Policy* and *De Corpore politico or the Fundamental Elements of Law Moral and Politik* appeared in 1650. They contain the main elements of Hobbes's mechanistic and materialistic view of the universe and of man, which forms the basis of his great work *Leviathan or the*

Matter Forme and Power of a Commonwealth (1651). *Leviathan* was rptd. in 1680. There are many modern edd. The best are those of A. R. Waller (text only, 1904), of W. G. Pogson Smith (with valuable introd. 1909), of M. Oakeshott (1946), and in Ev. Lib. The first of three treatises of which the *De Cive* had been the third was pub. in 1655 under the title *Elementorum philosophiae sectio prima de corpore*. The second part *Elementorum Philosophiae sectio secunda de homine* appeared in 1658. An English tr. of the *De Corpore* corrected by Hobbes also appeared in 1658. Hobbes became involved in controversies on two fronts after the publication of these works. On the one hand he was attacked by Bishop Bramhall (see p. 286) for his rigid determinism set forth in his tract *Of Liberty and Necessity*, pub. without Hobbes's permission in 1654, and on the other by some of the chief mathematicians of the day such as Seth Ward and John Wallis for his strictures on academic teaching and his own brilliant but amateurish mathematical theories. He was also drawn into controversy with the great chemist Robert Boyle. Thus it will be seen that his views were distrusted equally by the orthodox churchmen and the scientists. His *Bethemoth: The History of the Causes of the Civil Wars of England* was written about 1668, but, by the command of the King, Hobbes refrained from publishing it. It appeared in 1680. There is a modern ed. by T. Tönnies (1889). Another work entitled *An Historical Narration concerning Heresie* was written about 1668 but not pub. till 1688. Hobbes's other works include an Ecclesiastical History (1688) and an *Autobiography* (1679) both in Latin elegiac verse. He also tr. Thucydides and Homer.

Collective Editions

A collection of Hobbes's Latin works was pub. at Amsterdam in 1668. His collected *Moral and Political Works* appeared in London in 1750. The standard modern ed. is that of Sir W. Molesworth (16 vols. 1839-45).

Biography and Criticism

The 'short life' of Hobbes by his friend and admirer John Aubrey will be found in Aubrey's *Short Lives*, ed. A. Clark (1898, i, 321-423). It is one of the most delightful of seventeenth-century biographies. There is an excellent monograph by S. Croom Robertson in *Blackwood's Philosophic Classics* (1886). The valuable

German dissertation by F. Tönnies, *Hobbes, Leben und Lehren*, appeared at Stuttgart in 1896. Sir Leslie Stephen wrote the vol. on Hobbes for the E.M.L. Series (1903). There are monographs by G. E. G. Catlin (1922), F. Brandt (tr. from the German, 1928), and J. Laird (in The Leaders of Philosophy Series, 1934). There are also excellent short studies of Hobbes's writings by Sir James Stephen in *Horae Sabbaticae* (1892, Series II) and by Basil Willey in the *Seventeenth Century Background* (pp. 93-111). There is a valuable Bibliography ed. H. Macdonald and M. Hargreaves (Bib. Soc., 1952).

JOHN BRAMHALL (1594-1663)

John Bramhall, Bishop of Derry and afterwards Archbishop of Armagh, was one of Hobbes's most powerful adversaries in philosophic controversy. He attacked Hobbes's determinism in *A Defence of the True Liberty of Human Actions from antecedent and extrinsecall Necessity* (1655). As a reply to Hobbes's rejoinder he pub. *Castigations of Mr. Hobbes his last animadversions in the case concerning Liberty and Universal Necessity. With an appendix concerning the catching of Leviathan or the great Whale* (1658). He also wrote various works of religious controversy. His *Works* ed. J. Vesey were pub. at Dublin 1676. A modern ed. by W. J. Sparrow with life and letters appeared in 1842-45. There is a German dissertation by J. H. Loewe (Prague 1887), a biography by W. J. S. Simpson (1927) and an interesting essay by T. S. Eliot in *Essays Ancient and Modern* (1936).

JAMES HARRINGTON (1611-77)

Harrington, the famous republican thinker, wrote his political romance *The Commonwealth of Oceana* (1656) as a constructive criticism of Hobbes's political theory. Although it has little literary distinction *Oceana* has an important place on the development of political thought, particularly with regard to the conception of a 'free' state. There are modern edd. by H. Morley in *Morley's Universal Library* (1887) and by S. B. Liljegren (Lund, 1924). Harrington's other chief works were his *Aphorisms political . . .* (1659) and *Political Discourses tending to the introduction of a free . . . commonwealth in England* (1660). Harrington's *Works* were collected and pub. John Toland in 1700. A study of *Oceana* and its influence in America is to be found in *Harrington and his Oceana* by

H. F. R. Smith (1914). There is a life in the D.N.B. by Sir L. Stephen.

THOMAS STANLEY (1625-78)

Thomas Stanley, scholar and poet, pub. the first *History of Philosophy* in English in 1655-62. Later edd. appeared in 1687, 1701 and 1743. Although a compilation, mainly from Diogenes Laertius, the book is important because it helped to disseminate interest in the atomism of Democritus and Epicurus. For Stanley's Poems, see below, p. 349.

THE CAMBRIDGE PLATONISTS

GENERAL STUDIES AND SELECTION

J. Tulloch's *Rational Theology and Christian Philosophy in England in the Seventeenth Century* (1862) is a solid and valuable study embodying the outlook of a typical liberal theologian of the nineteenth century. F. J. Powicke's *The Cambridge Platonists* (1926) contains a series of lively stimulating sketches with numerous quotations, but is neither profound nor very accurate. E. Cassirer's *Die Platonische Renaissance in England und die Schule von Cambridge* (Leipzig, 1932), pub. as one of the *Studien der Bibliothek Warburg*, is a valuable German philosophical survey. Basil Willey's *The Seventeenth Century Background* (1934) contains some of the most penetrating and valuable criticism of the Cambridge Platonists that has hitherto appeared. Reference should also be made to the chapter in the C.H.E.L. by J. Bass Mullinger (VIII, xi), to W. R. Inge's *The Platonic Tradition in English Thought*, to J. Hunt's *History of Religious Thought in England* and to W. R. Sorley's *History of English Philosophy*. Much light is also thrown on the Cambridge movement by certain contemporary writings such as *The Diary and Correspondence of Dr John Worthington* ed. J. Crossley (Chetham Society, Manchester, 1847-86), and *The Correspondence of Anne Viscountess Conway, Henry More and their Friends, 1642-94* ed. M. Nicholson (1930).

E. T. Campagnac's *The Cambridge Platonists* (1901) is an anthology of selections from Whichcote, Smith and Culverwel with a useful introd.

INDIVIDUAL AUTHORS

BENJAMIN WHICHCOTE (1609-83)

Works and Life

Whichcote was the real founder of the so-called Platonist School of liberal and philosophical divines at Cambridge. He pub. nothing in his lifetime, but acquired a great reputation as a preacher and lecturer at Cambridge from about 1644 onwards. Burnet writes of him that, 'he was much for liberty of conscience . . . he studied to raise those who conversed with him to a nobler set of thoughts and to consider religion as a seed of a deiform nature'. The first collection of his sermons to be pub. was Θεοφορούμενα Δόγματα *or some Select Notions of . . . Benj. Whichcote* . . . 1685. The third Earl of Shaftesbury, the philosopher, pub. an ed. of his *Select Sermons* with an introd. in 1698. This ed. was rptd. by W. Wishart in 1742. John Jeffery pub. *Several Discourses* in 1701 (2nd ed. 1702) and the same editor printed in 1717 a sermon of Whichcote called *The true Notion of Place in the Kingdom of Church or Christ*, and in 1703 his *Moral and Religious Aphorisms*. The most complete collection of Whichcote's sermons (without the *Aphorisms*) was pub. in 1751 at Aberdeen in 4 vols., entitled *The Works of the Learned Benjamin Whichcote*. In 1753 Samuel Salter pub. a greatly enl. ed. of the *Moral and Religious Aphorisms* with eight very interesting and significant letters which passed between Whichcote and Dr Tuckney, well-known Puritan divine. An excellent modern ed. of the *Moral and Religious Aphorisms* by W. R. Inge appeared in 1930. The only modern rpt. from the sermons is the selection given by Campagnac in *The Cambridge Platonists* (1901). A modern critical ed. of Whichcote's works is needed.

There is a brief, but very interesting character study of Whichcote by Burnet in *History of His Own Times*, I, 187, and another by Tillotson in his Funeral Sermon on him. There are modern studies by B. F. Westcott in his *Religious Thought in the West*, by

Campagnac and by Powicke (op. cit.). There is a biography in the D.N.B. by J. Bass Mullinger.

JOHN SMITH (1618-52)

John Smith was, perhaps, the most brilliant and profound thinker among the Cambridge Platonists and a writer of great distinction. He pub. nothing during his short life, but in 1660, eight years after his death, his friend John Worthington pub. his *Select Discourses*, a series of ten philosophical sermons or lectures containing the finest flower of the thought of the Cambridge School, and described by Dr W. R. Inge as 'the best University sermons that I know'. The vol. also includes a sermon by Simon Patrick preached at Smith's funeral, and a brief account of his life and death. A second ed. of the *Select Discourses* appeared in 1673, and another ed. by H. G. Williams in 1859. An abridgement with a memoir by John King was pub. in 1820. Campagnac's *The Cambridge Platonists* contains large extracts. A modern critical ed. of Smith's *Discourses* is needed.

Most of our knowledge of Smith's life is derived from the funeral sermon and memoir pub. with the *Select Discourses*. There is a useful article on him by J. B. Mullinger in the D.N.B., and a particularly valuable critical account of his work by Basil Willey in his *Seventeenth Century Background*, pp. 138-54.

NATHANAEL CULVERWEL (? 1618-? 51)

Culverwel, like John Smith, was a pupil of Whichcote, an admirable writer and a powerful and original thinker. His chief work is *An Elegant and Learned Discourse of the Light of Nature* (1652). This notable essay was ed. John Brown (Edinburgh, 1857) with a biographical and critical introd. Copious extracts from it are rptd. in Campagnac's *The Cambridge Platonists*.

RALPH CUDWORTH (1617-88)

Works

Cudworth was the most important and influential philosopher of the Cambridge school. His early works are two theological treatises both pub. in 1642 called *The True Notion of the Lord's Supper* and *The Church in a Shadow*. In 1647 he pub. his memorable *Sermon preached before the House of Commons . . . Mar. 31, 1647*, one of the greatest sermons in the English language. It was rptd. often in the nineteenth century. The most recent ed. is that pub. in 1930 by the Facsimile Text Society, N.Y. Cudworth devoted many years to his great work which was designed to confute the materialism of Hobbes. This is *The True Intellectual System of the Universe*, an immense monument of erudition, which appeared in 1678. A rev. ed. by T. Birch with three sermons appeared in 1743 and an abridgement by T. Wise in 1706. In 1733 J. L. Mosheim pub. a Latin tr. with important notes. This was rendered into English by J. Harrison, whose version appeared in 1845. Cudworth also left two important treatises in MS.: (1) *A Treatise concerning Eternal and Immutable Morality*, which was pub. E. Chandler, Bishop of Durham in 1731 and rptd. by Harrison in his ed. of *The True Intellectual System* (1845); (2) *A Treatise of Free Will*, first pub. by J. Allen in 1838. An ed. of Cudworth's *Works* in 4 vols. was published at Oxford and London in 1829.

Biography and Criticism

The chief authorities for Cudworth's life are the memoir by T. Birch prefixed to the 1743 ed. of the *True Intellectual System*, and rptd. in the 1829 ed. of the *Works*, that by J. L. Mosheim in his Latin version, and the article by Sir L. Stephen in the D.N.B. The chief critical works on his philosophy are *The Philosophy of Ralph Cudworth*, by C. E. Lowry, N.Y., 1884; and J. Beyer's *Ralph Cudworth als Ethiker, Staatsphilosoph und Aesthetiker* (Bonn University Dissertation, Bottrop, 1935). See also B. Willey's *The Seventeenth Century Background* and H. J. Grierson's *Cross Currents in English Literature of the Seventeenth Century* (1929).

HENRY MORE (1614–87)

Dr Henry More, the most fantastic and mercurial of the Cambridge Platonists, was a man of great learning and tireless literary activity. His early writings are poems in which he expounds in Spenserian verse a compound of neoplatonism and Christianity. *Psychoznia Platonica, or a Platonicall Song of the Soul* appeared in 1642 and in 1647 *Philosophicall Poems*, including an enl. version of *The Song of the Soul*. A. B. Grosart included an ed. of this work in his Chertsey Worthies Library (1878), and there is a very good modern ed. by G. Bullough (1931) with a valuable introd. In 1652 he published *An Antidote against Atheism*, an attempt to confute Hobbes's materialism, and in 1656 *Enthusiasmus Triumphatus*, an exposure of the emotional types of religion fashionable under the Protectorate. In 1660 appeared *The Grand Mystery of Godliness* and in 1664 *The Mystery of Iniquity*. In the *Divine Dialogues* (1668), he attempts a popular exposition of his philosophy in a series of dialogues containing some of his most attractive writing. He admired Descartes at first and pub. his correspondence with him in 1662, but later he changed his opinion, and in his *Enchiridion Metaphysicum* (1668) denounces the Cartesian philosophy. More had pub. in 1662 a collection of his early works called *A Collection of Several Philosophical Writings of Dr. Henry More*. In 1679, believing that his writings would become philosophical classics, More tr. them all into Latin and pub. them in two large folio vols. called *Henrici Mori Cantabrigiensis Opera Omnia*.

There is a useful modern selection from More's works called *Philosophical Writings of Henry More*, ed. F. I. Mackinnon (N.Y., 1925) with an introd. and a complete bibliography of his writings.

Biography and Criticism

In the Latin introd. to his *Opera Omnia* of 1679 More gives some interesting details of his life. Richard Ward, Rector of Ingoldsby in Lincolnshire, pub. in 1710 his excellent *Life of the learned and Pious Dr. Henry More*. A second part of this work dealing with More's writings is preserved in MS. at Christ's College, Cambridge, and has never been pub. There is a useful modern rpt. of the 1710 ed. of Ward's *Life of More* ed. with an introd., notes and some selections from his writings by M. F. Howard (Theosophical Society, 1911). Much light is thrown on the circle of More and his friend, Lady Conway, in the letters printed by M. Nicholson in *The Correspondence of Anne Viscountess Conway* (1930).

PETER STERRY (1613-72)

Sterry was a pupil and friend of Whichcote and later a chaplain to Cromwell; he was a Cambridge Platonist, a puritan of the Independent party, a teacher of mystical doctrine, and a prose poet of rare quality. His works include eight sermons pub. at various dates between 1645 and 1660, and 3 vols. pub. posthumously among which special mention may be made of *A Discourse of the Freedom of the Will* (1675), notable for the magnificent plea for toleration in its preface. He also left a number of works in MS. now at Emmanuel College, Cambridge. There is a selection from the whole of Sterry's Works including the MSS. with a biographical and critical study by V. de S. Pinto (1934). See also the article by the same writer, 'Peter Sterry and his Unpublished Writings' in R.E.S., October, 1930.

JOSEPH GLANVILLE (1636-80)

Glanville was an Oxford man, but a great admirer of the Cambridge Platonists and his works are closely connected with theirs. He is not a profound philosopher, but an extremely interesting and significant thinker and writer, whose works represent very well 'the climate of opinions' (his own phrase) in the reign of Charles II. One of the most characteristic is his earliest book, *The Vanity of Dogmatising* (1661), a valuable expression of the new tolerant and 'philosophical' ideas that were coming into fashion at the Restoration. It is from this book that the story of Matthew Arnold's *Scholar Gipsy* is taken. It was rptd. by the Facsimile Text Society (N.Y., 1931). He recast it and pub. it under the significant title of *Scepsis Scientifica* in 1665. There is a modern ed. of this version by J. Owen (1885). Among his other works mention may be made of his work on witches (in which he firmly believed), first ed. 1666, called in the fifth ed. of 1681 *Sadducismus Triumphatus*; his essays on *Several Important Subjects in Philosophy and Religion* (1676) and his *Essay Concerning Preaching: Written for the Direction of a Young Divine* (1678).

There is a valuable study of Glanville by F. Greenslet entitled *Joseph Glanville, A Study in English Thought and Letters in the Seventeenth Century* (N.Y., 1900), and a German monograph by H. Habicht, *J. Glanville, ein speculativer Denker* (Zürich, 1936). See also the remarks on Glanville in Lecky's *The Rise of Rationalism in Europe* (1874) and B. Willey's *The Seventeenth Century Background* (1934).

CHAPTER XIII
METAPHYSICAL POETRY

NOTE ON THE TERM 'METAPHYSICAL POETRY'

THE term 'metaphysical' was first applied to poetry of the school of Donne by Dr Johnson in his *Life of Cowley*. He seems to have taken a hint from Dryden, who wrote of Donne that 'he seems to affect the metaphysics, not only in his satires, but in his amorous verses'. Passages in Spence's *Anecdotes* seem to show that the term was known to Pope. For critical expositions of the nature of the 'metaphysical' style, which seems to have begun with Donne and which continued to be fashionable till the middle of the seventeenth century, the reader is referred to the works listed below under 'General Studies'. The metaphysical school never entirely dominated English poetry. It had to contend with other traditions, Italianate Renaissance humanism, and the courtly and neo-classical movements. These strains were by no means mutually exclusive, and are often found in the same writer, and even in the same poem. The writers included in this section are a selection of those in whose work the 'metaphysical' element is prominent.

GENERAL STUDIES

The classic critique of the metaphysical school is to be found in Dr Johnson's 'Life of Cowley' in his *Lives of the Poets* (1783). The introd. to H. J. C. Grierson's *Metaphysical Lyrics and Poems of the Seventeenth Century* (1921), T. S. Eliot, 'The Metaphysical Poets' in *Homage to John Dryden* (1924, rptd. in *Selected Essays*, 1932), J. Smith, 'On Metaphysical Poetry' in *Determinations* (1934), F. R. Leavis, 'English Poetry in the Seventeenth Century', *Scrutiny*, IV, 1935, and 'The Line of

Wit' in *Revaluations* (1936) are short studies of great importance. Fuller critical works are G. Williamson, *The Donne Tradition* (Camb. Mass., 1930); Joan Bennett, *Four Metaphysical Poets* (1934); J. B. Leishman, *The Metaphysical Poets* (1934); M. Praz, *Studies in Seventeenth Century Imagery* (I, 1939; II, 1948); Helen C. White, *The Metaphysical Poets* (N.Y., 1936); T. Spencer and M. Van Doren, Studies in *Metaphysical Poetry* (N.Y., 1939); R. Tuve, *Elizabethan and Metaphysical Poetry* (Chicago, 1947); M. M. Mahood, *Poetry and Humanism* (1950), and L. L. Martz, *The Poetry of Meditation* (New Haven, 1954), and *Seventeenth Century English Poetry* ed. W. R. Keast (N.Y., 1962).

ANTHOLOGIES

The best general anthology is H. J. C. Grierson's *Metaphysical Lyrics and Poems of the Seventeenth Century* (1921). Other valuable collections are G. Saintsbury, *Minor Poets of the Caroline Period* (3 vols., 1905-21); R. G. Howarth, *Minor Poets of the Seventeenth Century* (Ev. Lib., 1931, rev. ed., 1953); P. Quennell, *Aspects of Seventeenth Century Poetry* (1933); L. B. Marshall, *Rare Poems of the Seventeenth Century* (1936); H. C. White, R. C. Wallerstein and R. Quintana, *Seventeenth Century Prose and Verse*, 1600-60 (N.Y., 1951), and Helen Gardner, *The Metaphysical Poets* (1957, rev. ed. 1961, also in P.B.). For other anthologies, see below, p. 342.

INDIVIDUAL AUTHORS

JOHN DONNE (1573-1631)

Donne's early lyrics, elegies and satires, 'pieces loosely ... scattered in his youth' as Walton calls them, were probably all written before 1600 and were widely circulated in MS. The only poems that he is known to have pub. in his lifetime are the two elegies on Elizabeth Drury, *An Anatomy of the World* (1611) and *The Second Anniversarie* (1612), both pub. together 1621 (facs. in Noel Douglas Replicas). The first collected ed. of his peoms, *Poems* by *I. D.*, appeared in 1633, and was rptd. in 1635 with considerable alteration and additions. H. Alford's ed. of the Sermons pub. in 1839 includes a poor text of the poems (see p. 334). Grosart pub. an ed. in 1872 and C. E. Norton another at N.Y. in 1895. E. K. Chambers's useful little ed. in M.L. appeared in 1896. The standard modern ed. is that of H. J. C. Grierson (1912 and 1929). *The Complete Poetry and Select Prose* is a useful one-vol. ed. J. Hayward (1929), and there is an Ev. Lib. ed. by H. I. A. Fausset (1931). There is also an important ed. of *The Divine Poems* ed. Helen L. Gardner (1952) and a useful one of the *Songs and Sonets* ed. T. Ridpath (1960). Donne's early prose work essays called *Paradoxes and Problems* should be studied in connection with his early poems. They were first printed in 1633 and in an enl. ed. in 1652. There is a modern ed. by G. Keynes (1923). His Latin skit *The Courtiers' Library or Catalogus Librorum Aulicorum* was first ed. by E. M. Simpson (with tr. by P. Simpson) in 1930. For Donne's other prose works see pp. 334–5.

Biography and Criticism

The classic *Life* of Donne is that of Izaak Walton, first pub. with the 1640 ed. of his sermons (see p. 321). In 1899, E. Gosse pub. his important *Life and Letters of John Donne*. C.H.E.L., VII, contains an important study by H. J. C. Grierson, and there is also a valuable introd. to Grierson's ed. of the *Poems*. M. Ramsay's *Les Doctrines Mediévales chez Donne* (1916) is a study of Donne's use of medieval philosophical doctrines, and *Donne the Craftsman* by Legouis (1921) and *The Monarch of Wit* by J. B. Leishman (1951) are important critical essays. There is much suggestive criticism in *A Garland for John Donne* ed. T. Spencer (Harvard, 1931). The religious writings of Donne are dealt with particularly in A. Jessopp's *John Donne* (Leaders of Religion Series, 1897). The standard critical work on his prose is E. M. Simpson's *A Study of the Prose Works of John Donne* (1924). S. T. Coleridge's *Notes on English Divines* should also be consulted. See also the works mentioned under 'General Studies' above and E. Rickword's fine study 'Donne the Divine', T.L.S., December 25th, 1924.

GEORGE HERBERT (1593-1633)

Herbert pub. nothing in his lifetime except a few poems in Latin and Greek in contemporary anthologies. On his deathbed he bequeathed to his friend Nicholas Ferrar a small MS. vol. of poems. This was *The Temple, Sacred Poems and Private Ejaculations*, first pub. in 1633. Numerous edd. were pub. up till 1709, and it is said that over 20,000 copies were sold by 1670. A few other poems in English and Latin (including the two sonnets addressed to his mother, pub. in Walton's *Life*) survive. In 1652 his delightful prose work *A Priest to the Temple, or the Country Parson* was pub. in a vol. called *Herbert's Remains* with a short *Life* of Herbert by Barnabas Oley, and a collection of proverbs called *Jacula Prudentum*. Later edd. of *The Country Parson* appeared in 1671 and 1675, modern edd. by H. C. Beeching (1908 and 1916).

Herbert's *Works* with notes by S. T. Coleridge were pub. by Pickering in 1835-36, and many times rptd.; with some editing by J. Yeowell in 1859. Another ed. by R. A. Wilmott appeared in 1854. Grosart ed. the complete works in his *Fuller Worthies Library* (1874). Two separate type-facs. of *The Temple* were pub. in 1876, and J. H. Shorthouse contributed an Introductory Essay to Fisher Unwin's type-facs. of 1882.

G. H. Palmer's ed. of the *English Works* (1905 and 1907) is the first serious attempt to discover the chronological order of the poems, and is very fully annotated. The standard modern ed. is *The Works of George Herbert* ed. F. E. Hutchinson (1941) with a valuable introd. and commentary. There are also edd. in W.C. and Ev. Lib.

Biography and Criticism

Izaak Walton's beautiful *Life of Mr. George Herbert* was pub. in 1670 and can be consulted in the modern edd. of Walton's *Lives* (see below, p. 321) and in *English Biography in the Seventeenth Century* ed. V. de S. Pinto (1951). Biographies are prefixed to the edd. of Hutchinson and Palmer, and there is a study of *George Herbert's Life and his Times* by A. G. Hyde (1906). For criticism see Coleridge's *Biographia Literaria* chs. XIX-XX; P. E. More's *Sherburne Essays* (4th Series, Princeton, 1906); T. S. Eliot's essay in *The Spectator*, March 12th, 1932, L. C. Knight's essay in *Explorations* (1946) and M. Bottrall, *George Herbert* (1954). For Nicholas Ferrar and the Little Gidding community see J. E. B. Mayor's *Nicholas Ferrar: Two Lives* (1855), A. L. Maycock's *Nicholas Ferrar* (1938) and *The Ferrar Papers* ed. B. Blackstone (1939). J. H. Shorthouse's romance *John Inglesant* should be read in the light of the study of its sources by W. K. Fleming in *The Quarterly Review* (July, 1925).

LORD HERBERT OF CHERBURY (1583-1648)

Lord Herbert, elder brother of George Herbert, was a poet of distinction as well as a historian and a philosopher. The first collected ed. of his *Occasional Verses* appeared in 1665. The standard modern ed. is that of G. C. Moore Smith (1923). Lord Herbert's poems are also included in R. G. Howarth's *Minor Poets of the 17th Century* (Ev. Lib.). For Lord Herbert's philosophical works, biography and criticism, see p. 283.

RICHARD CRASHAW (1612-49)

In 1634, the year when he took the B.A. degree at Cambridge, Crashaw pub. a vol. of Latin epigrams. The first vol. of his English verse, *Steps to the Temple, Sacred poems with other Delights of the Muses*, containing both religious and secular poems, appeared in 1646. A second ed. with many additions appeared in 1648. In 1652 his friend T. Car pub. in Paris a vol. called *Carmen Deo Nostro*, containing most of the poems in Crashaw's previous vols. with important additions. It also contains vignettes from Crashaw's own drawings. A poor second ed. appeared in 1670. Grosart printed *The Complete Works* in 1872-73. The standard modern ed. is that of L. C. Martin (1927).

The best accounts of Crashaw are L. C. Martin's in the introd. to his ed. and Austin Warren's in his *Richard Crashaw a Study in Baroque Sensibility* (Louisiana, 1939). See also the important critical study by M. Praz in his *Secentismo e Marinismo in Inghilterra* (Florence, 1925; Eng. tr. in *The Flaming Heart*, P.B., 1958) and B. Willey, *Richard Crashaw, a Memorial Lecture* (1949).

HENRY VAUGHAN (1622-95)

Vaughan's early poems appeared in two vols., *Poems with the tenth Satyre of Juvenal Englished* (1646) and *Olor Iscanus*, which apparently was ready for the press in 1647 but was not pub. till 1651. In 1650 appeared his great collection of religious poems *Silex Scintillans*. A re-issue of this vol. with a second part containing some of Vaughan's finest poetry appeared in 1655. There is a rpt. by H. F. Lyte (1847, 1883 and 1891), and facs. of 1650 ed. by

W. Clare (1885). In 1652 Vaughan pub. a beautiful devotional work in prose called *The Mount of Olives, or Solitary Devotions*, in 1654 *Flores Solitudinis*, trs. of religious works from the Latin, and in 1655 *Hermetical Physick*, a tr. of a Latin medical work. His last vol. of verse was *Thalia Rediviva: the pass-times and diversions of a Country Muse*, containing poems both by Henry Vaughan and by his brother, the mystical thinker, Thomas Vaughan (1622-66). Vaughan's works remained almost unknown till the early nineteenth century. His poems were collected and ed. Grosart in 1870-71. The standard modern ed. of *Vaughan's Works* is that of L. C. Martin (2 vols., 1914; rev. ed., 1 vol., 1957). The standard biography is F. E. Hutchinson's *Henry Vaughan* (1947). See also Edmund Blunden's essay *On the Poems of Henry Vaughan* (with trs. of the Latin poems, 1927), Elizabeth Holmes's *Henry Vaughan and the Hermetic Philosophy* (1932) and the studies by J. B. Leishman, Joan Bennett and M. M. Mahood (op. cit, p. 294).

THOMAS TRAHERNE (1634-74)

Thomas Traherne pub. only two books during his lifetime: *Roman Forgeries, or a true account of false records* (1673), a polemic against the Roman Catholic Church, and *Christian Ethicks, or divine morality* (1675), a work mainly in prose but including seven short poems. His *Serious and Patheticall Contemplation of the Mercies of God* was pub. anon. in 1699. He was entirely forgotten until a MS. of his poems was discovered by W. T. Brooke and pub. B. Dobell in 1903. Another MS. collection of his poetry, which had remained unnoticed in the B.M., was pub. H. I. Bell in 1910, *Traherne's Poems of Felicity*. An ed. of *The Poetical Works* ed. Gladys I. Wade (1932) contains all the known extant poetry in the orig. spelling. The definitive modern ed. is *Poems and Centuries* ed. H. M. Margoliouth (2 vols., 1958). A selection, *Felicities of Thomas Traherne* by Sir A. Quiller Couch appeared in 1934. In 1908 Dobell pub. for the first time Traherne's prose work *Centuries of Meditation* (rev. ed. P. J. Dobell, 1927), containing some of his most beautiful writing. *The Serious and Patheticall Contemplation* has been ed. R. Daniells (Toronto and O.U.P., 1941).

There are studies by Gladys Willett, *Thomas Traherne, an Essay* (1918), F. Löhrer *Die Mystik und ihre Quellen in Thomas Traherne* (1930) and Q. Iredale, *Thomas Traherne* (1935), and J. B. Leishman (op. cit. p. 294).

FRANCIS QUARLES (1592-1644)

Francis Quarles was a voluminous and popular writer of verse and prose. He pub. a number of Biblical paraphrases between 1620 and 1630 which he collected in *Divine Poems*, 1630. In the same year appeared his narrative poem *Argalus and Parthenia* founded on a story in Sidney's *Arcadia*. More of his religious verse appeared in *Divine Fancies* (1632). His most famous vol. *Emblemes*, a series of religious poems illustrated by cuts mainly from the designs of William Marshall, first appeared in 1635. It was frequently rptd. up to the middle of the nineteenth century (most recent ed. 1888). He pub. a similar vol. called *Hieroglyphikes of the Life of Man* in 1638. His other publications include religious manuals and royalist tracts in prose. The only collected ed. of Quarles's works is that of A. B. Grosart, *Chertsey Worthies Library* 1880-81. A memoir of Quarles by his wife is prefixed to his vol. called *Solomon's Recantation* (1645, rptd. 1739). There is an article by Sir S. Lee in the D.N.B. and an unpublished thesis by Gordon S. Haight at Yale University entitled *Francis Quarles and his Emblems*. See also Haight's article in R.E.S., xii, 1936 on *Francis Quarles in the Civil War*. There is a valuable study of *The Imagery of Francis Quarles's Emblems* by Eleanour James in *Texas Studies in English* (1943), which includes a survey of recent studies of Quarles in periodical literature. M. Praz's *Studies in Seventeenth Century Imagery* (1939) should also be consulted. There is a Bibliography of his *Works to the Year 1800* by J. Horden (O.B.S., N.S., II, 1953.

ABRAHAM COWLEY (1618-67)

One of the most precocious of English poets, Cowley wrote while he was at Westminster School a vol. of verse *Poeticall Blossomes*, pub. 1633, and *Love's Riddle, a pastorall comoedie*, pub. 1638. At Cambridge he wrote and pub. a Latin comedy *Naufragium Joculare* (1638). In 1647 appeared his famous and very popular collection of love poems *The Mistresse* (modern ed. by J. Sparrow, 1926). His comedy *The Guardian* written and acted at Cambridge in 1641 was not pub. till 1650. He recast it and pub. it under a new title as *The Cutter of Coleman-street* in 1663. In 1656 appeared a vol. containing some of his strongest and most characteristic work, *Poems*, including his Pindarique 'Odes', four books of his Biblical epic *The Davideis*, and such excellent shorter pieces as *The Chronicle* and the elegies on Hervey and Crashaw (there is a modern rpt. ed. A. R. Waller, C.U.P., 1905). His later poems include an *Ode upon the Blessed Restoration* and an *Ode on the Royal Society*, both included in *Verses lately written upon several occasions* (1663, rptd. with the *Poems* of 1656 by A. R. Waller, C.U.P., 1905). His *Works* in prose and verse were printed by his friend T. Sprat in 1668. This vol. was frequently rptd. A. B. Grosart pub. an ed. of Cowley's works in 1881. The standard modern ed. of *The English Writings* is that of A. R. Waller (2 vols., 1905-06). For Cowley's prose works, see p. 322.

Biography and Criticism

The earliest authority for Cowley's life is the biographical sketch prefixed by Sprat to the ed. of 1668. Dr Johnson's *Life of Cowley* in *Lives of the Poets* is especially notable for its powerful criticism. Recent important works are J. Loiseau, *Abraham Cowley, sa vie son œuvre* (Paris, 1931), and H. Nethercot, *The Muses' Hannibal* (1931). There are valuable studies of Cowley's poetry by H. W. Garrod in his *Profession of Poetry* (1928), and by G. Walton in *Metaphysical to Augustan* (1955). See also T. S. Eliot, 'A Note on Two Odes of Cowley' in *Seventeenth Century Studies Presented to Sir H. Grierson* (1938).

ANDREW MARVELL (1621-78)

With the exception of a few pieces Andrew Marvell's poems were not pub. till after his death. In 1681 there appeared a small folio entitled *Miscellaneous Poems by Andrew Marvell*. In most copies the pages containing the passages in praise of Cromwell and the Protectorate, *Horatian Ode*, *The First Anniversary*, and *A Poem on the Death of O. C.* were removed for political reasons. The unique copy in the B.M., however, contains these pages. A modern rpt. of the *Miscellaneous Poems* was pub. by the Nonesuch Press in 1923. After the Restoration Marvell wrote much prose and some verse satires. A large number of political satires in verse attacking the Court were circulated in MS. and ascribed to Marvell. Many MSS. of these poems still survive. Most of them were printed after the Revolution in *A Collection of the Newest and Most Ingenious Songs, Catches, etc., Against Popery* (1689); *The Second Part of the Collection of Poems and Affairs of State* (1689) and *Third Part of the Collection of Poems on Affairs of State* (1689), all rptd. in 1697 as *Poems on Affairs of State*. In these and later collections many of the most vigorous satires are attributed, probably rightly, to Marvell, though some of them cannot be by him, as they refer to events which took place after his death. (For a full discussion of the problems connected with these poems, see *The Poems and Letters of Andrew Marvell*, ed. Margoliouth, I, 207-15.) Marvell's prose written after the Restoration includes his letters to his constituents (first printed in 1776), and controversial works, the best of which is the witty pamphlet called *The Rehearsal Transpros'd* (1672). Marvell's Works were first ed. T. Cooke in 1726 (rptd. 1772). The important ed. of Edward Thompson appeared in 1766. A. B. Grosart ed. *The Complete Works* in his *Fuller Worthies Library* (1872-75). There is an ed. by G. A. Aitken of the *Poems and Satires* in M.L. The standard modern ed. is *The Poems and Letters*, ed. H. M. Margoliouth (2 vols., 1927).

Biography and Criticism

A. Birrell's *Andrew Marvell* (E.M.L.) is readable but superficial. The most important biographical and critical study is *André Marvell, poète, puritain, patriote* by P. Legouis (Paris, 1928). See also T. S. Eliot's essay in *Homage to John Dryden* (1924), and the valuable study by M. C. Bradbrook and M. G. Lloyd Thomas (1940, rev. ed. 1962).

RICHARD CORBETT (1582-1635)

The poems of Richard Corbett, Bishop of Oxford and later of Norwich, were collected in 1647 with the title *Certain Elegant Poems* (1647, 2nd ed. with additions, 1672). An ed. by O. Gilchrist was pub. in 1807. The standard modern ed. is *The Poems of Richard Corbett* ed. J. A. W. Bennett and H. R. Trevor-Roper (1955).

HENRY KING (1592-1669)

The *Poems, Elegies, Paradoxes and Sonnets* of Henry King, Bishop of Chichester, were pub. 1657. In 1843 J. Hannah pub. an ed. of King's *Poems and Psalms*, containing his sacred poems and J. R. Tutin's ed. of his *Selected Profane Poems* appeared in 1904. There are edd. of *The English Poems* by L. Mason (1914), in Saintsbury's *Minor Caroline Poets* (Vol. III) and by J. Sparrow (1925). There is a memoir in Hannah's ed. of 1843 and in 1913 L. Mason contributed a study of *The Life and Works of Henry King* to *Transactions* of the *Connecticut Academy of Arts and Science*, Vol. 18.

WILLIAM HABINGTON (1605-54)

Habington's *Castara. A Collection of Poems*, was pub. anonymously in 1634; the author's name appears in the second ed. of 1635. There are edd. by C. A. Elton, 1812, E. Arber in *English Reprints*, and K. Allot (1948). Habington also wrote a play, *The Queene of Arragon*, 1640. There is an article on him by A. H. Bullen in the D.N.B.

JOHN CLEVELAND (1613-58)

The earliest publication containing poems by Cleveland was *The Character of a London-Diurnall* with *Several select Poems By the same Author*, pub. anonymously in 1647. The poems include *The Rebell Scot, Rupertismus, the Epitaph on Strafford* and other notable pieces. This vol. went through at least fifteen edd. by 1669. In 1659 appeared an ed. called *John Cleveland Revived* containing much that is spurious; in 1661, *Poems by John Cleavland with additions never before printed*, and in 1677 *Clievelandi Vindiciae, or Clieveland's Genuine Remains*, the most authentic of the old edd. There is a modern ed. by J. M. Berdan (Yale, 1903 and 1911), and a text in Saintsbury's *Minor Caroline Poets*, Vol. 3.

For details of Cleveland's life see Berdan's introd. to his ed.

SAMUEL BUTLER (1612-80)

The first part of *Hudibras*, Butler's great satire, appeared in 1663, the second in 1664. A corrrected and amended issue of both these parts was pub. in 1674 and was followed by the 'third and last Part' in 1678-79. *Hudibras* was rptd. very often. Zachary Grey's ed. (Cambridge, 1744, 1745) contains Hogarth's illustrations. Grey pub. in 1752 supplementary *Critical, historical and explanatory Notes to Hudibras*. A vol. entitled *The Posthumous Works in Verse and Prose* (1715) is mainly spurious, but contains some genuine pieces. *The Genuine Remains in Verse and Prose*, pub. R. Thyer in 2 vols., 1759, contains the prose characters and some interesting shorter poems including *The Elephant in the Moon*, Butler's satire on The Royal Society. The standard modern ed. of *The Collected Works* is that of A. R. Waller (1905-8) and R.

Lamar (3 vols.). J. Bauer pub. in M.P., XLV, 1948, 'Verse Fragments and Prose Characters by Butler not included in Complete Works'. For biography and criticism, see J. Veldkamp, *Samuel Butler, the Author of Hudibras* (1923), D. Gibson, *Samuel Butler* (1932), E. A. Richards, *Samuel Butler in the Burlesque Tradition* (1937), R. Quintana, 'Samuel Butler, a Restoration Figure in a Modern Light', E.L.H., XVIII, 1951, the valuable remarks by W. Hazlitt in *English Comic Writers* (1819) and the important chapter on *Hudibras* in *Augustan Satire 1660–1750* by Ian Jack (1952).

CHAPTER XIV

THE LATER DRAMA UP TO THE CIVIL WAR

GENERAL STUDIES AND COLLECTIONS

(See above, pp. 219-21.)

INDIVIDUAL AUTHORS

BEN JONSON (1572-1637)

None of Jonson's early works, written perhaps for Henslowe's company between 1595 and 1597, survive. His earliest extant play may be the comedy of English rustic life called *The Case is Altered*, possibly written in 1597 and certainly acted by the Children of the Chapel before the end of 1598. It was pub. in 1609, modern rpt. in Y.S.E. Vol. 56, 1917. His reputation as a dramatist was made by the two great 'humour' comedies. *Every Man in his Humour* (acted in September 1598, pub. 1601), and *Every Man out of his Humour* (acted 1599 or 1600, pub. 1600). There are many modern edd. of *Every Man in his Humour*. The best are by C. H. Herford in R.E.C., Vol. 2, 1913; by P. Simpson (1919); by H. H. Carter in Y.S.E., 1921; and facs. in Bang, Vol. 10, 1905. *Every Man out of his Humour*, appropriately called on its title page a 'Comicall Satyre', is rptd. in M.S.R. and Bang, N.S. XVI, vii. The two plays connected with Jonson's quarrel with Marston and the 'war of the theatres' are *Cynthia's Revels* and *The Poetaster* both acted in 1600. *The Fountayne of Selfe-Love or Cynthia's Revels* was pub. in 1601 (rpts. in Y.S.E., 1912, and Bang, Vol. 22), and *Poetaster or the Araignement* in 1602 (rpts. in Y.S.E., 1905, and B.L.). The first of Jonson's learned Roman tragedies, *Seianus, his Fall*, was pub. in 1605 (acted in 1603 or 1604; modern edd. by W. E. Briggs in B.L., and in Neilson). In 1605 Jonson collaborated with Chapman and Marston in the amusing comedy of London life called *Eastward Hoe* for which the three authors were imprisoned.

About 1605 Jonson began to write masques for the court of James I, and in that year his great poetic and ironic comedy

Volpone was probably produced. It was pub. in 1607 with the title *Ben. Ionson, his Volpone or the Foxe* (modern edd. in Neilson and Y.S.E., 1919). *Epicœne, or the Silent Woman* was produced in 1609-10, and possibly printed in the same year. The earliest extant ed. is dated 1620 (modern edd. in Y.S.E., 1906 and by C. M. Gayley in R.E.C., Vol. 2). *The Alchemist*, acted in 1610, was pub. in 1612 (modern edd. in Y.S.E., 1903, in Neilson, by G. A. Smithson in R.E.C. and facs. in Noel Douglas Replicas). Jonson's second Roman tragedy, *Catiline, his Conspiracy*, was acted in 1611 and pub. in the same year (modern ed. in Y.S.E., 1916). His great realistic picture of London life, *Bartholomew Fair*, was acted in 1614, but not printed till it appeared in the collective ed. of Jonson's works pub. 1640 with a separate title dated 1631 (modern ed. in Y.S.E., 1904). *The Devil is an Ass*, another comedy, acted in 1616, also appeared for the first time in the 1640 ed. with title dated 1631 (modern ed. in Y.S.E., 1905). Jonson now abandoned the theatre, and wrote no more plays for nine years. Some of his finest masques were written during this period. During his last years, however, he produced a series of four comedies that are far inferior to the great works of his prime. They are *The Staple of Newes* acted in 1625, first pub. in the 1640 ed. with the 1631 title page; *The Newe Inne, or the Light Heart* . . . 'As it was never acted but most negligently play'd, by some, the King's servants, in 1629,' to quote Jonson's words on the title page of an ed. of 1631 (modern ed. in Y.S.E., 1908); *The Magnetick Lady* (acted in 1632, pub. in 1640 ed. of the Works, modern ed. in Y.S.E., 1914); and *A Tale of a Tub* (acted in 1632, pub. in 1640 ed. of the Works, modern ed. in Bang, 1913). The 1640 ed. of Jonson's Works also contains the beautiful unfinished pastoral *The Sad Shepherd, or a Tale of Robin Hood* (modern ed. by W. W. Greg in Bang, 1902), and a short fragment of a historical tragedy called *Mortimer, his Fall*. For Jonson's authorship of the 'additions' to *The Spanish Tragedie*, see p. 231. Some of his finest poetry is to be found in his beautiful masques mostly written to be acted at court. Among the best are *The Masque of Beauty* (1608), *The Masque of Blacknesse* (1608), *The Hue and Cry after Cupid* (for Viscount Haddington's wedding, 1608), *The Masque of Queenes* (1609), *A Masque of the Metamorphos'd Gypsies* (1621).

The earliest collected ed. of Jonson's Works appeared in a folio in 1616 containing nine plays. In 1640 this ed. was re-issued with a second vol. containing five more comedies and the fragments of the *Sad Shepherd* and *Mortimer his Fall*, together with Jonson's non-dramatic poems entitled *Underwoods* and his prose essays *Timber or Discoveries*. Three of the plays in his ed. have title pages dated 1631 (see above) and may have been originally issued as a supplement to the vol. of 1616. This collection was ed. Sir Kenelm Digby. It was re-issued in 1692. The first important modern ed. was that of W. Gifford (1816, later edd. 1846, 1871, 1875). Bang contains a rpt. of the 1616 ed. in Vol. 6, 1905. The standard edition of Jonson's *Works* is that of C. H. Herford, P. and E. Simpson, 11 vols. (1925-52). There are many smaller collections including *The Best Plays of Ben Jonson*, ed. Nicholson in the Mermaid Series, *The Complete Plays of Ben Jonson*, ed. Schelling in Ev. Lib., *Selected Works* ed. H. Levin (N.Y., 1938) and *Five Plays* (W.C., 1953).

There is a useful separate ed. of *The Masques and Entertainments* in the *Carisbrooke Library* ed. H. Morley. Numerous modern edd. of the poems have been pub. The best is *The Poems of Ben Jonson*, ed. B. H. Newdigate (1936). There is a facs. ed of the *Epigrams, Forest, Underwoods*, ed. H. H. Hudson (N.Y., 1936).

For *Timber or Discoveries*, see p. 319.

For *The Conversations with Drummond*, see p. 214.

Biography and Criticism

The most complete and authoritative account of Ben Jonson and his works is to be found in Vols. I and II of *The Works of Ben Jonson*, ed. Herford and Simpson ('The Man and his Work'). M. Castelain's *Ben Jonson l'homme et l'œuvre* (Paris, 1907) and Gregory Smith's *Ben Jonson* in E.M.L. may also be consulted, and there is a critical essay by T. S. Eliot (1934). L. C. Knights's *Drama and Society in the Age of Jonson* (1937) is a work of the highest importance. See also G. E. Bentley, *Shakespeare and Jonson, Their Reputations in the Seventeenth Century Compared*. 2 vols. (Chicago, 1945). There is *A Concise Bibliography* by S. A. Tannenbaum (N.Y. 1942).

FRANCIS BEAUMONT (1584-1616) and
JOHN FLETCHER (1597-1625)

The nature of the collaboration between these two famous entertainers of the early Stuart courtly audiences is very obscure.

It is almost certain that Philip Massinger had a hand in some of the plays attributed to them. Beaumont may be the sole author of *The Woman Hater* (1608) and seems to have written most, if not all, of the delightful dramatic parody called *The Knight of the Burning Pestle* (produced perhaps in 1607 and printed in 1613). The first ed. is anonymous. Two edd. pub. 1635 ascribe it to Beaumont and Fletcher. There are many modern edd., including an excellent one by F. W. Moorman in T.D. The beautiful pastoral drama called *The Faithful Shepherdesse* is by Fletcher alone. It was first acted in 1608 or 1609, and printed 1610, with Fletcher's name on the title page and commendatory verses by Beaumont. There are the modern edd. in Neilson and by F. W. Moorman in T.D. The most notable plays in which the two authors collaborated are the romantic comedy *Phylaster, or Love lyes a Bleeding* (produced before 1610, pub. 1620, modern edd. by F. S. Boas in T.D., by A. H. Thorndike in B.L., and in Neilson), *the Maide's Tragedy* (acted before 1611, pub. 1619, modern edd. by A. H. Thorndike in B.L., and in Neilson), and the other romantic tragedy called *A King and No King* (acted 1611, pub. 1916, modern ed. by R. M. Alden in B.L.). *The Two Noble Kinsmen*, acted 1613, is described on the title page as by Mr. John Fletcher and Mr. William Shakespeare (see p. 258).

The Tragedy of Bonduca, probably written between 1609 and 1611, but first printed in 1647 (Modern ed. by Sir W. W. Greg, M.S.R., 1952) is generally regarded as by Fletcher alone, and he was also probably the sole author of *The Tragedy of Valentinian* (written perhaps between 1610 and 1614, and first pub. in the 1647 ed.). The comedy of *The Scornful Ladie* (pub. 1616) is almost certainly by Beaumont and Fletcher. *The Tragedy of Thierry King of France and his Brother Theodoret* (pub. 1621) and *Bollo, Duke of Normandy or the Bloody Brother* (pub. 1639, modern ed. by J. D. Jump, 1948) are probably by Fletcher, Massinger and others. The lively comedy of *The Wild-Goose Chase* was omitted from the 1647 folio and pub. in 1652. In this ed. it is ascribed to Beaumont and Fletcher. The very popular comedy, *Rule a Wife and Have a Wife*, was pub. in 1640 and ascribed to Fletcher alone. Another excellent comedy, *The Beggar's Bush*, first appeared in the 1647 ed. and is ascribed to Beaumont and Fletcher. This list is only a selection from over fifty plays ascribed to these authors either separately or together in seventeenth-century edd. A full list will be found in W. W. Greg's *List of English Plays*, op. cit., p. 219 above.

A folio ed. of *The Comedies and Tragedies written by Francis Beaumont and John Fletcher* appeared in 1647. It contained all the plays pub. up to that date except *The Wild-Goose Chase*. A second folio containing fifty plays appeared in 1619. A number of other edd. appeared in the eighteenth and nineteenth centuries. There are two important modern edd., one by A. Glover and A. R. Waller (10 vols., text alone), and the other by A. H. Bullen (variorum ed., 4 vols. only, 1904-12). There is a selection of the *Best Plays*, ed. J. S. L. Strachey in the Mermaid Series and another ed. G. P. Baker in Ev. Lib. See also *Songs and Lyrics from the Plays of Beaumont and Fletcher*, ed. G. H. Fellowes (1928).

Modern criticism tends to attribute part of the play of *Henry VIII*, included in the Shakespeare Folio, to Fletcher. This theory was first propounded by Spedding (following a suggestion of Tennyson) in 1850.

Biography and Criticism

For Beaumont, see G. C. Macaulay, *Francis Beaumont* (1883) and C. M. Gayley, Beaumont the Dramatist (1914); for Fletcher, O. L. Hatcher, *John Fletcher, a Study in Dramatic Method* (Chicago, 1905) and the article by A. H. Bullen in the D.N.B. On the collaboration, see the articles by R. Boyle in E. S. (1882-87) and M. Chelli, *Étude sur la collaboration de Massinger avec Fletcher et son groupe* (Paris, 1926). The most important modern studies are B. Maxwell, *Studies in Beaumont, Fletcher and Massinger* (Chapel Hill, 1939), L. B. Wallace, *Fletcher, Beaumont and Company, Entertainers to the Jacobean Gentry* (N.Y., 1947), M. Mincoff, *Baroque Literature in England* (Sofia, 1947), and 'The Social Background of Beaumont and Fletcher in E.M., i, 1950, and J. F. Danby, *Poets on Fortune's Hill* (1952). See also A. H. Thorndike, *The Influence of Beaumont on Shakespeare* (Worcester, Mass., 1901), A. C. Sprague, *Beaumont and Fletcher on the Restoration Stage* (Cambridge, Mass., 1926) and J. H. Wilson, *The Influence of Beaumont and Fletcher on Restoration Drama* (Columbus, Ohio, 1928). There is *A Concise Bibliography* by S. A. Tannenbaum (N.Y., 1938), Supplement (N.Y., 1948)

GEORGE CHAPMAN (c. 1560-1634)

Chapman's first plays were comedies. *The Blinde Begger of Alexandria* (acted 1596, pub. 1598), *An Humerous dayes Myrth* (acted 1597, pub. 1599), *The Gentleman Usher* (acted 1602-4, pub. 1606. modern ed. by T. M. Parrott in B.L.,) *All Fooles* (acted ?1604, pub. 1605, modern ed. by T. M. Parrott in B.L.), and *Monsieur d'Olive* (acted 1604, pub. 1606). In 1604 was acted the first of his great tragedies on French history, *Bussy d'Ambois: A Tragedie*. It was pub. in 1607, modern edd. by F. S. Boas in B.L., in Neilson, and Rylands. In 1605 he collaborated with Jonson and Marston in *Eastward Hoe* (modern edd. by J. W. Cunliffe in R.E.C., Vol. II, and in Y.S.E., 1926). His two other important comedies, *May Day* (1611) and *Widdowe's Teares* (1612), were followed by his two other great tragedies on French history, *The Conspiracie, And Tragedie of Charles Duke of Byron* (1608), and the second play on Bussy d'Ambois, *The Revenge of Bussy d'Ambois* (1610, modern ed. by F. S. Boas in B.L.). A fourth play on French history called *The Tragedie of Chabot Admirall of France*, appeared in 1639, and is ascribed on the title page to George Chapman and James Shirley. It is probably mostly by Chapman. Chapman's other dramas include the Roman play, *The Warres Of Pompey and Caesar* (acted c. 1613, pub. 1631), *The Ball a Comedy* (1639, ascribed to Chapman and Shirley) and *Revenge for Honour* and *Alphonsus Emperour of Germany*, both ascribed to Chapman in edd. pub. in 1654.

For Chapman's trs. of Homer, see pp. 178-9, and for his poems p. 215.

R. H. Shepherd ed. a collection of *The Comedies and Tragedies of George Chapman* in 1873, and of the complete works in 1874-5. The standard modern ed. of the Plays is that of T. M. Parrott, 2 vols (1914). A third vol. containing the Poems was announced but never published. There is a *Selection of the Best Plays* ed. W. L. Phelps in the Mermaid series.

Biography and Criticism

Swinburne's long essay, *George Chapman* (1875, printed as introd. to Shepherd's ed.) is one of his finest critical works. There are also valuable notes in Lamb's *Specimens* and Coleridge's *Literary Remains*. More recent critical estimates are A. Acheson's *Shakespeare and the Rival Poet* (1903); Percy Allen's *Shakespeare and Chapman as*

Topical Dramatists (1929), and M. C. Bradbrook's *The School of Night* (1936). See also E. Muir 'Chapman' in his *Essays on Literature and Society* (1949), J. Jacquot, *George Chapman* (Paris, 1951) and E. Rees, *The Tragedies of Chapman* (Cambridge, Mass., 1954). There is a *Concise Bibliography* by S. A. Tannenbaum (N.Y. 1938).

JOHN WEBSTER (b. c. 1570-80)

Webster probably began his literary career by collaborating with other playwrights. *Appius and Virginia*, pub. 1654, but probably acted c. 1608, may be his first unaided work. The first of his great tragedies, *The White Divel; Or, the Tragedy of Paulo Giordano Ursini Duke of Brachiano*, was probably composed between 1609 and 1612. It was first pub. in 1612. There are modern edd. by M. W. Sampson in B.L. and by G. B. Harrison in T.D. His other notable work, *The Tragedy of the Duchess of Malfy*, was written in 1613-14, and pub. in 1623. There are modern edd. by M. W. Sampson in B.L., in Neilson, and by F. Allen in Methuen's English Classics. Webster was also probably part author of *The Devils Law-case* (pub. 1623). His name with that of W. Rowley appears on the title page of *Two Newe Playes:* viz., *A Cure for a Cuckold ... The Thracian Wonder* (pub. 1661), but it is unlikely that he had anything to do with them.

The first collected ed. of Webster is that of Dyce (1830, second ed. 1857); an ed. by W. C. Hazlitt also appeared in 1857. The standard modern ed. is *The Complete Works of John Webster*, ed. F. L. Lucas, 4 vols. (1927). There are many modern rpts. of the *White Devil* and *The Duchess of Malfi*, including one ed. J. A. Symonds in The Mermaid Series, *Webster and Tourneur*.

Biography and Criticism

E. E. Stoll, *John Webster* (1905), is scholarly and painstaking; Rupert Brooke, *John Webster and the Elizabethan Drama*, is readable and stimulating. The best modern study is C. Leech, *John Webster* (1951). See also T. Bogard, *The Tragic Satire of Webster*, (Berkeley, Cal., 1955).

CYRIL TOURNEUR (c. 1570-1626)

The two famous plays on which Tourneur's reputation rests were both pub. anonymously. They are *The Revengers Tragedie* (1607) and *The Atheist's Tragedie: or the Honest Man's Revenge* (1611).

Tourneur also pub. some elegiac poems. A play called *the Nobleman* written about 1612, said to be by him, is not extant.

His *Plays and Poems*, ed. Churton Collins, were pub. in 1878. The plays are in the vol. in the Mermaid Series, *Webster and Tourneur*, ed. J. A. Symonds. The standard ed. of the *Works* is that by Allardyce Nicoll (1930).

There is a biographical and critical introd. to Nicoll's ed. See also T. S. Eliot 'Cyril Tourneur' in his *Elizabethan Essays* (1934), U. M. Ellis Fermor, 'The Imagery of the Revengers Tragedie and the Atheists Tragedy', M.L.R., xxx, 1935, H. Jenkins, 'Cyril Tourneur', R.E.S., xvii, 1941, and P. Quennell, 'Tourneur', in *The Singular Preference* (1952). There is *A Concise Bibliography* by S. A. Tannenbaum and D. R. (N.Y. 1948).

THOMAS MIDDLETON (1580-1627)

Middleton's earliest pub. work was *Blunt Master Constable, Or The Spaniards Night-walke* (1602). Other comedies by him entitled *A Tricke to Catch the Old One; A Mad World my Masters*, and *The Famelie of Love* were pub. in 1608. He collaborated with Dekker in *The Roaring Girle, Or Moll Cut-Purse* (pub. 1611). His comedy, *A Chast Mayd in Cheap-side*, was acted in 1611, but not pub. till 1630. About 1621-22 Middleton's great tragedy, *The Changeling*, was probably acted. It was pub. in 1653 (modern ed. by N. W. Bawcott, 1958). *The Spanish Gipsie*, founded on two stories from Cervantes, probably belongs to the same period. It was also pub. in 1653. Middleton was the author of two powerful plays pub. together in 1657 and written at an unknown date. They are called *More Dissemblers besides Women* and *Women beware Women*.

His remarkable political allegory in dramatic form called *A Game at Chesse* was acted with great applause in 1624 and pub. in 1625 (modern ed. by R. C. Bald, 1929). Besides the works mentioned in this list he wrote other plays alone, and in collaboration with T. Rowley and others, masques and pageants for civil functions, and a series of vivid prose sketches called *The Black Booke* and *Father Hubburd's Tales*. A complete list of his works will be found in the article in the D.N.B. mentioned below. His play *The Witch* remained in MS. till 1778. It contains the complete text of two songs, the first lines of which are quoted in *Macbeth*. Middleton's works were first collected and ed. A. Dyce in 1840. Another ed. A. H. Bullen in 8 vols., appeared in 1885-86. There is a good selection by Havelock Ellis in the Mermaid Series. A modern critical ed. is needed.

Biography and Criticism.

Bullen's ed. contains a biographical and critical introd. and there is a valuable Life by C. H. Herford in the D.N.B. Swinburne has a characteristic study in *The Age of Shakespeare* and T. S. Eliot an important essay in *Elizabethan Essays* (1934). See also H. D. Sykes, *Sidelights on Elizabethan Drama* (1924), W. D. Dunkel, *The Dramatic Technique of Thomas Middleton in his Comedies of London Life* (Chicago, 1925); S. Schoenbaum, *Middleton's Tragedies* (N.Y. 1951); G. R. Hibbard, 'The Tragedies of Thomas Middleton and the Decadence of the Drama' R.M.S., I. 1957, and R. H. Barker, Thomas Middleton (N.Y., 1958). There is *A Concise Bibliography* by S. A. Tannenbaum (N.Y., 1940).

JOHN MARSTON (1576-1634)

Marston began his literary career by the publication of poems: *The Metamorphosis of Pigmalions Image* (1598, modern ed. 1927) and the satires called *The Scourge of Villanie* (1598, modern ed. in Bodley Head, Quarto, 1925). The second of these was pub. under the name of W. Kinsayder. His tragedies, a curious mixture of bombast and fine poetry, *The History of Antonio and Mellida. The first part* and *Antonio's Revenge*, were both pub. in 1602, and both probably acted in the preceding year. There are modern edd. of the Antonio and Mellida plays in M.S.R. Another tragedy by Marston called *The Malcontent* was pub. in 1604; additions to it by Webster appeared in a second issue of the same year. In 1605, having become reconciled with Ben Jonson, who had ridiculed his first tragedies, he collaborated with him and Chapman in *Eastward Hoe*. Marston's vigorous comedy *The Dutch Courtezan* was acted in 1603-4 and printed 1605. His other works include *Parasitaster or the Fawne*, founded on a tale of Boccaccio (1606), the comedy *What You Will* (1607) and the tragedy of *The Insatiate Countesse* (1613). He probably revised the anonymous dramatic satire *Histriomastix* (1610).

Marston's *Tragedies and Comedies collected into one volume* were pub. in 1633. There are collective edd. by J. O. Halliwell-Phillipps (1856), A. H. Bullen (1887), and H. H. Wood (*The Plays* in 3 vols., 1934-39). There are rpts. of *The Malcontent* in T.D. and of the

satires called *The Scourge of Villanie* ed. G. B. Harrison in the
Bodley Head Quartos.

Biography and Criticism

There are biographical and critical accounts of Marston in the
edd. mentioned above and an article by A. H. Bullen in the
D.N.B. The most recent works on him are by R. E. Brettle: *John
Marston Dramatist: Some New Facts*, in M.L.R., XXII 1927; *John
Marston Dramatist at Oxford*, in R.E.S., III 1927, and an Oxford
University dissertation, *John Marston*, an abstract of which appeared in *Abstracts of Dissertations for the Degree of D. Phil.*, Vol. I.
See also J. Peter, 'Marston's Plays' in *Scrutiny*, XVII (1934),
O. S. Campbell, *Comicall Satyre* (San Marino, 1938), and T. S.
Eliot in *Elizabethan Essays* (1934). There is *A Concise Bibliography*
by S. A. Tannenbaum (N.Y., 1940).

PHILIP MASSINGER (1583-1640)

Massinger's early work for the stage appears to have been done
in collaboration with other dramatists, chiefly John Fletcher.
There is little doubt that he had a considerable share in the
authorship of a number of plays in the Beaumont and Fletcher
folio of 1647. A table showing his probable participation in these
works is given in C.H.E.L., Vol. VI, Ch. 5, app.

He produced fifteen plays unaided, comedies, tragedies and
tragi-comedies. The most notable of these are *The Duke of Millaine*,
an Italianate tragedy, written about 1618, pub. 1623, modern ed.
by T. W. Baldwin, 1918; the vigorous comedy of manners *A New
Way To Pay Old Debts*, pub. 1632, probably acted before 1622
(this comedy kept its popularity all through the seventeenth and
eighteenth centuries and was often acted and rptd., modern edd.
by C. Stronach in T.D. and by A. H. Cruickshank, 1926); *The
Roman Actor, a tragedie*, pub. 1629, acted 1626, modern ed. by
W. L. Sandridge in *Princeton Studies in English; The Maid of Honour*,
an excellent tragi-comedy, acted 1626, pub. 1632; *The Great Duke
of Florence*, acted in 1627, pub. 1636, modern ed. by J. M.
Stockholm, 1933; *The City-Madam*, an admirable comedy of manners, pub. 1658, acted before 1632, modern ed. by R. Kirk,
Princeton Studies in English, 1934; *Believe as You List*, acted before
1631, remained in MS. till 1848, when it was printed by the Percy
Society. Modern ed, by C. J. Sisson in M.S.R., 1928.

Massinger's works were first collected and ed. T. Coxeter in 1759. W. Gifford's ed., pub. in 1805, and rptd. in 1813, and 1850, is still the standard collection. Other collected edd. are those of Hartley Coleridge (1840) and F. Cunningham (1871).

There is a selection of the plays in 2 vols. in the Mermaid Series, ed. A. Symons, and another by L. A. Sherman in *Masterpieces of the English Drama* (N.Y. 1912).

Biography and Criticism

There is a useful memoir in Gifford's ed. and a good article by R. Bayne in the D.N.B. The most important modern studies are A. H. Cruickshank's *Philip Massinger* (1920) and M. Chelli's *Le Drame de Massinger* (1923). See also study by H. W. Garrod in *The Profession of Poetry* (1928), tercentenary article in T.L.S., March 16th, 1940, D. J. Enright, 'Poetic Satire and Satire in Verse', *Scrutiny*, XVIII, 1952 and P. Quennell, 'Massinger' in *The Singular Preference* (1952). There is *A Concise Bibliography* by S. A. Tannenbaum (N.Y. 1938).

JOHN FORD (1586-1639)

Ford's first publication was an elegy on the Earl of Devonshire. He collaborated with Dekker and Rowley in the fine play called *The Witch of Edmonton* (pub. 1658, written c. 1621), and with Dekker in the masque called *The Sun's Darling* (produced 1624, pub. 1656).

The first unaided dramatic work was *The Lovers Melancholy*, acted in 1628, pub. 1629. His three most famous plays appeared in 1633. They are *The Broken Heart*, modern edd. by C. Scollard, 1895, by O. Smeaton in T.D., 1906, and by S. P. Sherman in B.L., 1916; *Loves Sacrifice;* and *Tis Pitty Shees a Whore*, modern ed. by S. P. Sherman in B.L.

His historical play, *The Chronicle Historie of Perkin Warbeck*, appeared in 1634, modern edd. by J. P. Pickburn and J. Le G. Brereton, 1896, and M. C. Struble, 1926. His last works were two comedies, *The Fancies, Chast and Noble* (1638) and *The Ladies Triall* (1639).

His works were collected by W. Gifford in 1827. A revision of this collection by A. Dyce was pub. in 1869. The standard modern ed. is *John Ford's Dramatic Works* ed. S. P. Sherman and H. de Vocht 2 vols. (Bang, N.S., 1908-27).

Biography and Criticism

There are important studies by M. J. Sergeaunt, *John Ford* (1936), G. F. Sensabaugh, *The Tragic Muse of Ford* (Alto Palo, 1944) and R. Davril, *Le Drame de Ford* (Paris, 1954). See also the articles by P. Ure in M.L.Q., xi, 1950 and Eng.St., xxxii, 1951, and P. Quennell's essay in *The Singular Preference* (1952). There is *A Concise Bibliography* by S. A. Tannenbaum (N.Y., 1941).

THOMAS HEYWOOD (c. 1574-1641)

Thomas Heywood, Lamb's 'prose Shakespeare', was perhaps the most industrious dramatic writer of the period and no less than 220 plays are ascribed to him. He was essentially a popular writer and many of his works were ephemeral productions, turned out rapidly for the players. Some of the most interesting are the following: *The Foure Prentises of London*, acted perhaps in 1592, printed 1615, modern ed. by B. Field, 1842; *The Royall King and The Loyall Subject*, acted perhaps in 1602, pub. 1637, modern ed. by K. W. Tibbals, 1906. *A Woman kilde with Kindnesse*, a fine drama of domestic life, acted 1603, pub. 1607, modern ed. by A. W. Ward in T.D.; in Neilson; and by K. L. Bates, 1919. *The Wise Woman Of Hogsdon*, acted perhaps in 1604, pub. 1638; a series of plays on classical subjects, *The Rape of Lucrece* (pub. 1608); *The Golden Age* (pub. 1611); *The Silver Age* (pub. 1613); *The Brazen Age* (pub. 1613), and *The Iron Age* (pub. 1632); the lively romantic comedy, *The fair Maid Of the West: Or, A Girle worth gold*, acted 1617, pub. 1631, modern ed. by K. L. Bates in B.L., 1917; *The English Traveller*, acted c. 1627, and printed 1633; and *The Captives; or The Lost Recovered*, first pub. by A. H. Bullen in O.E.P., 1884, ed. by A. C. Judson, 1921. Heywood also pub. non-dramatic verse and prose, including the very interesting *An Apology For Actors* (1612).

J. P. Collier and B. Field, ed. a number of the plays for the Shakespeare Society in 1842-51. The first complete ed. is that of Pearson (1874). A. W. Verity ed. the best plays for the Mermaid Series.

Criticism and Biography

There are three important modern works on Heywood: *Thomas Heywood, a Study in the Elizabethan Drama of Everyday Life*, by O. Cromwell (Y.S.E., 1928), *Thomas Heywood, Playwright and*

Miscellanist, by A. M. Clark, and *Thomas Heywood*, by F. S. Boas (1950). See also P. Ure, 'Marriage and Domestic Drama in Heywood and Ford', Eng.St., xxxii, 1951. There is a complete Bibliography by A. M. Clark in the O.B.S., I, 1925.

THOMAS DEKKER (c. 1572-1632)

Dekker's earliest extant play is *The Pleasant Comedie of Old Fortunatus*, acted 1599, pub. 1600, modern ed. in O.E.P., by H. Scherer (Munich, 1901), and by O. Smeaton in T.D. His delightful comedy of London life, *The Shomaker's Holiday Or The Gentle Craft*, was also acted in 1599, and pub. in 1600. There are many modern edd.: by A. E. Lange in R.E.C., Vol. III; by J. R. Sutherland in Nelson Playbooks and in McIlwraith. His *Satiro-mastix*, an episode in the 'war of the theatres', an attack on Jonson, appeared in 1602, modern edd. in Bang, Vol. XX, and by J. H. Penniman in B.L. In *The Honest Whore* (two parts acted 1604 and 1605, first part. pub. 1604, second, 1630), Dekker collaborated with Middleton. In *Westward Hoe* (acted 1604, pub. 1607) and *Northward Hoe* (acted 1605, pub. 1607), Dekker collaborated with Webster, in *The Roaring Girle or Moll Cut-Purse* with Middleton; and in the excellent play of English country life called *The Witch of Edmonton*, with Ford and Rowley (1658). Chambers's *Elizabethan Stage* contains a list of the plays certainly or conjecturally ascribed to Dekker.

Dekker's *Dramatic Works* were ed. R. H. Shepherd (1873). A complete ed. of *The Dramatic Works* in 4 vols. ed. F. T. Bowers is projected. Three vols. have appeared (1958). There is a selection of the plays ed. E. Rhys in Ev. Lib.

Biography and Criticism

There are two important modern studies of Dekker: *Thomas Dekker, a Study*, by M. L. Hunt in C.S.E. (1911), and *Thomas Dekker, a Study in Economic and Social Backgrounds*, by K. L. Gregg, in University of Washington *Publications in Language and Literature*. Vol. II, 1924. See also Mary L. Hunt, *Thomas Dekker* (N.Y., 1911) and H. Child, 'Thomas Dekker and the Underdog' in his *Essays and Reflections* (1948). There is *A Concise Bibliography* by S. A. Tannenbaum (N.Y., 1939), Supplement (N.Y., 1943).

RICHARD BROME (d. about 1652)

Richard Brome, at one time Ben Jonson's servant, was the author of fifteen comedies which foreshadow in some respects the Restoration comedy of manners. They include *The Northern Lasse* (1632), *The Antipodes*, and *The Sparagus Garden* (both 1640), and *A Joviall Crew; Or the Merry Beggars* (acted 1641 and pub. 1652). Two collections, each containing 'Five Newe Playes' by Brome, appeared in 1653 and 1659 respectively. R. H. Shepherd's ed. of *The Dramatic Works of Richard Brome* in 3 vols. was pub. in 1873. There is a German dissertation on him by E. K. R. Faust (Halle, 1887), an interesting article by J. A. Symonds in *The Academy*, March 21st, 1874. See also the study by A. C. Swinburne in *Contemporaries of Shakespeare* (1919) and C. E. Andrews, *Richard Brome, a Study of his Life and Works* (N.Y., 1913).

JAMES SHIRLEY (1596-1666)

From 1625 when his first play was licensed to the closing of the theatres, about forty dramatic pieces are recorded as by Shirley, and of these nearly all are still extant. For a full list, see the excellent bibliography in H. Nason's *James Shirley Dramatist*, 1915.

His best work is perhaps to be seen in his comedies of manners: *The Wittie Faire One* (1633); *The Gamester* (1637); *Hide Park* (1637); *The Lady Of Pleasure* (1637). *The Cardinal* (acted 1641, first printed in *Six New Plays*, 1653) is his best attempt at tragedy. *The Sisters* was the last play by Shirley, performed before the theatres were closed in 1642. It was not printed till 1653.

The first collection of Shirley's plays was *Six New Playes*, pub. in 1653. *The Dramatic Works* in 6 vols. ed. W. Gifford, with additional notes by A. Dyce, appeared in 1833. There is a selection of the plays by E. Gosse in the Mermaid Series.

Biography and Criticism

There is a good account of Shirley's life in the ed. of 1833. See also R. S. Forsythe's *The Relationship of Shirley's Plays to the Elizabethan Drama* (1912) and A. H. Nason's *James Shirley Dramatist, a Biographical and Critical Study* (1915). See also A. Harbage, *Cavalier Drama* (N.Y., 1936). There is *A Concise Bibliography* by S. A. and D. R. Tannenbaum (N.Y., 1946).

THE MASQUE AND THE PASTORAL DRAMA

A complete *List of Masques, Pageants and Entertainments* by W. W. Greg was pub. the Bib. Soc. in 1902. The two compilations of John Nichols, *The Progress and Public Processions of Queen Elizabeth* (3 vols. 1823), and *The Progresses, Processions and Magnificent Festivities of King James I* (4 vols., 1828) contain much valuable material. There are German studies by A. Soergel, *Die englischen Maskenspiele* (Halle, 1882), and R. Brotanek, *Dir englischen Maskenspiele* (Vienna, 1902); much more important are the fine French study, *Les Masques anglais* (Paris, 1909) by P. Reyher; Enid Welsford's *The Court Masque* (1927); and Allardyce Nicoll's *Stuart Masques and the Renaissance Stage* (1938). There is a useful anthology of *English Masques*, ed. with introd. by H. A. Evans (1897). See also A. Nicoll, *Stuart Masques and The Renaissance Stage* (1937).

The chief work on the pastoral plays is W. W. Greg's *Pastoral Poetry and The Pastoral Drama* (1906). There is an anthology of *English Pastorals* by E. K. Chambers (1895).

CHAPTER XV

SECULAR PROSE OF THE SEVENTEENTH CENTURY

(For Philosophical Works, see pp. 281–92.)

ESSAYS AND MISCELLANEOUS PROSE

ROBERT BURTON (1576/7-1639/40)

ROBERT BURTON, the 'fantastic old great man' of Lamb, pub. the first ed. of his famous book, *The Anatomy of Melancholy*, in folio in 1621. Five edd. appeared in Burton's lifetime, and three more in 1651, 1660 and 1676 respectively. No other ed. appeared till 1800. A. R. Shilleto's three-vol. ed. of 1893 was the first in which an attempt was made to track down the numerous quotations to their sources. There is a good modern cheap edd. in 3 vols. ed. Holbrook Jackson in Ev. Lib. and a selection, *Burton the Anatomist*, by G. F. C. Mead and R. C. Clift (1925). Burton's Latin comedy, *Philosophaster*, was first pub. from the MS. by the Roxburghe Club in 1862. There is a modern ed. with tr. by P. Jordan-Smith (Stanford, 1931). See the very important number of O.B.S., I (1927), devoted wholly to Burton and containing essays by Sir W. Osler, Professor E. Bensly and others. For comment and criticism see essays by C. Whibley in *Literary Portraits* (1904) and J. M. Murry in *Countries of the Mind* (1922). For 'melancholy', see L. Babb, *The Elizabethan Melody* (Michigan, 1951).

BEN JONSON (1572-1637)

Jonson's *Timber: or Discoveries made upon Men and Matter*, is a commonplace book of the highest interest and importance. It first appeared in the 1640-41 folio ed. of Jonson's works. There are modern edd. by Sir I. Gollancz in T.C. (1906); F. E. Schelling (1892); M. Castelain and G. B. Harrison in the Bodley Head Quartos (1923).

JOHN SELDEN (1584-1654)

John Selden, one of the greatest English scholars of his time, left an interesting collection of *pensées* pub. in 1689 by his secretary,

R. Milward, under the title *Table Talk . . . being the discourses of John Selden*. Later edd. appeared in 1696 and 1716, modern edd. by S. W. Singer (1847), by Sir I. Gollancz in T.C., and by F. Pollock (Selden Society, 1927). The last is the standard ed., and it contains a valuable life of Selden by Sir E. Fry.

SIR THOMAS BROWNE (1605-82)

Browne's earliest work, *Religio Medici*, was written about 1635 and circulated in MS. Two unauthorized edd. appeared in 1642, and in 1643 Browne pub. 'a true and full coppy'. This achieved immediate popularity and passed through eight edd. by 1685; a Latin tr. appeared in 1644. There are modern edd. by W. A. Greenhill (1881 and 1883), C. H. Herford (with other Writings, 1904), J. W. Murison (1922), J. O. Denonain (1953 and 1955) and L. C. Martin (with other Writings, 1965). In 1646 Browne pub. his longest work, *Pseudodoxia Epidemica* ('Enquiries into Vulgar and Common Errors'). After an interval of twelve years, inspired by the discovery of some sepulchral urns at Walsingham, he wrote *Hydriotaphia, Urne-Buriall*, his most memorable work (1658); appended to it was the fantastic essay *The Garden of Cyrus*, a discussion of the ubiquity of the quincunx. There are modern edd. of *Hydriotaphia* by W. A. Greenhill (1896) and W. Murison (1922) and a facs. in the Noel Douglas Replicas. Three posthumous works appeared after Browne's death: *Certain Miscellany Tracts* ed. Archbishop Tenison (1684), *A Letter to a Friend* (1690) and the fine unfinished *Christian Morals* ed. J. Jeffrey (1716, second ed. with Life by Dr Johnson, 1756).

The first collective ed. of the *Works* appeared in 1686. The first modern scholarly ed. with commentary was that of S. Wilkin, *Works and Letters*, vols. (1835-6, Bohn ed., 3 vols., 1852). The *Works* ed. C. Sayle, 3 vols. (1904-7), is a useful text. The standard modern ed. of *The Complete Works* is that of G. Keynes, 6 vols. (1928-31, 2nd rev. ed., 4 vols., 1965).

Biography and Criticism

The first life of Browne was that of Samuel Johnson (see above). Sir E. Gosse contributed a biography to E.M.L. (1905). Recent important studies are W. P. Dunn, *Browne, a Study in Religious Philosophy* (Minneapolis, 1926, rev. ed. 1950), O. Leroy, *Le Chevalier Thomas Browne (1605-82), médecin, styliste et metaphysicien*

(Paris, 1931), F. L. Huntley, *Sir Thomas Browne a Biographical and Critical Study* (Michigan, 1961), and Joan Bennett, *Sir Thomas Browne, a Man of Achievement in Literature* (1961). Some of the best criticism of Browne is to be found in S. T. Coleridge's *Literary Remains*, W. Hazlitt's *Lectures on the Age of Elizabeth*, Lytton Strachey's *Books and Characters*, Basil Willey's *The Seventeenth Century Background* and M. Praz's essay in his *Studi e svaghi inglesi* (Florence, 1937). Morris Croll, 'The Baroque Style in Prose' in *Studies in Philology in Honor of Frederick Klaeber* (Minneapolis, 1929) should also be consulted. There is a Bibliography by G. Keynes (1924).

IZAAK WALTON (1593-1683)

Walton's earliest publication of importance was his *Life of Donne*, which was prefixed to Donne's *LXXX Sermons*, pub. in 1640. It was pub. separately in a rev. form in 1658. His *Life of Sir Henry Wotton* appeared in the vol. called *Reliquiae Wottonianae* in 1651. It was enl. in later edd. His *Life of Hooker* appeared in the 1665 ed. of Hooker's Works. These lives were collected and pub. together in 1670 with a fourth, the beautiful Life of George Herbert, a separate ed. of which also appeared in the same year. Walton's fifth and last *Life*, that of Dr. Sanderson, Bishop of Lincoln, was prefixed to a collection of Sanderson's tracts, which appeared in 1678, and was issued in a rev. form with a collection of Sanderson's Sermons in 1681.

There are modern edd. of *Walton's Lives* by A. H. Bullen (1884); A. Dobson (1898); in T.C. (1898) and by G. Saintsbury in W.C. (1927). A new ed. by J. E. Butt and I. A. Shapiro is in preparation. A bibliography of the seventeenth-century edd. by J. E. Butt is included in O.B.S., II (1930). Walton's other great work, *The Compleat Angler or the Contemplative Man's Recreation*, was pub. 1653 anonymously, but the epistle dedicatory was signed Iz. Wa. Since then over 280 edd. have appeared. The fifth ed. included the excellent continuation on trout and grayling fishing by C. Cotton; modern edd. include those by Andrew Lang (1896, now in Ev. Lib.), R. Le Gallienne (1897, a delightful illustrated ed.) and J. Buchan (1901, now in W.C.). Facs. of the first ed. were pub. in 1893 and 1928. There is a bibliography in *A New Chronicle of the Compleat Angler* by P. Oliver (1936) and there is an ed. of *The Angler* and *The Lives* by A. W. Pollard (1901). *The Compleat*

Walton ed. G. Keynes (1929) includes besides *The Angler* and *Lives*, minor writings and letters.

Biography and Criticism

The most important works on Walton are R. H. Shepherd's *Waltoniana* (1878) and J. Martin's *Izaak Walton and his Friends* (1904). There is a discussion of Walton's biographical work in D. A. Stauffer's *English Biography before 1700*, and in J. E. Butt's essay, *Izaak Walton's Methods in Biography* (E.S.M.E.A., XIX, 1933).

ABRAHAM COWLEY (1618-67)

Cowley's essays were first printed in the 1668 ed. of his works as *Select Discourses by way of Essayes in Verse and Prose*. In 1661 he had published separately his fine *Vision concerning his late pretended Highness, Cromwell the Wicked*. There are many modern edd. of the prose works. The best are those of J. R. Lumby (rev. A. Tilley, 1923), and A. R. Waller (1906). For Cowley's poems, see p. 299.

SIR WILLIAM TEMPLE (1628-99)

Temple pub. in 1673 *An Essay on the Advancement of Trade in Ireland*. His very interesting *Observations upon the United Provinces of the Netherlands* appeared in 1673. It passed through many edd. and was rptd. in 1932.

The first part of his essays entitled *Miscellanea* appeared in 1680, the second in 1690-91. This included the famous essays upon *Ancient and Modern Learning*, *Upon Poetry* and *Upon the Gardens of Epicurus or of Gardening*.

The third part of *Miscellanea* appeared in 1701 after Temple's death. The three parts of *Miscellanea* were pub. Swift in 1705-8.

An ed. of Temple's Works appeared in 1720. A later ed. of 1740 included a Life of Swift by his sister Lady Giffard.

A selection of the essays ed. J. Nicklin appeared in 1911, and in 1930 G. C. Moore Smith pub. an interesting collection of early *Essays and Romances*, with the *Life* by Lady Giffard.

Biography and Criticism

As well as Lady Giffard's life there is an early life of Temple by A. Boyer (1714). There are also *Memoirs* by T. P. Courtenay

(1836), reviewed by Macaulay in his notable Essay on Temple (1838), two Oxford prize essays by M. L. R. Beavan and E. S. Lyttel respectively (1908), and a monograph by Clara Marburg: *Sir William Temple a seventeenth century 'libertin'* (1932). The best modern study is H. E. Woodbridge, *Temple, The Man and his Work* (N.Y., 1940).

GEORGE SAVILE, MARQUIS OF HALIFAX (1633-95)

George Savile, Marquis of Halifax, the famous 'Trimmer' (not to be confused with his younger contemporary Charles Montague, Earl of Halifax), was one of the most able and distinguished English prose writers of the later seventeenth century. His two most notable works are both 'characters'. *The Character of King Charles II* is one of the most acute and interesting of the historical 'characters', and his *Character of a Trimmer* is a development of the Theophrastan form and one of the most brilliant political pamphlets of the period. Both were written about 1685. *The Character of King Charles II* was pub. in 1750, and *The Character of a Trimmer* in 1688. His other works include two other important and influential pamphlets, *A Letter to a Dissenter* (1688) and *The Anatomy of an Equivalent* (1688). His aphorisms called *Political, Moral and Miscellaneous Thoughts and Reflections*, were not pub. till 1750. A vol. of his *Miscellanies* was pub. in 1700. It includes his delightful and popular essay, *The Lady's New-Year's-Gift: or Advice to a Daughter*. There is a good modern ed. of *The Works of Halifax*, ed. with introd. by Sir W. Raleigh (1912), and a valuable biography by H. C. Foxcroft in 2 vols. (1897). A shorter study by Miss Foxcroft entitled *A Character of the Trimmer* was pub. in 1946.

HISTORIES, BIOGRAPHIES AND MEMOIRS

GENERAL STUDY AND SELECTION

D. Nichol Smith, *Characters of the Seventeenth Century* (1918) contains a study of English historical writing of the seventeenth century, together with a selection of 'characters' from historical works of the period. V. de S. Pinto, *English Biography in the Seventeenth Century* (1951) is a collection of eight short seventeenth century biographies with a study of the development of English biography up to the end of the century.

INDIVIDUAL AUTHORS

LORD HERBERT OF CHERBURY (1583-1648)

Lord Herbert's history of *The Life and Raigne of King Henry the Eighth* appeared after his death in 1649. It was rptd. in 1672, 1682 and 1741.

He also wrote a most interesting *Autobiography* which was pub. 1764 by Horace Walpole. There are modern edd. by Sir S. Lee (1886 and 1907), and C. H. Herford (Gregynog Press, 1928).

For his philosophical works, and biography and criticism, see p. 283. For his poems, see p. 297.

EDWARD HYDE, EARL OF CLARENDON (1609-74)

Clarendon's great *History of the Rebellion*, the first important English history of contemporary affairs, was begun in 1646, when he was in the Channel Islands at the end of the first Civil War. The orig. draft took the narrative up to the Battle of Alresford in March 1644. In 1646 he also wrote an account of the affair in the West to defend himself before the Prince's Council. Between 1668 and 1670 he wrote a *Life* of himself, extending up to 1660, and in 1671, he reverted to his orig. intention, and wove all these narratives into a *History of the Great Rebellion*, making many alterations and omissions. This book was pub. after his death in 1702-4, when it was ed. his son, the Earl of Rochester and Dean Aldrich, who made some minor alterations. The orig. MSS. are in the Bodleian. After his banishment in 1667 Clarendon wrote the work called *The Life of Edward, Earl of Clarendon, being a continuation of the History of the Grand Rebellion from the Restoration to his Banishment*. This book, which was pub. in 1759, contains the parts of the *Life* not included in the earlier work together with a very interesting history of the early years of the reign of Charles II. For an account of Clarendon's shorter works see Sir C. H. Firth's article in the D.N.B. The first ed. to print *The History* from the orig. MSS. was that of B. Bandinel (1826). Edd. of both the *History* and the *Life* from the MSS. were pub. at Oxford in 1843 and 1849. The best modern ed. of the *History* is that of W. D. Macray (6 vols. 1888). The last ed. of the *Life* is that of 1859. There are numerous modern edd. of parts of the *History*. Among them mention may be made of T. Arnold's ed. of Book VI, *Characters and Episodes of the Great Rebellion*, ed. G. D. Boyle, and *War Pictures from Clarendon*, ed. R. J. Mackenzie. There is an excellent selection in W.C. ed. G. Huehns (1955).

Biography and Criticism

There is an important early life of Clarendon in Wood's *Athenae Oxonienses*. Sir C. Firth contributed a valuable article on him to D. N. B. Firth's articles on '*Clarendon*'s *History of the Great Rebellion*' in E.H.R., XIX (1904) and his lecture, *Edward Hyde as Statesman, Historian and Chancellor of the University* (1909) is indispensable. The standard biography is Sir H. Craik, *The Life of Edward, Earl of Clarendon* (2 vols., 1911). A more recent study is B. H. G. Wormald, *Clarendon 1640-1660* (1951). See also L. C. Knights, 'Reflections on Clarendon's *History of the Great Rebellion*' in *Scrutiny*, XV (1948).

GILBERT BURNET (1643-1715)

Although Burnet's great *History of My Own Time* deals largely with events after 1688 and was not pub. till the next century, several of his other works appeared during the period covered by this vol. and may be conveniently mentioned here. His *Memoires of the Lives and Actions of James and William Dukes of Hamilton* appeared in 1676, and his *History of the Reformation*, Vol. i, in 1679, Vol. ii, 1681 and Vol. iii, 1714. His two most interesting short works are *Some Passages of The Life and Death of John, Earl of Rochester* (1680) and his *Life and Death of Sir M. Hale* (1682). The book on Rochester is largely an account of Burnet's conversations with the dying poet, and is excellently written. It is rptd. in *English Biography in the Seventeenth Century* ed. V. de S. Pinto (1951). *The History of My Own Time*, one of the most lively and vigorous of English histories, was pub. in 1724-34. The best modern ed. is that of O. Airy (2 vols. O.U.P. 1897-1900). There is a good biography of Burnet by J. E. S. Clarke and H. C. Foxcroft (1907). See also G. P. Gooch, *Courts and Cabinets* (1944).

JOHN AUBREY (1626-97)

The only work of Aubrey pub. during his lifetime was a vol. called *Miscellanies*, which appeared in 1696. He left a large number of MSS. including accounts of the natural history of Wiltshire and Surrey, and a series of vivid sketches of eminent men made for Anthony à Wood who used them for his *Athenae Oxonienses*. The MSS. of these 'brief lives' of Aubrey are in the Bodleian. A selection called *Lives of Eminent Men* appeared in 1813. The standard ed. is *Brief Lives by John Aubrey*, ed. A. Clark (2 vols. 1898). *Brief Lives and Other Selected Writings* ed. A. Powell (1949) and *Brief Lives* ed. O. Lawson Dick (P.B.) are useful modern edd. See also A. Powell, *Aubrey and his Friends* (1948).

THOMAS SPRAT (1635-1713)

Sprat's *Life* of his friend Cowley was prefixed to the ed. of the poet's English Works which appeared in 1668, and was rightly described by Johnson as 'a funeral oration, rather than a history'. Sprat's most notable work is *The History of the Royal Society* (1667), an invaluable expression of some of the main currents of thought in the Restoration period. It was often rptd. down to 1764. There is an excellent modern ed. by Jackson I. Pope and H. W. Jones (St. Louis, Missouri, 1958).

LUCY HUTCHINSON (b. 1620)

Lucy Hutchinson's famous biography of her husband called *Memoirs of the Life of Colonel Hutchinson* was first pub. in 1806. There are good modern edd. by C. H. Firth (1885, rev. ed. 1906), and in Ev. Lib.

ANTHONY À WOOD (1632-95)

This great Oxford antiquarian pub. in 1674 his Latin *Historia et Antiquitates Universitates Oxoniensis*. An English tr. appeared in 1691. His most famous work, the *Athenae Oxonienses, an exact history of all the Writers and Bishops who have had their education . . . in Oxford . . . from 1500 . . . to 1690*, the first really important English biographical dictionary, appeared in 1691-92, second ed. 1721. The best ed. is that of P. Bliss (4 vols. 1820). Wood's other works include his very interesting *Diaries* printed in *The Life and Times of Anthony Wood* (ed. A. Clark, 5 vols.). There is a selection from the Diaries called

The Life and Times of Anthony à Wood, ed. Llewelyn Powys (1932, ed. in W.C., 1961).

ROGER NORTH (1653-1734)

Roger North's important works fall just outside the period covered by this book as far as their dates of composition and publication are concerned, but, as they belong to the period in respect of their style, spirit and subject matter, perhaps they may be mentioned here. His most interesting and valuable writing is to be found in his fine, racy biographies of his brothers, Francis North, Lord Guilford, the famous judge, Sir Dudley North, the great 'Turkey' merchant, and the Hon. and Rev. John North, a Cambridge don, and in his own autobiography. Roger North pub. nothing in his lifetime except *A Discourse of Fish and Fishponds* (1683). His *Life of the Rt. Hon. Francis North, Baron of Guilford* was pub. in 1742 and the two other Lives in 1744. An ed. of his *Lives of the Norths*, ed. A. Jessopp, appeared in 3 vols. in 1890. The same editor pub. *The Autobiography* in 1887. North's other works include the historical study called *Examen*, a critical reply to a Whig *Compleat History of England*, which appeared in 1740. A modern ed. of North's works is needed.

DIARIES AND LETTERS

SAMUEL PEPYS (1633-1703)

The only work pub. Pepys in his lifetime seems to have been his *Memories relating to the State of the Royal Navy* . . . (1690, modern ed. by J. R. Tanner, 1906). The MS. of his great Diary, written in shorthand between 1660 and 1669, was bequeathed by him to Magdalene College, Cambridge. It was first deciphered and transcribed by the Rev. J. Smith and pub. Lord Braybrooke in 1825. A new ed. freshly deciphered from the MS. by Mynors Bright appeared in 1875-79 with some of Pepys's correspondence. Both these early edd. omitted large parts of the orig. work. Most of these omissions were supplied in the excellent ed. of H. B. Wheatley, first pub. 1893-96 (6 vols., cheap ed. 1904). There are also edd. by G. Gregory Smith in The Globe Series, and in Ev. Lib. An abridged ed., *Everybody's Pepys*, appeared in 1927. J. Smith pub. in 1841 *The Life, Journals and Correspondence of*

Samuel Pepys, including the second diary giving an account of the Voyage to Tangiers in 1683. An ed. of the *Letters and Second Diary* by R. G. Howarth appeared in 1932. Two vols. of Pepys's correspondence have been pub. by J. R. Tanner in 1926 and 1929 respectively and an ed. of the *Letters* by H. T. Heath (1955). There are many books on Pepys. Among the best are J. R. Tanner, *Introduction to the Diary* (1925), A. Ponsonby's study E.M.L. (1928), A. Bryant's elaborate and scholarly work, *Samuel Pepys* 3 vols. (1933-38) and J. H. Wilson, *The Private Life of Mr. Pepys* (N.Y. 1959), a lively picture of the man and his times. See also R. L. Stevenson's essay in *Familiar Studies of Men and Books* (1882).

JOHN EVELYN (1620-1706)

Evelyn was a voluminous writer of ephemeral tracts. His *State of France*, (1652), *Character of England* (1659) and *Fumifugium* (a work on the smoke of London, 1661), are full of interest for the social historian. He also wrote technical tracts on engraving and agriculture. His *Miscellaneous Works* were collected and ed. W. Upcott in 1825. His famous *Diary* remained in MS. until 1818 when it was pub. W. Bray under the title *Memoirs Illustrative* of the *Life and Writings of John Evelyn*. Other edd. are those of H. B. Wheatley (1879 and 1906), and Austin Dobson (1906, 4 vols. also in Globe ed.). There is also an ed. in Ev. Lib. The standard modern ed. is that of E. S. de Beer, 6 vols. (1955; 1 vol. ed. with some omissions 1959). Evelyn's life of his friend Margaret Godolphin was pub. S. Wilberforce in 1847 (modern ed. in K.C.). Recent works on Evelyn are *The Early Life and Education of John Evelyn* by H. Maynard Smith (1920), *John Evelyn, Fellow of the Royal Society* by A. Ponsonby (1933), *Mr. Pepys and Mr. Evelyn* by Clara Marburg (Philadelphia, 1935), and *John Evelyn, a Study in Bibliophily and a Bibliography of his Writings*, by G. Keynes (1927). See also the essay by Virginia Woolf in *The Common Reader*.

DOROTHY OSBORNE (LADY TEMPLE) (1627-95)

Dorothy Osborne's letters to her future husband Sir W. Temple remained in MS. till the nineteenth century. A selection from them was pub. T. P. Courtenay in his *Memoirs of Sir William Temple* (1836) and a complete ed. by E. A. Parry (1888, now in

Ev. Lib.). The standard modern ed. with a memoir is that of G. C. Moore Smith (1928).

THE THEOPHRASTAN CHARACTER

The pithy description of a social type in prose called The Character was a favourite literary form in seventeenth-century England. It should be carefully distinguished from the historical 'Character' or portrait of an actual person, which was popular during the same period. The character sketches of types seemed to have been originally inspired by the ancient Greek characters of Theophrastus, the Greek philosopher, discovered by Casaubon the French scholar, and pub. by him with a Latin tr. in 1592. Perhaps the first English 'characters' of the Theophrastan type are Ben Jonson's short descriptions of the dramatis personae of *Every Man out of his Humour* (1600). The earliest English collection of characters seems to have been *The Characters of Vertues and Vices* by Joseph Hall (1608). In 1614 appeared the famous collection pub. with the second ed. of Sir T. Overbury's poem, *A Wife*. These 'witty characters' are probably the work of a number of authors, one of whom was almost certainly the dramatist John Webster. A modern critical ed. of *The Overburian Characters* ed. W. J. Paylor with a valuable introd. was pub. in Blackwell's *Percy Reprints* (1936). Nicholas Breton's *Characters upon Essaies Morall and Divine* (1615) is an interesting early attempt to combine the character and the essay. (For this and Breton's other collection of characters see p. 243.) The beautiful collection of characters by John Earle (afterwards Bishop of Salisbury) called *Microcosmographie* first appeared in 1628. There are many modern edd. including one by W. H. Rouse in T.C. and another pub. in 1933. The remarkable *Characters* by S. Butler, the author of *Hudibras*, were not pub. till 1759, when they appeared in his *Genuine Remains* (see p. 302). There is a modern ed. in vol. 2 of Butler's *Works*, ed. A. R. Waller. In the reign of Charles II were pub. a number of very able and interesting anonymous 'characters', such as *The Character of a Tavern*, *The Character of a Town Gallant* and *The Character of a Town Misse* (all 1675, rptd. in Aldington's collection, see below). There are several good modern collections of the old 'characters'. They include *Character Writings of the Seventeenth Century*, ed. H. Morley (1891), *A Book of Characters*, ed. R. Aldington (Broadway Library, 1924), which contains a most valuable introd. and *A Cabinet of Characters*, ed. Gwen Murphy (1925). Miss Murphy has also pub. *A Bibliography of English Character Books* (1925).

LITERARY CRITICISM

An excellent collection of most of the chief critical essays of this period will be found in *Critical Essays of the Seventeenth Century*, ed. with a valuable introd. and notes by J. E. Spingarn (3 vols., 1908-9). For Dryden's criticism see pp. 391-2.

FICTION

For accounts of the fiction of this period see *The History of the English Novel* by E. A. Baker, Vol. III (1924) and *The English Novel* by Sir W. Raleigh (1894).

The most ambitious attempts were the high-flown romances in the French style such as *Parthenissa* (1654-69) by R. Boyle, Earl of Orrery (1621-69) and *Aretina or the Serious Romance* (1660) by Sir G. Mackenzie (1636-91). There were also English trs. of the French romances of D'Urfée, Mlle de Scudéry, Calprenède and others.

Several dramatists experimented in prose fiction in the Restoration period. Aphra Behn's best stories, *The Fair Jilt* and *Oronooko or the Royal Slave*, were both pub. after her death in 1698 (modern edd. *The Novels of Aphra Behn*, ed. E. A. Baker, 1913, and in M. Summers's ed. of the *Works*, see p. 378). Crowne's *Pandion* (1665) is a poor heroic romance, but William Congreve's *Incognita* (1691-92, modern ed. by

H. F. B. Brett Smith in *Percy Reprints*, 1922), is a short story showing great promise. Francis Kirkman, a London bookseller (b. 1632), was a pioneer in the popular types of fiction, later developed by Defoe. Besides editing plays and the well-known collection of 'drolls' called *The Wits or Sport upon Sport* (1662), he tr. romances from the Spanish and French, and wrote the amusing autobiographical medley called *The Unlucky Citizen Experimentally Described* (1673), and the account of the swindler Mary Carleton, called *The Counterfeit Lady Unveiled* (1673). Ernst Bernbaum's *The Mary Carleton Narratives* (1914) is an important contribution to the study of late seventeenth century fiction. The picaresque romance called *The English Rogue* by Richard Head was first pub. in 1665. Kirkman re-issued it in 1666, and wrote a continuation of it, which he pub. in 1671. A modern ed. of *The English Rogue* including Head's original narrative and Kirkman's continuation was pub. in 1928. There is a useful modern rpt. of *The Counterfeit Lady Unveiled and Other Criminal Fiction of Seventeenth Century England* ed. S. Peterson (P.B., N.Y., 1961). See also B. Boyce, 'The Effect of the Restoration on Prose Fiction', *Tennessee Studies in Literature*, VI, 77-83, 1961.

TRANSLATIONS

Among the numerous English prose translations of the seventeenth century mention may be made of the great version of Rabelais by Sir Thomas Urquhart (1611-60), the first two books of which appeared in 1653 and a third in 1693 (completed by P. A. Motteux, 1708, modern edd. by C. Whibley in *Tudor Translations* [1900], in Ev. Lib. and W.C.); Charles Cotton's fine version of *Montaigne's Essays* (1685, modern edd. 1905 and 1923); and the numerous racy trs. of Sir R. L'Estrange, the best of which are, perhaps, *The Fables of Aesop and other eminent Mythologists* (1692, many later edd.), and *Twenty Select Colloquies of Erasmus* (1680), modern ed. Abbey Classics no. XVII (n.d.), introd. by C. Whibley.

CHAPTER XVI

RELIGIOUS PROSE OF THE SEVENTEENTH CENTURY

(This section is divided into three parts: [*a*] Bible Translations, [*b*] Anglican Divines, [*c*] Puritans and Quakers. The works mentioned here only represent a very small selection from the vast religious literature of the period. For the Platonists and Latitudinarians see above, pp. 287–92.)

BIBLE TRANSLATIONS

AFTER the rev. ed. of Cranmer's 'Great Bible', pub. 1541 (see above, p. 159), no important English version appeared till the reign of Elizabeth. Some English divines in exile on the continent during Mary's reign made the ultra-Protestant version called the Geneva Bible. It was preluded by an English version of the New Testament pub. at Geneva in 1557 probably by W. Whittingham, afterwards Dean of Durham. In 1560 the complete Geneva Bible tr. by W. Whittingham, A. Gilby and T. Sampson was pub. in London. It is significant that it was the first small Bible fit for private reading. Elizabeth permitted its use and granted an exclusive patent to John Bodley to print it for seven years, but Cranmer's 'Great Bible' was placed in the churches. A rev. version of this work was made by the Anglican Bishops under the supervision of Archbishop Parker and was pub. in 1568. This 'Bishops' Bible', a folio, became the standard Church Bible of the Elizabethan period while the Geneva or 'breeches' version, was commonly possessed by private persons. Shakespeare seems to have known both. Meanwhile the Romanists began to feel the lack of an English Bible with no Protestant bias and Gregory Martin, of the English Jesuit College at Rheims, was commissioned to produce a version of the New Testament for English Romanists. Martin's tr appeared at Rheims in 1582. The English College moved to

Douai in 1593 and the English New Testament was rptd. for the Douai College at Antwerp in 1600. In 1609-10 a Romanist version of the Old Testament was added to it. The complete Romanist version was therefore known as the Douai version.

At the Hampton Court conference of 1604 the Puritan party, through their spokesman Dr John Reynolds, urged the necessity of a new English version of the Bible. James I agreed to the suggestion, and ordered that a new tr. should be 'done by the best learned in both Universities, after them to be reviewed by the Bishops, and the chief learned of the Church; from them to be presented to the Privie-Councell; and lastly to be ratified by his *Royall Authoritie*'. About fifty scholars were appointed to carry out the work under the editorship of Miles Smith, afterwards Bishop of Gloucester, and Thomas Bilson, Bishop of Winchester. They were directed to use previous English trs., particularly the Bishops' Bible, but also Tyndale's, Coverdale's, the Geneva and other Protestant versions. They interpreted their instruction literally and occasionally used the Romanist Rheims version of the N.T. as well. Generally, however, they kept close to the Protestant versions, especially to Tyndale's, which has been rightly described as the very core of the English Bible. The Authorized Version, perhaps the greatest literary work ever produced by a committee, was pub. in folio and simultaneously in quarto in 1611, and was soon accepted by non-Romanist Englishmen of all shades of religious opinion, thus becoming by far the best known and most influential of English books. The most useful and scholarly English rpt. is that ed. by A. W. Pollard, with an excellent historical introd. Pollard has also ed. *The Records of the English Bible*, a rpt. of all the chief documents connected with early English Bible trs. The bibliography of A. V. is discussed in *A Description of the Great Bible* by F. Fry (1865) and by F. H. Scrivener in *The Authorized Edition of the Bible and the Subsequent Reprints* (1884). For the influence of the Romanist version, see J. C. Carleton's *Rheims and the English Bible* (1902). Among critical works reference may be made to *The Bible and English Prose Style* by A. S. Cook (1892), *The Bible as English Literature* by J. H. Gardiner (1905) and the excellent essays by Quiller Couch in *On the Art of Reading* and J. Livingstone Lowes in *Of Reading Books* (1929). See also *The English Bible* ed. V. F. Storrs (1938), a valuable collection of studies, and C. S. Lewis 'The Literary Impact of the Authorized Version' in *They Asked for a Paper* (1961).

ANGLICAN DIVINES
GENERAL STUDIES

To the works mentioned on p. 270 should be added Izaak Walton's *Lives* (for edd., see p. 321), S. T. Coleridge's *Notes on English Divines* (1853).

INDIVIDUAL AUTHORS

JOHN DONNE (1573-1631)

Donne's sermons were the most characteristic productions of the later part of his life. Six were printed in his lifetime. His last sermon, the famous *Death's Duell*, was pub. soon after his death in 1632, and in 1634 six more were pub. at Cambridge. In 1640 his son pub. a folio containing *LXXX Sermons*, in 1649 a second folio of *Fifty Sermons* and 1660 a third entitled *XXVI Sermons* but actually containing twenty-four. One hundred and sixty sermons by Donne were pub. in the seventeenth century. In 1839 H. Alford pub. an ed. containing 154 sermons with poems, devotions and letters; Alford's texts are unreliable and he admitted that he bowdlerized some sermons. A complete ed. in 10 vols. ed. G. R. Potter and E. M. Simpson is in progress. Vols. I, II, III, VI, VII and VIII have appeared up to date. There is an excellent vol. of Selections from the Sermons with introd. by L. Pearsall Smith (1919). In 1923 the Nonesuch Press pub. a beautiful printed ed. of *Ten Sermons*, ed. G. Keynes, and selected passages from the sermons and other prose writings are included in J. Hayward's *Complete Poetry and selected Prose of John Donne* (1929). Besides the early *Paradoxes and Problems* (see p. 295), Donne's prose works include a treatise on suicide called *BIAΘAN ATOΣ* written in 1608, but not pub. till 1646, modern ed. by J. W. Hebel (facs. ed. N.Y. 1930); *Pseudomartyr* (1610), a controversial work against the Romanists; a satire on the Jesuits called *Conclave Ignatii* (1611, facs. ed. by C. M. Coffin (N.Y., 1941)); and the beautiful series of religious meditations called *Devotions on Emergent Occasions*, written in 1623, pub. 1634, rptd. Pickering, 1834 (with the fine *Sermon in Commemoration of Lady Danvers*); modern edd. by John Sparrow (1923) and W. H. Draper in W.C. (1925).

For collected edd. and biographical and critical works see pp. 294-5.

THOMAS FULLER (1608-61)

Fuller, praised by Coleridge both for his wit, 'surpassing that of the wittiest in a witty age', and for his 'sound, shrewd good sense and freedom of intellect' was a voluminous and delightful writer. Among his most popular works were the *Historie of the Holy Warre* (1639, modern ed. 1840); *The Holy State* with the *Profane State* (1642, modern edd., 1840, 1841, 1884 and 1938, the last a valuable critical ed. with important introd. by M. G. Walten (N.Y., 1938). An extract is rptd. in Cambridge Plain Texts); the delightful 'penseés', *Good Thoughts in Bad Times* (1645) and the sequel *Good Thoughts in Worse Times* (1647), modern edd. by Pickering (1841) and by A. R. Waller (1902, 1904). His last publications were his two great historical works *The Church History of Britaine* with the *History of the University of Cambridge* and *The History of Waltham Abbey* (1655), modern edd. 1837, 1868, and by J. S. Brewer, 1840. Fuller began his great historical compilation *The History of the Worthies of England* in 1644. It was left unfinished at his death and hurried through the press by his son, appearing in 1662; modern edd. by J. Nichols, 1811 and P. A. Nuthall, 1840. A collection of his *Poems* was pub. by A. B. Grosart in 1868 and his Collected Sermons by J. Bailey and W. E. A. Axon in 1891. There is a very good selection with useful introd. by E. K. Broadus (1928).

Biography and Criticism

An anonymous *Life* of Fuller appeared in 1661 and is rptd. by Broadus. The standard *Life* is still that of J. E. Bailey (1874);

there is a briefer study by D. B. Lyman (1935). Reference should also be made to Lamb's note appended to his *Specimens from the Writings of Fuller* (Lamb's Works ed. Lucas, I, 454), and to Coleridge's *Notes on Fuller*. The best modern critical work is *The Formation of Fuller's Holy and Profane States* by W. E. Houghton Jr. (Harvard 1938). See also W. A. Addison, *Worthy Dr Fuller* (1951) and S. C. Roberts, *Fuller: a Seventeenth Century Worthy* (1953).

JEREMY TAYLOR (1613-67)

Jeremy Taylor, praised by Coleridge for his 'great and lovely mind', was one of the most eloquent and poetical of English preachers and a voluminous writer on religious subjects. His numerous publications begin with a *Sermon upon the Anniversary of the Gunpowder Treason*, pub. in 1638. In 1647 appeared his famous and eloquent plea for toleration, *A Discourse of the Liberty of Prophesying* (rptd. 1647, 1702, 1709 and 1817). Perhaps the flower of his lyrical prose is to be found in his two little devotional treatises, *The Rule and Exercises of Holy Living* (1650) and *The Rule and Exercises of Holy Dying* (1651). These two books were very popular and have often been rptd. There are many modern edd. including one by A. R. Waller in T.C. Among his collections of his sermons mention may be made of his *XXVIII Sermons preached at Golden Grove* (1651), and *XXV Sermons preached at Golden Grove* (1653). They were printed together in a folio called 'Ενιαυτος (1653). His other writings include sermons, prayers and meditations, controversial works, the *Ductor Dubitantium*, a huge book of casuistry designed to guide Anglicans in difficult cases of conscience and a beautiful *Discourse of the Nature, Offices and Measures of Friendship* (1657) addressed to Mrs Katherine Philips ('Orinda', the poetess). A modern rpt. appeared in 1920.

Taylor's *Whole Works* were first collected and ed. with a *Life* by R. Heber in 1822. A rev. ed. by C. P. Eden appeared in 1847-51. His *Poems* were pub. A. B. Grosart in 1870. There are two modern selections, one by Martin Armstrong (Golden Cockerel Press, 1923) and the excellent vol. called *The Golden Grove*, with valuable critical introd. by L. Pearsall Smith (1930). This vol. contains a complete bibliography by R. Gathorne Hardy.

Biography and Criticism

Short accounts of Taylor are given in a funeral sermon preached on him by Dr G. Rust in 1668, in D. Lloyd's *Memoirs of the Loyalists*

(1668), and C. Barksdale's *Remembrances of Excellent Men* (1670). Eden's revision of Heber's *Life* in his ed. of the Works is the best modern authority. There is a study by Sir E. Gosse in E.M.L. and a biography by W. J. Brown (1925). The best critical study is that of L. Pearsall Smith in his selection, *The Golden Grove*. Reference should also be made to the notes by Coleridge and to Hazlitt's *Lectures on the Literature of the Age of Elizabeth*, VII. See also C. J. Stranks, *The Life and Writings of Jeremy Taylor* (1952), the most authoritative and up-to-date study.

ISAAC BARROW (1630-77)

Barrow was one of the most learned and also one of the most popular divines of the reign of Charles II. He was an early champion of what he calls the 'simple and plain way' of preaching, as opposed to the florid, poetical style of such divines as Jeremy Taylor, which he described as 'sublimities above the apostolical spirit'. He was an eminent mathematician and pub. mathematical treatises in Latin as well as Latin poems. His most important English work are his sermons pub. after his death by John Tillotson, *Sermons preached upon several occasions* . . . 1678. Tillotson also pub. an ed. of Barrow's *Theological Works* in 1683-87 with a *Life* of Barrow by Abraham Hill. The standard modern ed. is that of A. Napier (9 vols. 1859), with memoir by W. Whewell. The *Life* by Hill in the ed. of 1683-87, rptd. in *English Biography in the Seventeenth Century* ed. Pinto (see above, p. 323), is brief, but one of the most delightful of seventeenth-century biographies. Whewell's memoir is a valuable sketch of Barrow's 'Life and Academical times'. The best modern study is P. H. Osmond, *Barrow: his Life and Times* (1944).

ROBERT SOUTH (1634-1716)

South was one of the favourite preachers of Charles II and his courtiers. His racy, vigorous sermons were admired by Dr Johnson, who nevertheless blamed him for his 'violence and sometimes coarseness of language'. He pub. collections of sermons in 1679, 1692 and 1715. His posthumous Works pub. in 1717 contain both sermons and an account of a journey to Poland. More of his sermons appeared in 1744 and a complete ed. in 1865.

The chief authorities for his life are the *Memoirs* pub. in the 1717 ed. of the *Posthumous Works* and the brief article in the D.N.B.

by A. Gordon. See also the very interesting passage on South in Boswell's *Life of Johnson* and the article by J. Sutherland in R.E.L. 1, i (1960).

JOHN TILLOTSON (1630-94)

John Tillotson, who became Archbishop of Canterbury in 1691, was one of the most popular preachers of the later seventeenth century, and with Dryden one of the great architects of the new plain style in English prose. Separate contemporary edd. of his sermons were very numerous. A collective ed. by R. Barker was pub. 1695-1704. In 1717 Barker pub. the *Works*, 'containing two hundred sermons and discourses on several occasions'. The best ed. of Tillotson's works is that of T. Birch, 1752, later ed. 1820. There is an excellent modern selection called *The Golden Book of Tillotson*, ed. J. Moffatt (1926). Birch's ed. includes a *Life*; there is a valuable survey by Alexander Gordon in the D.N.B., and a most useful biographical and critical introd. by Moffat in his *Golden Book*.

PLATONISTS AND LATITUDINARIANS

For the works of the principal divines of the Platonist and Latitudinarian Schools see above, pp. 287-92.

PURITANS AND QUAKERS

GENERAL WORKS

The standard *History of the Puritans* is by D. Neal (ed. Toulmin, 5 vols., 1822). E. Dowden's *Puritan and Anglican* (1901), J. Heron's *A Short History of Puritanism*, and O. M. Griffith's *Religion and Learning* (1935), may also be consulted. For the Quakers see G. W. C. Braithwaite's *The Beginnings of Quakerism* (1911), and T. Edmund Harvey's *The Rise of the Quakers* (1905, rev. ed., 1922).

There are also very suggestive remarks in R. H. Tawney's *Religion and the Rise of Capitalism*.

INDIVIDUAL AUTHORS

RICHARD BAXTER (1615-91)

Baxter, the famous moderate Presbyterian divine, was one of the most prolific writers of the seventeenth century and is said to have pub. 168 separate works ranging from folios to pamphlets. Besides these he left MSS. now in Doctor Williams's Library. *The Practical Works of the late reverend and pious Mr R. Baxter*, were pub. in 23 vols. by W. Orme in 1830 (second ed. in 4 vols. by Rogers, 1868). Baxter's best-known and most popular work was the famous book called *The Saint's Everlasting Rest* (1650). It has often been rptd. There are modern edd. by W. Young (1909 and 1928). His chief theological works were his *Christian Directory* and *Catholick Theologie* (both 1675). His *Poetical Fragments* (1681) contains some fine hymns, and is notable for the interesting criticism in its introductory Epistle to the Reader. His most enduring work is, perhaps, to be found in his autobiography pub. after his death by M. Sylvester under the title *Reliquiae Baxterianae* (1696). A useful abridgement by J. M. Lloyd Thomas was pub. in 1925 and is now obtainable in Ev. Lib. There are several important studies of Baxter by F. J. Powicke including the biography *The Reverend Richard Baxter Under the Cross* (1927).

JOHN BUNYAN (1628-88)

Bunyan pub. forty-three books during his lifetime, and several others by him were pub. posthumously. The greater part of this huge body of writings is now forgotten. It consists of sermons and treatises on Puritan theology. The sermon pub. in 1658 called *A Few Sighs from Hell, or the Groans of a Damned Soul*, one of his earliest works, contains the famous reference to Bunyan's reading before his conversion, 'a ballad, a newsbook, *George on Horseback* or *Bevis of Southampton*'. The earliest of his really important writings is the great autobiography *Grace Abounding to the Chief Sinners* (1666). It has often been rptd. There are modern edd. (with *The Pilgrim's Progress*) by Venables (1879, rev. M. Peacock, 1900) and by J. Brown (1907). The definitive modern ed. is that of R. Sharrock (1962). The first part of *The Pilgrim's Progress from this World to That which is to Come* appeared in 1678 (twelve edd. by 1689) and the Second Part in 1684. It was been rptd. very often, and there are many trs., abridgements and adaptations. Modern edd. include a facs. in Noel Douglas Replicas, the edd. by Venables and Peacock and J. Brown mentioned above and the very scholarly ed. by J. Wharey (1928, rev. ed. by R. Sharrock, 1960), which is the standard modern ed. of both parts. In 1680 Bunyan pub. *The Life and Death of Mr Badman* (modern edd. by J. Brown [1905] and B. Dobrée, W.C.), and in 1682 *The Holy War*, his most elaborate allegory (modern ed. by J. Brown, 1905).

The first attempt at a collected Bunyan was that of Charles Doe who pub. the first vol. of his ed. in 1692, but never completed it. Enl. edd. of Doe's vol. appeared in 1736-37 and 1767-68. The best modern edd. are those of G. Offor (3 vols., 1853 and 1862). Another by H. Stebbing appeared in 1859. There are a number of edd. of two or more works including 2 vols. in Ev. Lib. and G. B. Harrison's ed. of *The Pilgrim's Progress* and *Mr Badman* for the Nonesuch Press, 1928. A modern complete ed. is needed.

Criticism and Biography

Though Bunyan's work was admired by Swift, Johnson and Cowper, it was considered to be outside the pale of literature till the nineteenth century. The acceptance of Bunyan as a classic dates from Southey's ed. of *The Pilgrim's Progress* (1831) and Macaulay's Essay on Bunyan, which appeared as a review of it. The standard modern studies are J. Brown, *John Bunyan, his Life and Works* (1885, rev. ed. by F. Harrison, 1928) and H. Talon, *John Bunyan* (Paris, 1948, English tr., 1951). Valuable concise surveys are G. B. Harrison, *John Bunyan, a Study in Personality* (1928) and R. Sharrock, *Bunyan* (1954). See also W. Y. Tindall, *John Bunyan Mechanick Preacher* (1934) and the essays by J. Livingstone Lowes in *Of Reading Books* (1929), Sir C. H. Firth in *Essays Historical and Literary* (1938) and J. W. Mackail in *Studies in Humanism* (1938).

GEORGE FOX (1624-91)

George Fox, 'the apostle of the Quakers', pub. many books; a complete list will be found in Joseph Smith's Catalogue of Friends' Books. His most important work is his *Journal, or Historical Account of the Life of George Fox* (1694) ed. Thomas Ellwood, who wrote the portion for the years 1675-91. It was rptd. in 1891, 1901 and 1902, and in Ev. Lib., 1924. In 1911 an ed. was printed from a

MS. dictated by Fox covering the years 1650-75. *The Short Journal and Itinerary Journals* dictated by Fox in Lancaster Gaol were pub. N. Penney in 1925. There are studies of Fox by T. Hodgkin (in the Leaders of Religion Series), and A. N. Brayshaw (1919 and 1933). See also G. W. C. Braithwaite's *The Beginning of Quakerism* (1911).

WILLIAM PENN (1644-1718)

A list of Penn's numerous works will be found in the Bibliography by M. K. Spence (1932). *A Collection of the Works of William Penn*, ed. J. Besse, was pub. in 1726 (fourth ed. 1825). His most popular book *No Cross No Crown* appeared in 1669 and went through many edd. The most recent are by J. D. Hilton, 1902, and that pub. by the Society of Friends (1930). Some of his best writing is to be found in *Some Fruits of Solitude* (1693), modern edd. by E. Gosse (1900), J. Clifford (1905), and J. V. Cheney (1906). There is a Life of Penn by S. M. Janney (1852) and recent studies by M. R. Brailsford. *The Making of William Penn* (1930), by Bonamy Dobree, *William Penn, Quaker and Pioneer* (1932), and C. E. Vulliamy, *William Penn* (1934).

CHAPTER XVII

POETRY FROM CAREW TO OLDHAM

COLLECTIONS AND MODERN ANTHOLOGIES

VOLS. V–VIII of Chalmers contain a useful collection of texts. G. Saintsbury's *Minor Poets of the Caroline Period* (3 vols., 1905-21), includes texts of eighteen poets of the seventeenth century. Modern anthologies and books of selections are numerous. Among the best are *The Oxford Book of Seventeenth Century Verse* ed. H. J. C. Grierson and G. Bullough (1934), *Seventeenth Century Lyrics* ed. Norman Ault (1928, rev. ed., 1950) and *Minor Poets of the Seventeenth Century* ed. R. G. Howarth (Ev. Lib., 1931).

CONTEMPORARY ANTHOLOGIES

A. E. Case in his *Bibliography of English Poetical Miscellanies* (Bib. Soc., 1936), records the publication of 200 poetical miscellanies between 1602 and 1700. Special attention may be drawn to the following: *Parnassus Biceps* ed. Abraham Wright, pub. 1656, valuable modern ed. by G. Thorn Drury, 1927; *Choyce Drollery, Songs and Sonnets*, 1656, the first of a series of 'Drolleries' containing lively popular poetry often of excellent quality, rptd. J. W. Ebsworth, 1876 with pieces from other 'Drolleries'; *Westminster Drollery*, Pt. I, 1671, Pt. II, 1672, contains much notable poetry including the great 'Tom of Bedlam' song ('From the hagg and hungry Goblin') and *The Hunting of the Gods*, modern ed. by J. W. Ebsworth, 1876; *Covent Garden Drollery*, 1672, valuable modern ed. by G. Thorn Drury, 1928; *A Collection of Poems written upon several occasions published by several persons*, pub. Hobart Kemp, 1672, one of the most important collections of Restoration lyric verse, rptd. by T. Collins in 1673 and with additions by F. Saunders in 1693 and by D. Brown in 1701; *Dryden's Miscellany*, for this famous anthology see p. 388; and the well-known collections. N. Ault's *Seventeenth Century Lyrics* (see above, p. 342) contains a useful list of the chief miscellanies printed in four parts under various titles in 1688-89 and rptd. with additions as *Poems on Affairs of State* in 1697.

GENERAL STUDIES

One of the best studies of the 'Cavalier lyric' is the chapter by F. W. Moorman in C.H.E.L., VII, i. There is also an excellent chapter in the same work on *The Court Poets of the Restoration* by C. H. Whibley (VIII, viii). Courthope's *History of English Poetry*, Vol. III, should be consulted, and there are suggestive remarks in H. J. C. Grierson's *Cross Currents in English Literature of the Seventeenth Century* (1929), in the introd. to R. G. Howarth's *Minor Poets of the Seventeenth Century* (Ev. Lib.), and in *Revaluation* by F. R. Leavis (1936); see also *The Court Wits of the Restoration* by J. H. Wilson (Princeton, 1948) and *The Restoration Court Poets* by V. de S. Pinto (B.C.S., 1965).

INDIVIDUAL AUTHORS

THOMAS CAREW (?1594-1640)

Carew could be classed either as a 'courtly' or as a metaphysical poet. The only work of his pub. during his lifetime was his fine masque *Cœlum Britannicum*, acted at Whitehall, with costumes and scenery designed by Inigo Jones, in 1633, and pub. in 1634. *Poems by Thomas Carew Esquire* appeared in 1640 including most of his poems and the masque. An enl. ed. with eight additional poems was pub. in 1642 and a third ed. with three more poems in 1651, rptd. 1671. The only eighteenth-century ed. appeared in 1772 with a poor Life. A selection of the poems ed. J. Fry was pub. at Bristol in 1810, and in 1824 T. Maitland pub. at Edinburgh a limited ed. consisting of rpt. of the 1640 ed., with an appendix containing the additional poems pub. in 1642 and 1651. W. C. Hazlitt pub. an ed. of the Poems in 1870 and another ed. J. Ebsworth, appeared in 1893.

There is an ed. by A. Vincent in M.L. The best modern ed. is that of R. Dunlap with valuable introd. (1949). See also F. R. Leavis, *Revaluation*, op. cit., pp. 15-17, 37-38.

SIR JOHN SUCKLING (1609-42)

Only a few of Suckling's poems appeared in his lifetime. His first play, *Aglaura*, was pub. in folio in 1638; another play, *The Discontented Colonel*, was pub. in 1640, and in 1646 with a different title as *Brennoralt*. The delightful *Ballad upon a Wedding* was first printed in *Wit's Recreation*, a miscellany pub. in 1640. All his works of any importance were included in a vol. called *Fragmenta Aurea, A collection of the Incomparable Pieces written by Sir John Suckling* (1646). This includes his poems, letters, three plays (the two mentioned above and *The Goblins*), and a tract on Socinianism. It was rptd. as *The Works of Sir John Suckling* several times in the seventeenth and eighteenth centuries. In 1836 appeared *Selections from the Works of Sir John Suckling*, with a life by Alfred Inigo Suckling. An ed. of the Poems, Plays, etc., by W. C. Hazlitt appeared in 1874. Modern edd. include *The Works* in prose and verse, ed. A. Hamilton Thompson, 1910, and the Poems (1933). The text of the Poems is included in R. G. Howarth's *Minor Poets of the Seventeenth Century* (Ev. Lib.).

There is a Life of Suckling by A. I. Suckling prefixed to his *Selections* of 1836, a valuable article by T. Seccombe in the D.N.B., and criticism by F. W. Moorman in C.H.E.L., VIII. 1. See also 'The Singing Cavalier', T.L.S., May 9th, 1942.

THOMAS RANDOLPH (1605-35)

Randolph, one of the most promising and admired of early seventeenth-century poets, pub. in 1630 two 'shows' acted at Cambridge called *Aristippus; or the Joviall Philosopher* and *The Conceited Peddler* and the comedy (also acted at Cambridge) called *The Jealous Lovers* (1632). Three other plays by him were performed in his lifetime: *Hey for Honesty*, an adaptation from Aristophanes, performed at Cambridge; *The Entertainment*, known later as *The Muse's Looking Glass*, and *Amyntas*, his beautiful pastoral play, both performed in London in 1630. In 1638 his brother pub. an ed. of his *Poems with the Muses' Looking-Glasse and Amyntas*; this ed. was rptd. several times in the seventeenth century. *Hey for Honesty* appeared in 1651. An ed. of the *Poetical and Dramatic*

Works, ed. W. C. Hazlitt (2 vols.) appeared in 1875, and a very scholarly modern ed. of the *Poems and Amyntas* by J. J. Parry (Yale, 1917). There is also an excellent and beautifully printed ed. of the *Poems* by G. Thorn Drury (Haslewood Books, 1929).

The best accounts of Randolph and his works are to be found in the introds. to the edd. of Parry and Thorn Drury and, in the valuable Warton Lecture, *Thomas Randolph*, by G. C. Moore Smith (Br. Ac., 1927).

RICHARD LOVELACE (1618-?57)

Except for some lines engraved under a portrait of Voiture in a tr. of *Letters and Affaires*, which appeared in 1657, the whole of Lovelace's extant poetry has come down to us in two little vols. called *Lucasta* (1649), and *Lucasta, Posthume Poems* (1659). Some contemporary MSS. of the famous song, *To Althea from Prison*, are extant. No second ed. of Lovelace's poetry appeared till the early nineteenth century, when S. W. Singer rptd. the edd. of 1649 and 1659 in 1817 and 1818 respectively. In these edd. passages that were thought to be improper were expurgated. W. C. Hazlitt included an ed. of Lovelace's poetry in *The Library of Old Authors* (1864, rptd. 1897). In 1906 the two *Lucasta* vols. were rptd. fairly accurately in the *Unit Library*, afterwards included in Hutchinson's *Popular Classics*. The standard modern ed. is that of C. H. Wilkinson, *The Poems of Richard Lovelace* (2 vols., 1925). This ed. contains a very full and authoritative biographical introd. and commentary (1 vol. ed., 1930).

ROBERT HERRICK (1591-1674)

Before 1648 Herrick had printed a few lyrics in books by other authors pub. in the reign of Charles I: *A Description of the King and Queene of Fayries* (1635); *The Poems of Thomas Carew* (1640); *Poems by Wil. Shakespeare Gent* (1640); *Witts Recreation refined* (1645), and *Comedies and Tragedies written by Francis Beaumont & John Fletcher* (1647). The famous collection of his poems called *Hesperides; or the Works both Human & Divine of Robert Herrick Esq.*: appeared in 1648. Besides the *Hesperides* proper or secular poems, it includes the collection of sacred verse called *Noble Numbers*, bearing a separate title page dated 1647. *Lachrymae Musarum, The Tears of the Muses*, the vol. of elegies pub. in 1649, contained *The New Charon*, an elegy by Herrick together with contributions by

Marvell and Dryden. A large number of the poems in *Hesperides* were rptd. in various seventeenth-century anthologies and songbooks. Versions of some of them (sometimes different from those printed in *Hesperides*) also survive in MS. collections. No second ed. of *Hesperides* appeared in the seventeenth century and the biographical and critical notices of Herrick in Anthony à Wood, Phillips and Winstanley, are meagre and inaccurate. Dryden, although he was distantly related to Herrick, never mentions him in his critical works. For over a century he seems to have been forgotten, although it is said that some of his poems were handed down by oral tradition among the country people of Dean Prior in Devonshire, where he spent a large part of his life as a country parson. It was not until the end of the eighteenth century that his poetry was rediscovered. In 1796-97 J. Nichols drew attention to it in the *Gentleman's Magazine*, and soon after Dr N. Drake praised it in his *Literary Hours*. In 1810 G. F. Nott pub. the first modern ed., a selection from the *Hesperides*; in 1823 a complete ed. by T. Maitland appeared at Edinburgh, and in 1846 Pickering pub. an ed. with introd. by S. W. Singer. Nineteenth-century edd. include those of W. C. Hazlitt (1869), A B. Grosart (1876), Palgrave (a selection, 1877), A. W. Pollard (M.L., with introd. by Swinburne, 1891), and Gollancz in T.C. F. W. Moorman's ed. of *The Poetical Works* (1915, text only 1921) is now replaced by that of L. C. Martin (1956).

Moorman's excellent monograph, *Robert Herrick, a Biographical and Critical Study* (1910) is the most reliable and exhaustive biographical and critical study. See also the chapter on Herrick by the same author in C.H.E.L., VII, 1. See also S. Musgrove, *The Universe of Herrick* (Auckland, 1950). There is *A Concise Bibliography* by S. A. and D. R. Tannenbaum (N.Y., 1949).

GEORGE WITHER (1588-1667)

George Wither (called 'wretched Withers' by Pope) was a belated Elizabethan in his poetry, though he survived till the reign of Charles II. He was imprisoned for a satire, *Abuse Stript and Whipt* (1613), and while he was in the Marshalsea wrote his pastoral, *The Shepheard's Hunting* (1615). In 1622 he pub. his *Juvenilia* and *Faire Virtue or the Mistresse of Philarete*. These vols. contain most of his best poetry. The excellent poem on Christmas appears in the *Faire Virtue* vol. His later works are mainly religious verse. Wither's works were rptd. by the Spenser Society (1871-73), and an ed. by F. Sidgwick (2 vols.) appeared in 1903. There is also a selection by H. Morley (1891).

SIR WILLIAM DAVENANT (1606-68)

Davenant's most important non-dramatic poetry is to be found in his unfinished epic, *Gondibert* and in some of his lyrics. In 1638 he pub. a collection called *Madagascar with other Poems*. *Gondibert An Heroick Poem*, was pub. in London in two edd. in 1651. The famous and important Preface to *Gondibert* with Hobbes's letter to Davenant in reply to it had already appeared with a few stanzas of *Gondibert* in Paris in 1650. The 1652 edd. contains the first two books and part of the third. The commendatory verses by Waller and Cowley prefixed to this ed. are of great interest and significance. In 1673 five years after Davenant's death, a collected ed. of his writings called *The Works of Sir William Davenant Kt.* was pub. in folio. This book contains *Gondibert* with part of a continuation of the poems not previously printed, *Madagascar* with other Poems, the plays and *Poems on Several Occasions, Never before Printed*. R. Anderson's *Works of the British Poets* (1795) includes *Gondibert*, *Madagascar*, and selections from Davenant's other non-dramatic poems. The same pieces are printed in Chalmers's *English Poets*, vol VI (1800). There is another rpt. of *Gondibert* in Southey's *Selected Works of the British Poets* (1841). Dr C. M. Dowlin of the University of Pennsylvania has in preparation a modern ed. of *Gondibert* based on the two edd. of 1651 and the text in the folio and 1673.

There are accounts of Davenant in Aubrey's *Brief Lives* and Wood's *Athenae Oxonienses*. There are criticisms of Gondibert in Scott's *Life of Dryden* (1808), Isaac D'Israeli's *Quarrels and Calamities of Authors* (1812-13), and Sir E. Gosse's *From Shakespeare to Pope* (1885). The most complete biographical and critical study is A. Harbage's *Sir William Davenant Poet Venturer 1606-68* (Philadelphia, 1935). C. M. Dowlin's dissertation on *Davenant's Gondibert its Preface and Hobbes's Answer* (Philadelphia, 1934) is planned as an introd. to a projected ed. of *Gondibert*. The Preface to *Gondibert* is rptd. in Spingarn's *Critical Essays of the Seventeenth Century* (II, 1-53). See also E. C. Marchant, *Sir William Davenant* (1936) and A. H. Nethercot, *Davenant, Poet Laureate and Playwright Manager* (Chicago, 1938).

EDMUND WALLER (1606-87)

Edmund Waller, generally considered during the eighteenth century to have been in the words of Dick Minim (with Denham) one of the 'first reformers of English numbers', pub. his first collection of poems in 1645 (3 edd.) in the same year, two printed for Humphrey Moseley, who also pub. Milton's early poems in the same year. Other poems by Waller appeared at different times between this date and his death. The famous song, 'Go, lovely Rose', was first printed in a miscellany called *Ayres and Dialogues* (Vol. II, 1655), and his eulogy of Cromwell, *A Panegyric to my Lord Protector*, appeared in the same year. His poem on Cromwell's death was pub. in 1659, with verses on the same subject by Dryden and Sprat, and his poem on the Restoration, *To the King Upon his Majesty's Happy Return* (the subject of the famous anecdote) in 1660. His *Instructions to a Painter* (1666) is a complimentary poem to the Duke of York on his victory over the Dutch in 1665. It was forerunner of the satiric poems with similar titles, ascribed to Marvell and Denham (see p. 300 and below). His *Divine Poems* appeared in 1685, and, after his death, in 1690, a collection called *Poems Part II*, including his alteration of *The Maid's Tragedy* and various poems with some speeches, ed. with a very eulogistic preface by Dr (afterwards Bishop) Atterbury. Waller's poems were often rptd. in the eighteenth century. The most important ed. was that of Elijah Fenton with a *Life of Waller* (2 vols., 1729). The best modern ed. is that of G. Thorn Drury (2 vols., M.L.). The chief biographical and critical studies of Waller are Fenton's *Life*, Johnson's *Life* (in the Lives of the Poets), and Thorn Drury's introd. to his ed. See also F. W. Bateson, *English Poetry* (1950) pp. 165-74.

SIR JOHN DENHAM (1615-69)

Denham's first two publications both appeared in 1642. They were the heroic play called *The Sophy* and *Cooper's Hill*, his famous 'local' poem in heroic couplets, which was re-issued with additions in 1650, and in a corrected ed. in 1655. In 1656 he pub. a version of the second book of the *Aeneid* called *The Destruction of Troy*, which he wrote in 1636, with an interesting preface. His *Poems and Translations, with the Sophy* appeared in 1667-68. In 1669 appeared his *Cato Major of Old Age*, a versified paraphrase of

Cicero *De Senectute*. It was included in the fourth ed. of the Poems pub. in 1704. The satires, pub. in *The Second Advice to a Painter . . . In Imitation of Mr Waller* (1667); *The Second and Third Advice to a Painter . . . In Answer to Mr Waller* (1667), and *Directions to a Painter*, 1667, are all ascribed to Sir John Denham on the title pages. It is unlikely, however, that he wrote them. See the *Poetical Works*, ed. Banks, pp. 327-31.

There is a good modern critical ed. of Denham's *Poetical Works* by T. H. Banks (1928), including a bibliography and an app. with doubtful poems.

THOMAS STANLEY (1625-78)

Thomas Stanley, an original poet of some distinction, was also a brilliant verse translator from the French, Italian, Spanish, Greek and Latin. Edd. of his *Poems* were pub. in 1647-48 and 1651. A collection of his verse was included by Saintsbury in his *Caroline Poets*, op. cit., vol. III. An excellent complete ed. of his *Poems and Translations* (including his prose version of Pico della Mirandola's *A Platonick Discourse Upon Love*) ed. G. B. Crump was pub. in 1962. For his *History of Philosophy*, see above, p. 287.

CHARLES COTTON (1630-87)

Besides his tr. of Montaigne and his continuation of *The Compleat Angler* (see p. 331 and p. 321), Cotton wrote much prose and verse both orig. and tr. His burlesque of Virgil, imitated from Scarron, called *Scarronides, or the First Book of Virgil Travestie* appeared in 1664, rptd. with a burlesque of the Fourth Book in 1670. His *Poems on Several Occasions*, highly praised by Wordsworth and Coleridge, appeared in 1689. There are modern edd. by J. Beresford (1923) and J. Buxton (1958).

KATHERINE PHILIPS (the Matchless Orinda) (1631/2-64)

Katherine Philips's tr. of *Pompey a Tragedy* from the French of Corneille appeared in two edd. in 1663. Her *Poems* ('by the Incomparable Mrs K. P.') were pub. in a pirated ed. in 1664. An authorized and enl. ed. of the *Poems* with her trs. of *Pompey* and also *Horace* was pub. in 1667. The latter tr. was left unfinished by her and completed by Sir John Denham. This collection was rptd. in 1669, 1678 and 1710. The text of the *Poems* of 1678 (without the plays) is rptd. by Saintsbury in his *Minor Poets of the Caroline Period*, Vol. I. There is also a selection by J. R. Tutin (1904). The most complete account of Katherine Philips is to be found in *The Matchless Orinda* by P. W. Souers (Harvard, 1931).

SIR CHARLES SEDLEY (1639-1701)

Sedley collaborated with his friends Waller, Buckhurst, Godolphin and Filmer in a tr. of Corneille's tragedy *La Mort de Pompee*, which appeared in 1664 as *Pompey the Great a Tragedy*. His comedy *The Mulberry Garden*, containing one of his best songs, was pub. in 1668. In 1677 appeared his 'heroic' tragedy, *Antony and Cleopatra*, which he later recast on more strictly classical lines. The later version called *Beauty the Conquerour*, was not pub. till after his death. His second comedy, *Bellamira or the Mistress*, founded on *The Eunuch* of Terence, was acted and printed in 1687. *The Grumbler*, his clever adaptation of the famous French farce *Le Grondeur*, by Brueys and Palaprat, was first printed in the 1722 ed. of his works. Another play, *The Tyrant of Crete*, printed in the same ed., is simply a shortened version of an old piece called *Pallantus and Eudora*, by H. Killigrew, and there is no reason to suppose that Sedley had anything to do with it. Sedley's best work is to be found in his lyrics of which at least thirty were printed in Kemp's *Collection* of 1672 (see p. 342). Three trs. by Sedley from Ovid's *Amores* were also printed in Dryden's *Miscellany Poems* of 1684, and a number of his later lyrics appeared in *The Gentleman's Journal*, one of the first English literary periodicals, ed. P. Motteux, 1691-94.

The first collected ed. of his poems (with *Beauty the Conquerour*) appeared in 1702. It was rptd. with various additions (not all by Sedley) in 1707 and 1709-15. An ed. in 2 vols. of *The Works* appeared in 1722, including the poems, plays, speeches and some spurious pieces both in verse and prose with a short memoir, probably by Defoe. This ed. was rptd. in 1776 and 1778. The standard modern ed. is *The Poetical and Dramatic Works*, ed. V. de S. Pinto (2 vols., 1928), with a complete bibliography. The most complete account of Sedley is contained in *Sir Charles Sedley, a Study in the Life and Literature of the Restoration*, by V. de S. Pinto (1927).

JOHN WILMOT, EARL OF ROCHESTER
(1647-80)

Rochester, the most notable poet among the literary courtiers of the Restoration, probably never authorized the publication of any of his writings. Some of his poems, however, appeared during his lifetime as broadsides and in miscellanies. One of his most powerful works, *A Satyr against Mankind*, seems to have been first published as a folio broadside in June, 1679, though it had apparently been circulating in manuscript as early as the spring of 1676. The first published collection of his poems was a badly printed little book entitled *Poems on Several Occasions. By the Right Honourable the E. of R-*, which appeared in the autumn of 1680, shortly after his death. It professed to be printed at Antwerp and was obviously regarded as a pornographic publication; it contains a number of poems which are not by Rochester. No less than ten editions of it have been traced. A facs. ed. of the copy in the Henry E. Huntington Library, California, was pub. at Princeton in 1950 with a valuable bibliographical introd. by J. Thorpe. In 1685 Andrew Thorncome pub. a collection based on the foregoing with some omissions and alterations entitled *Poems on several occasions by a late Person of Honour*, and in the same year Rochester's tragedy *Valentinian* also appeared with an important preface by his friend Robert Wolseley. In 1691 Jacob Tonson pub. *Poems on Several Occasion; with Valentinian a Tragedy written by the Right Honourable John late Earl of Rochester* with a Preface by Thomas Rymer. This ed. contains, besides twenty-three genuine poems which had appeared in the 'Antwerp' edd., sixteen others previously unpublished including some of Rochester's best lyrics. Unfortunately some of Rochester's poems seem to have been excluded by Tonson on moral grounds and some of his texts are bowdlerized. Besides the poems and *Valentinian*, this ed. includes Rochester's amusing prose satire 'Alexander Bendo's Bill' (modern ed. in *The Famous Pathologist* by Thomas Alcock and John Wilmot, Earl of Rochester ed. V. de S. Pinto, 1961). Tonson's ed. was rptd. in 1696, 1705, and in 1714 together with a collection of Rochester's letters. These had appeared in two vols. of *Familiar Letters* pub. 1897. Other letters of Rochester are extant in the original MSS in the B.M. His lively correspondence with Henry Savile was pub. in *The Rochester-Savile Correspondence* ed. J. H. Wilson (Columbus, Ohio, 1941) with a valuable introd. and commentary. *The Miscellaneous Works of the Right Honourable the late Earls of Rochester and Roscommon* (1707) contains some genuine poems of Rochester previously unpublished and a group of his satires appeared in the various edd. of *Poems on Affairs of State* (1689, 1697). A number of edd. of the poems, all more or less unreliable, appeared during the eighteenth century. The first attempt at a modern ed. was *The Collected Works* ed. J. Hayward (1920), a useful but undiscriminating collection containing almost every piece of published verse and prose rightly or wrongly attributed to Rochester. *Poems by John Wilmot, Earl of Rochester* ed. V. de S. Pinto (M.L., 1953, 2nd, rev. ed., 1964) is the first attempt to establish a critical canon of the genuine poetry and also the first ed. to make use of the important manuscript material in the Portland collection in Nottingham University Library and in Harvard University Library. It contains a biographical and critical introd. and an Appendix of poems ascribed to Rochester on doubtful authority.

Biography and Criticism

For Burnet's contemporary biography see p. 325. *John Wilmot, Earl of Rochester: his Life and Writings* by J. Prinz (Leipzig, 1927) contains valuable biographical information and a very full bibliography. The most complete and up-to-date account of Rochester is *Enthusiast in Wit, a Portrait of John Wilmot, Earl of Rochester* by V. de S. Pinto (1962). See also V. de S. Pinto, 'John Wilmot, Earl of Rochester and the Right Veine of Satire', E.S.M.E.A., N.S. vol. 6 (1953, rptd. in *Seventeenth Century English Poetry* ed. W. R. Keast, N.Y., 1960) and 'Rochester and Dryden', R.M.S., V, 1961, F. Whitfield, *Beast in View* (Camb. Mass., 1939); valuable studies of *A Satyr against Mankind* are those of S. F. Crocker in *West Virginia Univ. St.* III, *Philological Papers*, vol. 2, May, 1937, and T. H. Fujimura in S.P., LV, October, 1958.

CHARLES SACKVILLE, EARL OF DORSET (1638-1706)

Charles Sackville, first Lord Buckhurst and afterwards Earl of Dorset, Dryden's Eugenius in *The Essay of Dramatic Poesy*, was the author of a number of lyrics and satires which have never been collected in a single vol. Most of them were first printed in various miscellanies. His famous ballad 'written at sea in the first Dutch War' must have been written in 1664 as Pepys had a copy of it on January 2nd, 1664/5. The oldest extant text, however, is in the collection called *Wit and Mirth*, Vol. V, 1714. Other poems of Dorset were printed in Kemp's *Collection* of 1672 (see p. 342), and in the succeeding miscellanies based upon it, in *Poems on Affairs of State*, in the 1707 ed. of Rochester's *Works* and later edd. of Rochester. *The Works of the most Celebrated Minor Poets* (2 vols., 1749 and 1751) includes the poems of Roscommon, Dorset, Halifax and others. Johnson's *English Poets* (1779) also includes a selection from Dorset's poems. A useful check-list of Dorset's Poems by Helen A. Bagley, was pub. in M.L.N., XLVII, 454–61 (November 1932), and 'Some Additions to the Poems of Lord Dorset' by R. G. Howarth appeared in M.L.N., L, 457-9 (November 1935). The best account of Dorset is *Charles Sackville, Sixth Earl of Dorset, Patron and Poet of the Restoration* by Brice Harris (Illinois, 1946).

JOHN OLDHAM (1653-83)

Dryden in a famous elegy recognized Oldham as one of his chief predecessors in English satire, and praised him as the 'Marcellus of our tongue'. The well known *Satyrs upon the Jesuits* (1681) was one of several vols. of Oldham's verse which were pub. during his lifetime. His *Poems and Translations* appeared in 1683 and *Remains in Verse and Prose* in 1684. His popularity in the early Augustan period is attested by the fact that edd. of his *Works* were pub. in 1684, 1686, 1693, 1694, 1695, 1698, 1703, 1704, 1710 and 1722. Dr Johnson thought of editing him at one time, but unfortunately this project was never carried out. Edward Thompson's ed. of his *Compositions in Prose and Verse . . . to which are added Memoirs of his Life, and explanatory notes* (1770) is a poor compilation. A selection ed. R. Bell was pub. in 1854 (2nd ed. 1871). Bell's selection was rptd. in 1960 as *The Poems of John Oldham* with a valuable introd. by Bonamy Dobrée. Harold F. Brookes has pub. a *Bibliography of John Oldham the Restoration Satirist* with an important introd. in O.B.S., Vol. V, pt. I, 1936.

CHAPTER XVIII

JOHN MILTON (1608-74)

COLLECTIVE EDITIONS OF VERSE AND PROSE

THERE are two collective edd. of Milton's works. The older, *The Works of John Milton in Verse and Prose* ed. J. Mitford, appeared in 1851, and includes almost everything that Milton wrote except the posthumous *De Doctrinâ Christianâ*. Original spelling is preserved and the Latin, Greek, and Italian writings are given in the orig. language only. There is a *Life* and index but no commentary. The standard modern ed. is *The Works of John Milton* (18 vols., general editor Frank Allen Paterson) pub. the Columbia University Press, N.Y., 1931. It includes all Milton's extant works and English trs. of the Latin, Greek and Italian writings are given with the original texts.

MANUSCRIPTS

The Cambridge Manuscripts

This famous MS., preserved at Trinity College, Cambridge, is a thin folio containing on 47 pages copies of Milton's *Arcades, Comus, Lycidas* (apparently a first draft with many cancelled and altered passages) and other poems and sonnets together with a list of characters and scenario for a play called *Paradise Lost*, a long list of 33 possible subjects for an epic or drama from Biblical and early English history, short sketches of four projected tragedies on Biblical subjects and notes on 5 Scotch stories (one of which is *Macbeth*) and on two other Biblical subjects. The whole MS. is in Milton's own hand except for some of the sonnets which are in the hands of ammanuenses. The first pub. account of the MS. was given by T. Birch in his ed. of the *Prose Works* of 1637.

There is a facs. ed. W. Aldis Wright (1899) and another ed. F. A. Patterson (1933). This MS. is one of the most interesting extant records of the plans and workmanship of a great poet.

Comus

A stage copy of *Comus* in MS. (probably that of Henry Lawes) is preserved among the Bridgewater MS. (now in the Henry Huntington Library, California). It is probably an acting version and differs from Milton's version in the Cambridge MS. and from the edd. pub. in 1637, 1645, and 1673. It was first printed by Todd in his ed. of 1798. There is a modern ed. by Lady Alix Egerton with facs. of two pages (1910).

Paradise Lost

A MS. of *Paradise Lost*, Book I in the hand of an ammanuensis and corrected by other hands under Milton's direction, is now in the J. P. Morgan collection, N.Y. It was submitted to the licenser of the press, contains his *imprimatur* and it was used for setting up the type of the first ed. of 1668. A facs. ed. with introd. by Helen Darbishire was pub. in 1931.

The MS. of Milton's Latin work on Christian Doctrine found its way to the Public Record Office, where it is still preserved. It consists partly of a copy made for publication by Milton's friend, Daniel Skinner, and partly of the orig. MS. taken down by Jeremie Picard at Milton's dictation.

POETICAL WORKS

Collections

The first pub. collection of Milton's poems was a small 8vo which appeared on January 2nd, 1645, *The Poems of Mr. John Milton, Both English and Latin . . . Printed . . . for Humphrey Moseley . . .*, containing *On the Morning of Christ's Nativity, L'Allegro, Il Penseroso, Arcades, Comus, Lycidas* and other poems in English, Latin and Italian. Moseley in his short preface states that he was encouraged to publish the book by the recent success of Waller's 'choice pieces' (see above, p. 348). It was rptd. in 1673 with some additional poems in English and Latin and the prose *Tractate on Education* (see below, p. 363). Facs. edd. of the 1645 ed. were pub. in the *Tudor and Stuart Library* and the Noel Douglas Replicas (both 1924). There is a valuable modern ed. of *The Poems of Mr John Milton: the 1645 Edition* ed. C. Brooks and J. E. Hardy (N.Y., 1951). Although *Paradise Regained* was first pub. with *Samson Agonistes* in 1671 and was rptd. with *Paradise Lost* in 1692, no other ed. that can be called a 'collection' appeared till 1693 when *The Poetical Works* were pub. in a folio ed. a Scottish scholar called Patrick Hume. This was the first attempt at an annotated ed. and contains a commentary on *Paradise Lost*. In the same year Tonson, the famous publisher, issued an ed. of *Paradise Lost, Paradise Regained and the Smaller Poems*. Numerous edd. of the poetical works appeared in the eighteenth century, beginning with Tonson's ed. of 1705 in 2 vols. in 4vo. Tonson's most important ed. was the finely printed *Poetical Works* of 1620 in 2 vols., 4to, ed. T. Tickell with Addison's essays on *Paradise Lost* and a valuable index. A list of 300 subscribers is prefixed to it and it ranks with Pope's *Homer* as one of the great publishing ventures of the period. Elijah Fenton's valuable ed. with a *Life* appeared in 1725. The most important and scholarly ed. of the eighteenth century was Bishop Newton's (3 vols. 1749-52), the first 'variorum' ed. with principal notes of previous editors and a new *Life*. The great achievement of Miltonic scholarship in the late eighteenth century was Thomas Warton's masterly ed. of the *Minor Poems* (1785, 2nd enl. and rev. ed. 1791). In 1801 H. J. Todd pub. the first of his important edd. (the 'second variorum'). The 2nd ed. of Todd's work appeared in 1809 with considerable additions, a third and fourth in 6 vols. in 1826 and 1842 respectively and a fifth in 4 vols. in 1852. Todd's commentary is of the greatest value representing the fruits of over a century of Miltonic scholarship. He was the first editor to use the Cambridge MS. and his ed. is still in many ways the best. Among the many later edd. of the poetical works mention may be made of R. C. Browne's (*English Works* only, 2 vols. 1870); D. Masson's monumental ed. (3 vols. 1874, 2nd rev. ed. 1890) with its offspring the Golden Treasury ed. and Globe one vol. ed.; H. C. Beeching's Oxford ed. (text only, original spelling, 1904); 1938 with trs. of Latin and Italian poems from the Columbia ed. and Readers' Guide by W. W. Skeat; W. Aldis Wright's Cambridge ed. (1903; textual notes and modernized spelling); W. V. Moody's American Cambridge ed. (1899; rev. E. K. Rand with new trs., 1924); H. J. C. Grierson's Florence Press ed. (2 vols.; poems in chronological order, spelling partly modernized, 1925); *The Students' Milton* ed. A. Patterson (N.Y., 1930, 1933); *Complete Poetry and Selected Prose* ed. E. H. Visiak (1937); *The English Poems* ed. C. Williams (W.C., 1941); *The Complete Poetical Works in Facsimile* ed. H. F. Fletcher (4 vols., Urbana, 1943-48); *The Poetical Works* ed. H. Darbishire (2 vols., 1952-55); *The Complete English Poems* ed. J. Gawsworth (1953) and *Poems* (with important textual introd. and bibliography) ed. B. A. Wright (Ev. Lib., 1956).

Selections

Milton, Poetry and Prose ed. A. M. D. Hughes (with essays by Johnson, Hazlitt and Macaulay, 1920); *Selections from the Prose and Poetry* ed. J. H. Hanford (Boston, 1923); *The Portable Milton* ed. D. Bush (N.Y., 1949); *Selected English Poems* ed. L. D. Lerner (P.B., 1953).

INDIVIDUAL POETICAL WORKS

The Epitaph on Shakespeare

The first poem of Milton to be pub. was his epitaph on *The Admirable Dramatick Poet W. Shakespeare* prefixed to the 1632 Folio of Shakespeare works (see p. 248). In the 1673 ed. of Milton's *Poems* it is dated 1630.

L'Allegro and Il Penseroso

These poems which first appeared in the 1645 ed. of Milton's *Poems* were not printed separately till 1740, when they were set to music by Handel. There are many later separate edd. For the date of composition of *L'Allegro* and *Il Penseroso* see E. M. Tillyard's E.A. pamphlet, *Milton L'Allegro and Il Penseroso* (July 1932, No. 82).

Comus

The first ed. of *Comus* was pub. in 1637 apparently by Henry Lawes, the musician who produced the mask in 1634. It was rptd. in the edd. of 1645 and 1673. Numerous edd. were pub. in the eighteenth, nineteenth and twentieth centuries. There were two eighteenth-century adaptations for the stage, one by J. Dalton (1738) and another by G. Coleman with music by Dr Arne in 1772. Performances are recorded in almost every year from 1738 to 1890. See Alwin Thaler, *Milton in the Theatre* in S.P. XXII, 1920. The text of the Bridgewater MS. was first printed in Todd's edd. (see p. 356). Among later separate edd. mention may be made of those by O. Elton (1902), C. T. Onions (1904) A. W. Verity (1909) and E. H. Visiak (with the music, 1938).

Lycidas

Lycidas was first printed in the collection of elegies on the death of Edward King called *Obsequies to the Memory of Mr. Edward King* (included in the vol. called *Justa Edouardo King naufrago ab Amicis mœrentibus* . . . pub. 1638). Milton rptd. it in a rev. form in the ed. of 1645. In the eighteenth century it was arranged as 'a musical entertainment' by W. Jackson in 1767. There are modern separate edd. by F. A. Paley, (1874), H. B. Cotterill (1902), H. M. Percival (1914) and W. Bell (N.Y., 1938). There is a facs. ed. by E. C. Mossner

(N.Y., 1939). In a monograph, *Lycidas* by W. Tuckwell (1911) the text of the Cambridge MS. is printed in full.

The Sonnets

Five of Milton's English sonnets first appeared in the ed. of 1645 and ten more were added in the ed. of 1673, one of which had already appeared prefixed to Henry Lawes's *Choice Psalms* in 1648. The sonnets to Cromwell, Fairfax and Vane, and the second sonnet to Cyriack Skinner were omitted from the ed. of 1673 for political reasons and were not pub. till 1694 when E. Phillips printed them in a very garbled form in his *Life of Milton* prefixed to the *Letters of State* (see p. 367). The full text of these sonnets was preserved in the Cambridge MS. The first separate ed. of the sonnets was that of Mark Pattison (1883). Since then several edd. have appeared, the best of which is that of J. S. Smart (1921), with valuable introd. and commentary.

The Minor Poems

The Minor Poems pub. Milton in 1645 and 1673 were rptd. by Tonson in 1695, and again often in the eighteenth century. The first critical annotated ed. was that of T. Warton (see p. 356). The best modern edd. include Verity's very fully and learnedly annotated Pitt Press ed. (1891-1912), O. Elton's useful small ed. (1910), H. C. Beeching's (1923), and *The Poems of John Milton: the 1645 Edition* ed. C. Brooks and J. E. Hardy (N.Y., 1951).

The Latin and Italian Poems

These first appeared in the edd. of 1645 and 1673. J. Langhorne pub. anonymously his tr. of the Italian poems in 1776. William Cowper's tr. of the *Latin and Italian Poems* ed. W. Hayley appeared in 1808. The best modern separate ed. of the Latin poems is that of W. Mackellar (text and tr., New

Haven, 1930). W. W. Skeat's tr. of *Milton's Lament for Damon and other Latin Poems* ed. E. H. Visiak was pub. in 1935.

Paradise Lost

The first ed. of *Paradise Lost* was a 4to vol. pub. 1667, *Paradise Lost, a Poem Written in ten books By John Milton* . . . There are no less than nine issues of this ed. with variation of the title and preliminary pages. Some are dated 1667, some 1668, and some 1669. In the later issues the address of *The Printer to the Reader*, *The Argument*, and Milton's *Note on the Verse* are inserted. The second ed. pub. in 1674 contains the rev. version of the poem in 12 books with the portrait of Milton and commendatory verses by Barrow in Latin and Marvell in English. This was the last ed. pub. Milton and provides the standard text. A third ed. appeared in 1678, and a fourth in folio with illustrations in 1688. This was pub. J. Tonson and was the second English book to be pub. by subscription, the first having been *Walton's Polyglot Bible*. In 1692 *Paradise Lost* was pub. in a folio with *Paradise Regained*. It is said that over one hundred separate edd. of *Paradise Lost* were pub. in the eighteenth century as compared with fifty of Shakespeare's plays and seven of *The Faerie Queen*. An additional proof of its popularity is found in the fact that it was arranged four times for an oratorio, once for Handel and once for the *Creation* of Haydn. Good edd. appeared in 1711 (Tonson) and 1725 (ed. Fenton). Richard Bentley, the great classical scholar, pub. an ed. in 1732 based on the unwarrantable assumption that the orig. text had been corrupted by an editor who took advantage of Milton's blindness. Bentley made hundreds of emendations, most of which only reveal his own bad taste. Only two of his emendations have been generally accepted, and a few others are considered by J. W. Mackail as probably correct. There is a study of *Bentley's Milton* by J. W. Mackail (Br. Ac.). John Hawkey's Dublin ed. of 1747 is a carefully rev. and finely printed text and the 4to ed. pub. at Glasgow in 1750 is also worthy of note. A scholarly ed. of Book I pub. Capel Lofft in 1792 restores the original spelling and punctuation. Among the many edd. of the nineteenth century mention may be made of James Prendeville's (with learned commentary, 1840), R. Vaughan's folio ed. with Doré's illustrations (1866), Pickering's fine rpt. of the first ed. (1783) and Masson's facs. of the first ed. (1877). Good separate modern edd. are those of A. W. Verity (fully annotated, 1910), A. F. Cowling and H. F. Hallet (1926), J. Isaacs (text of the 1667 ed., 1937) and P. Hofer and J. R. Winterich (with Blake's illustrations, N.Y., 1941).

Paradise Regained and Samson Agonistes

These poems were first pub. together in 1671, and were rptd. in 1680. A folio ed. appeared in 1688. Many edd. of *Paradise Regained* with or without *Samson Agonistes* were pub. in the eighteenth and nineteenth centuries. Modern separate edd. include A. J. Wyatt's (1898), L. C. Martin's (1923), and E. H. Blakeney's finely-printed ed. with valuable commentary (1932). *Samson Agonistes* was less popular than *Paradise Regained* in the eighteenth century. Atterbury suggested to Pope that he should revise and 'polish' Milton's tragedy for the stage, but Pope wisely declined. Modern edd. include those of S. C. Collins (1883), H. M. Percival (1890), E. K. Chambers (1897) and C. T. Onions (1905), and A. W. Verity (1892), V. Hammer (Florence, 1931) and A. J. Wyatt and A. J. F. Collins (with the Sonnets, 1932).

PROSE WORKS

Collections

The first collection of Milton's prose was a folio entitled *The Works of Mr. Milton*, pub. in 1697 and including only *The Doctrine and Discipline of Divorce*, *The Reason of Church Government urg'd against Prelacy*, and *ΕΙΚΟΝΟΚΛΑΣΤΗΣ* each with a separate title page. The second, pub. in 1697-98 is the important collection ed. J. Toland in 3 folio vols. entitled *A Complete Collection of the Historical, Political and Miscellaneous Works of John Milton, both English and Latin, with som papers never before published*. It contains nearly all Milton's prose with Toland's *Life*.

Two important collections of the prose appeared in the eighteenth century, the earlier ed. T. Birch, in 1738 and the later, a rev. ed. of this work ed. T. Birch and R. Barrow, in 1753. In 1806 Charles Symmons pub. his ed. of *The Prose Works* in 7 vols. with trs. of the Latin works. R. Fletcher's popular ed. of the *Prose Works* appeared in 1838, and an American ed. in 2 vols. by R. Griswold in 1847. The most complete ed. of the nineteenth century was that of J. A. St. John in Bohn's Universal Library (5 vols. 1848-53), which was the first collection to include the *De Doctrinâ Christianâ*. Latin works are given in tr. and spelling is modernized. The text is not reliable. The definitive modern ed. is *The Complete Prose Works* ed. D. M. Wolfe (8 vols., New Haven, 1953).

Selections

One of the earliest selections from Milton's prose is that ed. J. A. St. John in 2 vols. (1836). Among the numerous modern selections are the excellent *Prose of Milton* ed. R. Garnett (1894), *Milton's Prose* ed. J. M. Wallace (W.C.), *Areopagitica and other Prose Works* ed. C. E. Vaughan (Ev. Lib.), *Milton on Himself*, ed. J. S. Diekhoff (N.Y., 1939) and *Prose Selections* ed. M. Y. Hughes (N.Y., 1951).

SEPARATE PROSE WORKS

The Anti-Prelatical Tracts

Milton began his work as a pamphleteer with five contributions to the controversy concerning episcopacy which raged in London in 1641-42. The first, *Of Reformation touching Church Discipline in England* . . ., appeared in June 1641; the second, a reply to Bishop Ussher, pub. anonymously in June or July 1641, was *Of Prelatical Episcopacy and whether it may be deduc'd from the Apostolic Times*; the third is a defence of the group of Puritan ministers who wrote under the name of Smectymnuus against Bishop Hall, and is called *Animadversions on the Remonstrant's Defence against Smectymnuus*. It also appeared in the summer of 1641. In March 1642 Milton returned to the attack on episcopacy in *The Reason of Church Government urg'd against Prelaty* and at about the same time he pub. a reply to an attack by Hall, called rather clumsily *An Apology against a Pamphlet called 'A Modest Confutation of the Animadversion of the Remonstrant agaaist Smectymnuus'*.

The Divorce Pamphlets

Milton pub. four tracts on Divorce between the summer of 1643 and the spring of 1645; the earliest, probably written at the time when his first wife left him, was *The Doctrine and Discipline of Divorce*, pub. before August 1st, 1643 (second ed. 1644). In July 1644 Milton pub. *The Judgment of Martin Bucer concerning Divorce*, in March 1645 appeared his *Tetrachordon*, an examination of four scripture passages bearing on the subject, and his *Colasterion*, a reply to an anonymous answer to his first Divorce pamphlet.

Of Education

Milton's small 'tractate' *Of Education to Master Samuel Hartlib* appeared anonymously in June 1644 and again with the early poems in 1673 (see p. 359). It was not rptd. till 1723. There are modern edd. by E. E. Morris (1895), Oscar Browning (1905), O. M. Ainsworth (Cornell Studies in English, 1928) and F. Schlupp (Würzburg, 1935).

Areopagitica

Milton's great pamphlet on the freedom of the press evoked by an Ordinance of Parliament establishing a censorship in

June 1643, was pub. in November 1644 with the title *Areopagitica; A Speech of Mr. John Milton for the liberty of Unlicenc'd Printing to the Parliament of England*. It was not rptd. till 1738. Other edd. followed in 1772, 1780 and 1791. T. Holt White's elaborately annotated ed. appeared in 1809. There are numerous modern edd. of which the best are those of J. W. Hales (1874) and Sir R. Jebb and A. W. Verity (1918), Facs. ed. *Areopagitica 1644* (N.Y., 1934).

The Anti-Monarchical Pamphlets

Milton's first printed attack on monarchy was probably written at the time of the trial of Charles I and was pub. with the title *Of the Tenure of Kings and Magistrates* in February 1649. Immediately after the King's death the famous anonymous book *ΕΙΚΩΝ ΒΑΣΙΛΙΚΗ, The True Portraiture of his Sacred Majesty in his Solitudes and Sufferings* was pub. and had an immense circulation. Milton, now Latin secretary to the Council of State, was commissioned to answer it, and his reply, called *ΕΙΚΟΝΟΚΛΑΣΤΗΣ*, appeared in October 1649. Second edd. of these two anti-monarchical pamphlets of Milton appeared in 1650. There is an excellent modern ed. of *Of the Tenure of Kings and Magistrates* by W. T. Allison (N.Y., 1911).

The Three 'Defensiones'

Commissioned by the Commonwealth to reply to Salmasius (Claude Saumaise) a French scholar who had written a Latin defence of Charles I, Milton pub. in March 1651 a Latin tract *Ioannis Miltoni Angli pro populo anglicano defensio contra Claudii anonymi, alias Salmasii defensionem regiam*. This work designed for foreigners, had a great success abroad, was rptd. three times in 1651 and again in 1652 and 1658. An English version by Joseph Washington was pub. in 1692. The second Latin 'defensio' was evoked by a tract called *Regii Sanguinis Clamor ad Coelum* by Peter du Moulin in which the distinguished scholar, Alexander More or Morus, was supposed to have had a hand. Milton's reply, *Ioannis Miltoni pro populo anglicano defensio secunda contra infamen libellum anonymum* appeared in the spring of 1654, and is the greatest of his Latin pamphlets. An English tr. by F. Wrangham was pub. in 1655. More replied in a pamphlet pub. at the Hague, and Milton defended himself in a third Latin tract *Prose Defensio*, pub. 1655 in London and rptd. at the Hague in the same year. No English tr. appeared till the publication of one in the Columbia ed. Milton's *Works*.

Later Ecclesiastical Pamphlets

Milton pub. two pamphlets on ecclesiastical questions in 1659. The first, dealing with the question of toleration, entitled *A Treatise of Civil Power in Ecclesiastical Causes* appeared in February and in May when the restored 'Long Parliament' was discussing disestablishment and tithes, Milton pub. his views on these matters in his vigorous *Considerations Touching the Likeliest means to remove Hirelings out of the Church*.

The Tract on a Free Commonwealth

After the collapse of the Protectorate in 1659, when the question of the future form of government was being widely discussed, Milton drew up his plan for a reformed English Commonwealth in *The Ready and Easy Way to Establish a Free Commonwealth*, pub. in February or March 1660. In April he pub. a brief reply to a Dr Griffith, who had advocated the restoration of Charles II, called *Brief Notes on a late Sermon . . .* A second rev. ed. of *The Ready and Easy Way* appeared in 1660. There is a rpt. in the Ev. Lib. ed. of Milton's prose.

The History of Britain

This work, written probably between 1648 and 1655, was not pub. till 1670. A long digression in Book III comparing the state of Britain after the Roman evacuation with its condition at the end of the Civil War was excised by the Censor but pub. separately in 1680 as *Mr. John Milton's Character of the Long Parliament and the Assembly of Divines*. The *History* was rptd. in 1677 and 1695, and in Toland's ed. of the prose works pub. in 1697-98 (see p. 362). Toland's text contains material not found in the first three edd. and apparently derived from a copy of the 1670 ed. annotated by Milton. See *Milton as a Historian* by Sir C. Firth (1908)

Tracts published after the Restoration

Milton contributed one pamphlet to the discussions which followed Charles II's *Declaration of Indulgence* of March 1672. It is a plea for a 'united Protestant front' called *Of true Religion, Heresy, Toleration and the growth of Popery*. It was rptd. in 1826. In 1674 Milton pub. an English tr. of a Polish manifesto in Latin called *A Declaration of the Election of this present King of Poland, John III*.

Miscellaneous Prose

A complete list of Milton's minor prose works will be found in J. Holly Hanford's *Milton Handbook*. They include a Latin grammar pub. 1669; Latin letters written by Milton when he was Secretary to the Council of State pub. under the title *Literae Pseudo-Senatus Anglicanae* in 1676, English trs. *Republican Letters* (1682) and *Letters of State* ed. E. Phillips (1694); and a popular account of Russia called *A Brief History of Moscovia*, probably written under the Commonwealth or early Protectorate, and pub. in 1682, modern edd. by Prince Mirsky (1918) and R. R. Cawley (Princeton, 1941). Milton's *Commonplace Book* was discovered in 1874 and pub. in that year by A. J. Horwood. His *Private Correspondence and Academic Exercises* ed. E. M. Tillyard were pub. in 1932.

The De Doctrinâ Christianâ

This important Latin work containing a system of theology constructed by Milton on the basis of passages of scripture and the writings of various divines was finished by Milton about 1661, but was not pub. by him. The MS. was apparently bequeathed to his friend Daniel Skinner, who copied part of it, and sent it to Elzevir, the Dutch publisher, with a view to publication. He was warned, however, that the publication of the book would be fatal to his political ambitions, and he gave up the project. The MS. found its way to the Public Record Office, where it was discovered by the Keeper, Robert Lemon, in the reign of George IV, who entrusted Bishop Charles Sumner with the task of transcribing, translating and editing it. Sumner's ed. including Latin text and English tr. appeared in 1825. For an analysis of the *De Doctrinâ Christianâ*, and an account of its relationship to Milton's epics see D. Saurat's *Milton, the Man and the Thinker* (1924, 2nd rev. ed. 1944) and A. Sewell's *Milton's De Doctrinâ Christianâ* (E.S.M.E.A., XIX, 1934).

BIOGRAPHY

The earliest pub. *Life of Milton* appeared in Anthony à Wood's *Fasti Oxonienses* of 1691, and was based on two unpublished sources, a collection of notes sent to Wood by Aubrey in 1681, and an anonymous MS. *Life of Milton* now in the Bodleian. Helen H. Darbishire has shown that this anonymous *Life* was almost certainly by John Phillips, Milton's nephew. Aubrey's vivid notes will be found in his *Brief Lives*, ed. Clark (II. 60-72). Milton's other nephew Edward Phillips wrote a *Life* which he prefixed to his ed. of the *Letters of State* (1694, see p. 359). In 1697-98 John Toland's important and interesting *Life* appeared in his ed. of the Prose Works (see p. 362). All these early *Lives*, together with J. Richardson's (see below) have been carefully ed. with introd. by Helen Darbishire in her *Early Lives of Milton*

(1932). Numerous *Lives*, many of them of the 'honeysuckle' variety condemned by Dr Johnson appeared in the eighteenth century. Jonathan Richardson's, however, prefixed to his *Explanatory Notes and Remarks on Milton's Paradise Lost* is of great importance and contains much new information. There is a copy of this book, annotated in MS., probably by the author, in the London Library. Other notable eighteenth-century *Lives* are those of T. Birch and Bishop Newton in their ed. and Dr Johnson's trenchant study in *Lives of the Poets* (1781). Nineteenth-century *Lives* include those of Todd and Mitford prefixed to their edd. and D. Masson's enormous *Life of John Milton narrated in connection with the Political, Ecclesiastical and Literary History of his Time* (7 vols. including index, 1849-80). A parallel work to Masson's is the German study by A. Stern, *Milton und seine Zeit* (Leipzig, 1877-79). There are numerous modern one-vol. biographies. The best are by Mark Pattison (1880), Richard Garnett (1890), W. P. Trent (1899), Sir W. Raleigh (1900), D. Saurat (1924), E. M. Tillyard (1930), J. H. Hanford, *John Milton, Englishman* (1949) and K. Muir, *John Milton* (1955). They all include critical surveys of Milton's writings. For modern studies of various details and aspects of Milton's life and character see the bibliographies appended to Saurat's *Milton the Man and the Thinker*, and to Hanford's *Milton Handbook*. *The Life Records of Milton* ed. J. M. French (4 vols., New Brunswick, 1949-1956) is an invaluable collection of documents relating to Milton's life.

CRITICISM

Miltonic criticism begins in the seventeenth century with Dryden's remarks in his Prefaces (see W. P. Ker's ed. of Dryden's Essays), Patrick Hume's commentary (see p. 356), and Toland's eulogy in his *Life of Milton* (see p. 367).

Addison's famous series of essays on *Paradise Lost* first appeared in the *Spectator* from December 31st, 1711 to May 3rd, 1712. They were rptd. separately in 1719 and had a great effect in popularizing Milton. The *Explanatory Notes and Remarks on Milton's Paradise Lost . . . with the Life of the Author* by the two Jonathan Richardsons appeared in 1734 (see p. 368) and is, perhaps, the first English monograph on an English poet. Much of the best Miltonic criticism of the eighteenth century is to be found in the various edd. An account of William Lauder's attack on Milton, whom he accused of plagiarism and of the forgeries by which he supported this attack, will be found in the standard biographies. Johnson's Miltonic criticism started with papers in *The Rambler* on Milton's versification and on *Samson Agonistes*. His *Life of Milton* in *The Lives of the Poets* contains the famous criticisms, which aroused much controversy, but which, in spite of a colouring of prejudice, are of permanent value.

William Blake in his *Marriage of Heaven and Hell* and elsewhere in his works has some illuminating comments on Milton's work and character. The great romantic poets and critics, Wordsworth, Coleridge, Lamb, Hazlitt, Landor, Keats, Shelley and De Quincey, all paid notable tributes to him. Special attention is drawn to Coleridge's comparison between Milton and Shakespeare in *Biographia Literaria*, Ch. XV, to Shelley's remarks in his *Defence of Poetry*, and to Keats's in his *Letters*. Macaulay's famous essay appeared in 1825 as a review of Sumner's ed. of the *De Doctrinâ Christianâ*. Among the vast mass of nineteenth-century studies mention may be made of W. Bagehot's essay in his *Literary Studies* (1879), of David Masson's on *Milton's Devil* in his *Essays Biographical and Critical* (1856), rptd. in *The Three Devils* (1874), of Matthew Arnold's *Milton in Essays in Criticism* (second series, 1888) and *A French Critic on Milton* in *Mixed Essays* (1879), of Tennyson's poem in alcaics, and of his illuminating remarks recorded in Hallam Tennyson's *Memoir*, and of the monographs of Mark Pattison (1879) W. P. Trent (1899), Richard Garnett (1890), and Sir Walter Raleigh (1904). Lascelles Abercrombie's criticism of Milton's epics in his monograph *The Epic* (1912) is of the highest importance. Since 1917 a new and remarkable school of Miltonic criticism has come into existence; in the words of Professor D. Saurat it 'considers Milton as a Renaissance Thinker and Artist and no longer as a Puritan', and, to use an expression of Professor J. S. Smart, it has tried to get him 'completely and resolutely demassonized'. Bibliographies of studies based on this conception of Milton are to be found in App. D of Saurat's *Milton, The Man and The Thinker*, and at the end of J. Holly Hanford's *Milton Handbook*. The most important contributions to the work of the new school are S. B. Liljegren's *Studies in Milton* (Lund, 1918), and his various articles in E.S. and other periodicals, J. Holly Hanford's *The Youth of Milton* (in *Studies in Shakespeare, Milton and Donne*, Ann Arbor, 1925), in articles by J. H. Hanford, E. Greenlaw and E. Chauncy Baldwin in M.L.N., M.P., S.P. etc., and Denis Saurat's books, *La Pensée de Milton* (Paris, 1920), *Blake et Milton* (Bordeaux, 1922), *Milton the Man and the Thinker* (London, 1924), and *Milton et le Matérialisme Chrétien* (Paris, 1928). The new conception of Milton was pushed to fantastic lengths in the writings of H. Mutschmann *Der andere Milton* (1920) and *Milton und das Licht* (1922).

Important scholarly works standing quite apart from this group are R. D. Haven's exhaustive account of *The Influence of Milton on English Poetry* (Harvard, 1922), E. H. Visiak, *Milton Agonistes* (1923), E. M. Tillyard, *Milton* (1930) and *The Miltonic Setting* (1938), Sir H. J. C. Grierson, *Milton and Wordsworth* (1937) and F. E. Hutchinson, *Milton and the English Mind* (1946) Adverse criticism of Milton, doubtless to some extent a reaction against the excessive adulation of older critics, finds expression in an important body of work in the present century, beginning, perhaps, with certain remarks of Ezra Pound (see Ezra Pound, *Literary Essays* ed. T. S. Eliot, 1954) and with T. S. Eliot's description of Milton's blank verse in *The Sacred Wood* (1920) as a 'Chinese Wall' erected across English poetry. Eliot's early adverse criticism of Milton is to be found in 'A Note on the Verse of Milton' in E.S.M.E.A., XXI, 1935; it was, however, considerably modified in his British Academy Lecture, *Milton* (Br. Ac., XXXIII, 1947). Other acute and thoughtful adverse criticisms are to be found in F. R. Leavis, *Revaluation* (1936) and *The Common Pursuit* (1950), and in A. J. A. Waldock, *Paradise Lost and its Critics* (1947, P.B., 1961). L. Pearsall Smith in *Milton and his Modern Critics* (1940) reviews adverse criticisms and replies to them. Milton's art is ably defended by C. S. Lewis in his *Preface to Paradise Lost* (1941, rev. ed. 1942) and C. Williams in his Introd. to his W.C. edition of the *English Poems*. Two short studies of great value are W. Menzies, *The Last Poems*, E.S.M.E.A., XXIV, 1938, and J. B. Leishman, *L'Allegro and Il Penseroso in their relation to Seventeenth Century Poetry*, ibid., N.S. 4, 1951. Other important critical studies are G. Wilson Knight, *The Burning Oracle* (1939) and *Chariot of Wrath* (1942); C. M. Bowra, *From Virgil to Milton* (1944); D. Bush, *Paradise Lost in our Time* (Ithaca, 1945); B. Rajan, *Paradise Lost and the Seventeenth Century Reader* (1947); D. C. Allen, *The Harmonious Vision* (1954); F. T. Prince, *The Italian Element in Milton's Verse* (1954); F. Kermode, *The Living Milton* (1960); Rosamund Tuve, *Images and Themes in Five Poems of Milton* (1960), and W. Empson, *Milton's God* (1961). D. Wolfe, *Milton on the Puritan Revolution* (N.Y., 1941) is a valuable and exhaustive study of the political significance of Milton's work. His prosody can be studied in R. Bridges, *Milton's Prosody* (1894, rev. ed. 1921) and in S. E. Sprott, *Milton's Art of Prosody* (1953). J. H. Hanford, *A Milton Handbook* (1928) is an excellent short guide and introduction to the study of Milton.

BOOKS OF REFERENCE

The best Milton concordance is that of J. Bradshaw (London, 1894). C. G. Osgood's *The Classical Mythology of Milton's Poems* (N.Y., 1900, rev. ed., 1925) is a valuable dictionary of Milton's references to classical mythology. There is a *Lexicon to the English Poetical Works of John Milton* by Laura Lockwood (N.Y., 1907), *A Concordance of the Latin, Greek and Italian Poems* by Lane Cooper (Halle, 1923), and *A Geographical Dictionary of Milton* by Allen H. Gilbert (New Haven, Connecticut, 1919).

There are useful bibliographies in the edd. of Todd and Masson and in R. Garnett's *Milton* (1890); the last contains a list of magazine articles, reviews, etc. *Milton, a Topical Bibliography*, by E. N. C. Thompson (New Haven, Connecticut, 1916) is a valuable work arranged by 'topics' (e.g., 'biography', 'puritanism', etc.). Under each 'topic' works on Milton are arranged chronologically. See also D. H. Stevens, *A Reference Guide to Milton 1800 to the Present Day* (Chicago, 1930).

CHAPTER XIX

RESTORATION DRAMA (1660-88)

SOME GENERAL STUDIES

EARLY accounts of plays and dramatists are to be found in Gerard Langbaine's *An Account of the English Dramatick Poets* (1691, second enl. ed. by Gildon, 1699; there are important MS. annotations by William Oldys in a copy of the 1691 ed. and others by J. Haslewood in a copy of the 1699 ed. in the B.M.), D. E. Baker's *The Companion to the Playhouse* (1764), rev. ed. called *Biographia Dramatica* (1782), and J. Genest's *Some Account of the English Stage* (1832). Among critical essays of the nineteenth century the most important are Lamb's *The Artificial Comedy of the Last Century* in *Essays of Elia* (1823), Hazlitt's study in his *Lectures on the English Comic Writers* (1819), Leigh Hunt's Preface to his ed. of Wycherley, Congreve, Vanbrugh and Farquhar (1840) and Macaulay's review of this work in his essay on *The Comic Dramatists of the Restoration* (1841). Allardyce Nicoll's *History of Restoration Drama* (1923, rev. ed. 1952) is the most complete modern survey. J. Palmer's *The Comedy of Manners* (1913) and Bonamy Dobrée's *Restoration Comedy* (1924) and *Restoration Tragedy* (1920) are valuable and stimulating modern critical works. W. L. Chase's *The Heroic Play* (N.Y., 1903) deals with one particular development of Restoration drama. Important American studies are J. W. Krutch, *Comedy and Conscience after the Restoration* (N.Y., 1924, rev. ed., 1949), K. M. Lynch, *The Social Mode of Restoration Comedy* (Ann Arbor, 1926), T. H. Fujimura, *The Restoration Comedy of Wit* (Princeton, 1952) and N. N. Holland, *The First Modern Comedies* (Harvard, 1959). For a modern adverse view see 'Restoration Comedy' by L. C. Knights in his *Explorations* (1945). J. Wilcox's *The Relationship of Molière to Restoration Comedy* (N.Y., 1938) is a notable essay in comparative literature. Other important studies are C. V. Deane, *Dramatic*

Theory and the Rhymed Heroic Play (1931); A. E. Parsons, 'The English Heroic Play,' M.L.R., III, 1938; C. Leech, 'Restoration Comedy, the Earlier Phase', E.C., I, April 1951; J. Wain, 'Restoration Comedy and its Modern Critics', E.C., VI, October 1956; F. W. Bateson, 'L. C. Knights and Restoration Comedy', E.C., VII, April 1957; C. D. Cecil, 'Libertine and *Précieux* Elements in Restoration Comedy', E.C., IX, July 1959.

For conditions in the theatre reference should be made to Pepys's *Diary* ed. H. B. Wheatley; Colley Cibber's *Apology for his Life* (1740, ed. R. W. Lowe with *Supplement* by A. Aston, 2 vols., 1889); J. Downes, *Roscius Anglicanus* (1708, ed. M. Summers, 1928); R. W. Lowe, *Thomas Betterton* (1891); Eleanoure Boswell, *The Restoration Court Stage* (Harvard, 1932) and J. H. Wilson, *All the King's Ladies, Actresses of the Restoration* (Chicago, 1958). Bibliographies are 'A Hand-List of Restoration Plays', A. Nicoll, *A History of Restoration Drama*, App. C, and *A Check-List of English Plays* by G. L. Woodward and J. G. McManaway (1945).

COLLECTIONS

Early collections of Restoration plays (with later works are to be found in such dramatic anthologies as *A Collection of Plays* (1719), Bell's *British Theatre* (1776-78), Sharpe's *British Theatre* (1804), Mrs Inchbald's *British Theatre* (1808), R. Cumberland's *British Drama* (1826) and J. Cumberland's *British Theatre* (1829). Leigh Hunt's famous collection (which evoked Macaulay's *Essay*) was pub. in 1851 and includes *the Dramatic Works of Wycherley, Congreve, Vanbrugh and Farquhar. Dramatists of the Restoration*, ed. J. Maidment and W. H. Logan (14 vols., Edinburgh, 1872-79) includes the dramatic works of Sir W. Davenant, John Wilson, John Tatham, John Lacy, Sir Aston Cockayne and John Crowne. Smaller modern collections are *Representative Dramas from Dryden to Sheridan* ed. F. and J. W. Tupper (1914); *Restoration Comedies* ed. M. Summers (1921); *Five Restoration Tragedies* ed. B. Dobrée (W.C. 1928); *Restoration Plays* ed. E. Gosse (W.C., 1912, rev. ed. 1932); R.E.C. vol. IV (N.Y., 1936); *British Dramatists from Dryden to Sheridan* ed. G. H. Nettleton and A. E. Case (Boston, 1939); *Restoration Plays* ed. B. Harris (N.Y., 1953); *Six Restoration Plays* ed. J. H. Wilson (Camb. Mass., 1959); *Five Heroic Plays* ed. B. Dobrée (W.C., 1960).

INDIVIDUAL AUTHORS

ABRAHAM COWLEY (1618-67)

Cowley's early play *Love's Riddle, a Pastorall Comædie*, was written when he was at Westminster School and pub. in 1638. His comedy, *The Guardian*, was acted before the Prince of Wales at Trinity College, Cambridge, in 1641, and printed 1650. He re-wrote it after the Restoration and the new version entitled *Cutter of Coleman Street*, was acted 1661, and printed 1663. It is rptd. in R.E.C., vol. IV, with a critical essay by H. A. Beers.

SIR WILLIAM DAVENANT (1606-68)

Davenant's plays produced before the Civil War include *Albovine King of the Lombards, a Tragedy* (1629), *The Platonick Lovers, The Witts* (both 1636), and *Love and Honour* (1649). During the reign of Charles I he also produced a number of Masques for the court, such as *The Temple of Love* (1635), *The Triumphs of the Prince D'Amour* (1636), and *Luminalia* (1637). These works, like Ben Jonson's masques, were written to order as court entertainments. The next phase in Davenant's dramatic career begins when he had returned to England under the Protectorate, and had persuaded the authorities to lift their ban on the drama sufficiently to allow him to stage some semi-private performances at Rutland House. His dramatic works staged under the Protectorate are *The First Day's Entertainment at Rutland House* (1657); *The Siege of Rhodes, Made a Representation by the Art of Prospective in Scenes and the Story Sung in Recitative Musick* (1656).(The first English opera), *The Cruelty of the Spaniards in Peru* (1658) and *The History of Sir Francis Drake* (1659). His post-Restoration Plays include *The Rivals* and the *Man's the Master* (both pub. 1668) and *The Playhouse to Lett* and *The Law against Lovers*, which were not printed till they appeared in the folio ed. of his works pub. 1673. He adapted two of Shakespeare's plays for the Restoration Theatre, *The Tempest or the Enchanted Island* (with Dryden, acted 1667, pub. 1670) and *Macbeth* (acted 1664, pub. 1674). The only modern ed. of Davenant's plays is that of Maidment and Logan in their *Restoration Dramatists* (5 vols., 1773). For biography and criticism see p. 347.

SIR SAMUEL TUKE (d. 1674)

Tuke was the author of the very popular and successful play called *The Adventures of Five Hours*, an adaptation from the Spanish made by express command of Charles II. This play pub. in 1663, was Pepys's favourite: 'the best for variety and the most excellent for the continuance of the plot to the end'. Beside it *Othello* seemed to him 'a mean thing'. There is a modern ed. by B. Van Thal with introd. by M. Summers (1928) and another by A. E. H. Swaen (Amsterdam, 1927). Allison Gaw in a monograph pub. 1917 (Baltimore) discusses *Sir Samuel Tuke's Adventures of Five Hours in Relation to the Spanish Plot and to Dryden*.

ROGER BOYLE, EARL OF ORRERY (1621-79)
Works

This mediocre but influential dramatist, the pioneer of the rimed heroic tragedy, pub. six plays during his lifetime. They were *The History of Henry the Fifth* and *The Tragedy of Mustapha* (both pub. 1668); *Two New Tragedies, The Black Prince* and *Tryphon* (1669); *Guzman a Comedy* (1669), and *Mr. Anthony a Comedy* (1671). Works pub. after his death include *Herod the Great* (1694); *Altemira* (1701) (produced in an earlier version as *The Generall* in 1664) and *The Tragedy of King Saul* (1703). *The Tragedy of Zoroastres*, an unpub. work of Orrery, survives in a MS. in the B.M. (Sloane, 1828). Orrery's *Dramatic Works* were printed in 2 vols., 1739. There is a valuable modern ed. by W. S. Clark (2 vols., 1937).

Biography and Criticism

There is a Life of Orrery by T. Henderson in D.N.B. The most up-to-date information, however, is to be found in the Introd. to Clark's ed. See also articles by Clark in R.E.S., II (1926), VI (1930), and M.L.N., XLII (1927), XLIV (1929). There are unpublished theses on Orrery by Clark at Harvard (*Harvard*

Summaries of Theses, II, 1930) and W. F. Payne in London University.

THOMAS OTWAY (1652-87)

Otway's plays were pub. in the following order: *Alcibiades* (1675), *Don Carlos, Prince of Spain* (1676), *Titus and Berenice* (with a farce adapted from Molière called *The Cheats of Scapin* (1677), *Friendship in Fashion* (1678), *The History and Fall of Caius Marius* (1680), *The Orphan or the Unhappy Marriage* (1680), *The Souldier's Fortune* (1681), *Venice Preserved, or a Plot Discovered* (1682), *The Atheist or the Second Part of the Souldier's Fortune* (1684). Collected edd. of Otway's Works appeared in 1691, 1712 and at later dates in the eighteenth century. There is a good selection of his plays in the Mermaid Series, ed. Hon. Roden Noel, and two modern complete edd., one by Montague Summers (1926), and the other by J. C. Ghosh (2 vols., 1932). Ghosh's ed. is by far the better of the two, and is likely to remain the standard modern text.

There are many separate edd. of *The Orphan* and *Venice Preserved*. *Venice Preserved* is obtainable in the T.D. (ed. Gollancz) and the two tragedies together in B.L., ed. McClumpha.

Biography and Criticism

There are lives by Langbaine in his *English Dramatick Poets* with notes by Oldys in the B.M. copy, and by Johnson in *The Lives of the Poets*. There is a pleasant but inaccurate sketch by Sir E. Gosse in his *Seventeenth Century Studies*; more valuable are a dissertation by E. Schumacher (Berne, 1924), a study by Roswell G. Ham in his *Otway and Lee* (Yale, 1931) and Aline M. Taylor's interesting monograph, *Next to Shakespeare: Otway's 'Venice Preserved' and 'The Orphan' and their History on the London Stage* (Durham, N.C., 1950).

GEORGE VILLIERS, 2ND DUKE OF BUCKINGHAM (1628-87)

Buckingham's one important dramatic work was the famous burlesque of the 'Heroic' plays called *The Rehearsal*. He is said to have been helped in its composition by Matthew Clifford, Samuel Butler and Thomas Sprat. It was first acted at Drury Lane in December 1671 and pub. in 1672. The third (rev. and enl.) ed. appeared in 1675. It was often rptd. in the eighteenth century and in various nineteenth-century collections. There are modern annotated edd. by E. Arber in his *English Reprints*, M. Summers (1914), by A. G. Barnes (with Sheridan's *The Critic*) (1927) and by G. R. Noyes in his *Selected Dramas of John Dryden* (N.Y., 1910). Buckingham's other dramatic works are a lively adaptation of Fletcher's *The Chances* (1682) and a farce on the Battle of Sedgmoor included in his *Miscellaneous Works* of 1704 and 1715. See J. H. Wilson, *A Rake and his Times* (N.Y., 1954).

JOHN WILMOT, EARL OF ROCHESTER (1647-80)

Rochester's one complete extant play is *Valentinian: A Tragedy* (a rewriting of the play by John Fletcher with the same title), acted after his death in February 1683/4 and pub. (2 edd.) in 1685. B.M. Add. MS. 28692 (another copy of which, apparently a rough draft, is in the Folger Shakespeare Library, Washington, D.C.) is a small folio containing, in a scribe's hand, a version of *Valentinian* called *Lucina's Rape* together with 'A Scaen of Sir Robert Howard's Play', written by Rochester for a play called *The Conquest of China* planned but never completed by Howard in 1672. Rochester's 'Scaen' is an impressive fragment in vigorous heroic couplets. Both *Valentinian* and the 'Scaen' are printed in J. Hayward's ed. of Rochester's *Collected Works* and the 'Scaen' and selected passages from *Valentinian* in V. de S. Pinto's ed. of the *Poems* (see pp. 351-2). There is also a fragment of a comedy in Rochester's own hand in the Portland MSS. in Nottingham University Library, printed in V. de S. Pinto, *Enthusiast in Wit* (1961), pp. 111, 112. For criticism of Rochester's dramatic works see Pinto, op. cit., pp. 108-12, 159, 160.

APHRA BEHN (1640-89)

Characteristic works of this prolific dramatic author and the tragi-comedies called *The Forc'd Marriage* (1671) and *The Young King* (1683), the comedies, *Sir Patient Fancy* (1678) and *The Feigned Courtezans* or *A Night's Intrigue* (1679), and the tragedy *Abdelazer or the Moors Revenge* (1677). Collected edd. of the plays were pub. in 1702 and at subsequent dates in the eighteenth century. There is a modern ed. of her works by M. Summers (6 vols., 1915). *Selected Writings* ed. R. Phelps (N.Y., 1950) contains one play together with stories and poems. For her prose fiction see p. 330. There is a short study of her by the Hon. V. M. Sackville West,

Aphra Behn or the Incomparable Astraea (1927), and fuller ones by S. Woodcock, *The Incomparable Aphra* (1948), and E. Hahn, *Aphra Behn* (1951).

SIR GEORGE ETHEREGE (1634-91)

Etherege's earliest play, *The Comicall Revenge or Love in a Tub* was acted and pub. 1664. *She Wou'd if She Cou'd* was acted in 1667-68, and pub. 1668. His masterpiece *The Man of Mode or Sir Fopling Flutter* was acted and pub. 1676. Tonson pub. collected edd. of Etherege's plays in 1704 and 1715. A. W. Verity's limited ed. of the *Plays and Poems* appeared in 1888. The standard modern ed. of the plays is that of H. F. Brett Smith (2 vols., 1927). Etherege's *Letter Book*, containing copies of his letters while he was ambassador at Ratisbon, is extant in MS. (B.M. Add. MS. 11513). It has been ed. by S. Rosenfeld (1928). An account of a 'Second Letter Book of Etherege' (MS. at Harvard) by S. Rosenfeld was pub. in R.E.S., N.S. III, 1952. Etherege's *Poems* have been excellently edited by James Thorpe (Princeton, 1963).

Biography and Criticism

The best biographies of Etherege are those by B. Dobrée in his *Essays in Biography* (1925) and H. F. B. Brett Smith in the introd. to his ed. of the *Plays*, op. cit. Dale Underwood, *Etherege and the Seventeenth Century Comedy of Manners* (Yale, 1957) is a monograph of the highest value for the study both of Etherege and of Restoration comedy in general.

NATHANIEL LEE (1649-92)

Works

Lee's plays include *The Tragedy of Nero, Emperor of Rome* (1674), *Sophonisba, or Hannibal's Overthrow* (1675), *The Rival Queens or the Death of Alexander the Great* (1677) (his most popular work), *Mithridates, King of Pontus* (1678), *Caesar Borgia* (1650) and *Theodosius or The Force of Love* (1680). He collaborated with Dryden in *Oedipus, A Tragedy* (1678) and *The Duke of Guise* (1682). His works were pub. in 2 vols, 1713, and in 3 vols. 1722, later ed. 1734. *The Rival Queens* was often acted in the eighteenth and early nineteenth centuries, and was much altered and adapted. Altered versions appear in Bell's *British Theatre* and elsewhere.

An excellent modern ed. of Lee's *Works* by T. B. Stroup and A. L. Cooke was pub. in 1954-55 (2 vols., Brunswick, N.J.).

Biography and Criticism

There is an article on Lee by Sir S. Lee in the D.N.B. and a study of his life and writings in Roswell G. Ham's *Otway and Lee* (Yale, 1931).

THOMAS SHADWELL (1642-92)

Shadwell's plays were pub. in the following order: *The Sullen Lovers or the Impertinents* (1668), *The Royal Shepherdess* (1664), *The Humourists* (1671), *The Miser* (1672), *Epsom Wells* (1673), *The Tempest* (an opera based on Shakespeare's play, 1674), *Psyche* (an opera, 1675), *The Libertine* (1676), *The Virtuoso* (1676), *The History of Timon of Athens* (adapted from Shakespeare, 1678), *A True Widow* (1679), *The Woman Captain* (1680), *The Lancashire Witches and Teague O'Divelly the Irish Priest* (1682), *The Squire of Alsatia* (1688), *Bury Fair* (1689), *The Amorous Bigotte with the Second Part of Teague O'Divelly* (1690), *The Scowrers* (1691). *The Volunteers or the Stock Jobbers* (1693). His non-dramatic works include *The Medal of John Bayes* (1682), a scurrilous attack on Dryden; a tr. of Tenth Satire of Juvenal, and various worthless official poems written when he was Poet Laureate. A collected ed. of his plays appeared in 1720. Saintsbury ed. a good selection from his plays for the Mermaid Series. B.L. includes an ed. of *Epsom Wells* and *The Volunteers* by D. M. Walmsley. The only complete modern ed. is that of M. Summers (5 vols., 1927).

Biography and Criticism

There is a short account of Shadwell's life prefixed to the ed. of 1720, a useful article in the D.N.B. by G. Aitken and a valuable monograph by A. S. Borgman (Harvard, 1928). See also Saintsbury's introd. to his Mermaid ed. and R. G. Smith 'Shadwell's Impact on Dryden', R.E.S., XX, 1944, 'Shadwell and the Ladies and the Change in Comedy', M.P., XLVI, 1948, and 'French Sources for Six English Comedies', J.E.G.P., XLVII, 1948.

JOHN WILSON (1627-96)

Wilson's four plays are *The Cheats* (1664), *Andronicus Comnenius* 1664), *The Projectors* (1665) and *Belphegor or the Marriage of the*

Devil (1691). The only complete ed. is that of Maidment and Logan (op. cit. p. 374). There is a modern ed. of Wilson's *The Cheats* by M. C. Nahm based on the MS. of the play in Worcester College Library (Blackwell, 1935). Concerning this MS., see F. S. Boas's *Shakespeare and the Universities* (1923). There is a good article on Wilson in the D.N.B. by T. Seccombe.

SIR ROBERT HOWARD (1626-98)

This politician, virtuoso and author, Dryden's brother-in-law, pub. *Four New Plays* in 1665. They are *The Surprisal*, *The Committee* (comedies) and *The Indian Queen* and *The Vestal Virgin* (tragedies). Dryden collaborated with Howard in *The Indian Queen*. Howard's tragedy *The Great Favourite or the Duke of Lerma* was pub. 1668. *The Five Plays* were rptd. in 1692, 1700 and 1722. There is an interesting study of *Dryden and Howard* by D. D. Arundell (1929). The definitive biography is H. S. Oliver, *Sir Robert Howard* (Durham, N.C., 1963).

JOHN DRYDEN (1631-1700)

For Dryden's plays see pp. 389-91.

SIR CHARLES SEDLEY (1639-1701)

For Sedley's plays see p. 350.

JOHN CROWNE (1640-1712)

Works

A complete list of Crowne's numerous dramatic works will be found in G. P. Winship's *Bibliography of John Crowne* (1922). The most notable are, perhaps, *The History of Charles the Eighth of France* (1671), *The Country Wit* (1675), *The Destruction of Jerusalem* (2 pts. 1677), *City Politiques* (1683) and *Sir Courtly Nice or It Cannot Be* (1685). His dramatic works were collected by Maidment and Logan in their *Dramatists of the Restoration*. *Sir Courtly Nice* was rptd. by M. Summers in his *Restoration Comedies* (1921).

Biography and Criticism

There is a monograph on John Crowne by Arthur F. White (Cleveland, Ohio, 1922), a monograph on 'Crowne's Place in Restoration Comedy' by Sir A. W. Ward in R.E.C., Vol. IV, and an account of the production of his masque of *Calisto* in Eleanoure Boswell's *Restoration Court Stage*, op. cit.

WILLIAM WYCHERLEY (1640?-1714)

Wycherley's first play, *Love in a Wood* was probably acted in the spring of 1671, and was pub. in 1672. *The Gentleman Dancing Master*, his second work, the plot of which is partly borrowed from a play by Calderon, was acted in the winter of 1671-72, and pub. in 1673. *The Country Wife*, his most brilliant production, was acted in 1672 or 1673 and pub. in 1675. His fourth and last comedy, *The Plain Dealer*, was probably acted in 1674, and was pub. in 1677. Wycherley pub. nothing else till 1704, when his folio vol. of *Miscellany Verses* appeared. This publication seems to have led to his friendship with the young Pope, who helped Wycherley by correcting some of his verses. This co-operation led to a quarrel (see Pope's *Letters* and the accounts of the affair given in the critical works cited below). After Wycherley's death his *Posthumous Works in Verse and Prose* were pub. by Major R. Pack in 1728. Neither this nor the 1704 collection have been rptd. Collective edd. of Wycherley's plays appeared in 1713, 1720, 1731, 1735 and 1768. They were included by Leigh Hunt in his ed. of *Restoration Comedies*, and there are modern edd. by W. C. Ward in the Mermaid Series, and by M. Summers (4 vols., 1924). There is an excellent ed. of *The Country Wife* and *The Plain Dealer* by G. B. Churchill in B.L. *The Plain Dealer* is rptd. in R.E.C., vol. IV, with a critical essay by A. Beljame and H. S. Symmes.

Biography and Criticism

Studies of Wycherley include a German thesis by Klette, *Wycherley's Leben und dramatische Werke* (Münster, 1883), an excellent French monograph by C. Perromat, *William Wycherley Sa Vie —Son Oeuvre* (Paris, 1921), and a detailed critical biography by Willard Connely, *Brawny Wycherley* (1930).

The accounts of Wycherley in Voltaire's *Lettres sur les Anglais* and in Spence's *Anecdotes*, and the criticisms by Leigh Hunt in the introd. to his ed. by Macaulay in his essay on *The Comic Dramatists of the Restoration*, and by Hazlitt in his *Lectures on the English Comic Writers* should also be consulted. See also J. Wilcox, *The Relation of Molière to Restoration Comedy* (N.Y., 1938) and E. E. Williams, 'Furetière and Wycherley', M.L.N., LIII, 1958. See also P. F. Vernon, *William Wycherley* (B.C.S., 1965).

ELKANAH SETTLE (1648-1724)

Elkanah Settle, Dryden's 'Doeg', was a prolific and popular dramatic author. Among his numerous works the most famous are perhaps the 'heroic' plays *Cambyses, King of Persia* (1670), *The Empress of Morocco* (pub. with 'sculptures' or engravings, 1673, the first illustrated English play), *Ibrahem* (1676), and *The Female Prelate Being the History of the Life and Death of Pope Joan* (1680). He also wrote the famous opera, *The Fairy Queen* (adapted from Shakespeare's M.N.D.), for Purcell's music, and, among other 'drolls' or puppet plays, *The Siege of Troy*, which was frequently performed at Bartholomew Fair and is represented in Hogarth's picture of *Bartholomew Fair* painted in 1733. There are modern edd. of *The Empress of Morocco* and *The Female Prelate* by M. Summers (1935). There is an ed. of *The Preface to 'Ibrahem'* by H. Macdonald (Luttrell Soc., 1947).

SIR JOHN VANBRUGH (1664-1726)

Vanbrugh's three comedies, *The Relapse or Virtue in Danger*, *Aesop* and *The Provok'd Wife* were all pub. in 4to edd. in 1697. His later works include three comedies, *The False Friend* (1702), *The Confederacy* (1705) and *The Mistake* (1706) with a fragment of a fourth *A Journey to London*, completed by Colley Cibber as *The Provoked Husband* (1728). He collaborated with Congreve and Walsh in an adaptation from Molière (see below) wrote two farces called *The Country House* and *The Cuckold in Conceit*, and adapted Fletcher's *The Pilgrim*, performed with Dryden's *Secular Masque* in 1700. Collected edd. of Vanbrugh's plays appeared in 1730 and at subsequent dates in the eighteenth century. There are also many edd. of separate plays which were often acted and altered. R. B. Sheridan adapted *The Relapse* under the title of *A Trip to Scarborough* (1793).

There are modern edd. of Vanbrugh's plays by W. C. Ward (2 vols., 1893), by A. E. H. Swain in the Mermaid Series. *The Complete Works*, ed. Bonamy Dobrée and G. Webb (4 vols., 1927-28) is the standard modern ed. The Provok'd Wife is rptd. in R.E.C., vol. IV, with a critical essay by A. Thaler.

Biography and Criticism

Early accounts of Vanbrugh's life are summarized in Baker's *Biographia Dramatica*. A valuable article on him by A. Ashpital appeared in the 8th ed. of the *Encylopaedia Britannica* (1860) and there is an important *Life* prefixed to Ward's ed. G. H. Lovegrove's *The Life, Work and Influence of Sir John Vanbrugh* (1902), deals mainly with his work as an architect. The best modern studies are Bonamy Dobrée's in *Essays in Biography* (1925) and Lawrence Whistler's in *Sir John Vanbrugh Architect and Dramatist* (1938). See also the critical notices by Leigh Hunt in his *Comic Dramatists of the Restoration*, Hazlitt in *English Comic Writers* and H. T. E. Perry in *The Comic Spirit in Restoration Comedy* (1925).

WILLIAM CONGREVE (1670-1729)

Works

William Congreve's five famous plays were pub. in the following order: *The Old Batchelor* (1693), *The Double Dealer* (1694), *Love for Love* (1695), *The Mourning Bride*, a tragedy (1697) and *The Way of the World* (1700). His later dramatic works are *The Masque of Paris* (1701), *Monsieur de Pourceaugnac or Squire Trelooby* (an adaptation from Molière made in collaboration with Walsh and Vanbrugh, 1704), and *Semele*, an opera (1710). His works were pub. in 3 vols. in 1710 and often as subsequent dates in the eighteenth century. Individual plays, especially *Love for Love*, *The Mourning Bride* and *The Way of the World* were often rptd. in the various dramatic collections. There is an ed. of the plays by A. C. Ewald in the Mermaid Series, another in 2 vols. with introd. by G. S. Street (1895) and of the complete works by M. Summers (4 vols., 1923). The best modern edd. are those of *The Comedies* by J. W. Krutch (N.Y., 1927) and of the *Works* by F. W. Bateson (1930) and by Bonamy Dobrée (2 vols., W.C.).

There are a number of separate modern edd. of *The Way of the World* including one by W. P. Barrett in the T.D. (1933) and an important one in R.E.C., Vol. IV. For Congreve's novel *Incognita* see p. 330.

Biography and Criticism

Sir E. Gosse's *Life of Congreve* with bibliography by J. P. Anderson first appeared in 1888 and again in a rev. ed. in 1924. There are more recent biographies by D. C. Taylor (1931) and J. C. Hodges (1941). See also the preface of Leigh Hunt to his ed. Palmer's study in *The Comedy of Manners*, the very suggestive remarks in Hazlitt's *Lectures on the English Comic Writers* and Meredith's *Essay on Comedy*, the prefaces in Dobrée's ed., the important essay by G. R. Noyes in Gayley and Thaler's *Representative English Comedies*, Vol. IV., and K. M. Lynch, *A Congreve Gallery* (Camb., Mass., 1951).

THOMAS SOUTHERNE (1660-1746)

Southerne's dramatic career begins with the tragedy of *The Loyal Brother or the Persian Prince* (1682). His comedy, *Sir Anthony Love or The Rambling Lady* appeared in 1690. His two most popular works were *The Fatal Marriage or the Innocent Adultery* (1694) and the tragedy, *Oronooko* (1695) founded on Aphra Behn's novel *The Royal Slave* (see p. 330). This play was frequently acted in the eighteenth century and was altered and adapted by David Garrick and Francis Gentleman. Collected edd. of Southerne's works appeared in 1721 (2 vols.) and 1774 (3 vols.). A modern ed. is needed. There is a study of Southerne by J. W. Dodds: *Thomas Southerne, Dramatist* (Yale, 1933).

CHAPTER XX
JOHN DRYDEN (1631-1700)

COLLECTIVE EDITIONS

THE first complete ed. of the works of Dryden in verse and prose was that of Sir Walter Scott (18 vols., 1808). It includes practically all Dryden's poetry, prose, plays and tr. with 'notes, historical, critical and explanatory', and Scott's *Life of Dryden*. A second ed. appeared in 1821. A rev. ed. of this work by G. Saintsbury was pub. at Edinburgh in 1882, and is known as the Scott-Saintsbury ed. A new complete ed. of *The Works of John Dryden* Gen. Editor, H. T. Swedenberg. It is now in process of publication by the University of California Press. Vol. I (Poetry) and VIII (first vol. of plays) have appeared up to date (1965).

COLLECTIONS OF POETRY

A very imperfect collection of Dryden's poems called *Poems on Various Occasions and Translations from Several Authors* was pub. by Tonson in a folio in 1701. In 1743 the same publisher printed *Original Poems and Translations by Dryden*, ed. T. Broughton. Other incomplete collections were pub. in the eighteenth century at Dublin and Glasgow. The most ambitious ed. of the eighteenth century was that of Samuel Derrick: *The Miscellaneous Works of John Dryden* (4 vols., 1760) with a Life and notes. It includes practically all the works in verse except the plays. The poetical works were included in various collections of the English poets such as those of Johnson (1790), Anderson (1793), Park (1806-08) and Chalmers (1810). A valuable ed. in 4 vols. with notes by Joseph and John Warton, designed to supplement Malone's ed. of the prose works appeared in 1811. Mitford edited Dryden's poems for the Aldine Series (5 vols., 1830, rptd. Boston, 1854), and a useful ed. by R. Bell appeared at Edinburgh in 1854. W. D. Christie's Globe ed. and J. Sargeaunt's Oxford ed. are both useful texts with valuable introds. A valuable 1 vol. ed. of the *Poetical Works* is that of G. R. Noyes (N.Y., 1909, rev. ed. 1950). This ed. includes biographical and critical introd. and a thoroughly reliable annotated text of all the poems and trs. with the orig. prose prefaces, etc. An admirable ed. on a large scale is that of J. Kinsley, *The Poems of John Dryden* (4 vols., 1958, 1 vol. ed. of *The Poems and Fables*, 1961).

SELECTIONS

The following are the most notable among the numerous selections from Dryden's works: *Dryden Poetry and Prose* ed. D. Nichol Smith (1925); *The Best of Dryden* ed. L. I. Dredvold (N.Y., 1933); *Poems of John Dryden* ed. B. Dobrée (Ev. Lib., 1934); *Poêmes Choisis* ed. P. Legouis (Paris, 1946; English text with French tr.); *Selected Poems* ed. G. Grigson (1950); *Poetry, Prose and Plays* ed. D. Grant (1952); *John Dryden* ed. D. Grant (P.B., 1960); *Selected Works* ed. W. Frost (P.B., N.Y., 1964).

INDIVIDUAL POETICAL WORKS

Dryden's chief poetical works were pub. at the following dates: *Lachrymae Musarum, The Tears of the Muses* (1649; a collection of elegies on Lord Hastings including Dryden's early lines *Upon the Death of Lord Hastings*); *Heroique Stanzas Consecrated to the Glorious Memory of his most Serene and Renowned Highnesse Oliver Late Lord Protector of this Common-Wealth* in *Three Poems Upon the Death of his late Highnesse Oliver Lord Protector* etc. (1659); *Astraea Redux. A Poem on the Happy Restoration & Return of his Sacred Majesty Charles the Second* (1660); *To his Sacred Majesty, A Panegyric on his Coronation* (1661); *To My Lord Chancellor presented on New-Years-day*

(1662); *To my Honour'd Friend, Dr. Charleton* (lines prefixed to Charleton's *Chorea Gigantum*, a book on Stonehenge, 1663); *Annus Mirabilis: The Year of Wonders, 1666, An Historical Poem* (1667, type facs., 1927); *Ovid's Epistles, translated by Several Hands* (1680) (tr. by Dryden and others); *Absalom and Achitophel, A Poem* (1681); *The Medall, A Satyre against Sedition* (1682, facs. rpt., 1924); *Prologue to his Royal Highness, Upon his first appearance at the Duke's Theatre since his Return from Scotland* (broadsheet, 1682); *To the Dutchess On her Return from Scotland* (broadsheet, 1682); *Mac Flecknoe, or a Satyr upon the True-Blew-Protestant Poet, T.S.* (1682; written in 1678); *The Second Part of Absalom and Achitophel, A Poem* (by Tate and Dryden, 1682); *Religio Laici or a A Laymans Faith, A Poem* (1682); *Miscellany Poems ... By the Most Eminent Hands* (1684); *Sylvae ... Or, the Second Part of Poetical Miscellanies* (1685); *Examen Poeticum: Being the Third Part of Miscellany Poems*(1693); *The Annual Miscellany: For the Year 1694. Being the Fouth Part of Miscellany Poems* (1694). (Four vols. of an anthology of contemporary verse orig. and tr. by Dryden and others; Tonson continued the series after Dryden's death, and the fifth and sixth parts appeared in 1704 and 1709 respectively. It is sometimes known as 'Dryden's' or 'Tonson's Miscellany'. *Examen Poeticum* [1693], the third of the miscellanies contains *A Song for St. Cecilia's Day*, 1687, it was printed as a broadside in 1687); *Threnodia Augustalis: A Funeral-Pindaric Poem Sacred to the Happy Memory of King Charles II* (1685); *To the Pious Memory of the Accomplisht Young Lady Mrs. Anne Killigrew* (in *Poems* by Mrs. Anne Killigrew, pub. after death, 1686); *The Hind and the Panther. A Poem, in Three Parts* (1687); *Britannia Rediviva: A Poem on the Birth of the Prince ...* (1688); *Eleanora A Panegyrical Poem* (1692); *The Satires of Decimus Junius Juvenalis. Translated into English Verse* (by Dryden, Tate, and others, 1662); *An Ode on the Death of Mr. Henry Purcell* (broadside, 1696); *The Works of Virgil: Containing His Pastorals, Georgics and Aeneis* (1697); *Alexander's Feast; or The Power of Music* (1697, facs. rpt., 1925); *Fables Ancient and Modern; Translated into Verse, from*

Homer, Ovid, Boccace, & *Chaucer: with Original Poems* (1700); *The Pilgrim, a Comedy . . . with several Additions. Likewise a Prologue, Epilogue, Dialogue and Masque Written by the late Great Poet Mr. Dryden* (1700; contains the famous 'Secular Masque' by Dryden written to celebrate the opening of the eighteenth century). Besides these poems Dryden also pub. numerous prologues and epilogues to plays by himself and other dramatists as well as songs and other verses, original and translated, in contemporary anthologies, etc. They will be found in the various collective edd. His notable epistle *To My Dear Friend Mr. Congreve* was prefixed to the first ed. of Congreve's *The Double Dealer* (1694, see above, p. 384). Henry Morley pub. a separate ed. of the *Fables* in *The Companion Poets* (1891), and J. C. Collins's ed. of *The Satires* appeared in 1893. There is a separate ed. of *Absalom of Achitophel,* ed. W. D. Christie, rev. C. H. Firth (1911), an ed. of *The Songs of John Dryden* (with facs. of contemporary musical settings), ed. C. L. Day (Harvard, 1932) and an ed. of *The Prologues and Epilogues* ed. W. B. Gardner (N.Y., 1951).

PLAYS

Dryden's first play to be acted (1662-63) was a comedy, *The Wild Gallant* (pub. 1669). His tragi-comedy, *The Rival Ladies,* was acted and pub. in 1664. His heroic tragedies begin with *The Indian Emperour, or the Conquest of Mexico,* acted 1665 pub. 1667, a sequel to *The Indian Queen,* in which Dryden collaborated with Howard (see p. 381). It was followed by *Secret Love, or The Maiden-Queen* (1667), the two comedies *Sir Martin Mar-all, or The Feigned Innocence* (1667), and *An Evening's Love, or The Mock Astrologer* (acted 1668, pub. 1671). His second heroic tragedy *Tyrannick Love, or The Royal Martyr,* was acted in 1669, and pub. in 1670, and the two parts of *The Conquest of Granada* (acted 1670-71) were pub. in 1672. In 1670 was pub. *The Tempest, or the Enchanted Island,* the adaptation by Dryden and Davenant (acted 1667). The comedies, *Marriage à la Mode,* and *The Assignation or Love in a Nunnery*, were both acted in 1672 and pub. in 1673. *Amboyna*, the topical 'tragedy', was acted and pub. in 1763. *Aurung-Zebe*, the last of Dryden's heroic riming tragedies, was acted in 1675 and pub. in 1676, and the unacted opera based on *Paradise Lost* called *The State of Innocence*, was pub. in 1677. In the same year Dryden's greatest tragedy, *All for Love; or The World Well Lost*, was first acted (pub. 1678). His comedy, *The Kind Keeper*, or *Mr. Limberham*, was acted 1677-78 and pub. 1680. *Oedipus*, the first play in which Dryden collaborated with Lee (see p. 379) was acted and pub. in 1679, and his adaptation of *Troilus and Cressida* in the same year. The comedy called *The Spanish Fryar or the Double Discovery*, appeared in 1681 (acted 1679-80), and *The Duke of Guise*, the second play by Dryden and Lee in 1683 (acted 1682). Dryden's first attempt at an opera was *Albion and Albanius*, acted and pub. in 1685. His first play to be produced after the Revolution was the tragedy *Don Sebastian, King of Portugal* (acted 1689, pub. 1690). His last comedy, *Amphitryon; or the two Socias*, was acted and pub. in 1690, with music for the songs by H. Purcell. *King Arthur: or The British Worthy*, a *Dramatic Opera*, appeared in 1691, and *Cleomenes, The Spartan Heroe, a Tragedy*, in 1692. Dryden's last play was *Love Triumphant; or, Nature Will Prevail* (1694). In 1701 appeared *The Comedies, Tragedies, and Operas written by John Dryden, Esq.*, in two folio vol. pub. Tonson. Congreve's ed. of *The Dramatick Works* in 6 vols. was first pub. in 1717 and rptd. 1735 and 1762. The chief plays of Dryden to hold the stage in the eighteenth and early nineteenth centuries were *All for Love, Oedipus, The Spanish Fryar, Don Sebastian* and *Amphitryon*. These plays were often rptd., sometimes in altered forms, in the dramatic collections.

All Dryden's plays were rptd. by Scott in his ed. and again in the Scott-Saintsbury ed. There is a good selection with introd. by Saintsbury in the Mermaid Series (2 vols.), a valuable ed. of *Selected Dramas of John Dryden with the Rehearsal* ed. G. R. Noyes (Chicago and N.Y., 1910), and a complete ed. of the *Dramatic Works*, ed. M. Summers (6 vols., 1931-32).

All for Love is included in F. Tupper's *Representative British Dramas from Dryden to Sheridan* and other modern collections. There are separate edd. by W. A. Clarke, Jr. (San Francisco, 1929, a facs. of the Bridgewater copy of the first ed.). There is a valuable ed. of *The Spanish Fryar* in R.E.C., vol. IV.

PROSE WORKS

Dryden's most important prose work to be pub. separately was his famous *Essay of Dramatic Poesy*, pub. in 1668, with the title *Of Dramatick Poesie, An Essay by John Dryden, Esq*. His other important critical works all took the form of essays, pub. with his own poems, plays, and translations. Among the most notable of these are the Preface to *Annus Mirabilis* (1667), 'A Defence of An Essay of Dramatic Poesy' prefixed to the second ed. of the *Indian Emperour* (1668); 'Of Heroic Plays, An Essay' prefixed to the *Conquest of Granada* (1672); 'Defence of the Epilogue, Or, An Essay on the Dramatique Poetry of the last Age' printed at the end of the Second Part of *The Conquest of Granada* (1672); 'The Author's Apology for Heroique Poetry and Poetique' prefixed to *The State of Innocence* (1677); 'The Grounds of Criticism in Tragedy' prefixed to *Troilus and Cressida* (1679); The Preface to *Sylvae* (or the 'Second Miscellany', 1685); the Dedication of *Examen Poeticum* (or the 'Third Miscellany', 1693); 'A Discourse Concerning the Original and Progress of Satire' (prefixed to the tr. of Juvenal, 1693); 'A Parallel of Poetry and Painting' (prefixed to Dryden's prose version of Du Fresnoy's *De Arte Graphica*, 1695); and the Preface to the *Fables*, perhaps Dryden's most notable critical preface (1700). His other prose works are mostly controversial pieces or trs. They include *Notes and Observations on the Empress of Morocco* (the joint work of Dryden, Shadwell and Crowne, and attack on Settle, 1674), *His Majesties Declaration Defended* (1681), ed. G. Davies, Los Angeles, 1950); 'The Life of Plutarch' (prefixed to a tr. of Plutarch's *Lives*, 1683); *The History of the League*, tr. from the French of Maimbourg (1684);

A Defence of Papers Written by the Late King, etc. (a controversial Essay directed against Stillingfleet, the Anglican divine, 1686); *The Life of Saint Francis Xavier*, tr. from the French of Bouhours (1688); A 'Character of St. Evremont', prefixed to *Miscellany Essays of Monsieur St. Evremont* (1692); *The Art of Painting*, tr. from a French version of Du Fresnoy's Latin poem *De Arte Graphica* (1695); *The Life of Lucian* (prefixed to a tr. projected by Dryden and finally pub. in 1711). Dr. Johnson printed in his *Life of Dryden* valuable MS. notes made by Dryden on Thomas Rymer's *Remarks on the Tragedies of the last Age*; these had already appeared in *The Works of M. Francis Beaumont and M. John Fletcher* (7 vols., 1711).

The first collective ed. of Dryden's Prose Works was that of Edmond Malone: *The Critical and Miscellaneous Works of John Dryden* (3 vols. in 4, 1800). It includes all Dryden's pub. prose works, his letters and Malone's life. Important modern edd. are *Essays of John Dryden*, selected and ed. W. P. Ker (2 vols., 1900), and *Dryden Of Dramatic Poesy and Other Critical Essays* ed. G. Watson (2 vols., Ev. Lib., 1962). *Dryden and Howard, 1664–1668*, ed. D. D. Arundell (1929) includes the text of *The Essays of Dramatic Poesy* and other controversial matter by Dryden and Howard. There are many small modern collections of his prose works and edd. of *The Preface to the Fables*, ed. A. Mawer (Tutorial Series), in O.P.T., and ed. W. H. Williams (1908). H. Morley pub. an ed. of *The Discourses on Satire and Epic Poetry* (1888), and there is an ed. of *The Defence of an Essay on Dramatic Poetry* by A. Mawer (1910). A finely printed ed. of *An Essay of Dramatic Poesy* (1928) is preceded by T. S. Eliot's *Dialogue on Poetic Drama*. The *Letters* ed. C. E. Ward were pub. at Durham, N.C., in 1942.

BIOGRAPHY AND CRITICISM

There is a short account of Dryden by Congreve in his dedication to the Duke of Newcastle of *The Dramatick Works*

(1717) and a perfunctory life in *Lives of the Poets* (1753; attrib. to T. Cibber, really by R. Shiels). Dr. Johnson's famous life in his *Lives of the Poets* (1783) is notable both as biography and criticism. E. Malone's 'Life of Dryden' prefixed to his ed. of *The Critical and Miscellaneous Works* (1800), though not well written, is also of the highest value. Sir Walter Scott's *Life of John Dryden* occupies the first vol. of his ed. (1808) and is a fine, sane, scholarly work. George Saintsbury contributed a characteristic monograph to E.M.L. (1881). More recent biographies are K. Young, *John Dryden, a Critical Biography* (1934); A. M. Crinò, *John Dryden Poeta Satirico* (Florence, 1957; in Italian) and C. E. Ward's very full, accurate, if somewhat pedestrian, *The Life of John Dryden* (Chapel Hill, N.C., 1961).

Among contemporary criticisms of Dryden the most notable are those of Thomas Rymer in his Preface to the tr. of *Rapin's Reflections on Aristotle's Treatise on Poesie* (1674), of Gerard Langbaine in his *Account of the English Dramatick Poets* (1691) and of Rochester in his *Allusion to the Tenth Satyr of the first book of Horace* (? 1677). Early eighteenth-century opinions are to be found in Addison's *Poem to Mr. Dryden*, his *Account of the Ancient English Poets*, and his allusions in the *Spectator*, *Tatler* and *Guardian*, and also in Voltaire's *Lettres Philosophiques* and his *Siècle de Louis Quatorze*, but no elaborate critical survey appeared till the appearance of Johnson's *Life*, which is also a critical essay of the highest importance. Goldsmith in his 'Poetical Scale' in the *Literary Magazine* for 1758 gave Dryden 18 marks for genius, 16 for judgment, 17 for learning, and 18 for versification, while Pope receives 18, 18, 15 and 19, Milton 18, 16, 17 and 18, and Shakespeare 19, 14, 14 and 19. Wordsworth's remarks in his *Essay Supplementary to the Preface to Lyrical Ballads* represent the reaction against Dryden's methods in the early eighteenth century, but he was ably defended by Scott in his *Life*, by Hazlitt in his *Lectures on the English Poets* and by Byron in *Don Juan*. Macaulay's Essay appeared as a review of an ed. of Dryden's poems in the *Edinburgh Review* in 1828. One of the fairest and most thoughtful studies of the nineteenth century was the essay by James Russell Lowell in *My Study Windows* (1871). Some of the best modern criticism of Dryden is to be found in A. W. Verrall's *Lectures on Dryden* (1914). The best critical monographs of the twentieth century are A. W. Verrall, *Lectures on Dryden* (1914), M. Van Doren's very valuable *Dryden: a Study of his Poetry* (N.Y., 1920, rev. ed. 1946) and D. Nichol Smith's Clark Lectures, *Dryden* (1950). Important shorter studies are those of Sir W. Raleigh, 'Dryden's Political Satire' in *Some Authors* (1923), T. S. Eliot in *Homage to John Dryden* (1924), C. S. Lewis in *Rehabilitations* (1939) and E. M. W. Tillyard in *Five Poems* (1948). For an adverse view see R. Bridges, 'Dryden on Milton' in his *Collected Essays*, X (1932). The following are some notable works dealing with special aspects of Dryden's work and life: L. I. Bredvold, *The Intellectual Milieu of John Dryden* (Ann Arbor, 1934), a masterly study of the philosophic background of Dryden's poetry; N. B. Allen, *The Sources of Dryden's Comedies* (Ann Arbor, 1938); P. Legouis, 'Corneille and Dryden as Dramatic Critics' in *Seventeenth Century Studies Presented to Sir H. Grierson* (1938); J. M. Osborn, *Dryden: Some Biographical Facts and Problems* (N.Y., 1940); F. L. Huntley, *On Dryden's Essay of Dramatic Poesy* (Ann Arbor, 1951); W. Frost, *Dryden and the Art of Translation* (Yale, 1955); J. Söderlind, *Verb Syntax in Dryden's Prose* (Uppsala, 1951-58).

BIBLIOGRAPHIES

The standard bibliography is H. Macdonald, *Dryden: a Bibliography of Early Editions and Drydeniana* (1939). It is supplemented by J. M. Osborn in 'Macdonald's Bibliography of Dryden: an Annotated Check-List of Selected American Libraries', M.P., XXXIX, 1951. See also S. H. Monk, *Dryden: a List of Critical Studies, 1895-1948* (Minneapolis, 1950), supplemented by W. R. Keast in M.P., XLVIII, 1951.

INDEX

Index to proper names in the Introduction and to names of Authors and books (where these receive separate treatment) in the Students' Guide to Reading. Figures in italic type refer to pages in the Guide.

A

Abercrombie, Lascelles, 97
Academic Plays, *224–7, 235*
Adlington, William, *186*
Alexander VI, Pope, 38
Alexander, Sir William, *226*
Alleyn, Edward, 56–7
Ammianus Marcellinus (translation), *185*
Amurath III, 44
Amyot, Jacques, 49, *179*
Andrews, H., 110n.
Andrewes, Bishop Lancelot, 71, *270–1*
Apuleius (translation), *186*
Aquinas, St Thomas, 1
Ariosto, 12, 47, 51, (translations), *189–90*
Aristotle, 2, (translations), *178, 181*
Armado, 34
Armin, Robert, 113
Arthur, King, 48
Arthur, Prince (Tudor), 6, 17
Arthur, Prince, 52
Ascham, Roger, 31, 49, *146–7, 188, 245*
Ashley Cooper, Anthony, 1st Earl of Shaftesbury, 78, 100
Ashmore, John, *183*
Aubrey, John, 102, *326*
Augustine, St (translations), *186*
Authorized Version, see Bible Translations
Autolycus, 106

B

Bacon, Francis, 37, 80, 83–5, 90, *244–5, 281–3*
Bacon, Roger, 83
Baïf, Jean Antoine de, 126
Bajazeth, 58

Baldwin, William, 47, 117n., *165, 170–1*
Bale, Bishop, *223*
Ballads, *217–18*
Bandello (translations), *187–8*
Banister, J., 110
Barclay, Alexander, 185
Bardi, Count, 126
Barker, Granville, 56
Barrow, Isaac, *337*
Baxter, Richard, 73, 82, 103, *339*
Beaumont, Francis, 87, *306–8*
Beaumont, Sir John, 183
Bede (translation), *186*
Bedinfield, Thomas, *189*
Behn, Aphra, *330, 378–9*
Belleforest (translation), *188*
Belvedere or the Garden of the Muses, *203*
Bembo, Pietro, 11, 13
Bernard, R., *184*
Berners, Lord, see Bourchier, J.
Bibiena, Bernardo, 11
Bible Translations, 24–6, 86, *157–160, 332–4*
Bidle, J., *182*
Billingsley, H., *181*
Blake, William, 83, 89, 97
Blow, John, 112
Boccaccio, 47, (translations) *187–8*
Boethius, 106
Boiardo (translation), *189*
Boileau, 93
Boleyn, Anne, 16, 18, 22, 30
Bolton, Edmund, *193*
Bossuet, 75
Bottom, 105
Bourchier, John, Lord Berners, *191*
Boyle, Robert, 92
Boyle, Roger, Earl of Orrery, *330, 376–7*

395

INDEX

Bradford, John, *187*
Bramhall, Bishop, 92, *286*
Breton, Nicholas, 36, *242-3*, *329*
Brinsley, J., *182*
Britton, Thomas, 110
Brome, Richard, *317*
Brooke, Lord, see Greville, Fulke and Greville, Robert
Browne, Sir Thomas, 85-6, 91, *320-1*
Browne, William of Tavistock, *217*
Brutus of Troy, 48
Bryan, Sir Francis, 10
Bryskett, Lodowick, *189*
Buckhurst, Lord, see Sackville, Charles
Buckingham, Dukes of, see Villiers, George
Bunyan, John, 28, 73, 77, 103, *339-40*
Burbage, James, 56-7, 112
Burbage, Richard, 56-7, 60
Burnet, Gilbert, 95, 101-2, *325*
Burton, Robert, 82, *319*
Butler, Samuel, 100, *302-3*, *329*
Byrd, William, 67, 122
Byron, Duke of, 64
Byron, Lord, 13

C

Cabot, John, 8, 38
Cabot, Sebastian, 39
Caccini, 127
Caesar, Julius (translations), *186*
Calvin, John, 29, 75
Camarata, The, 126-7
Cambridge Platonists, 92, 102, *287-92*
Camden, William, 40, *187*, *197-8*
Campeggio, Cardinal, 17
Campion, Thomas, 67, 114, 124-7, *183*, *204*, *216-17*, *246*
Candish, R., *181*
Carew, Sir Peter, 108
Carew, Richard, *189*
Carew, Thomas, 80, 128, *343-4*
Carlisle, Bishop of, 62
Cartwright, Thomas, *273-4*

Cary, Lucius, Lord Falkland, 73, 80
Casaubon, Meric, *181*
Case, J., 104n
Castiglione, Baldassare, 11, 20, 107, 119, (translation), *188*
Catherine of Aragon, 16, 17, 29
Catullus (translations), *183-4*
Cavendish, George, *194*
Cecil, Sir William, 30, 32, 40
Cervantes (translations), *190*
Chaloner, Sir Thomas, *186*
Chambers, Sir E. K., 69n.
Chambers, R. W., 21
Chancellor, Richard, 39
Chapman, George, 64-5, *178-9*, *215-16*, *309-10*
'Characters', *329-30*
Charles I, 72-5, 78, 95
Charles II, 76-8, 91, 94, 98
Charles V (Emperor), 17
Charnock, Prior Richard, 4
Chaucer, Geoffrey, 1, 3, 11-14, 47, 50-3, 116
Cheke, Sir John, 31, 46, *145*
Chillingworth, William, 73
Churchyard, Thomas, *171*
Cibber, Colley, *374*
Cinthio, Giraldi (translation), *188*
Clarendon, Lord, see Hyde, Edward
Claudian (translation), *184*
Clement VII, Pope, 17
Cleveland, John, *302*
Cobb, John, 128n
Coleridge, S. T., 7
Colet, John, 4, 7, 21, *144*
Columbus, 3, 4, 8
Common Prayer, Book of, 26-7, *161*
Congreve, William, 66, 103, *384-5*
Cope, Anthony, *185*
Corbett, Richard, Bishop, *301*
Cortez, 37
Costard, 61
Cotton, Charles, *331*, *349*
Courte of Venus, The, *149*
Courville, Thibaut de, 126
Coverdale, Miles, 24, 26, *159-60*

INDEX

Cowley, Abraham, 94, 99, 102, 129, *299–300, 322, 375*
Cranmer, Thomas, Archbishop, 24, 26, 27, 29, 31–2, *160–1*
Crashaw, Richard, 82, *297*
Creech, Thomas, *184*
Cromwell, Oliver, 73–4, 77, 87, 99, 110
Cromwell, Thomas, 20, 23, 31
Crowley, Robert, 5
Crowne, John, *381*
Cudworth, Ralph, 102, *289–90*
Culverwel, Nathaniel, *289*

D

Dacres, Edward, *189*
Danby, Earl of, see Osborne, Thomas
Danett, Thomas, *191*
Daniel, John, 112, 124
Daniel, Samuel, *211–12, 246*
Dante, 12, 47, 115
Davenant, Sir William, 87, 94, 111, *347–8, 375–6*
Davies, John, 39
Davison, Francis, *204*
Davison, Walter, *204*
Davison's Poetical Rhapsody, 204
Day, Angel, *181*
Defoe, Daniel, 103
Dekker, Thomas, 64, *242, 316*
Deloney, Thomas, 105, *240*
Demosthenes, 2, (translations), *180–1*
Denham, Sir John, 94, *182, 348–9*
Descartes, Réné, 90, 92–3, 99
Desdemona, 113
Devereux, Robert, Earl of Essex, 42
Digges, Leonard, *184*
Dolman, John, *185*
Donne, John, 69–70, 80–3, 85, 88, 91, *294–5, 334–5*
Dorset, Earl of, see Sackville, Charles, and Sackville, Thomas
Douglas, Gavin, 16
Dowland, John, 67, 124, 127, *204*

Dowland, Robert, 127
Drake, Sir Francis, 41, 42, 50, 56–57, 70
Drant, Thomas, *183*
Drayton, Michael, *212–13*
Drolleries, 342
Drummond, William, *213–14*
Dryden, John, 98–102, 111
 Collective edd, *386–7*
 Poems, *387–8*
 Plays, *389–91*
 Prose, *391–2*
 Biography, Criticism, etc. *392–4*
Du Bartas (translation), *192*
Du Bellay, 50–1, (translations), *192, 207*
Dudley, Robert, Earl of Leicester, 35, 36, 49, 52, 60
Dymock, Edward, *190*

E

Earle, John, *329*
Eden, Richard, *200*
Edward III, 24
Edward, IV, 4
Edward, VI, 26–9, 32
Edwards, Richard, 55, 109, *226*
E.K., 51
Elderton, William, 105
Eldred, John, 42–3
Eliot, T. S., 83, 91
Elizabeth I, 16, 30–7, 40, 44, 47, 51–2, 56, 71–2, 105, 108, *185*
Elyot, Sir Thomas, 107, *145, 177–8*
England's Helicon, 203
England's Parnassus, 203
Epictetus (translations), *181*
Erasmus, 4, 6, 8, 12, 18, 23, 28, 50, 77, *141* (translations), *186–7*
Etherege, Sir George, 77, 102, *379*
Euclid (translations), *181*
Euripides (translations), *178*
Evelyn, John, 76n., 102, *328*

F

Fabyan, Robert, *193*
Fairfax, Edward, *189*

398 INDEX

Fairfax, Sir Thomas, 74
Falkland, Lord, see Cary, Lucius
Falstaff, 62, 105
Fanshawe, Sir Richard, *182–3*, *190*
Farrant, Richard, 112
Faustus, Doctor, 83
Feiling, Keith, 74
Fenton, Sir Geoffrey, 49, *187–8*
Ferrabosco, Alfonso, 111, 127
Feste, 113
Ficino, Marsilio, 2
Fish, Simon, 19, 20, *157*
Fisher, Saint John (Bishop), 8, 22, *143–4*
Fitch, Ralph, 42–3
Fleming, Abraham, *182*
Fletcher, Francis, *201*
Fletcher, Giles, *214*
Fletcher, John, 87, *306–8*
Fletcher, Phineas, *214*
Florio, John, *191*
Fontenelle, Bernard de, 90
Ford, John, 87, *314–15*
Forde, Emmanuel, *240–1*
Fortescue, Thomas, *190*
Fox, George, 28, 75, 103, *340–1*
Foxe, John, 29, *156*
Francis, St, 1
Fuggers, The, 4
Fuller, Thomas, *335*

G

Gale, Thomas, *181*
Galen (translation), *181*
Gascoigne, George, 46–7, *171–3*, *178*, *225*
Gentillet, Innocent (translation), *191*
Gilbert, Sir Humphrey, *200*
Glanville, Joseph, 102, *292*
Golding, Arthur, *182*, *186*
Googe, Barnabe, *174*
Gorges, Sir Arthur, *184*
Gorgious Gallery of gallant Inventions, A, 46, *169*
Gosson, Stephen, 105n., *245*
Grabut, Louis, 76
Grafton, Richard, *178*, *196*

Grantham, Henry, *188*
Great Bible, The, 26, *159*
Green, J. R., 21
Greene, Robert, 57, 60, *230–1*, *238–239*
Greneway, Richard, *186*
Greville, Fulke, Lord Brooke, *214–215*, *226*
Greville, Robert, Lord Brooke, *283–4*
Grey, Lady Jane, 29
Grey, Bishop William, 6
Grierson, Sir Herbert, 89n., 103
Grimald, Nicholas, *154–5*, *185*
Grindal, William, 31
Grocin, William, 4
Guarini (translations), *189–90*
Guazzo, Stephen (translation), *189*
Guevara, Antonio (translation), *190*

H

Habington, William, *302*
Hakluyt, Richard, 43, *198–9*
Halifax, Marquis of, see Savile, George
Hall, Arthur, *178*
Hall, Edward, 48, *193–4*
Hall, Joseph, *329*
Hamlet, 62
Handeful of pleasant delites, A, *168*
Handel, George Frederick, 129
Harborne, Sir William, 43
Harington, Sir John, the elder, *174*
Harington, Sir John, *189*
Hariot, Thomas, *201*
Harrington, James, *286–7*
Harvey, Gabriel, 50, 52, *246*
Hawes, Stephen, 10, 13, 51
Hawkins, Sir John, 41, 42, *200*
Hawkins, Sir Richard, *200*
Hawkins, Sir Thomas, *183*
Head, Richard, *331*
Healey, John, *186*
Heliodorus (translation), *181*
Henry VII, 4, 6, 7, 11, 19, 22, 31

INDEX

Henry VIII, 6-7, 9-12, 16-18, 20-4, 26, 28-9, 31-2, 34, 36, 54
Henry, Prince, 127
Herbert, George, 73, 82, 85-6, 89, *295-7*
Herbert, Lord, of Cherbury, 118, *283, 297, 324*
Herodotus (translations), *180*
Herrick, Robert, 80-1, 86, *345-6*
Hervet, Gentian, *178*
Heywood, Jasper, 55, *184*
Heywood, John, 10, 55, *223-4*
Heywood, Thomas, *315*
Hill, Abraham, *337*
Hippocrates (translations), *181*
Hobbes, Thomas, 90-3, 99, 101, *284-6*
Hoby, Sir Thomas, 107n., *188*
Holbein, Hans, 38
Holinshed, Raphael, 48, 61, *194-5*
Holland, Philemon, *180, 185-7*
Holyband, C., 109n.
Homer, 16, 51, 100, (translations), *178-9*
Homilies, First Book of, 27, *160*
Hooker, Richard, 37, 73-4, 77, 86, *274-5*
Hooper, Bishop John, 32
Horace, 16, (translations), *183*
Howard, Henry, Duke of Norfolk, 23
Howard, Henry, Earl of Surrey, 10, 15, 23, 30, 46, 55, 117, *148-51, 153-4, 181*
Howard, Sir Robert, *381*
Howell, Thomas, *174, 182*
Hughes, Thomas, *226*
Hutchinson, Lucy, *326*
Hyde, Edward, Earl of Clarendon, 80, 94, 102, *324-5*,

J

James I, 60, 71-2, 80-1, 112
James II, 78
Jenkinson, Anthony, 39
Jerome, St, 25

Jewel, Bishop John, 271-2
John of Gaunt, 61
Johnson, Samuel, 80, 83
Jones, Inigo, 111
Jones, Robert, 112
Jonson, Ben, 59, 66, 80, 111, 127, 129, *183, 216, 304-6, 319*
Julius II, Pope, 17

K

Kemp, Will, 105
King, Bishop Henry, *301-2*
Kinwhelmersh, Francis, 178, 225
Kirkman, Francis, *331*
Kyd, Thomas, 60, *189, 231-2*
Kyffin, Maurice, *184*

L

Langland, William, 28
Lanier, Nicholas, 111
Latimer, Hugh, 5, 24, 27, 29, 32, *159*
Laud, Archbishop William, 74-5, 82
Lawes, Henry, 128, *355*
Lawes, William, 128
Lawrence, D. H., 89
Lee, Nathaniel, *379-80, 390*
Leeds, William, 42
Leicester, Earl of, see Dudley, Robert
Leishman, J. B., 82
Lejeune, Claude, 126
Leland, John, *197*
Lely, Sir Peter, 76
L'Estrange, Sir Roger, *331*
Livy (translations), *185*
Lloyd, Humfry, *181*
Locke, John, 78-9
Lodge, Thomas, *234, 239, 245*
Lollards, 24-5
Longus (translation), *181*
Louis XIV, 79
Lovelace, Richard, 118, *345*
Lowe, Peter, *181*
Lucan (translations), *184*
Lucretius (translations), *184*
Lully, Jean Baptiste 76, 111

Luther, Martin, 18, 24
Lydgate, John, 13, 47, 51
Lyly, John, 60, *228–9*, 237

M

Mabbe, James, *190*
Machaut, Guillaume de, 116
Machiavelli, Niccolo, 20
Mackenzie, Sir George, *330*
Magellan, Ferdinand, 38
Marco Polo, 39
Marcus Aurelius (translation), *181*
Markham, Jervis, *215*
Marlowe, Christopher, 57–60, *183–4*, *215*, *228–30*
'Marprelate', 'Martin', *275–7*
Marston, John, 64, *312–13*
Martial, 16, (translations) *181*
Marvell, Andrew, 100, *300–301*
Mary I, 28–31, 47, 108
Mary, Queen, of Scots, 33
Masque, The, *318*
Massinger, Philip, 64, 83, *313–14*
Masuccio (translation), *187*
Matthew, Sir Tobie, *186*
Maudit, Jacques, 126
Maynard, Sir John, 80
Medici, The, 3
Medici, Guiliano di, 11
Medwall, Henry, 9, *222*
Melville, Sir James, 108
Mendoza, Diego Hurtado de (translation), *190*
Mercutio, 61
Mexia, Pedro (translations), *187*, *190*
Middleton, Thomas, 64, 87, *311–12*
Milton, John, 67, 75, 77, 86–9, 95–8, 103, *354–72*
  Collective editions, *354*
  Manuscripts, *354–5*
  Early Poems, *355–60*
  Paradise Lost, *360–1*
  Paradise Regained and *Samson Agonistes*, *361*
  Prose, *361–7*
  Biography, Criticism, etc., *367–372*

Mirror for Magistrates, A, 47, 50, 55, *165–6*
Monk, General George, 76
Montaigne, Michel de, 82, 83, 85, 90, (translations), *191*, *331*
Montemayor, Jorge (translation), *190*
More, Henry, 102, *290–1*
More, Sir Thomas, 4, 5, 8–10, 16, 21, 23, 30, 32, 45, 50, *141–3*, *222*
More, William, 118
Morley, Lord, see Parker, Henry
Morley, Thomas, 123
Morton, Cardinal, 6, 9
Motteux, Peter, *331*
Mountjoy, Lord, 6
Mulcaster, Richard, 50–1
Munday, Anthony, *234–5*, *241*

N

Nashe, Thomas, *234*, *239–40*
Navagero, Andrea, 11
Nevyle, Alexander, *184*
Newbery, John, 42
Newman, Cardinal John Henry, 26
Newton, Sir Isaac, 103
Newton, Thomas, *184*
Nichols, Philip, *201*
Nicolls, Thomas, *178*
Norfolk, Duke of, see Howard, Henry
North, Roger, 109, *327*
North, Sir Thomas, 48–9, *179–80*, *189–90*
Norths, Lives of the, 102, *327*
Norton, Thomas, 55, 61–2, *225*
Notari, Angelo, 127
Nuce, Thomas, *184*

O

Odoric of Pordenone, 39
Oldham, John, 101, *353*
Osborne, Dorothy (Lady Temple), *328–9*
Osborne, Thomas, Earl of Danby, 78

INDEX

Othello, 62
Otway, Thomas, *377*
Overbury, Sir Thomas, *329*
Ovid (translations), *182–3*

P

Painter, William, *187*
Palace of Pleasure, The, *187*
Paradise of daynty devises, The, 46, 117, *169*
Parker, Archbishop Matthew, 48, 50, *196–7*
Parker, Henry, Lord Morley, *189*
Parker, Martin, 105
Parker Society's Publications, The, *156*
Parnassus, England's, 170, *203*
Parnassus Plays, The, 105, *235*
Patrick, Simon, *192*
Paynell, Thomas, *187*
Peele, George, 112, *232–3*
Pembroke, Countess of, *226*
Penn, William, 102, *341*
Pepys, Samuel, 102, 110, *327–8*
Petrarch, 12, 13, 15, 115, 123, (translations), *189*
Pettie, George, *237*
Phaer, Thomas, *182*
Philip II, 29
Philips, Katherine, *349–50*
Phoenix Nest, The, *203*
Pizarro, 37,
Pius V, Pope, 33
Plato, 2, *181*
Plautus, 54 (translations), *184*
Plutarch, 61–2, (translations), *179–80*
Pliny (translations), *186*
Pollard, A. W., 25
Polybius (translations), *180*
Prayer-book, see *Common Prayer, Book of*
Preston, Thomas, *226*
Prince, The (Il Principe), 20
Prynne, William, 86
Ptolemy, 1
Purcell, Henry, 111
Purchas, Samuel, *199–200*

Puttenham, George, 11, 15, 118, 125, *246*
Pynson, Richard, 15

Q

Quarles, Francis, *299*
Quince, Peter, 105

R

Rabelais, François (translation), *331*
Ralegh, Sir Walter, 37, 42, 49, 68–9, *201*, *210*, *243–4*
Randolph, Thomas, 80, *344–5*
Rastell, William, 9, 30, 54, *143*, *222*
Redford, John, *222*
Return from Parnassus, The, see *Parnassus Plays*
Richard II, 24
Rider, Henry, *183*
Robin Hood Plays, *227*
Rochester, Earl of, see Wilmot, John
Rojas, Fernando de (translation), *190*
Ronsard, Pierre, 50, 119–20, (translations), *192*
Rosseter, Philip, 112, *216*
Rowland, David, *190*
Rowlands, Samuel, *243*
Ruskin, John, 26, 89

S

Sackville, Charles, Lord Buckhurst, later Earl of Dorset, 94, *352–3*
Sackville, Thomas, Earl of Dorset, 47, 53, 55, *166*, *174–5*, *225*
Safiyeh, Sultana, 44
Sagudino, 109
Sallust (translation), *185–6*
Sanderson, Bishop Robert, 86
Sandys, George, *183*
Sanford, J., *181*
Savile, George, Marquis of Halifax, 102, *323*
Savile, Sir Henry, *186*

Sedley, Sir Charles, 94, 102, 350, 381
Selden, John, 80, 319-20
Seneca, 54, (translations), 184-6
Settle, Elkanah, 383
Shadwell, Thomas, 102, 111, 380
Shaftesbury, Earl of, see Ashley Cooper, Anthony
Shakespeare, William, 5, 13, 37, 44, 48, 50, 56, 60-4, 86-7, 91, 112-14, 248-69
  Collective edd., 248-52
  Plays, 252-4
  Poems, 254-7
  Doubtful and Apocryphal Plays, 257-9
  Life and Personality, 259-61
  Criticism, etc., 261-9
Shelton, Thomas, 190
Shirley, James, 317
Sidney, Sir Philip, 15, 23, 33, 46, 49, 53-4, 58, 118, 205-6, 238, 245
Skelton, John, 10, 177, 223
Smith, John (Platonist), 77, 102, 289
Smith, John, Captain, 201
Songes and Sonettes, see *Tottel's Miscellany*
Song-Books, Elizabethan, 204-5
Sophocles, 2, 88
South, Robert, 337-8
Southerne, Thomas, 385
Southwell, Robert, 210-11
Speed, John, 196
Spenser, Edmund, 23, 37, 45, 47, 50-4, 58, 60, 70, 88, 207-9
Sprat, Thomas, 92, 93n., 94, 326
Stanley, Thomas, 287, 349
Stanyhurst, Richard, 182
Stapleton, Thomas, 186
Stapylton, Robert, 182
Starkey, Thomas, 145
Sterry, Peter, 86, 291-2
Stony, John, 42
Stow, John, 48, 195-6
Strafford, Earl of, see Wentworth, Thomas
Straparola (translation), 187
Studley, John, 184

Suckling, Sir John, 80, 118, 344
Suetonius (translation), 185
Surrey, Earl of, see Howard, Henry
Swift, Jonathan, 63
Sylvester, Joshua, 192

T

Tacitus (translations), 186
Tamburlaine, 58
Tasso (translations), 189
Tavener, Richard, 187
Tawney, R. H., 73n.
Taylor, Jeremy, 73, 75, 336-7
Temple, Sir William, 102, 322-3
Terence, 54, (translations), 184
Theocritus, 51, (translation), 179
Thorne, Robert, 39
Thucydides (translations), 178, 180
Tillotson, Archbishop John, 102, 338
Tiptoft, John, Earl of Worcester, 6, 185
Tofte, Robert, 189
Tottel, Richard, 30
Tottel's Miscellany (Songes and Sonettes), 30, 150-1
Tourneur, Cyril, 310-11
Traherne, Thomas, 82, 298
Translations, 177-92, 331
Trissino, Giovanni, 11, 245
Tudor Translations, The, 177
Tuke, Sir Samuel, 376
Tusser, Thomas, 175-6
Twyne, Thomas, 182
Tyndale, William, 18, 24-6, 157-8

U

Udall, Nicholas, 54, 184, 225
Underdowne, Thomas, 181, 183
Urbino, Duke of, 11
Urquhart, Sir Thomas, 331

V

Vanbrugh, Sir John, 383-34
Vasco da Gama, 3, 37

INDEX

Vaughan, Henry, 82, *297–8*
Vaux, Thomas, Lord, 10, *155*
Vellutello, 13
Vespucci, Amerigo, 8
Vicars, John, *182*
Villiers, George, 1st Duke of Buckingham, 72
Villiers, George, 2nd Duke of Buckingham, *377–8*
Virgil, 16, 30, 47, 51, (translations), *181–2*
Vives, Johannes Ludovicus, *187*

W

Waller, Edmund, 94, *348*
Walsingham, Thomas, 33
Walton, Izaak, 85–6, *295*, *321–2*
Ward, Richard, *291*
Warham, Archbishop William, 6
Warner, William, *184*
Warton, Thomas, *148*, *359*
Watson, Thomas, *206–7*
Webbe, William, *246*
Webster, John, 64–5, 87, *310*, *329*
Wells, H. G., 76
Wentworth, Thomas, Earl of Strafford, 73–4
Whetstone, George, *188*
Whichcote, Benjamin, 102, *288–9*
Whittington, Robert, *185*
Wilkins, John, 92
Wilkinson, John, *178*
Willes, Richard, *200*

Willey, Basil, 85
William III, 79–80
Wilmot, John, Earl of Rochester, 76, 94–5, 102, *351–2*, *378*
Wilmot, Robert, *225*
Wilson, John, *380–1*
Wilson, Thomas, *146*, *180–1*, *185*
Wither, George, *346–7*
Wolsey, Cardinal Thomas, 7, 17, 20
Wood, Anthony à, *326–7*
Wordsworth, William, 85, 89
Wotton, Sir Henry, 86
Wren, Sir Christopher, 76
Wroth, Sir Thomas, *182*
Wyatt, Sir Thomas, 10–11, 14–15, 23, 45–6, 95, 119, *148–53*
Wyclif, John, 24
Wycherley, William, 77, 102–3, *382*

X

Xenophon (translation), *180*

Y

Yonge, Nicholas, 109
Young, Bartholomew, *188–90*

Z

Zenocrate, 58
Zwingli, Ulric, 29